THE BUSINESS OF MARKETING RESEARCH

THE BUSINESS OF MARKETING RESEARCH

First Edition

Marco Vriens, Douwe Rademaker, and Rogier Verhulst

cognella®
SAN DIEGO

Bassim Hamadeh, CEO and Publisher
Angela Schultz, Senior Field Acquisitions Editor
Michelle Piehl, Senior Project Editor
Casey Hands, Production Editor
Emely Villavicencio, Senior Graphic Designer
Greg Isales, Licensing Associate
Natalie Piccotti, Director of Marketing
Kassie Graves, Vice President of Editorial
Jamie Giganti, Director of Academic Publishing

Printed in the United States of America.

cognella® ACADEMIC PUBLISHING
3970 Sorrento Valley Blvd., Ste. 500, San Diego, CA 92121

BRIEF CONTENTS

DETAILED CONTENTS

ACTIVE LEARNING

This book has interactive activities available to complement your reading. Your instructor may have customized the selection of activities available for your unique course. Please check with your professor to verify whether your class will access this content through the Cognella Active Learning portal (http://active.cognella.com) or through your home learning management system.

cognella® | ACTIVE LEARNING content

PREFACE

This book has two audiences in mind. One, undergraduate and master's students in marketing and marketing research. Two, marketing practitioners, both on the client and supplier side. For these audiences the currently available books on marketing research have several shortcomings that our book aims to address. There are currently two types of marketing research books on the market. One type is written from an academic perspective and a second type is written by practitioners. The marketing research books written from an academic perspective often have lots of details about various methodological and statistical topics. The contents of these books are very similar. First, in our view, these books allocate too much attention to topics that, in the day-to-day world of marketing research professionals, are not so important that they justify entire chapters. For example, they often have an entire chapter on sampling, or they may dedicate pages to outline the formulas and equations for a t-test or an ANOVA. Marketing, and marketing research professionals will most likely simply not need it. They do need to know why sampling is important or why a t-test can help in decision making, but for these topics they do not need to know the how. Second, these books are not aligned with commercial practice in terms of the type of activities that practitioners *do* need to do. Hence, students will arrive in their jobs unprepared for the reality. A second type of marketing research book is written by practitioners, and these books generally do not include foundational topics (such as the basics of analytics, or the basics of common marketing research approaches) that students need to be familiar with. Without some basic and foundational understanding students will be ill prepared to evaluate what they are doing or will be unable to evaluate what others will bring to them.

Both types of books have significant shortcomings. This book was motivated and designed to close these gaps. The authors, collectively, have worked in business and academics, and are in executive marketing research positions and hence have a unique and realistic perspective on what it takes to do effective and impactful marketing research.

HOW OUR BOOK IS DIFFERENT

We have outlined the general complaints from the business world in Vriens (2012) and Vriens, Brokaw, Rademaker, and Verhulst (2019). The key complaints and areas in need of improvement that are addressed in our book include the following:

1. Client interaction skills. Marketing research is a people's job: You will have to work with suppliers, internal marketing researchers, marketers, executives, or all of the above. The role of a marketing research executive is to have impact. And that means that your partners have to trust you and your work.
2. Communication skills. Generating the marketing research results is only half the job. These results need to be communicated persuasively and with impact. In most books this topic of storytelling is almost entirely missing. We dedicate an entire chapter to it, and we address it throughout the book.
3. Better ability to extract actionable insights. Many books explain how techniques work or how to design a survey, but the interpretation of data and results and how to connect the dots across various data points and studies is missing. We discuss this insight-generating process and have included exercises that allow students to practice this vital skill.
4. More practical analytics. Though our audience doesn't need to know the formula for a t-test or the closed-form equation of a linear regression model, they do need to know what types of marketing problems can be addressed through analytics, and they do need to have an ability to judge the quality of analyses.
5. Customer satisfaction and brand studies. These are the two most important types of marketing research projects. Customer satisfaction is critical, as it often is a key metric on executive scorecards and often the biggest line item in a marketing research budget. Branding is vital as this is often where the firm creates its competitive advantage and finds it new paths to growth.

This textbook contains many practical examples and anecdotes but also is steeped and grounded in academic rigor. We aimed to combine the best of both worlds (i.e., we discuss commercial practices that likely any marketing undergraduate or MBA student will encounter in their professional career).

However, the discipline of marketing research is not static and neuro-marketing methods are increasingly part of the commercial toolbox. We have included a small chapter on this topic, but no single course and no single book can cover everything. We hope this book will be a great resource for both marketing students and marketing practitioners.

Marco Vriens	Douwe Rademaker	Rogier Verhulst
mvriens@msn.com	Douwe.rademaker@ipsos.com	Rverhulst@linkedIn.com

REFERENCES

Vriens, M. (2012), *The insights advantage: Knowing how to win*. I-Universe publishing.

Vriens, M., Brokaw, S., Rademaker, D., & Verhulst, R. (in press). Rethinking the marketing research curriculum: Bridging the academics-practitioners gap. *International Journal of Market Research 65*(5), 492–501.

CHAPTER 1

INTRODUCTION: THE BUSINESS OF MARKETING RESEARCH

1.1 WHAT AM I GOING TO LEARN?

The budget allocated to marketing research is usually much smaller than the budget allocated to marketing. Nevertheless, marketing research (and increasingly analytics) is a very substantial business (globally roughly $ 44 billion), both for companies who have a marketing research department and for suppliers who offer their marketing research services to such companies. Understanding the structure of the marketing research business and the magnitude in which it can impact a company's financial success is the topic of this chapter. Specifically, we discuss the following: (1) Why do firms and organizations embark on doing marketing research and why are they willing to make substantial investments in this function, (2) How do we define marketing research, (3) How is the marketing research business structured, (4) How does marketing research add value to the firm (i.e., the research value chain), (5) How can companies leverage marketing research strategically, (6) What are the emerging trends, and lastly, (7) How do external disruptions (e.g., Covid-19 Pandemic) affect the industry?

1.2 WHY MARKETING RESEARCH?

Why marketing research? Facebook, Alibaba, WhatsApp, LinkedIn, Pinterest, WeChat, Weibo, Twitter, YouTube, Instagram. Consumers leave their feelings, their emotions, their consumer preferences and a lot more all over the internet. And more data is coming from an increasing number of connected appliances and products like fridges, dishwashers, cars, toothbrushes, security systems. With all this data, we should know more about our consumer's behavior than a simple questionnaire or a simple focus group could ever know.

So, why bother with marketing research? With all this information in the palm of our hands, is this the end of the marketing research business as we know it (i.e., mostly surveys and focus groups)? Will marketing research become obsolete like so many other products and services (Yellow Pages, the tape recorder, manually resetting pins at a bowling hall, etc.)?

In this book, we will show to you that, in fact, it is quite the opposite. We live in the golden age of marketing research. Companies need to be increasingly "consumer centric" to remain relevant in today's disruptive markets. Consumer centricity is based on a deep understanding of customers and competitors. This understanding comes from marketing research and related functions such as competitive intelligence and analytics. Companies embark on doing marketing research because they want to better meet the needs of their customers and make themselves more appealing to customers than their competition. In short, they want to make better marketing decisions. This doesn't mean that every decision that is based on, or utilized by, marketing research will be a better decision. It does mean that in general firms will do better when their decisions are based on marketing research. See Vriens (2012) for an extensive review on how the successful implementation and use of marketing research and analytics leads to superior financial results and market positions. Throughout this book we provide numerous case studies of where and how marketing research benefitted a firm.

Not surprisingly, marketing research skills are important to marketing and business students and will amplify their ability to make effective decisions and hence will be an important element in their individual career success. Schlee & Harich (2010) found that marketing research was the second most important area that students should have conceptual knowledge in—second only to consumer behavior but more essential than promotion and advertising, sales, and pricing. This held true for entry- and mid-level jobs and upper management jobs.

1.3 WHAT IS MARKETING RESEARCH?

We know that marketing research is a vital business success driver. But marketing research involves many disciplines. As a multidisciplinary function, marketing research requires skills in consumer behavior, psychology, data collection, statistical analysis, Big Data, business understanding, and communication and persuasiveness.

So how do we define marketing research? There are various ways to answer this question. We can define it by (a) its overall objective, (b) the four basic activities a marketing and marketing research professional should think about and work on, and (c) the types of marketing research.

1.3.1 Definition Based on Objective

Various formal definitions have been suggested; for example Malhotra (1992) defines marketing research as "the systematic and objective identification, collection, analysis and dissemination of information for the purpose of assisting management in decision making related to the identification and solution of problems and opportunities in marketing" (p. 379; see also Malhotra, 1993). Our formal definition of marketing research is that it help companies or organizations advance their goals through the following:

1. Collecting data, information, and insights, sometimes by analyzing or synthesizing data or analyses, about society, markets, consumers, or customers
2. Articulating the actions that a company or organization should consider as a result of this data, information, or insight
3. Being an active partner in the activation of the data, information, or insight

This definition shows that marketing research is related and overlaps with the analytics function, Big Data, and competitive intelligence functions.

The definition mentions data, information, and insights. These are terms that should be defined as well. Loosely, we could define data as any direct observation we have about our market or our consumers. For example, the average age of the customers who buy our brand is 55 years old. Information is when we do something with this data. For example, the average age of consumers who buy a competing brand is 35 years old, so our competition has a much younger audience. Insight is a bit harder to define. To illustrate the concept of insight, consider the following definitions:

> Thoughts, facts, data, or analysis of facts and data that induce meaning and further understanding of a business challenge and create an urgency to act or rethink a business challenge in terms of its problems or solutions (Vriens, 2012, p. 2).
>
> An insight is a revelation of a significant tension between consumers' aspirations and what they perceive as available, which can be turned into a business opportunity.
>
> New information giving you actionable ideas to drive your business in the stated desired direction and provide competitive advantage (Cooper, 2006, p. 262).

We note that internal clients have a need for raw data, information, and insights. However, because decision makers are usually too busy to process or interpret data and information themselves, the marketing researcher will be more impactful if they can digest all the data and information and turn these into (actionable) insights.

There is an important distinction between the "order-taker" approach and the "trusted advisor" approach; you will encounter both approaches in marketing research. An order-taker approach refers to situations where the internal client "orders" specific research from the internal marketing researcher (e.g., "I want you to commission and execute some focus groups") or the internal marketing researcher takes a business problem from the internal client, doesn't question it, and immediately designs a study to solve the problem. In both situations there is typically little to no interaction between the internal marketing researcher and internal client. There are situations where such an engagement model can work, but we believe collaboration and interaction between internal clients and internal marketing researchers (and even external suppliers) are usually very productive (we return to this topic later in the chapter).

1.3.2 Definition Based on Market Researchers' Activities

Marketing research can be defined by four basic activities and these have to do with the types of knowledge we have and the types of knowledge we don't have: (a) what we know we don't know, (b) what we know we know, (c) what we don't know we know, and (d) what we don't know we don't know.

What we know we don't know refers to situations we can articulate what it is we don't know. For example, how many consumers in our target market are aware of our new product or our new brand? To address a question like this, I could commission survey research among consumers in my target audience and simply ask respondents what brands come to mind when they think about the category. In these situations, we are usually able to draft a survey with questions that will give us the answers we need.

What we know we know refers to data and insights that the firm already has (and of which you are aware of) but nothing or not enough has been done with it. The task for the marketing (research) professional is to determine if these results justify certain business actions, and if they do the marketing researcher should consider getting decision makers in the firm to act on these results.

What we don't know we know is related to the previous activity: The firm may have done research or have data that you are not aware of. Finding out about this is important for two reasons: (a) In any new marketing research project you are considering what could benefit from this existing research (i.e., we can become more efficient in what additional data and information we really need), and (b) such data and results may need to be activated. Not doing so may leave opportunities on the table.

What we don't know we don't know is probably the most enigmatic-sounding activity. This activity refers to recognizing that we may not even know what we don't know. For example, few people probably would have expected the sudden global Covid-19 pandemic. In marketing research this means we may not fully know what questions to ask in our marketing research data collection. For example, consumers may have something on their minds that we are not even aware of (see Table 1.1.). One can, of course, always make the case that there is something "we don't know, that we don't know." In the end it is going to be a judgment call as to whether this unknown unknown is significant. If it is, marketing researchers should start with qualitative research (e.g., focus group, personal in-depth interviews). In commercial marketing research this is not always done but one should think about this element.

1.3.3 Definition Based on Purpose

We can define marketing research by its main purpose. For example, we can distinguish between exploratory research, descriptive research, and predictive research.

Exploratory research, as the name suggests, means we have little prior knowledge, we have few if any hypotheses, and we expect there might be a substantial amount of "what we don't know that we don't know." This means we might not (fully) know what types of questions to ask or how to ask them. We might not know what topics to address. Often, exploratory research will utilize qualitative research approaches such as focus groups and in-depth personal interviews. However, even if we have quantitative data (e.g., survey data, internal transactional records, even Big Data) we might "explore" the data by utilizing a variety of analyses just to find out "what the data are telling us."

Descriptive marketing research is done when we know what we don't know (see Table 1.1) and in this type of research we merely describe a situation in numerical terms. What percentage

TABLE 1.1 Case in Point: LinkedIn Entering a New Market

When LinkedIn decided to expand its paid services offering to small business owners it had no prior knowledge about its needs and wants and what the current challenges are. This made it very difficult to understand where to even start with doing research. Traditional research using a discussion guide in 1:1 or focus groups or designing structured questions is often biasing in and of itself. The questions are predisposed in tone and voice and many are leading—leading respondents to think or frame answers in a fixed and biasing way despite the best intentions of the interviewer or no matter how well-trained an interviewer is to reduce these types of biases. Big Data and several emerging text analytics techniques have made it possible to sort of "drop in" on any conversation that is happening organically on the Internet. For example, at LinkedIn we have hired a firm to scrape unstructured comments, articles, and blogs from the Internet over a set period of time to better understand the struggles and challenges of small business owners. Specifically, we used text analytics to analyze discussion forums, blogs, and social media discussions where small business owners congregate to better understand the daily struggles and get a closer understanding of how LinkedIn may be able to better serve this segment. The words and the way they describe the issues they encounter on a daily basis would have been impossible to elicit with traditional research. It helped LinkedIn to better understand how to address this audience and engage them in the right way with the right content and messaging. It also provided the foundation for doing more traditional follow-up research to develop the right solutions for this segment. This is another example of how the field of market research is rapidly evolving to take full advantage of emerging techniques for deeper exploration.

of our target audience is using our brand, what percentage considers our brand, who are the consumers who are aware and consider us in terms of age, gender, etc.?

As ones moves from the exploratory stage to descriptive to predictive, the research becomes more structured. With exploratory research we may have a rough idea in mind as to what we want to accomplish, but we may not know what questions to ask or how. With the descriptive stage, we typically know what questions to ask and how to ask them. We may not, however, have a specific conceptual model in mind that stipulates how various variables are related to each other. In predictive research we do have some notion as to how variables are related to each other, and we know what we would like to predict. This is the most structured situation. We know what questions to ask, how to ask them, and we have a model of consumer behavior. The goal is to quantify that model and see how much it can predict our variable(s) of interest.

We note that any given research project may have elements that are exploratory, descriptive, and predictive. For example, a large soft drink company needed to increase its market share in fast-food restaurants in Turkey. They did market research to gain a deep understanding of the use of its drinks in fast-food channels and use that knowledge to increase their brand's preference. The market research agency designed a three-phased marketing research project that included individual qualitative interviews (exploratory) with users of fast-food restaurants to uncover motivations and barriers, quantitative research to understand meal and beverage usage and preferences (descriptive), and neuroscience research (eye tracking and EEG) with individual fast-food customers to help design menus and menu boards in terms of background, price, product, and claim. A predictive model was used to predict what menu design would yield the highest increase in beverage consumption (predictive). The soft drink company quickly took action, and their new design led to 32% year-over-year increase in revenue. We discuss these three types of research more extensively in Chapter 7.

1.4 THE MARKETING RESEARCH INDUSTRY

The marketing research industry is a large and growing industry and has enjoyed decades of almost continuous year-over-year growth, fueled by Big Data and analytics trends (Davenport & Harris, 2007; Lilien, Roberts & Shankar, 2012) and there are no signs of it slowing down. The Bureau of Labor Statistics projects a 19% increase in market research analysts' positions over a 10-year time span (compared to 7% for other occupations). Related fields such as analytics and Big Data are expected to grow even stronger (Houghton Schertzer, & Beck, 2018; Sieben, 2016). ESOMAR estimated that the size of the marketing research industry was north of $44 billion.

1.4.1 The Marketing Research Ecosystem

There are several constituents in the marketing research industry. We distinguish between client organizations and external suppliers. External suppliers include: (a) full service marketing research firms, (b) field agencies, (c) niche market research firms, (d) advertising agencies, and (e) consulting firms. There are two ways to get consumer insights: The companies can do it themselves or they can outsource to a specialized marketing research specialist. Recent developments in data availability, Big Data analysis, new ways to understand consumer needs and behaviors, and the increasing need for advice and consultancy have upset the industry and opened the market to new players like consultancies, behavioral and neuro research firms, data collection agencies, Big Data companies, and many others. We will first discuss the players in the ecosystem and then disruptions and the impact on the marketing research industry.

1.4.2 Clients

In client companies we see various roles and teams that are important for a marketing researcher to be aware of, namely: (1) the internal marketing researcher, (2) the internal client or clients (the direct internal customer and the person or team whose budget funds the research, and (3) other stakeholders and decision-makers (including senior executives) who may not have contributed to paying for the research but who may benefit from it or can own some of the recommendations that came out of the research.

The Internal Market Researcher

The internal marketing researcher or the marketing research team, the person, or the team, who is responsible for the management and production of marketing research. This can be done fully in house or with help from external suppliers (more on this in Chapter 2). Internal marketing research teams can vary from a single person to a small group of marketing researchers, to teams consisting of hundreds of professionals. Internal marketing researchers can be organized in a central marketing research team, a central team, or a team attached to other business groups such as a strategy, marketing, or sales team, or a hybrid form. There are pros and cons to each, but a central team certainly has some distinct advantages (see Vriens & Grover, 2006).

Companies like American Express, for example, used to have two floors of hundreds of market research specialists in their New York headquarters. These research teams were responsible for acquiring deep consumer insights about payments, credit card usage, and how people shop. There were teams doing statistical analysis on all this data, teams responsible for acquiring databases with consumer data, and teams responsible for writing consumer insight reports for business units who were responsible for coming up with new innovative credit card solutions, payment plans, interest rates, and so forth. For budget and efficiency reasons, these teams have over the years been reduced to a much smaller group, and most of their work is now outsourced to outside agencies.

At LinkedIn, the internal market research function is centralized and split into two sub-functions. One sub-function is focused on engaging with internal clients. Their responsibility is to build a deep understanding of the business, and they are aligned to teams in marketing, business operations, product development, and sales. They are responsible for identifying the business problems, designing the right research, analyzing and reporting consumer insights, making recommendations, and influencing business decision makers. The other sub-function is focused on the research operations—the fielding of surveys, providing data analytical support, and bringing together different data sources. The advantage of these two sub-functions is that each function is specialized in answering both the what and the why and can bring together disparate data sources more effectively for deeper insights. The two teams can analyze existing behavioral data (for example, site engagement or purchase behavior) and profile data and combine that with why behaviors are happening. Many companies are starting to adopt this model to address a disruptive trend, which we elaborate on in the next section.

These internal market research experts can also use external suppliers to execute research projects. Typically, an RFP (request for proposal) is sent out to various marketing research suppliers. These suppliers then submit a proposal, and the company awards the project to the one with the best proposal (this can be "best" in term of the best research design, best price, best timing, best credentials, best global footprint, or a combination). The internal marketing researchers then supports the process and helps communicate the results to the decision maker.

Internal clients

Second is the internal client or internal client team—the person/team whose budget funds the research (usually to pay the project fee for an external supplier to execute the research). It is not unusual to have multiple internal clients who are all contributing to a specific study (sometimes referred to as tin cupping). This happens especially with expensive studies such as brand tracking or customer satisfaction tracking studies. We can distinguish several principal internal clients:

- The corporate marketing team and sometimes separately the brand team
- The product and product marketing teams
- The marketing managers in subsidiaries
- The R&D team
- The sales team
- The media and demand generation marketers who develop strategies for targeting audiences and how advertising dollars are spent
- Business operations, including the financial team, factory operations, quality control, and so on
- Senior executives, decision makers who either report directly to the CEO or have cross-functional responsibilities (this is a unique set of stakeholders. We discuss this further in Chapter 3.)

Many clients will reside in the marketing department. In fact, it is not uncommon for the marketing research team to reside within the larger marketing team. Across these diverse stakeholders dozens of business questions need to be answered. For example, what are the needs and the unmet needs of our customers, how can we develop a unique value proposition, what ideas for new products should be pursued and prioritized, who are we competing with, how strong is our brand, are we positioned in the best way, can our market be segmented, how satisfied are our customers (vis-à-vis the competitors' customers, etc.; see Vriens & Grover, 2006, p. 22-23 for details). The specific needs can substantially vary company by company. In consumer-packaged goods industries, for example, branding is considered core to a company's success. For example, Coca-Cola is only responsible for a limited number of steps to make a Coke. They outsource and license its recipes, production, sales, and bottling to bottling companies. The areas it invests in heavily are branding and R&D. The key stakeholders are therefore mostly concentrated in branding, and marketing and research areas arise mostly from these areas. At LinkedIn, there are many different businesses, and needs arise around a wide spectrum of topics and issues. At any given time, different stakeholders require support, and priorities shift, which means that the market research team needs to be organized around diverse skill sets and build expertise around a wide spectrum of approaches and domains.

Other Internal Stakeholders

Third are the other internal stakeholders and decision makers. Other internal stakeholders can reside in the same groups as the internal clients. They are different from internal clients because they did not pay for the research from their budgets and, in most cases, were not part of the broader internal market research effort: they may not have engaged with the internal marketing researchers during the production of the marketing research project. Research reports or specific insights are generally distributed beyond the original internal clients to a wider group of internal stakeholders.

The marketing team may have commissioned a market segmentation study. If some of the results of that project are relevant for sales, the marketing research team may connect with the sales department to make sure the relevant findings are conveyed to the sales team. An example we encountered in our practice: A segmentation study was done for a large global oil company to help them rethink the positioning of their brand. The head of the forecourt retail business of this oil company noticed how he could apply the segmentation research to his business and successfully used it to help him grow his business.

Note: In the remainder of this book we may use the terms "internal clients," "internal stakeholders," and "business decision-makers" interchangeably. Internal clients are also stakeholders. They all need to make decisions and they all need information and insights to make these decisions as good as possible.

1.4.3 External Suppliers

There is a wide selection of shapes and colors to choose from. We can distinguish the following types:

1. Full-service large marketing research firms able to do all aspects of a marketing research project (i.e., anything from data collection, [both qualitative and quantitative] to cleaning and analyzing the data, to the final reporting and presentation). Some full-service firms have global capabilities and have a presence in many countries and hence can do all kinds of research.
2. Advertising agencies. Even though their primary service is developing advertising, it is not that unusual for advertising agencies to also do the marketing research. Typically, though, this will be marketing research to support advertising strategy or execution.
3. Fieldwork companies who are only responsible for data collection (e.g., focus group companies specialized in qualitative focus groups, companies specialized in brand tracking research or customer satisfaction research, etc.).
4. New agencies with a specialist focus:
    a. Specialized firms in certain types of research (e.g., firms specialized in marketing mix modeling or eye tracking, conjoint analysis/discrete choice modeling, virtual reality and augmented reality [VR/AR], behavioral science, shopping, and so on).

b. Data platform companies: These can include firms that offer easy data collections tools (e.g., Qualtrics), or firms that help integrate (and analyze) different data sources. There are the Big Data owners like Amazon, Alibaba, Facebook, and Google who offer consumer insights to clients for a price.
c. Do-it-yourself platforms (like Zappistore), where companies can run simple research programs with very limited support from an agency but at a very low cost.

5 Consulting firms. Management consultancies are moving into the marketing insights area instead of their traditional areas of profit improvement, operational effectiveness, and organizational restructuring.

1.5 THE MARKETING RESEARCH VALUE CHAIN[1]

It is useful to think about how precisely marketing research adds value to a company. Figure 1.1 (adapted from Corte-Real, Oliveira & Ruivo, 2017 and Vriens, 2012) outlines the marketing research value chain.

As Figure 1.1 indicates, to be successful we need people, tools, and processes. The role of marketing research is to transform consumer data that exists in various forms (in consumers' minds, in internal stakeholders, in industry experts' minds, in databases, etc.) into knowledge, insights, and actionable opportunities for the client/company to spot new business opportunities, become more efficient, grow business, or gain a competitive advantage (see Vriens, 2012) through the use of various tools and techniques described in this book. Processes can further improve and facilitate this.

FIGURE 1.1 The Marketing Research and Analytics Value Chain

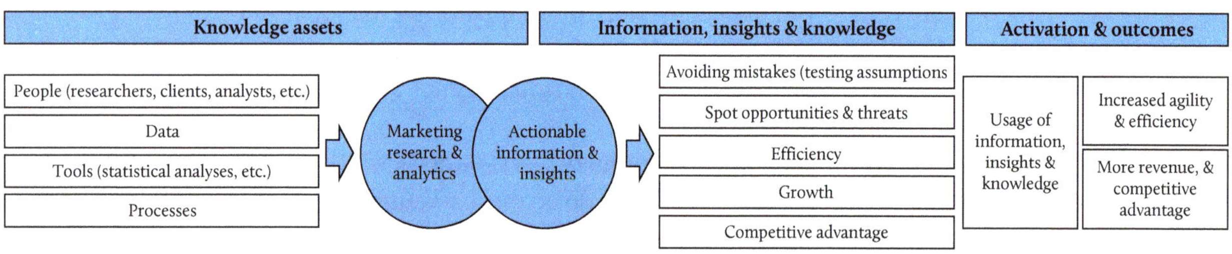

As Figure 1.1 shows, we distinguish between (a) avoiding mistakes, (b) spotting opportunities and threats, (c) efficiency insights, (d) growth insights, and (e) insights than can lead to competitive advantage. This framework is discussed in Vriens (2012), and we believe it is useful because it doesn't limit marketing research to marketing insights. Business mistakes are still often made (e.g., see Clancy & Krieg, 2000). Mistakes can happen by relying too much on intuition or by making assumptions that are not tested, for example: assuming everyone has seen your product launch; they may not have. Spotting threats or opportunities has more

1 This section is based on Vriens, Chen, & Vidden (2019) but is adapted to a marketing research context.

to do with trend spotting. That is not typically a structural part of what marketing research does, but it should be. Efficiency insight is the bread and butter of marketing research—which product ideas are best, which ad will resonate most, what price will work best, what products should we have in our portfolio, which customers are most profitable, and so on. These all boil down to being more efficient. Another product idea might have worked as well or maybe not, or another ad might have done the trick just not as well, and so on. Growth insights go a little (or sometimes a lot) further than efficiency insights. These are insights that can help the company grow their market share or their market. And, competitive advantage insights, probably most rare, enable the firm to scope out a position that competitors cannot copy or cannot easily copy and hence give the firm a longer-term advantage.

Often, companies distinguish between product development insights and go to market insights. For example, a research project aimed at testing new product ideas would be a product development project. Researching the effectiveness of ads would be considered a go-to-market project.

A second part of the marketing research and analytics value chain is the activation of information, insights, and knowledge. This transformational process to business growth shows that the marketing research function is an important link in companies' value chains.

1.5.1 Reactive Versus Proactive Value Creation[2]

Much of the marketing research that is done or commissioned by an internal marketing research team is driven by requests coming from internal clients. Typically, an internal client has a business problem and reaches out to the internal marketing research team to help find insights that can help solve their business problem.

However, the internal market research team needs to be proactive and anticipate potential future insights needs beyond these direct requests from internal stakeholders, for several reasons. First, there may simply not be enough time available to do any research if a problem arises and a decision needs to be made. Second, new approaches need to be piloted and tested. Third, there are often cases where the internal clients will not ask for a specific approach because they don't know that it exists. Fourth, most marketing research and analytics projects are one-off activities. This makes it virtually impossible to generate market insights or knowledge that be valid over a longer time period and that can be used on more than one occasion. Therefore, to be able to move to a more continuous infusion of insights, one needs to invest in building foundational insights. Such insights typically have more longevity than ad hoc insights. Last, even if clients and stakeholders believe they have enough insight it is important to be proactive to protect them from any potential "blind spots" they might have. Business decision-makers usually have significantly prioritized their activities, and hence the set of decisions they feel they need to make. They may have mentally blocked out an entire area. If that area offers attractive opportunities to meet customers' needs, management needs to be aware and gauge the likelihood that the competition will jump on that opportunity.

---

2 This section is adapted from Vriens (2012).

Stakeholders also need to have an open mind and avoid that they are simply kicking off research that confirms their agenda (i.e., the ideas they intuitively believe in). They must be open to research that negates strongly held beliefs. We have seen plenty of examples where research was pushed aside when the findings were questioning the status quo. Marketing researchers need to be strong to maintain the purity of the research when the findings are provocative and controversial.

1.6 TOWARD STRATEGIC IMPACT

For companies to be successful in today's disruptive markets, they need to be increasingly consumer centric. Strategic growth decisions should be based on sound and robust consumer insights, and marketing research needs to play a strategic role in a company. Companies generally agree that consumer insights should form the basis for strategic decisions, but in practice marketing research does not have a strategic place in the organization. Presentations of the findings of large strategic research projects are often not attended by senior managers or business unit heads. Similarly, marketing research reports are not read and end up in a closet gathering dust, while strategic decisions are made without the necessary consumer insights, leading to failed new product launches, or worse, directing companies' limited resources in the wrong directions (e.g., see Clancy & Krieg, 2000).

What can companies do to avoid this pitfall? How can companies ensure that their company is truly consumer centric and strategic decisions are based on robust consumer insights?

We see three ways to ensure consumer centricity:

1. Create an organizational structure where marketing insights play at a strategic role in the organization.
2. Make sure the leader of marketing research is a strategic insights partner to the business.
3. Tell a story with each market research engagement and drive impact in the organization.

1.6.1 A Consumer-Centric Organization

If a company claims to be consumer centric, it needs to have the consumer at the heart of its organization. Consumer needs must be the driving force behind strategic choices like portfolio decisions, brand strategy, innovation choices, and defining consumer experiences. That also means that consumer insights need to play a central role in strategic decisions. Then why, in many organizations, is marketing research a mid-level function and why are marketing research leaders not board-level positions?

For a company to be truly consumer centric, its marketing research team should be integrated in its strategic planning team, and the leader should have a senior seat at the table where strategic decisions are taken—a role equal to the chief marketing manager or the chief strategist.

But the reality is that sales, marketing, and product are the key functions in many organizations. For example, a company will cease to exist without a product or a salesperson to sell the product, and the same cannot be said of market research. These are the functions that are most critical to propel the business forward. Market research is often part of the marketing organization, which can be limiting in the types of questions and problems it solves, but it can be the right home as long as the market research function and process are closely embedded into other key functions and its value and purpose is clear to the stakeholders in and outside of marketing. In this position it will play an important internal consultative role to the product and sales decision makers even if it is not elevated to the C suite. It takes time and education to establish that influential role, but it also requires organizations to hire for diverse skills sets. At LinkedIn, for example, we hire not based purely on raw technical market research and data analytical competencies but also based on communication skills, the ability to influence and persuade, and general business acumen (e.g., Vriens, 2012).

To have the most influence a market research team is best organized if it does the following:

- Transcends organizational walls with company-first mentality to bring disparate teams together to solve problems holistically. Therefore, it should be a function that is independent of product and sales so that it remains objective and pure.
- Owns and runs strategic research programs for measuring customer satisfaction and loyalty—a key aspect for knowing if an organization is customer centric. Many organizations today have such a program in place and its executives are paying close attention to it. It often forms the jumping-off point into many other interesting and strategic research projects, further elevating the market research function.
- Forms strong, independent allies. Market research in many organizations is a relatively small team, but it can enable many parts of the organizations in a strategic way if it creates shared objectives and breaks down organizational silos. It can create leverage through joining forces with business operations, corporate development, analytics, and so on to align around key insights and push initiatives that drive growth, despite not being part of the formal product or sales organization. For example, in 2017, LinkedIn decided to expand its offering to SMBs. Initially it was an initiative that the marketing team took on. As part of marketing, the marketing research team scoped out several projects, but it quickly became clear that other teams were trying to answer related questions but coming at it from different angles. Business operations was trying to size the market based on government labor sources; the user experience team was focusing on the user experience of SMBs, and marketing research was trying to understand the wants and needs of this segment. At first, there was little coordination between the teams, and it was difficult for each team to get traction and to get the organization to act on the insights. It wasn't until the teams started working together, combined their findings, and created a comprehensive story that the executive team started to act.
- Is centrally organized. This allows the pooling of resources and expertise and offers meaningful career paths. A decentralized market research function where researchers are spread across the organization has the advantage that researchers build more domain expertise, but they lack career progression, and the insular nature of it limits

efficiency and the ability to zoom out and provide impactful insights. As individuals they also will lack clout. Decentralization of this function only makes sense if the units are operating independently. For a more detailed discussion of this topic, see Vriens and Grover (2006).

It is important for aspiring market researchers to understand how market research is organized as it has implications on the career being pursued. A decentralized function may limit the exposure to different research methods, coaching, and business expertise. Depending on objectives, one should weigh these trade-offs and have a clear sense of how success is being measured for the market research team and what its standing is within the organization—a trusted advisor who thinks critically about foundational problems versus an organization that simply takes orders and executes mostly tactical research (e.g., see Jones, 2004; Grover & Vriens, Chapter 1). New hires should proactively seek answers to these questions during the interview process.

1.6.2 A Strategic Insights Partner

Having a functional and organizational position in the company is not enough to have impact. Equally important is to have personal impact as a marketing research professional. Your role, your job, or your place in the organization does not necessarily mean you will be listened to. More important is your behavior, your attitude, and your professionalism. The same goes for a marketing research executive in a research firm. To be effective, to ensure your client listens to your recommendations, you need to behave like a strategic insights partner. And, just like any other function, market research is a "team sport," and it's rare that one individual brings all the characteristics to be effective; different people on the team will play different roles depending on the stage of a research project.

- It's important that a well-structured team hires for a mix of different strengths balanced across (a) technical issues and problem solving, (b) organization, (c) communication, and (d) collaboration and relationship-building skills. Successful market research teams have expertise across all four, and while everyone needs to be competent to a degree in each area, more experienced people tend to engage internal clients more directly. Market researchers at all levels quickly find themselves interacting with the most senior executives and need to hone their client management skills. Most teams tend to put too much emphasis on one area, which causes gaps around communication and understanding the business.
- Market research teams need to invest in building a diverse team that includes members who represent their target customers in thinking and culture; they need to have affinity with the groups they study and represent these diverse customer groups.

But what does it mean to behave like a strategic insights partner? Becoming a strategic insights partner takes time and practice. Below, we give you a simple framework and some simple exercises to help you get started on this journey.

The framework has four elements, each playing an important role:

- Be a reliable partner
- Form an emotional connection
- Think bigger
- Have a strong executive presence

Reliability is like the foundation of a house. Without a strong foundation, any house will eventually crumble. Reliability is your reputation; it is something you should start working on early in your career and build it like you build and maintain the foundation of your house. Your house may get leaks, a window may crack, a pipe may burst, but if foundations are strong, everything can be repaired. It is similar with reliability. You can make mistakes in your career, you are even expected to make mistakes, as long as you are seen as a reliable partner by your clients and your colleagues.

Reliability is a combination of credibility and trustworthiness. In other words, know what you are talking about and keep your word. The first one takes time, and the second one takes the right attitude. It is true that it takes time to build expertise and credibility. But trustworthiness starts immediately. Meet deadlines, keep promises, admit mistakes, and be honest in your client relationships.

A foundation alone does not make a house. The main pillar to become a strategic insights partner is to build an emotional connection. Without an emotional connection, your client or boss will not see you as a strategic partner and likely will not listen to you or act on your recommendations.

An emotional connection is created by courage and empathy. Have the courage to have and share an opinion that may differ from your audience. Having the courage to speak up, to go in an opposite direction, to give a provocative or an unorthodox recommendation makes people want to listen to you. They may not agree, but they will be engaged and excited. Nobody gets excited to hear what they already know or to have people agree with them all the time. A strategic insights partner needs to have courage to let the facts lead the recommendations, not what the client wants or expects to hear.

Courage without empathy leads to arrogance. The second element of building an emotional connection therefore is *empathy*. The definition of empathy is the ability to step in someone else's shoes. It means seeing the world from someone else's perspective. A strategic insights partner needs to consider how its findings and recommendations will be perceived by the client. Will they be happy with the results? Will the recommendations be hard to implement in the organization? Is it going the be a political battle for your client to get your recommendations acted on? How can you help your client overcome these difficulties? This does not mean you should change your recommendations, but you should consider what they mean for your client. Your orientation should be on your client, not on yourself.

A good tool to help you build empathy is to develop an empathy map for your client before you present or discuss the findings of a marketing research program (see Figure 1.2).

FIGURE 1.2 The Empathy Map

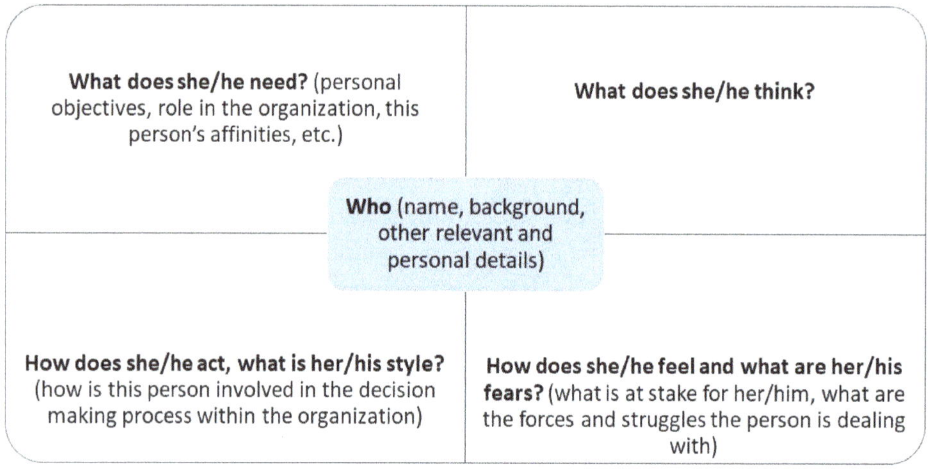

An empathy map will force you to think in more detail about the person who will receive the results of your marketing research project. It will help you step in the shoes of your client. The map has five boxes. In the middle you write down the client's data. This data includes name, education background, but also his or her favorite sport team, restaurant, and anything else that you may be aware of and that can be useful at some point. Then, in the top two boxes, you write down the client's personal objections and ambitions, what they think about their company and your company, the role of the research project, and so on. In the bottom two boxes you write down the person's style of work and communicating and their feelings and fears. This empathy map will help you be more considerate in your communications with your client.

The roof of the house of becoming a strategic insights partner is to think beyond the topic of research and think about the impact on the business of your client. That means you need to understand your client's business model and how they make money and make sure your conversations and discussions are around helping the client grow its business. That also means you should do your homework and understand the client's challenges, its main competitors, its new launches, its campaigns, and whatever has been in the news in the past months.

And finally, once you are seen as reliable, have a strong relationship, and demonstrate that you can think bigger, you need to be able to project an executive presence. This doesn't happen all the time, but most market researchers will be faced with an executive sooner rather than later given the strategic importance of the projects they work on. Often these are tiny moments but are key in making or breaking your career. It's that one meeting in front of executives that can make a difference in whether your insights are accepted and that will create the image of you and the function that you represent. Executives are very different types of stakeholders, and that's why we call them out. They are pressed for time and very sharp/confrontational; otherwise, they wouldn't have made it to that level, impatient and inquisitive. When you get invited to a C-suite meeting, often a formal presentation or read out is not the right way to engage that audience. You need to be able to quickly communicate the key findings orally and address questions live without becoming defensive. Executives do not like to be presented to and get distracted quickly (e.g., Gilbert, 2013). It requires a great deal of improvising depending on how the discussion goes; specifically, you need to be flexible to adapt and change the structure of your talk depending on where the executives want to focus. You often don't have more than 30 minutes, so it's important that you are well prepared and have all of the back-up notes and figures memorized. When questions arise it's important you stay focused on answering the question first, before going deeper. If further questions arise you divulge more. Too many researchers make the mistake of trying to be exhaustive, and it is important to stay concise: be brief, be bright, be gone.

This knowledge and focus will make you an equal partner to your client and further build your status of a strategic insights partner.

Now that you are a reliable, empathetic, courageous insights partner who can think beyond research and think about business implications, you are ready to deliver impactful marketing research projects beyond simple data or insights.

Figure 1.3 shows a summary of the strategic insights house.

FIGURE 1.3 Strategic Insights Partner House

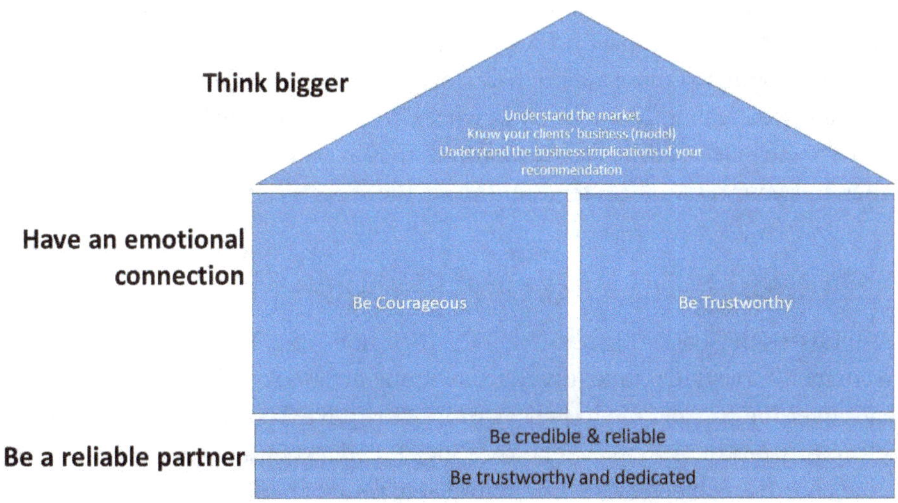

1.6.3 The Engagement Impact Model

As a strategic insights partner, your job is to have impact with each marketing research project under your responsibility. A common mistake in presenting the findings and insights of a marketing research program is to overburden the audience with data. After analyzing the data and finding many interesting insights, you need to suppress the need to present every insight you have found from your analyses. Instead, you need to go back to your business question and the research question and ask yourself, “What is the story you want to tell?” Notwithstanding that marketing research professionals should know better by now, experienced researchers prepare large deck of tables for their clients instead of telling inspiring stories, and clients still complain about marketing researchers preparing 300 pages of PPT slides and expecting them to, somehow, find nuggets of insights in all this data. But clients are not archaeologists, digging through caves for clues. So, how do we prepare an exciting story? How do we create an inspiring marketing research report? In Chapter 3 we discuss in depth how to communicate and activate research findings and insights.

So, how do we prepare an exciting story? How do we create an inspiring marketing research report? There are three things to consider when preparing a report: think of a relevant structure for your story, add contextual insights, and be creative in your delivery to inspire your audience. We will investigate storytelling in more detail in Chapter 3. With marketing research, the proof is whether your recommendations have real and positive impact on the organization. What can you do to increase the chance that your insights have impact? What can you do to make the recommendations in your report will be acted on?

A very powerful solution is to be very clear in your report about the expected impact of your recommendations. Unfortunately, this is also the most difficult element to convince researchers to add to the report. Researchers love data and consumer insights; they are slightly less comfortable with recommending what their clients should do. But they are very uncomfortable telling the client the impact they expect to get from these recommendations. The issue with predicting impact is that it is based on many assumptions, and researchers don’t like assumptions as these are not based on real data. Assumptions are based on experience and gut feeling, but they are exactly what clients are looking for. At some point your client will have to make a decision based on what they expect to happen. And as a marketing researcher, it is your task to help the client make these decisions.

1.7 FIVE TRENDS IN THE MARKETING RESEARCH INDUSTRY

Like any industry, the marketing research industry is not static. The industry underwent the move from mail surveys to phone survey, from phone surveys to online surveying. However, the trends over the past decade have been more disruptive. People have more options and channels to buy products than ever before. Social media is influencing consumers everywhere, and consumers spend more time than ever in front of multiple screens (mobile, tablet, laptop), but less time in front of a television. Technological breakthroughs (like AI and VR) give companies new ways to engage with their consumers. And consumer data is increasingly streaming from products like connected appliances and cars.

There have been larger and smaller trends disrupting the marketing research industry in various ways. One might say they all have in common the idea that the adoption of anything new is driven by the need to get a bigger return on investments in marketing research and analytics. See Figure 1.4 for five disruptive trends; these are discussed next, along with some smaller trends.

FIGURE 1.4 Five Disruptive Trends in Marketing Research

1.7.1 The Analytics Trend

Analytics has emerged as potential powerful growth driver (e.g., Davenport & Harris, 2007; Lilien et al., 2012). The analytics trend refers to an increased inclination by firms to utilize existing data and increasingly utilize analytics and advanced analytical tools to extract insights (Vriens, Chen, & Vidden, 2018). There are multiple reasons why the trend took off. One reason is that there was a general increase in the availability of data: (a) Firms have gotten better in capturing and managing internal data; (b) online interviewing has lowered the costs of surveys, so firms have often a lot more survey data at hand; (c) do-it-yourself research has added to the availability of data; and (d) firms can scrape the comments and thoughts consumers share online via social media. Two, there have been many proof points that advanced analytics can deliver profits (Davenport & Harris, 2007; Vriens, 2012; Vriens, Chen, & Vidden, 2018).

Asics for example, was slowly but surely losing share against Nike. It had launched a new campaign focused on controlling your run. The campaign showed data streaming of an athlete in the ad while they were running. The campaign was focused on the consumer insight that amateur runners are rational people who have a plan and a focus to accomplish a specific health goal, whether it is getting fit or completing a marathon. Nike focused its campaigns on serious and professional runners, so Asics's positioning seemed like a good plan. The marketing research program Asics conducted a scan of conversations on social media around the topic of running. Then they looked for motivational running themes in these conversations using artificial intelligence. But they also analyzed the data over time to see if these conversations changed in the past 2 years. They found three significant themes.

One was around aspirational professional running. These were conversations around making serious times in marathons, the best shoes for specific types of underground roads, where you can find the best speed hike trails in the United States, and so on. This was a significant and stable conversation theme on social media, as Nike was the dominant brand in this theme. Another theme was around control. These conversations were about how often you should change your shoes, what time of the day is the best for running, how long (in minutes) people would run each day, what to eat before a run, and so on. Though a significant conversation, the theme seemed to dissipate over time, and many smaller brands were fighting for attention in this space. Another small but fast-growing theme on social media was around the excitement of becoming your personal best, beating yourself each time you go out and run. This theme was around your personal fight to get better, faster, and stronger. It's not about competition, just competition with yourself. This space was not dominated by any brand yet. Asics decided to change its campaign and focused on this small but growing motivational theme. The campaign showed a person running and winning from its own shadow. This example shows how new developments in text analytics using advanced AI techniques helped Asics position its brand better against its competitor.

1.7.2 The Big Data Trend

This trend is somewhat related to the analytics trend. Big Data usually is characterized by three v's: volume, variety, and velocity. Volume may be measured by petabytes, exabytes, or zetabytes (Erevelles, Fukawa, & Swayne, 2016), "truly big in size," both in terms of large n and large p (see Vriens, Chen, & Vidden, 2018). Large n refers to a large number of respondents or data points (see Buhlmann, Drineas, Kane, & Van der Laan, 2016); for example, a document Vriens et al., 2018) analyzed 875,000 posts and comments scraped from online sources. Large p refers to a large number of variables; for example, Sadilek, Kautz, & Silencio (2012) developed a model to predict the spread of the flu with an initial set of several million predictors.

Variety refers to having available more diverse datasets. A firm may have tons of survey data, scanner data, qualitative data, internal data on customer transactions, and secondary data, including any data they have scraped from online sources. In addition, Big Data is often unstructured. For Big Data to be useful in all its varieties requires special equipment, software, and statistical models. Also, executives will likely expect even more from marketing research because of their firms' additional investments in data, analytics, and Big Data.

Velocity refers to the fact that Big Data can come in continuously. Twitter feeds run nonstop; so do Facebook posts and anything else where consumers can post their thoughts and feelings.

Though the initial impetus to Big Data was the internet, the next wave of Big Data will come from the Internet of Things (IoT): connected fridges, toasters, ovens, and coffee machines; connected electronic cars, interactive movies, store cards. Massive amounts of consumer data are streaming from all corners of the world.

This trend has been so disruptive because it has become an alternative to survey research. Companies started to realize that they may be sitting on data that already hides the answer they were looking for. So, firms adopted a "secondary-first" philosophy, meaning no primary research is allowed to be commissioned until one has checked that the answer cannot be found in data the firm already has. Velocity has also been a force of disruption. When firms need answers fast, say overnight, there is no way a survey approach will be feasible; quickly setting up some focus groups will not work. What is feasible is to scrape consumer comments from the internet and run a quick analysis. That may not be perfect data, but it can contain enough information for a firm to decide if there is a problem that needs further study.

1.7.3 Stretching the Marketing Research Budget Trend

The increased competitive nature forces many companies to find opportunities to save costs. Though total marketing budgets are not necessarily being cut, companies are trying to stretch their budgets further by trying to get more value for their money. Companies do this by using do-it-yourself platforms. And though these solutions may not answer 100% of their business objective, it will answer 80% of their question for 20% of the costs. And, sometimes, this is good enough.

Another way to stretch the budgets further is to simplify the need for insights, for example by focusing on a limited set of marketing KPIs to track. Take a large consumer goods company that decided to reduce its four tracking research programs (global brand, corporate reputation, communication, and social media tracker) to one tracking program that focuses only on those questions that have shown predictive value (high correlation with market share). Part of this trend is that many companies understand that they already have a lot of consumer insight from previous marketing research, customer satisfaction, and CRM databases, social media, and many other sources. A simple way to reduce costs is to first see what you already know and focus new research on the gaps in your knowledge. It sounds like a no-brainer, but many companies do the same research over and over.

A third trend is to automate the marketing research process where possible. For example, increasingly companies want to see the results of their research downloaded on an insights dashboard that end users can access to see the latest scores on key measures like brand equity (see Table 1.2).

TABLE 1.2 Case in Point: Marketing Research Automated

A hotel asks people when they check-out to quickly complete a simple satisfaction survey online while they wait for the check-out procedure to complete. The results of the satisfaction survey are immediately and automatically analyzed and relevant data send to relevant teams. The cleaning crew gets a notification that the bathroom floor is slippery and they immediately go to the room to clean the floor. The positive score for the person that served breakfast results in an immediate congratulatory email to the server. The repair team is sent to fix the TV in the room and the customer gets a than kyou note with a summary of actions that have been taken to fix the issues mentioned in the survey. A completely automated program. These programs are sometimes called Enterprise Resource Planning (ERP) tools.

1.7.4 The Use of Mobile Technology and Video

The past decade has seen the emergence of several new tools and techniques, allowing marketing researchers to get closer to consumers' motivations, needs, and behaviors. We have seen an increase in mobile interviewing (or device-agnostic interviewing), the use of video in data collection, implicit measures, eye tracking, and so on. See, in Table 1.3, how one FMCG company used video to get insights into the laundry detergent market.

TABLE 1.3 Case in Point: The Use of Mobile and Video

A head of consumer insights of a global laundry detergent company wanted to better understand how people do their laundry to find new and better detergent products. Working with a Marketing Research agency, a sample of 1,000 men and women completed a 90-minute online questionnaire asking them all kind of questions on the last three times they had done the laundry. After analyzing the results, the findings did not yield anything new or interesting. Laundry is a tedious and automated task for most people, and most people don't think about what they do or how they make decisions on separating colored from white for example. Also, many people will not be very excited about completing a 90-minute survey. Another approach was needed to get closer to people's real thoughts and behaviors around doing the laundry.

The next Marketing Research program was different. Respondents were asked to use their mobile phone to film their laundry process and use voice-to-text to comment on the process while they were doing the laundry. Cameras were installed in the laundry room of a small group of people and other people were asked to wear Google glasses to record the laundry process from a consumer perspective. AI and video analytics were used to analyze thousands of hours of video and unstructured comments. This approach showed very interesting behavioral differences between men and women that could be used in product development. For example, what many men consider white would be classified as colored wash by many women. A new laundry detergent targeted to men doing the laundry that protect misclassified white wash was successfully launched in the market as a result of this study.

This example shows how mobile phones help the Marketing Research specialist to get closer to the consumer moment of choice, usage, and decision and therefore get better results. But also the use of video better helps to get closer to people's real needs instead of a questionnaire where people sometimes rationalize their behavior.

1.7.5 Behavioral Economics and Neuro Marketing Trends

The global marketing research firm Ipsos (one of the world's largest marketing research firms) has separate business units for neuroscience and behavioral science. Both departments are heavily loaded with PhDs. And there are many other firms specializing in this area, including Nielsen, who pioneered many approaches using neuroscience. Neuroscience and neuro marketing research refer to the set of tools that taps into consumers' brainwaves, eye movements, and skin resistance. Most of these responses are involuntary (i.e., it is very hard or impossible to purposely control these). The appeal of the neuroscience approach stems from its ability to answer questions that are impossible to answer with traditional marketing research methods and, more practically, can yield robust and valid insights from a small sample of consumers (Telpaz, Webb & Levy, 2015) using less than 20 respondents, while at the same time yield better predictions (Venkatraman et al., 2015).

The appeal of behavioral economics lies in its ability to identify subconscious or irrational influences on consumer choice behavior. By some estimates, about 50% of what consumers feel about any number of topics cannot be expressed through explicit survey questions. Furthermore, we now better understand that many decisions we make are both rational and emotional (Sharp, 2010; Thaler, 2015). In fact, research has demonstrated that we often make irrational choices. In one experiment, Thaler (2015, p. 39) demonstrated that when respondents were given an option to drive an extra 20 minutes to save $5 on a $15 item, they were more likely to do so compared to when a higher-priced item of $125 went on sale with a $5 discount. In both cases it is the same $5 savings, but in relative terms a $5 savings "feels" more significant on a $15 versus a $125 purchase, warranting the extra 20-minute drive. We are starting to understand a lot more about how the brain and mind works and how we encode and decode information consciously and unconsciously. The brain stores information through neurons that are firing and wiring together. Our brain cells communicate with one another via synaptic transmission; one brain cell releases a chemical that the next brain cell absorbs. This transmission process is known as "neuronal firing" and creates neural maps of associations around particular experiences, actions, and anything related to our senses. For example, when we first learned to drive a car many of the actions were very deliberate and conscious. As we gained more experience the brain was building a neural network through repeated experiences, to the point where these actions became more automated, effortless, and unconscious. This same process takes place when we encounter brands and logos or any experience related with a company. For example, the purpose of advertising is to engage an audience and then create and refresh mental associations through repeated exposures and create automated responses that drive purchase behavior. For example, when we encounter a visual of the golden arches against a red background, McDonald's wants us to elicit associations with a hamburger and hunger and motivate us to come into their restaurant.

Priming is an example of a research area that has shown how context (be it conscious or subconscious) can affect consumer preferences. For example, Chartrand, Huber, Shiv, &Tanner (2008) exposed respondents to retailer images (Walmart or Nordstrom) during only a split second, too short to be able to consciously register these images. Next, the respondents had to choose between two brands of socks. Respondents choices were affected by the retailer they had been exposed to.

Another example is the use of neuroscience in understanding advertising campaign effectiveness. LinkedIn has started using neuroscience to determine not only the effectiveness of a campaign to engage a certain audience and land specific messages but also whether it activates competitors and whether it's sufficiently distinct. For example, it's unavoidable that when we see a campaign for Burger King it also activates McDonald's; both are part of the same neural map of associations in our mind. Vriens et al. (2003) found advertising paid for by a brand also improves awareness of a competing brand. Companies often don't realize how strongly connected their brand is to other dominant brands that play in the same category. To truly answer whether a campaign is distinct and gets strongly tagged to your brand you have to apply neuroscience to discover these types of insights; otherwise, a company could be making costly mistakes on campaigns that are not distinct enough.

Tools like brand scans, virtual reality headsets, biometrics, artificial intelligence, automated video intelligence, and behavioral analytics, help the market researcher to get closer to people's deeper feelings and behaviors. They are sometimes referred to as system 1 tools. System 1 tools are tools that help understand people's unconscious needs and motivations. A good example is biometrics. Simple tools can measure people's heartrate or level of sweat on their skin while watching television advertising, for example. These biometrics show people's excitement and their involvement during the ad and track people's eye movements. They can detect how you process this information and what kind of unconscious connection your brain makes.

Another example is to ask the respondent to rate a brand on a number of attributes but instead of looking at the scores, we measure the speed at which the respondent answers the question. The rational is that the faster a response to a question, the more the respondent is emotionally engaged with this attribute and therefore the more it is connected to the brand. This is called individual response time (IRT) (see Vriens & Martin Alves, 2017).

These are just a few of the exciting new tools and techniques to help marketing researchers.

1.7.6 The Trend for More Advisory Services

With this data challenge comes the need for consultancy support. Many clients are asking for more than a research report. They need advice on databases, data analysis, activating consumer insights, online insights dashboards, and building end-to-end platforms. But there is also an increasing need for consultative advice on how to build and activate brands in this new mobile and connected world. How do you stay relevant to this new mobile consumer with no brand loyalty? Who buy products on their mobile, looks for unique experiences, while at the same time shopping for the product with the lowest price? It is a lucrative market, and many consultants are successfully exploiting this new field. These new companies are stealing market share from the traditional research companies. As a result, traditional research companies are looking for new ways to remain relevant. Some companies choose a larger global footprint, others for a new, more digital offer, and some focus on a specific offer like brand tracking or customer satisfaction.

1.8 HOW EXTERNAL DISRUPTIONS AFFECT THE MARKET RESEARCH INDUSTRY

This book was written in the midst of the COVID-19 crisis. The COVID-19 crisis has affected people across the globe with a loss of loved ones and many more people beating a nasty illness. People across the globe have been locked down in their homes for weeks, only to go out for bare necessities or a short walk around the block. This leads to both welcomed and unwelcomed consequences. People are spending more time with their family, have more time for themselves but also sense a feeling of stress, anxiety, and a sense of isolation. Also, as we are writing this book, bars and restaurants are still closed and large events, like the Olympics and music concerts have been postponed or canceled. This has greatly affected consumer behavior. Some categories have seen a uptick, like medical products, food (and cooking ingredients), online services like education and entertainment, and dairy and beverages, especially wine and beer. But other categories have seen a big decline like sports clothing, offline activities, beauty products, real estate, travel, tourism, and personal care products (according to an Ipsos survey in China in March 2020 among 1100 respondents).

So far, we have seen five impacts from this contextual COVID-19 disruption on the Market Research industry, some positive and some negative. The first impact is an urgent need for insights into this changing consumer behavior and the effect on brand preferences. Many companies want to understand how consumers are changing their behaviors and attitudes, but they also want to know which of these behaviors are durable. How are consumers changing their long-term routines? Will this disruption lead to a steep change in eCommerce? Will online education become a more standard tool for schools and universities? Will people continue to spend more time in the kitchen to prepare family meals? And is it changing brand preferences? Most companies are walking a fine balance of coming across as emphatic and focusing on growing sales. Many companies offer flexibility in contracts and payments, changing their operations to help build facemasks or ventilators or offering their hotels as temporary hospitals. KLM has retrained some flight attendants to be temporary nurses to support local hospitals. At the same time, they are responsible to try to ensure business continuity. It is expected that companies who stay true to their mission and avoid coming across as "tone deaf" and not being perceived as "ambulance chasers" are most likely to persevere and create a strong brand connection. At LinkedIn we are also seeing members and customers interacting more closely with their stronger ties, checking in on their immediate peers and colleagues. We are also seeing more companies launching virtual events and using live videos to communicate with their customers and employees. All these behaviors will have a long-term impact on product roadmaps and branding.

A second impact is driven by companies need for immediate cashflow. Companies need to have consumer insights fast and these insights need to help drive their business immediately. That means a focus on very fast, or even real-time, consumer insights. And market research companies are quickly building and launching agile market research solutions.

As a third impact, we see a move away from strategic research to more tactical research. Companies like to know how they can sell more products now, rather than rethinking their strategic brand portfolio. Large segmentation studies are put on hold and replaced by pack studies, shopping studies and innovation research.

A fourth impact is a move to online research. Doing research in a time of "social distancing" means a shift from face to face research and focus groups to mobile and online research, online communities and virtual workshopping. Contrary to traditional ideas, ideation workshops and even more strategic segmentation workshops can be done effectively through virtual platforms.

And finally, the fifth impact is a reduction in research budgets. Companies facing financial distress as a result of a reduction in consumer demand, are slowing down all expenses that they deem lower priority. Precise data on reduction in marketing research spend is not yet available, but we expect it to be 15% to 30% in the first quarter of 2020. As a result, many large market research firms have temporarily reduced payroll with salary cuts and lay-offs. At the moment of writing this book, it is unclear which research and consultancy companies will survive this crisis, but the research industry ecosystem is likely to be different post COVID-19.

1.9 QUIZ AND EXERCISES

1. How can we define marketing research?
2. Think of an example of "what you don't know that you don't know." In what sort of situations are you most likely to encounter this?
3. What is the difference between the "order-taker" approach and the "trusted advisor" approach?
4. In the chapter we discussed five trends. Is there overlap between these trends? Try to think of two sets of two trends where you can see an overlap.
5. What would be a downside of a company doing their marketing research in house? What would be an upside?
6. Can you think of some marketing problems where we might need an exploratory and predictive approach?
7. What element of the marketing research value chain will be most important in a mature market?
8. What types of decisions will a marketing manager or a brand manager encounter? Try to list as many decisions as possible.
9. Think about someone you know and create an empathy map.
10. What are your barriers to become a trusted insights partner and what can you do to overcome these barriers?

11. A company wants to conduct a brand study to help improve its brand equity. Think about three possible business reasons why the clients would want to conduct such a brand equity study.
12. Explain in your own words what is meant by the terms mutually exclusive and collectively exhaustive.
13. Why would the use of mobile (smart) phones or tablets in marketing research lead to better return on investments?
14. Analyze the marketing research industry using Porter's (2008) five competitive forces framework.

REFERENCES

Buhlmann, P., Drineas, P., Kane, M. & van der Laan, M. (2016). *Handbook of big data*. Chapman & Hall.

Chartrand, T.I., Huber, J., Shiv, B., 7 Tanner, R.J. (2008). Nonconscious goals and consumer choice. Journal of Consumer Research, 35, 2, 189–201.

Clancy, K. and P. C. Krieg. 2000. Counter-Intuitive Marketing. New York: The Free Press.

Cooper, T. (2006). Enhancing insight discovery by balancing the focus of analytics between strategic and tactical levels. *Database Marketing and Customer Strategic Management, 13*(4), 261–270.

Corte-Real, N., Oliveira, T., & Ruivo, P. (2017). Assessing business value of Big Data analytics in European Firms. *Journal of Business Research, 70*, 379–390.

Davenport, T. H., & Harris, J. G. (2007). *Competing on analytics: The new science of winning*. Harvard Business School.

Erevelles, S., Fukawa, N., & Swayne, L. (2016). Big data consumer analytics and the transformation of marketing. *Journal of Business Research, 69*(2), 897–904.

Gilbert, F. (2013). Speaking up: Surviving executive presentations. Berrett Koehler publishers Inc., Oakland, CA, USA.

Grover, R. & Vriens, M. (2006). Trusted advisor: How it lays the foundation for insights. In: Grover, R. & Vriens, M. (eds.). Handbook of Marketing Research, Sage Publications. Thousand Oaks, CA.

Houghton, D.M., Schertzer, C. & Beck, S. (2018). The MSCA Program: Developing analytics unicorns. Marketing Education Review, 28 (1), 41–51.

Jones, S. (2004). Problem-definition in marketing research: facilitating dialog between clients and researchers. Psychology & Marketing, 2, 2, 83–92.

Lilien, G. L., Roberts, J. H., & Shankar, V. (2012). Effective marketing science applications: Insights from the ISMS-MSI practice prize finalist papers and projects. *Marketing Science, 32*(2), 191–363.

Malhotra, N. K. (1992). Shifting perspective on the shifting paradigm in marketing research: A new paradigm in marketing research. *Journal of the Academy of Marketing Science, 20*(4), 379–387.

Malhotra, N. K. (1993). *Marketing research: An applied orientation*. Prentice Hall.

Porter, M. E. (2008, January). The five competitive forces that shape strategy. *Harvard Business Review*, 25–40.

Sadilek, A., Kautz, H., & Silenzio, V. (2012). *Predicting disease transmissions from geo-tagged micro-blog data*. Association for the Advancement of Artificial Intelligence.

Schlee, R. P., & Harich, K. R. (2010). Knowledge and skill requirements for marketing jobs in the 21st century. *Journal of Marketing Education*, *32*(3), 341–352.

Sharp, B. (2010). *How brands grow: What marketeers don't know.* Oxford University Press.

Sieben, K.C. (2016). Labor markets in 2040: Big data could be a big deal for job seekers. Monthly Labor Review, U.S. Bureau of Labor Statistics, February: https://doi.org/10.21916/mlr.2016.6.

Telpaz, A., Webb, R., & Levy, D. J. (2015). Using EEG to predict consumers' future choice. *Journal of Marketing Research*, *52*(4), 511–529.

Thaler, R. (2015). *Misbehaving: The making of behavioral economics*. Norton.

Venkatraman, V., Dimkoa, A., Pavlou, P. A., Vo, K., Hampton, W., Bollinger, B., Herschfield, H. E., Ishinara, M., & Winer, R. S. (2015). Predicting advertising success beyond traditional measures: New insights from neurophysiological methods and market response modeling. *Journal of Marketing Research*, *52*(4), 436–452.

Vriens, M. (2012). *The insights advantage: Knowing how to win*. I-Universe.

Vriens, M., Grigsby, M., & Franses, P. H. (2002). Time series models for advertising tracking data. *Canadian Journal of Marketing Research*, *20*(2), 62–71.

Vriens, M., & Grover, R. (2006). Structuring marketing research departments for optimal impact. In R. Grover & M. Vriens (Eds.), *Handbook of marketing research: Uses and misuses* (pp. 18–32). SAGE.

Vriens, M., & Alves, M. A. (2017). Modeling the implicit brand: Capturing the hidden drivers. *Journal of Product and Brand Management, 26*(6), 600–615.

Vriens, M., Chen, S. Kaulartz, S., & Vidden, C. (2017). Assessing the impact of a brand crisis using Big Data: The case of the VW diesel emission crisis. *DMA Annual Analytics Journal*, 107–118.

Vriens, M., Brokaw, S., Rademaker, D. & Verhulst, R. (2019). The marketing curriculum: Closing the practitioners-academics gaps, 61, 5, 492–501.

Vriens, M., Chen, S., & Vidden, C. (2018). *From data to decision: Handbook for the modern business analyst*. Cognella.

CHAPTER 2

THE MARKETING RESEARCH PROBLEM AND PROCESS

2.1 WHAT AM I GOING TO LEARN?

In this chapter we focus on the process of a marketing research project up until the research deliverables. Of course, the work of the marketing researcher or marketing research team doesn't stop there. There is still the activation of research, which will be discussed in Chapter 3.

Figure 2.1 shows the elements of the marketing research process.

FIGURE 2.1 The Marketing Research Process

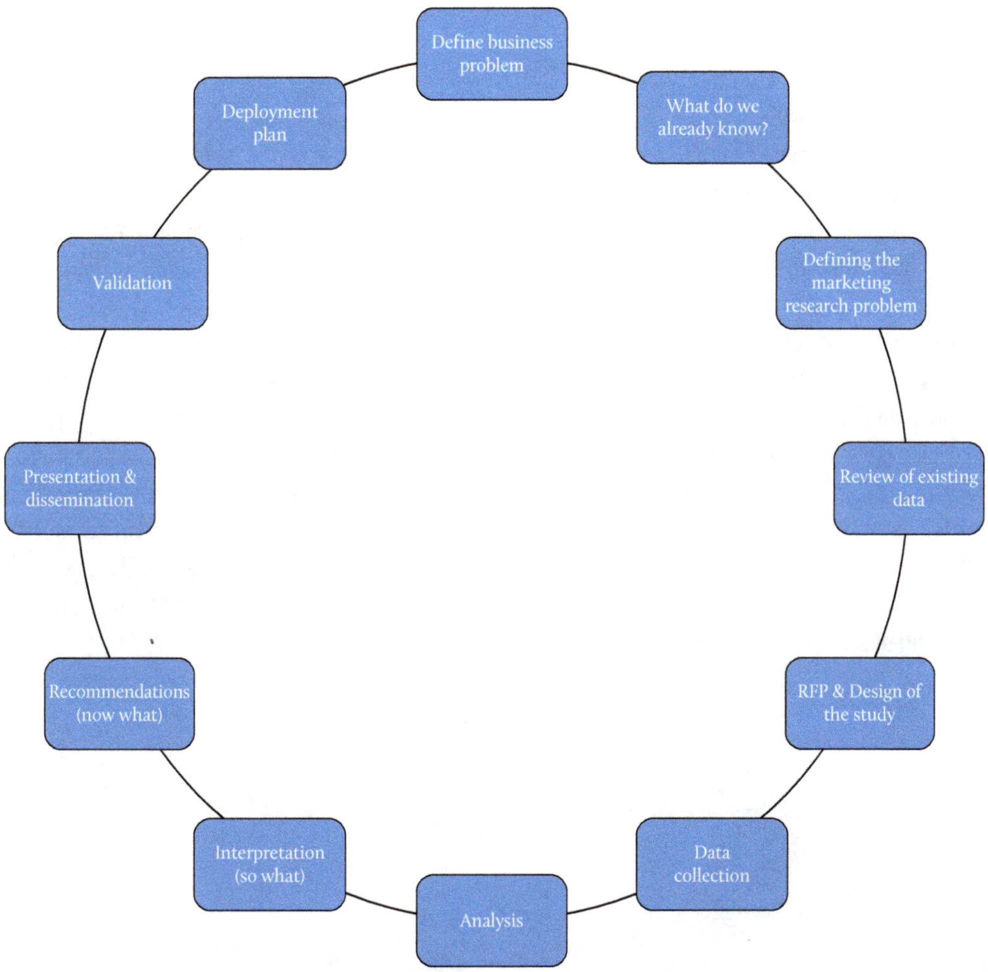

The marketing research process includes the following actions:

- Formulate a marketing or business problem, including a feasible decision.
- Review what is already known and formulate hypotheses if feasible. Not in all situations will it be feasible to articulate hypotheses. However, looking at what is already known not only gives part of the solution, it will also help define the marketing research problem more specifically.
- Define the marketing research problem. Note that there are different constructs for a marketing or business problem versus a marketing research problem (see Green, Tull & Albaum, 1988 for some examples).
- Review what data obtained that can help provide answers to the marketing research problem by re-using or re-analyzing this data, and then decide what further data is needed.
- Develop a research brief, or request for proposal (RFP), and design the study (this can be done with the help of external suppliers). If an external supplier does this, they will develop a proposal, and this typically also involves putting a project team together (internally and on the side of the external supplier). We discuss this in Chapter 2.
- Commission the study and start the data collection (we cover data and data collection in Chapters 4–7, 10 and 11).
- Clean the data, prepare it for analysis, and analyze. This analysis has a process itself (see Vriens, Chen, & Vidden, 2018). We discuss this in Chapters 5–10.
- Interpret the data (the so what); this is a key step that often gets skipped or short-changed. Chapter 8 deals with this topic.
- Complete the now what step: What specifically is being recommended? We discuss this in more detail in Chapters 3 and 8.
- Build a presentation for the internal client and work on further dissemination of the results (see Chapter 3).
- Possibly include a validation step.
- Keep internal marketing researcher or marketing research team an active participant in the deployment or activation of the research results or insights (we discuss this in Chapter 3).

There is an important distinction between the "order-taker" approach and the "trusted advisor" approach; you will encounter both approaches in marketing research. An order-taker approach refers to situations where (a) the internal client "orders" specific research from the internal marketing researcher (e.g., "I want you to commission and execute some focus groups") or (b) the internal marketing researcher takes a business problem from the internal client, doesn't question it, immediately designs a study to solve the problem. In both situations there is typically little to no interaction between the internal marketing researcher and internal client. There are situations where such an engagement model can work, but we believe collaboration and interaction between internal clients and internal marketing researchers (and even external suppliers) are usually very productive (we return to this topic later in the chapter).

2.2 THE BUSINESS PROBLEM AND THE MARKETING RESEARCH PROBLEM

Marketing research (and analytics) are support functions; they exist so that they can help with providing data, information, insights, and market knowledge to decision makers in a company so that they in turn can make better decisions. These decision makers can be part of the marketing team (e.g., product marketing managers, brand managers, CMOs, etc.) or other departments and teams (R&D team, PR team, sales team, etc.). We can roughly distinguish between two scenarios: (1) Specific problems and (2) Broad problems.

One, in some cases, a problem and corresponding decision has already been identified by management. An internal client may contact the internal marketing researcher with a specific question. The answer to such a question is directly related to the decision that needs to be made. For example, "Should we introduce this new product?," "How much can we charge for this feature?," etc. Such problems are very structured. Structured here means, we already have a pretty good idea as to how to go about. For example, say management needs to decide whether a new product should be introduced. The end goal clear: Make the right decision regarding the introduction of the new product. Also, it is not that hard to figure out how we could go about: i.e., we could commission a survey where we show respondents the new product or describe it in some detail and then ask respondents how likely they would be to buy this product if it were available on the market. We can then, in advance if needed, state a threshold beyond which the company should decide to introduce the new product and below which they should refrain from doing so.

Two, in other cases, internal clients may articulate a broader business problem that is less structured. For example, sales of our favorite beer variety, maybe a dark ale, have gone down, or we have a business challenge in that our CEO wants a new brand we introduced to grow by 5% next year. In both cases it is less clear what type of marketing research we should do. Maybe they should do a Usage & Attitude study (see Chapter 7), maybe a market segmentation study, maybe qualitative, etc. However, without any additional information, without even knowing what types of decisions the firm is willing to consider, it is hard to determine a good research approach. There is a risk, if we proceed to hastily to over-scope the problem: i.e., we will collect more information than we need. So, instead, we need to be cautious and be mindful. We should avoid *the solutions trap: a trap we are all vulnerable to.* If someone asks you for advice, it is a natural tendency to offer a solution immediately. However, when we are dealing with broad, unstructured problems we should resist that urge and instead ask ourselves a few questions first, e.g.: (1) What else do we know about the problem, (2) Does anyone on the firm have an hypothesis, (3) Have the internal stakeholders thought about what decisions they are willing and able to consider and are these decisions feasible, etc.? It has been argued that decision makers do not always know what the precise problem is (Chapman, 1989). Internal clients may provide vague requests and lack an understanding about what to expect from the research. According to Minto (2010), 60% of data collection and analysis is wasted in typical explorative research. Therefore, scoping and defining the right business problem and the right marketing research question is a vital component of the marketing researchers' job. As Green, Tull & Albaum (1988) state, "Translating a management problem into a marketing research problem typically means there need[s] to be communication between the internal marketing researcher and the internal client (see Norman, 2013, p. 31; see also Andreases, 1987). Norman (2013) wrote, "A brilliant solution to the wrong problem can be worse than no solution at all: solve the correct problem" (p. 218). Norman (2013) also wrote that good designers never start by trying to solve the problem given to them; they start by trying to understand what the real issues are and studying people and what they are trying to accomplish. We would argue that everyone, especially market researchers who try to solve problems, should take a similar attitude and take an original problem as a suggestion, not a final statement, and then think broadly about the underlying issues.

So, how can you do that: find the right problem and the right marketing research question to ask. There are two ways to go about this: the deductive and the inductive approach (Grover & Vriens, 2006). The deductive approach to marketing research resembles the scientific approach one progresses from:

- A literature review or determination of what we already know. This may or may not include a theory (we won't dive into what is and isn't a theory, but from a practical point of view let's define a theory as a statement as to how various variables (or concepts) are related to each other (these relationships can be causal or not)
- Formulation of hypotheses (these follow usually directly from the theory)
- Data collection and analysis to confirm or reject the hypotheses

The deductive scientific method for asking effective questions is a hypothesis-based approach, which we will explain in greater detail. Sometimes this process is also referred to as the "five why's" approach (Norman, 2013). Repeatedly asking the why question to get at the core of a problem or solution.

Using an inductive approach can be viewed as more data driven. We start with collecting data and making observations, and from these specific instances we aim to build a theory. In commercial marketing research we encounter both types of approaches, and they may even coexist in any given project.

Having a clear understanding up front about what the problem and underlying hypotheses are and how to go about answering them saves time and money. It's not surprising that many management firms take a hypothesis-based approach when they engage their clients so that its clear what problem gets solved and the firm can work backward from a set of hypotheses that are vetted with the client.

2.2.1 An Example

Say Company A sells software. They have a high-end version and a low-end version. Sales of their low-end software product has been declining over the past three quarters. The CEO is getting concerned and wants this researched. So, he meets with the CMO (chief marketing officer) and gives the CMO the assignment to solve this problem (this example is derived from Grover & Vriens, 2006). This is a broad business problem: We don't know what is causing this decline, it could be many things. Given that this is a broad problem, we want to avoid the solutions trap. It would be a mistake to immediately contact an external supplier and ask them to come up with a research proposal. Without any more information an external supplier could propose a broad research project. For example, they could commission a U&A study where we ask respondents about what software products they use, what, what brands they know, how they feel about these brands, and so on. This could very easily result in a long survey with hundreds of questions.

Instead, the CMO decides to go talk to some salespeople in the company and look over some other research the marketing research team has done over the past year. In other words, the CMO is trying to determine what is already known. Now, suppose that the salespeople are having trouble selling the low-end software product, even though it is better than a low-end software product from Competitor B. They also state the reason is because even though B's product is not as good as A's, it interoperates better and more intuitively with Microsoft (MS) Office. Now the problem has become a lot more structured and specific. We could even state a hypothesis: The reason consumers prefer Brand B over Brand A is because B is better in interoperability with MS Office. This hypothesis could be tested in a study. More importantly, we can already think about some possible decisions Company A could make: (a) make the interoperability with MS office more intuitive, (b) design training for customers that explains how the software product can interoperate with MS Office, and (c) lower the price. These three alternatives can easily be tested and researched in a very focused research project, and it would also have the advantage that decisions have already been articulated and don't need to be thought of after the research. Namely, if respondents react negatively to training, and price does not sway them, then, clearly, they need to improve their product. Hence, proceeding in the way outlined greatly increases the chances that the research will be used. If there is no clear understanding across all parties (internal market research, client, and supplier) in how the research results will be implemented, the research will lead to frustration and become unsuccessful. Following is an outline of a process that will greatly reduce this risk.

2.2.2 More About Hypotheses and Issue Trees

Using prior knowledge (i.e., what we already know) is, in essence, making use of a hypothesis. There are many benefits to a hypothesis-based approach:

- More efficient data collection and analysis by focusing on the most important data (eliminates "nice to haves")
- Identifies analytical dead-ends quickly and avoids analysis paralysis
- Aligns everyone in the organization around what hypotheses the research is trying to test
- Provides a graphical roadmap of how the problem breaks down and a framework for how the findings will get presented

The goal of a hypothesis-based approach is to break down a research problem into logical issues and guide the research (see Table 2.1 for a definition of a hypothesis).

TABLE 2.1 The Definition of a Hypothesis

What is a hypothesis?

- A preliminary assumption—for example: "Small business customers are more price sensitive"
- An assertion about a problem or issue that can be tested by further data collection and analysis. A hypothesis is either true or false and the effective research will help test these
- A declarative sentence that states the solution to an issue based on: Limited available information from syndicated or prior research
- Intuition/experience

Let's elaborate on this. Recall that we should not take an initial business problem as given. Among the key stakeholders there needs to be a common understanding of the business context, prior research, challenges, and what the research is trying to accomplish; having a one-sentence declaration that starts with a why or how question provides the necessary focus and clarity and is the first step for getting a successful research project off the ground. This often requires multiple discussions, and the process is iterative in nature. For example, in 2016 LinkedIn experienced a deceleration in its hiring solutions business; this business is focused on selling paid services and tools to recruiters to help them be more effective in sourcing candidates for their organizations. It was unclear why the business was softening. The sales and marketing organization asked the internal market research team to help investigate. The organization quickly jumped to the conclusion that LinkedIn was losing business to an upcoming new competitor who had recently been aggressively advertising its job board. It became the main headline and a classic example of confirmation bias. Confirmation bias is the tendency to search for, interpret, favor, and recall information in a way that confirms one's preexisting beliefs or hypotheses. People display this bias when they gather or remember information selectively or when they interpret it in a biased way that favors their beliefs. In this case, a strong competitive belief or a belief that at any time competitors can come and steal business clouded people's judgments.

However, the competitor's target audience was very different from the one LinkedIn was focused on—large enterprise customers versus smaller companies. Before diving in we needed to better understand the problem:

- Did customers have reduced budgets allocated to LinkedIn?
- Was overall revenue declining because customers switched partially to other brands?
- Did they spend less than the prior year but remained LinkedIn customers?
- Did a slowdown in customer acquisition cause the problem?
- Did all customers on average decline or was there variation across different customer types?
- Did LinkedIn add fewer customers who were spending less?

In essence, these explanations can all be considered initial hypotheses. It quickly became clear that there was not a common understanding of the exact problem. Setting aside any preconceived notions, the market research team first sat down with the key decision makers and business operations to better understand what was going on by looking through internal sales data. It encouraged everyone to think broadly and think about all problems that the business could be facing. After various discussions, LinkedIn created an issue tree. An issue tree, sometimes also called a logic tree, is a graphical breakdown of a question that dissects it into its different components vertically and that progresses into details as it reads to the right, such as in Figures 2.2 and 2.3.

FIGURE 2.2 The Issue Tree

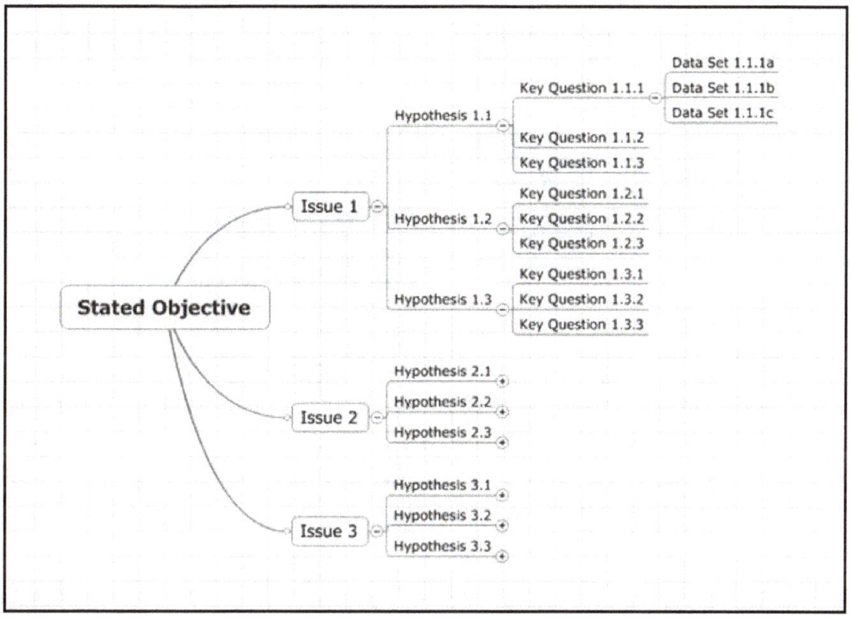

Issue trees are useful to identify the root causes of a problem as well as to identify its potential solutions. They also provide a reference point to see how each piece fits into the whole picture of a problem. This has several benefits. First, they provide a roadmap of the problem. By including all possible answers to the key problem statement, researchers reduce the possibility that key aspects get overlooked. Also, issue trees spell out the various alternatives in minute detail. They are useful in managing the problem-solving effort, structuring people's thinking, and offsetting any confirmation bias. The process of developing an issue tree should be a group exercise that includes all stakeholders and decision makers who have close knowledge of the business, prior research, and market dynamics. It is important that divergent thinking occurs and that stakeholders don't get stuck with the familiar and not think outside the box.

FIGURE 2.3 Example of an Issue Tree

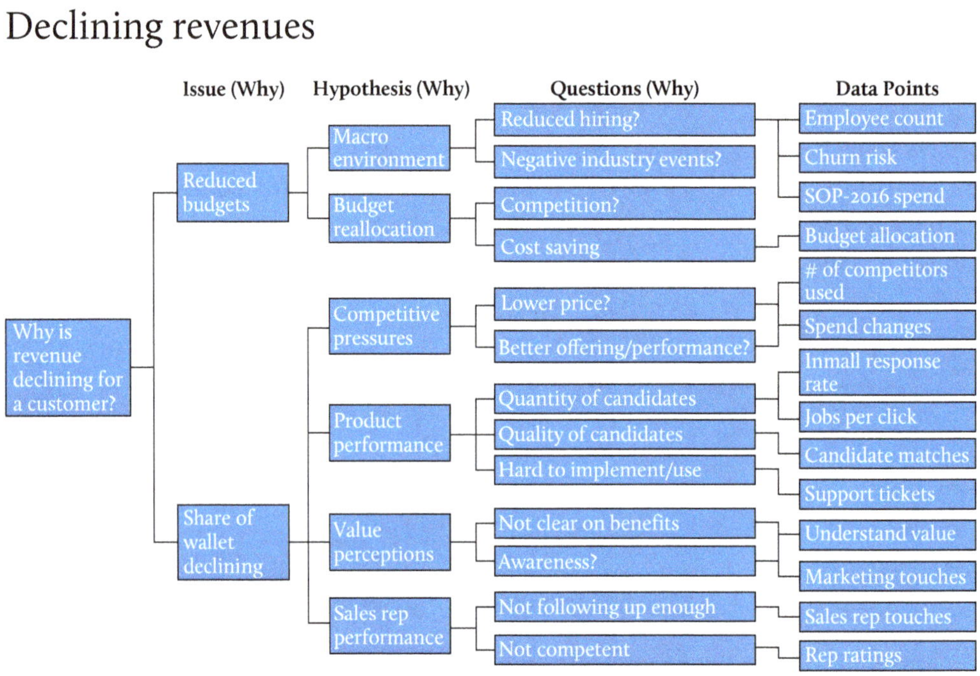

In LinkedIn's case we brainstormed many issues that could be underlying the reasons as to why revenue was declining. It is important at this step to not get into the details too quickly but provide a high-level answer to the main problem statement. In our case we determined that two overarching issues needed further investigation and formed the main branches of our tree: (a) reduced budgets, clients have for whatever reason less budget to spend than the prior year, and (b) smaller wallet share, clients still have the same or an even higher budget than last year but LinkedIn was getting a smaller share of it. At this stage it's tempting to get refined very quickly and break down the issue further, but that often leads to unnecessary complexity. In general, you do not want more than three to five issues.

Once you have identified the key issues, you continue to ask a why or how question to delve deeper into the underlying hypotheses. Why do clients have reduced budgets? Why is the share of their wallet for LinkedIn getting smaller? It's important to brainstorm as many answers to these questions as possible and then narrow it down to the three to five most salient.

Divergent thinking is a useful tool here. It is a thought process used to generate creative ideas by exploring many possible answers. It is often used in conjunction with convergent thinking, which comes directly after the divergent thinking process and uses logical steps or a set of conditions to narrow the number of issues. For example, a condition could be that an issue or hypothesis needs to be significant enough to have a material impact on revenue by impacting the majority of customers versus an issue affecting only a few customers. Or, if it's done with a large group of stakeholders, stack ranking issues based on the number of times the hypothesis was mentioned. By contrast, divergent thinking typically occurs in a spontaneous and free-flowing manner such that many ideas are generated in a group exercise using sticky notes and a whiteboard. Many possible options are explored in a short amount of time, and connections are drawn to group similar issues together. After the process of divergent thinking has been completed, the ideas and information are organized and structured using convergent thinking.

As you come up with your list make sure to write and select hypotheses that do the following:

- Describe a (assumed) causal relationship between the issue and the hypothesis; for example, share of wallet is declining because of heightened competition
- Aid in evaluating potential strategies/actions so that the outcomes from your research will be actionable; for example, the hypotheses when combined help determine how to combat the competition and reverse the declining trend in revenue but only if tested true
- Are testable and specific; for example, we can measure each of the hypotheses to determine if they are true or false
- Are comprehensive and exhaustive when taken together with other hypotheses (capture the most important aspects of why share of wallet may be declining [or not])

In LinkedIn's example, we focused our brainstorming activities on the two branches separately and started with thinking through all the reasons as to why client's budgets could have been reduced. The answers to these questions became the hypotheses (see Figure 2.3). We identified two hypotheses:

1. The macro environment is worsening.
2. Customers are re-prioritizing and reallocating budget to different areas.

The hypotheses we came up with for why share of wallet decreased are as follows:

1. The competition has a more attractive offering.
2. LinkedIn's products are not performing as expected.
3. Customers perceive LinkedIn as offering less ROI.
4. Sales reps are not performing well.

After the identification of a set of potential hypotheses, we can start thinking about the specific questions. In this step you list the assumptions or questions that need to be true to prove your hypotheses. You continue to ask the why or how question for each hypothesis that you came up with. Then you generate the key questions to prove or disprove the hypotheses, and every question should be answerable by collecting and analyzing the data. For example, in order for us to answer the question of whether the competition has a more attractive offering we need to understand its price structure and business model and how the product is performing, so these are two questions the research needs to address. As you can see, this process helps guarantee that you are asking the right questions and thereby dramatically reduces wasted efforts. It helps guarantee that you collect and analyze only the relevant data.

Once the questions have been decided, you are ready to determine, for each question, what data needs to be collected and with what method to accept, reject, or modify the hypotheses. You will quickly discover that for some of these data points you may not have to do any new net research and the information is easily accessible through syndicated research, such as the state of the macro economy. Other information needs to be obtained from internal systems. This step will provide a good sense for how difficult it is to collect the right information to solve the right problem.

Issue trees and the process of developing them help you stay organized, bring stakeholders along, and provide solution clarity. If you follow this process, you will be much more successful than if you take internal client requests and orders for face value without critically evaluating the right questions to ask. In summary, for issues trees to be effective, they need to obey five basic rules:

- Consistently answer a why or how question
- Progress from the key question to the analysis as it moves to the right
- Have branches that are mutually exclusive and collectively exhaustive (MECE)
- Use an insightful breakdown (divergent thinking is a critical skill)

An important side effect of this process is that it forces you to learn more about the business and helps bring stakeholders together to build effective relationships. This will pay dividends once the results of the research come back. The issue tree, in essence, becomes the structure of your report and how you organize your slides. You will notice that you face far less resistance since you have brought everyone along using a common framework and language. Now you are ready to translate the issue tree into a research brief and solicit proposals that will generate actionable research outcomes.

2.3 RFPs AND PROPOSALS (THE CLIENT SIDE)

Before starting a marketing research project, it is important to carefully consider what you want to accomplish, especially when other people and/or marketing research partners are involved. Most companies that work with an external supplier use a Request For Proposal (RFP), or *brief*, to brief potential partners (the terms RFP and brief are somewhat interchangeable). This RFP is also used to make sure that all internal stakeholders (decision makers, budget holders, and the people who will use the results of the research) are on the same page about the goals and expectations of the research. External suppliers that have been selected to receive this RFP (usually three to five agencies) use this RFP to prepare a research proposal for the client. After a client receives all proposals, they review these research proposals in terms of how well the research solution will address the business problem, what the reputation of the research firm is including the reputation of the specific researchers the suppliers has identified as will be executing the project and the overall price. Then they choose the one they feel gives them the best value. The supplier with the best proposal will get to work on the marketing research project.

2.3.1 Developing an RFP

As mentioned, the objective of the RFP is to make sure that all stakeholders, internally and externally, have a good understanding of the purpose of the research, the business issue that will be addressed, and results and guidelines such as timing and available budget. Most briefs have the following six sections:

1. *Some relevant background on the company*: A short description of the company, products, or services the company sells and possibly the key challenges this company faces in the market.
2. *Background for why research is needed*: The business question that needs to be addressed by the marketing research, the key decisions the clients plan to make with the results of the research, and what the research is going to be used for. For example, "The results of this research will guide our cosmetics strategy and make marketing plans and communication for both brands accurate and efficient."
3. *Research objectives, suggested methodology, and recommended sample*: The business issues are not the same as the research details. In this section, the client can clarify the research they think is needed to solve this business issue.

    - Start with the *research objectives;* for example, understand hair typologies, purchase dynamics by category, consumption dynamics, how consumers want to feel/look, and their mood.
    - Follow with *suggested methodology*, for example, stage 1 qualitative groups and ethnographies and stage 2 quantitative groups.
    - End with thoughts on *sample and geography*; for example, focus on the United States and China. In each market we propose a sample of 500 interviews with women by different age groups and social classes in the quantitative phase.

4. *Some details on expected deliverables:* It is important for clients to be precise with what they expect to receive. Is it just a written PPT (Power Point) report or also a presentation or workshop where the results are presented and where the recommendations are discussed? Is a separate report needed for each country? Do the countries need separate presentations of the results?
5. *Cost estimate and budget:* Be precise on how to see the cost estimate (the price) so that you can compare apples to apples when you receive different proposals. Do you want to see one overall cost estimate? Or a cost estimate per country? Do you want the costs broken down by phase (for example, a separate price for the qualitative and quantitative research)? Some firms may give you some hints as to what their budget is, though in most cases the client will not share this information with the suppliers.
6. *Due date/time frame:* The RFP needs to clearly show the different milestones. When do you expect to receive the proposal? In general, a supplier needs 1 to 2 weeks to prepare a proposal, depending on the difficulty of the marketing research program. For large research projects, say a 20+ country international tracking study more time may be given and needed. When will you make a decision? Most clients need a week to come to a

decision after they receive all proposals. When do you expect the research to start? And, more importantly, when do you need to have the final report/presentation/workshop?

When the brief is finished, make sure you get input and approval from all your internal stakeholders. Then send it out to the marketing research suppliers you have shortlisted as potential partners. Give these suppliers a time to call you to discuss the proposal and ask questions. You can ask the suppliers to send their questions in advance so that you can prepare (and get feedback from internal stakeholders). Then the suppliers can prepare their proposal. See Figures 2.4 and 2.5 for two examples of briefs.

FIGURE 2.4 Example RPF

Objective

The objective of this Market Research project is to develop a global consumer segmentation with an A&U overlay. This should cover all major categories and brands.

The key objective of the segmentation is to help us identify and size consumer targets, based on their involvement and knowledge of the spirits category. As the majority of our brands are challengers, we will need to bear in mind in most cases we will not have high awareness levels.

A few key questions:

- What fundamental consumer segments are there in the marketplace?
  - What are different ways consumers related to the various spirits categories?
  - What are the different clusters of consumers based on their repertoire, and attitudes towards the different spirits categories?
- What drives choice in the moment of consumption?
  - What are key drivers/barriers to engaging with spirits segments for each type of consumer?
  - How do these drivers and barriers vary by category (e.g. vodka vs whiskey)?
  - How do individual categories and brands relate to these consumers in each market?
- How do the consumer segments interact (or how engaged) with key cultural influences? E.g. music, film, politics, influencers.
- What is the size of the (future) prize? That is, translate the consumer research into sales or other figures, as well as a future forecast.

Information about your company and approach

1. General company background (what do you do, what your strengths are)
2. Your expertise/experience in segmentation
   a. What is your experience in global segmentations? Which regions/countries?
   b. At a high level, how would you tackle our challenge?
   c. What is unique about the way you would approach our segmentation, or about segmentations in general?
3. What is your company's experience in beer?
4. How would you integrate our prior motivational/need state studies?
5. How do you work with your global clients to provide consulting and implementation support?
6. What countries do you routinely conduct primary quantitative research?
7. How would you integrate other capabilities of your company to provide a robust segmentation?

2.3.2 Reviewing Proposals

The client's task is to choose a supplier from a shortlist of proposals and presentations. How are these decisions made and what criteria do they use? How a client will review and appreciate a proposal will probably vary by client, and it may not always be a fully objective process. For example, if a supplier has done previous projects for the client, this may give them an advantage, and if there are only small differences between the proposals, they may be awarded the project. However, if your task is to review proposals, we believe there are some criteria that can be used:

FIGURE 2.5 Example RPF

Research Brief

Study Title	Bread/Grains Consumer Perception Research Study
Background	Consumer health perception of bread/grains has been called into question due to the rise of various sources that state that bread/grains contribute to weight gain and other health related issues. GB has established an objective to change consumer's perception about bread/grains by +50% by 2020.
Type of research	Quantitative, multi-country.
Objective	Understand what consumers perception of bread/grains is today, and benchmark it against several other categories for reference.
Key questions to answer (3 max)	• What % of the target consumer group thinks that bread/grains are healthy/unhealthy? • What % of the target consumer group thinks that categories x, y & z are healthy/unhealthy? • How might their opinion about bread/grains be changed?
Information required	The key pieces of information needed are the overall health perception that consumers have about bread/grains, and why they feel the way that they do (healthy as well as unhealthy). The quantitative data of how they perceive bread/grains will be as important as why they perceive it to be so.
Success criteria	Success will be measured by how much improvement is made to the consumer perception of bread/grains over the next 5 years. A benchmark needs to be established that will be used to measure success in 2020.
Next steps	As a result of this research, GB will use the information to help improve the perception of bread/grains over the next several years. Another study will be conducted in 2020, perhaps sooner
Target	• Adults 18-65 (sub-segment?) • HHI- will vary by country • Canada, USA, Mexico, LAS Countries (4 studies total) • Consumers that perceive bread/grains to be unhealthy. (1 cell/country) • Consumers that view bread/grains as healthy. (1 cell/country)
Delivery date	November 1, 2016
Budget	To be shared by individual countries, proportionately.

1 *How different are the quoted prices?* For any given project, different suppliers may quote very different prices. For one, the price a supplier comes up will depend on the methodology they propose. Second, even if the methodology is exactly the same, quotes can widely vary. One of the authors worked in the central marketing research team for Microsoft and compared across several similar projects (e.g., three focus groups, interviewing 300 people in the United States, etc.) and found that Microsoft had worked with some and quotes varied substantially (e.g., one supplier charged more than twice than other suppliers). That is not the say that the lowest quote is always the best. You, as the internal marketing researcher, need to have insight into what it takes to execute a project properly. If a supplier's quote is too low, then this is reason for caution: Does this supplier really know what it takes to execute this project?

2. *Does the proposed approach answer the business and marketing research questions?* This is clearly a very important factor. Any supplier who does not make their approach clear needs to be viewed with caution.
3. *Track record and experience:* Has the supplier outlined their experience with their proposed approach? If they propose a conjoint analysis, then how many of those studies have they done, and were their clients for such projects happy with their work?
4. *Timing*: Does the proposal respect the timing that the project requires? You, as an internal marketing researcher, will have your own internal client, and they will operate under tight internal deadlines. If these deadlines are missed, that will be considered a major fail, not just for the supplier, but for you as well.
5. *Sample sources:* If the project includes third-party panel providers who provide the sample, the client needs to know the subcontractors and what process is in place to guarantee a reliable sample. Details about the panel need to be made transparent (e.g., panel composition, how the panel is recruited, what quality checks are applied, etc.).
6. *References*: Does the supplier have references (i.e., do they have other clients who are willing to provide a testimonial for the supplier you are considering)?

Often, the marketing insights team will assess the proposals on quality and timing. Sometimes, if it is a large project, the client may ask two finalists to present their proposal. This is a good opportunity to introduce the team that will be working on the project. Intangible and personal relationship factors matter a great deal. If two final suppliers are similar in terms of the objective value their proposals offer, it may come down to the chemistry between the team and the supplier. Once suppliers are rank ordered, the procurement department takes over the negotiations with the suppliers to try to get the price down.

2.4 THE PROPOSAL (THE SUPPLIER SIDE)

Upon receiving an RFP, there are seven steps a marketing research supplier will go through:

1. Reach out to the client
2. Prepare a team
3. Design a research methodology
4. Get the costs and decide on a price
5. Write the proposal
6. Present the proposal
7. Follow up

2.4.1 Reaching Out to the Client

The first thing to do when you receive a request for a proposal is to thank the client. Nothing beats a simple thank you. Remember, the client has shortlisted you as one of the suppliers to receive the RFP. This is a vote of confidence, and you should show your gratitude for this confidence. The next step is to reach out and have a conversation with the client about the RFP. Even if you think you think the RFP is clear, a conversation will build a trusting relationship with the client. Trust is important in all phases of the research project but especially in the beginning when the problem is still being scoped out and in the end when the client needs to act on the insights (Vriens, 2012) (see Table 2.2).

TABLE 2.2 Case in Point: The Importance of Trust

Lack of trust makes it harder to find out what the real business problems are, and makes it much harder to get the consumers of insights—executives and other decision-makers—to act on the insights. Yet I have seen many firms where the relationship between marketing research and marketing, and marketing research and other departments such as R&D, Finance, or Operations, is either non-existing or problematic. One study (Souder, 1981) found that if the interface between marketing and R&D was harmonious, 51 percent of new products were successful. This success rate fell to 32 percent under conditions of mild disharmony and to 11 percent under severe disharmony.

How do we become trusted? There are at least four controllable factors that drive trust between individuals or teams:

1. *Expertise/domain knowledge.* This refers the technical expertise pertaining to research, data, and analytics, but it also pertains to the knowledge an individual has about the business one is generating the insights for. The latter is extremely important, as it enables one to put the generated insights in to a relevant context and make them actionable.
2. *Professionalism.* This includes traits such as integrity, dependability, and reliability. It involves project management skills and the ability to *deliver on the explicit promise*. For example, if one promises to have insights by end of day tomorrow, those insights should be delivered by then.
3. *Delivering on the implicit promise.* The implicit promise refers to the notion that somehow insights professionals are expected to solve the right problem even if the problem is not articulated correctly.
4. *Reputation and positive past experiences.* Trust is rarely present on day one. In most cases, one has to gradually build trust by delivering on both explicit as well as implicit promises. The more people believe you provide solid insights, the more your reputation will grow, and that will improve the base level of trust you get when connecting with new stakeholders. Whenever there is no prior engagement, or much less engagement, the role of reputation becomes critical. Insights that are not the result of a specific request might need to be shared with consumers of insights, with whom there may not be an ongoing engagement. In those cases reputation will be an enabler to get these insights acted on (See Moore, Deshpande & Zaltman, 1993).

There are always subtleties or political issues that the client forgot or was not willing to include in the proposal. Also, it gives you an opportunity to better understand the business issues and what the client plans to do with the research in their own words. It will give you a chance to ask the available budget, if it is not mentioned in the RFP, and ask for any expectations in terms of methodology, sample size, and so forth. And, finally, you can get an idea if the client is open to innovative solutions and techniques, and you can try out some different approaches and see how the client reacts before you decide on a methodology.

2.4.2 Preparing a Team

When you are clear on the RFP and have discussed it with the client, you should get a team together who can work with you on the proposal, and the first decision to make is on the team leader (i.e., who is in charge of the overall proposal process and will lead client discussions). Once the team leader has been determined, you need to think of the expertise you need on your team.

- *Costing expertise*: The costing expert is in charge of getting the costs of the proposed marketing research program together so that a price can be estimated.
- *Data collection expertise*: The data collection expert advises on how to get the consumer feedback for the research. Are you considering interviewing consumers from a respondent panel or analyzing posts and blogs on social media? Do you plan face-to-face in-store or telephone interviews? Will you interview people from the client's customer database or recruit respondents via pop-ups on relevant websites? To help decide you need to ensure you have data collection expertise in your team
- *Analytical/statistical expertise:* Most research programs need an analytical or statistical expert to advise and help with multivariate analysis. Every market research firm employs senior analytical and statistical experts for support
- *Content expertise*: Other than a statistical expert, most research firms also employ so-called content experts. These people may have expertise in branding, customer satisfaction, advertising, polling, and so on. They are brought in to help teams think of a methodology that is the best fit to answer the client's business questions
- *Visual design expertise:* An undervalued skill is the visual design skill. An expert in this area can help elevate the look and feel of the deliverables, whether it is a PPT proposal, a proposal website, a proposal video, or another creative deliverable.

The first task of the team leader is to kick off with a team meeting and assign roles, responsibilities, and deadlines. Remember, the proposal deadline is not flexible and often not negotiable. The proposal needs to be at the client desk before the deadline. Missing this deadline is the best way to lose your chance of winning the marketing research project.

2.4.3 Designing a Research Methodology

Now that there is a team, you need to agree on a methodology design. Are you proposing a 15-minute mobile questionnaire, a 45-minute online questionnaire, a 5-minute pen-and-paper diary, a focus group, or an analysis of the client's database? What analyses are you proposing? The key here is to show how what you propose will answer the client's research questions.

Each of these designs will lead to a very different price. You can only start calculating the costs for the proposal after you have nailed the methodology.

So, get the team together and brainstorm on the best methodology for the RFP and think about what coming up with a solution that is reliable and robust yet creative and unique. Remember, you want your proposal to stand out from the competition. Try to push yourself in applying the latest tools and techniques. Use shorter, mobile questionnaires if feasible. Be brave in your recommendations. Err on the side of innovation. This book will give you many ideas of methodologies and analysis that will help you stand out from the crowd. However, always try to understand your client as much as possible: Is the person, or is their company, open to innovation? Are they price sensitive? Who is likely the competition (what other firms might have gotten the RFP)? These are all factors can that can play a role.

2.4.5 Getting the Costs and Deciding on a Price

The next step is to get the costs for running your proposed methodology. Reach out to the panel supplier, focus group company, social media companies, and your partners in different companies to get their costs. Don't be afraid to negotiate to lower the price (within reason). Every penny you save from your suppliers helps you get a lower price for your proposal or more profit for you. But remember that these are your long-term partners. Don't force your hand in negotiations. In the end, everyone in the value chain needs to come out as a winner. After a successful negotiation, both partners need to walk away happy.

Determining the selling price for a project is both an art and a science. Suppliers can use a variety of pricing approaches. They can use a cost-plus approach or a value-based approach. Often, the price is the result of a mixture of such approaches. The cost-plus approach can be done using spreadsheet. First, all cost sources are identified:

- All out-of-pocket costs are identified (e.g., renting facilities, sample, any subcontractors, etc.)
- Field costs (cost of the interviewing)
- Analytic team's expected hours (the number of hours is multiplied by the hourly rate of the person(s) doing the analyses)
- Project management expected hours
- Overall cost, plus a percentage of profit margin

Often, the supplier will assess whether the final price is reasonable and may further tweak the price offered to the client.

2.4.6 Writing a Proposal

Before you start putting all the pieces together (i.e., research methodology, price quote, what your firm's credentials are, etc.) think of an "edge," a theme, a framework, something creative that holds the proposal together. For example, for a large segmentation program, a team used a music metaphor as an edge for the proposal. The title was "A Different Beat," and the team showed different "beats" in chapters and how different segments would get a different beat, a different value proposition. Another example is the Censydiam framework that Ipsos uses in some of its brand studies. Censydiam is a motivational framework that recognizes eight different motivational branding archetypes. It is a useful and unique framework to give a proposal an edge.

In addition to the already discussed elements, a proposal usually also has a section where the supplier recaps the client's brief, demonstrate they understand the client's business, and last, but not least, puts a lot of effort in making sure the proposal looks visually appealing. It is best to brainstorm with the visual design expert to help think of a theme for the proposal. With this theme, the visual designer can start working on a proposal PPT template.

Now it is time to start writing. A proposal generally has six sections:

1. *Executive summary:* The executive summary is one page that briefly describes the background, the proposed solution, and why the client should choose your proposal. A good framework to use in writing this one-pager is situation-complication-resolution. The situation briefly describes the client's background, and the complication describes the business question. This is normally a problem that needs to be addressed. The resolution is a brief description of the proposed methodology and how it helps answer the business question.
2. *What we heard:* The first real section of the proposal presents the business question and the related research questions.
3. *Point of view:* The next section should show a unique point of view related to the business question. For example, if the business question is related to brands, you can write your point of view on how you think brands grow or refer to a credible source for your framework or approach. If you want to introduce a system 1 solution in your methodology, you can discuss the need for behavioral and system 1 techniques to get closer to consumer needs.
4. *Proposed methodology:* In this section you describe, in detail, the research methodology, sample structure, and type of data collection you propose.
5. *Example deliverables and case study:* Show some examples of analyses you propose to do and one or two case studies where you applied a similar methodology. This will bring your proposal to life and proves that you have done this before. A case study is one page that shows (a) the business question, (b) the methodology you used, and (c) the impact on the organization.
6. *Timing and investments:* Finally, you show the timeline of the various elements in your proposed methodology and the price/estimation.

When all elements are put together, make sure you proofread the proposal for spelling mistakes and consistency. Also, spend time improving the look and feel of the proposal. Add pictures (in line with the template and theme you choose for the proposal) and simplify the amount of text (and the titles) on the each of the pages. Push yourself. Remember, you're in competition, and you need to come out as the winner. Your proposal needs to be the best.

So, look at it one more time and be critical on yourself. Don't stop until you're completely satisfied with the result. Then, send the proposal to the client.

2.4.7 Presenting the Proposal

Often, the client invites a few shortlisted suppliers to present the proposal in person to a team of stakeholders in the organization. The client will do this if they are not sure which proposal to choose and want an opportunity to meet with the suppliers and ask questions. This is the opportunity for a supplier to prove that their proposal and team stands out from the competition. This is your chance to shine.

A presentation should not be an afterthought. Too many suppliers come to a proposal presentation unprepared and bore the audience by projecting each PPT page on a big screen and reading the text with their back turned to the audience. Then they run out of time, fast forward the last few pages in a rush, and leave no time for questions and discussion. Instead, think about your audience. They are people too. They like to be entertained, inspired, and engaged. As a simple rule, the client will likely not remember much of what you said, but they will surely remember how you made them feel.

So, how do you inspire your audience? How do you excite them? Here are a few tricks to improve your presentation skills:

- *Manage your time:* Make sure you keep your presentation to no more than 75% of the time allotted. If the client gives you 1 hour for the presentation, make sure you use no more than 45 minutes and leave at least 15 minutes for questions and discussions. As a rule, do not use more than one PPT page per minute. A 45-minute presentation means you can use no more than 45 slides in your presentation.
- *Prepare the slides:* Presentation slides are not the same as pages from the proposal. An audience doesn't read much when you present. That means you need to reduce text on the presentation slides to an absolute minimum and add more pictures, frameworks, and so on. Test yourself; if it takes you more than 20 seconds to read the text on a slide, then you need to reduce the text.
- *Assign roles:* Make sure that everyone who comes to a presentation has a role to play. You can have one, two, or three presenters (one to open and close, one to discuss the point of view, and one to discuss the sample structure and methodology, for example) and one person to take notes.
- *Prepare and practice:* As a rule, make sure you prepare with the team. Give a test presentation to a fake (internal) audience and ask for feedback. The better you prepare, the more you can relax during the real presentation and can focus on the client when you present.
- *Relax*: It is very important to try to relax during the presentation. That starts when you walk into the room. Say hi to people, have a simple conversation about the weather, the local sports team, your kids, about getting stuck in traffic, anything to start building a bond with your audience before you start. Then, when you start, open with a

funny anecdote or a simple joke (people pay more attention to you when they have a smile on their face). And please do not have your hands in your pocket when you present. You have nothing to hide and nothing to hold when you present. Try to use the range of your voice when you present. Use your voice as if you're talking with your friends. Many people, when nervous, put up their boring voice when they present. There are some simple tricks to help you improve your presentation voice that will be described later.

- *Surprise*: Think about how you can add a surprise to the presentation to make it truly memorable. Sprinkle a little magic in the room. For example, during a presentation to a haircare client, a supplier brought two actors, one doing the other person's hair in a fake hair studio. It was a way to show an insight about the use of their products in professional hair care studios. In another example, a supplier used a heart as a theme in a "brand love" proposal. Before the presentation, the team sprinkled little hearts over the table in the client room and brought little chocolates in the form of hearts for everyone. In a presentation to a famous retailer, the team came in dressed in clothes bought in one of the stores. They did not mention it, but at the end the client noticed and was pleasantly surprised. Some suppliers do qualitative interviews at their own expense and show a little video with some consumer feedback before the start of the presentation.

Exercise

A simple exercise is to read aloud a children's book using crazy voices for each of the characters, the same way you would for a 3-year-old to keep him or her entertained. Then, use the same range of voices when you give a presentation. Sound crazy? Try it and note the difference.

2.4.8 Follow-Up

The proposal is delivered, the presentation is done, but you are not done yet—not until the client has made their final decision. The phase between the presentation and the final decision is important. In this phase it is your task to stay in touch with the client. Send an e-mail with extra information, answers to some questions that were raised in the presentation, and so on. You want to remain on the client's mind during the decision-making process. No news is generally bad news.

When the client awards you the project, thank the client for the project. Also, for future learning, ask the client why they choose you. Make sure to thank the team that helped you win this project and celebrate; ring a bell, open a bottle of champagne, go out for lunch, dance, scream, but never miss an opportunity to celebrate.

In case the client did not choose for you, ask why. Learn from it and improve your next effort.

2.5 QUIZ AND EXERCISES

1. What is the difference between a specific problem and a broad problem?
2. You need to determine how satisfied the customers of the Wells Fargo branch in your city are. What hypotheses could you come up with?
3. You are doing an independent research project and you are interested in the topic of branding. You know that things like brand awareness and brand positioning are important. What hypotheses can you think of?
4. What is an issue tree?
5. Is the following statement a hypothesis: "How can a business grow its revenue by 12%?"
6. What if the hypotheses prove to be false? Is this considered a failure of your research?
7. Think about someone you know and create an empathy map.
8. What are your barriers to becoming a trusted insights partner and what can you do to overcome these barriers?
9. A company wants to conduct a brand study to help improve its brand equity. Think about three possible business reasons for clients to conduct such a brand equity study.
10. Explain in your own words what is meant by mutually exclusive and collectively exhaustive.
11. You are approached by Warner Bros. in Los Angeles. Piracy is a big problem. They want recommendations as to how to reduce piracy incidents. You are thinking about developing a survey. How can the scientific approach help you and what steps would you take before even thinking of writing a draft for a survey?
12. What is the biggest mistake you can make in marketing research?
13. You just received an RFP from a Fortune 500 client. They are requesting a bid for a segmentation study in 5 countries: U.S., Brazil, France, India, and Japan. How do you go about? Describe the steps you will take.
14. You are a marketing research manager at Proctor & Gamble, and you have just received a request from one of your internal clients to go commission a survey study. They are worried about poor sales that a new type of laundry detergent is generating (the expectations were high, but the product did not live up to its hype). How do you go about?

REFERENCES

Chapman, R.G. (18989). Problem-definition in marketing research studies. Journal of Consumer Marketing, 6, 2, 51-59.

Gilbert, F. (2013). *Speaking up, surviving executive presentations*. Berrett Koehler.

Gladwell, M. (2011). *Outliers: The story of success*. Little, Brown & Company.

Clancy, K., & Krieg, P.C. (2002). Counter-intuitive marketing. Free Press.

Green, P. E., Tull, D. S., & Albaum, G. (1988). *Research for marketing decisions* (5th ed.) Prentice Hall.

Grover, R., & Vriens, M. (2006). Trusted advisor: How it lays the foundation for insights. In R. Grover & M. Vriens (Eds.), *Handbook of marketing research: Uses and misuses* (pp. 3–17). SAGE.

Jones, S. (2004). Problem-definition in marketing research: Facilitating dialog between clients and researchers. *Psychology & Marketing, 2*(2), 83–92.

Minto, B. (2010). The pyramid principle: Logic in writing and thinking. Pearson.

Norman, D. (2013). *The design of everyday things: Revised and expanded edition*. Basic Books.

Vriens, M., & Grover, R. (2006). Structuring marketing research departments and processes for maximum impact. In R. Grover & M. Vriens (Eds.), *Handbook of marketing research: Uses and misuses* (pp. 18–32). SAGE.

Vriens, M., Brokaw, S., Rademaker, D. & Verhulst, R. (2019). Re-thinking the marketing research curriculum, 61, 5, 492-501.

Vriens, M., Chen, S., & Vidden, C. (2018). *From data to decision: Handbook for the modern business analyst*. Cognella.

CHAPTER 3

DELIVERABLES, COMMUNICATION, AND ACTIVATION

3.1 WHAT AM I GOING TO LEARN?

Communication of marketing and activation of marketing research results is an activity any marketer and marketing researcher should prepare themselves for. Any marketing research that goes unused has no value (e.g., Porter & Miller, 1985). "We want decision-makers to consume the insights, and be open to adjust, correct, or replace their mental model[1]" (Vriens, Chen & Vidden., 2018, p. 53). Don't think too lightly about the deliverables and the communication and activation of these deliverables. After all the hard work is done (the actual research), it may be tempting to put a bow on it (i.e., create a PPT deck, present it, and be done with it). We need to think about deliverables, communication, and activation comprehensively. In Figure 3.1 we show the three pillars of the engagement that need to be managed: (a) quality of the initial deliverables, (b) quality of the communication, and (c) quality of the impact.

1 A mental model is a person's belief about how the world, or, in our case, belief about consumers and the market. Some of these beliefs may be true; others may be incorrect.

FIGURE 3.1 The Engagement Model

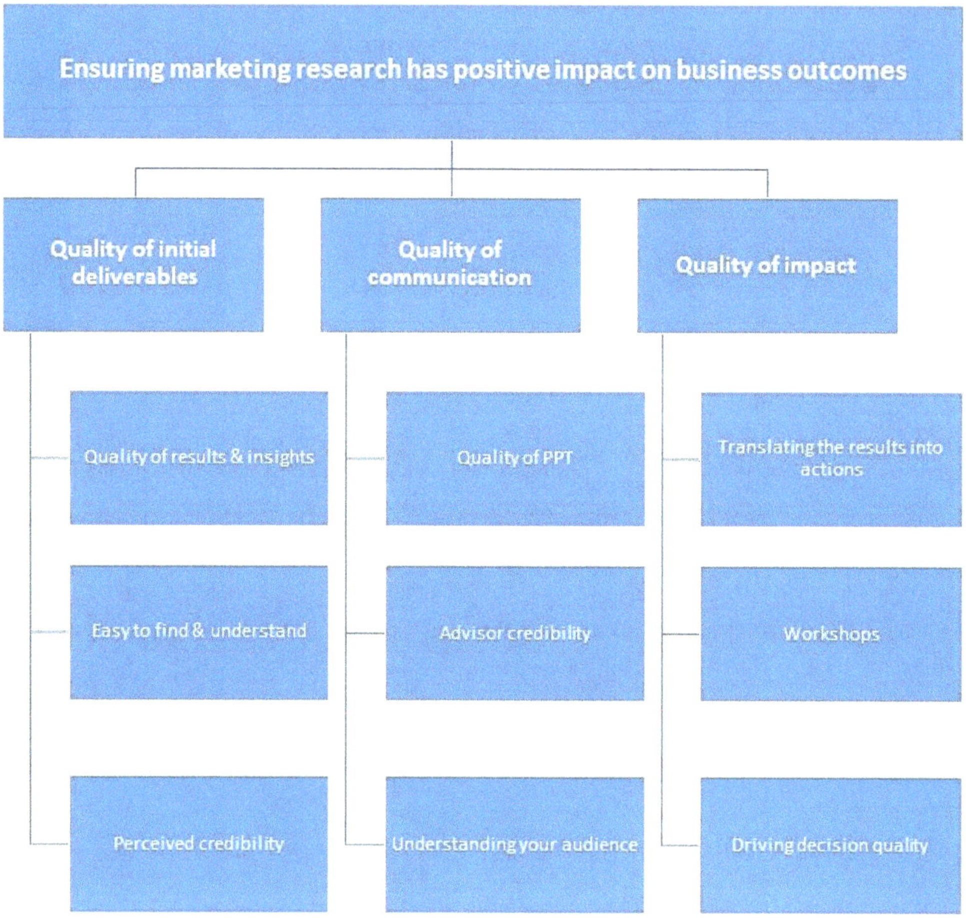

3.2 QUALITY OF DELIVERABLES

At the beginning of a project an agreement between the client and the marketing researcher is made as to how (i.e., in what format) the results will be delivered to the client; this is referred to as deliverables. After the data has been collected and analyzed, the marketing research team creates a set of deliverables that they intend to share or present to their internal client (the person or team whose budget funded the research) and possibly other stakeholders (i.e., those decision makers in the firm who did not directly fund the research but could still use the results of the research). The results of marketing research can be shared via (a) a PowerPoint (PPT) deck with tables with the factual results, along with several deeper analyses of that data (bivariate and multivariate analyses); (b) insights (these can be called out in the PPT, and major insights are sometimes communicated to a broader audience via e-mail);

(c) an Excel file with detailed results (this often the case in segmentation studies, more on this in Chapter 7); or (d) an interactive decision-support tool.

A PPT deck with the results presented is quite often the standard deliverable. Only those results that the team believes contribute to illuminating the business problem or marketing research question will be included in this deck. Whatever the format in which the results are delivered, we need to ensure the following:

1. That insights are extracted from the raw data, basic data tables, and analyses
2. That the internal clients and other stakeholders know that these results and insights exist and understand these results
3. That the internal clients perceive the results and insights as credible (Vriens, 2012)
4. That the data, analyses, and insights are woven into a compelling and inspiring story that can be remembered and inspire the client to act (more on this in the next section)

3.2.1 Extracting Insights

In one study among executives (Egan et al., 2009) one respondent commented, "I am so tired of getting reams of data from the research work. I need to know the one or two insights that affect my brand" (p. 9). One of the authors of this book recalls many such complaints, and one, a senior manager of a global CPG company, phrased it as follows: "Most of the reports I receive from my suppliers are basically large books of tables with lots of data and some interesting insights very well hidden in the big report. My latest segmentation research PPT report had 260 pages, dense with data and charts. It took my team many days to go through the report to find insights and many more days to translate these insights into actionable recommendations." Most reports have great insights and ideas, he said, but they are just very hard to find. Some research on decision making has suggested that insights are more influential than data or raw statistical results such as regression coefficients (e.g., Lavis et al., 2003; Weiss, 1991).

It is the task of the marketing researcher to tell a story, to make the most important things easy to find. Make the most important news immediately apparent and make it really simple for the reader to understand "what it all means" and "what they should do" so that they can act on it and impact their business.

Companies are always looking for consumer insights to help them grow their business. Marketing research projects aim to find insights. Great innovations are based on relevant consumer insights. The word "insight" is heavily used in the marketing research industry, but not everyone agrees on what it means. In Chapter 2 we gave a few definitions. When you Google for a definition of "consumer insights," you get over 44 million hits, with almost as many different definitions. For the purpose of this chapter, let's use the definition given in Vriens (2012):

> Thoughts, facts, data, or analysis of facts and data that induce meaning and further understanding of a business challenge and create an urgency (tension, added) to act or rethink a business challenge in terms of its problems or solutions. (p. 2)

The key words in this definition are "tension" and "sense of urgency." It needs to show a consumer problem to be resolved. Without tension, it is an obvious truth (e.g., consumers are interested in chocolate; consumers drink less beer in favor of wine; consumers choose more often low-sugar and low-calorie variants; etc.). Even though these examples can be interesting facts and show knowledge of the market, they are not consumer insights.

A good way to formulate tension is to use the "I/consumers ... but ... therefore ... framework." It starts with what is perceived as currently available (I), followed by the consumer's aspiration (but) and the impact this tension has (therefore). See the following examples:

- I know that I need to drink half a liter of water a day, but I don't have the time or I forget to drink enough water; therefore, I always feel like I am not accomplishing my daily health goals.
- I know that sugar is not healthy, but I don't know how to reduce sugar from my daily diet; therefore, I am stuck with my regular full-sugar dinners.
- Consumers love chocolate, but they understand it has too many calories; therefore, they are searching for low-calorie chocolate options.

A great consumer insight sparks innovation. It should immediately make you think of ideas on how to resolve the tension. For example, read the previous insights again and try to come up with ideas to remove these tensions with a new innovative product idea.

Another way to think about this is that insights that spark innovation tell you why customers make the choices they do (Christensen et al., 2016). Christensen et al. proceed by saying that the challenge is that the masses of data organizations collect are not organized in a way that enables them to reliably predict which ideas will succeed. The data is along the lines of "this customer looks like that one;" "this product has similar performance attributes as that one;"' or "68% of customers say they prefer version A over B"—but none of these are insights. They are observations that lack an answer as to why customers, for example, prefer A over B. This makes it extremely difficult for an organization to act on it and decide what innovation needs to take place. What further compounds this issue is that most data that gets collected (and note that we are specifically saying data and not insights) is not causal. Causality really matters for innovation to happen because it suggests that it's solving a real problem. Another classic example related to the difference between causality and correlation comes from Silver (2012): "Ice cream sales and forest fires are correlated because both happen in the summer. But there is no causation: you don't light a patch of the Montana brush on fire when you buy a pint of Haagen-Dazs" (p. 187). This notion of needing there to be causality once again underscores how important it is to think carefully, upfront, about what problems and questions you are trying to answer.

So, when sifting through the data from the marketing research, look for these insights that have a causal relationship to the original problem statement. Companies get excited and inspired with these insights, as the innovations that are based on such insights result in immediate business growth opportunities.

Finding insights are like finding the pearls in oysters. They are there: to find them you have to open many oysters. Once you have found the insights, you need to string them together in a necklace. In the next section, we will discuss how we string the pearls together in a coherent and inspiring story.

One final note on insights: Insights have features one should be aware of:

1. *They differ in value.* Some have big implications with potentially a major financial impact on the firm (see case studies in Vriens, 2012, pp. 41–66). Other insights can be smaller and may not be worth pursuing. However, there is still value in keeping track of the smaller ones as several smaller insights can sometimes build to a bigger insight.
2. *They differ in terms of how specific or broad they are.* Some insights are very specific and suggest a very specific type of action. Other insights are broader, and there is no single way they should be acted on. For example, U-Haul recognized that those shopping for moving trucks shop on price (i.e., they want the best daily rate). However, once they have rented a truck, they are not price sensitive for other shopping they do in the U-Haul rental office (e.g., buying boxes, tape, labels, etc.; see Gadiesh & Gilbert ,1998).
3. *They differ in terms of how validated they are.* Just because you believe you found an insight does not automatically mean it is also valid (i.e., if you act on it what you think is going to happen, it does not mean it will actually happen).
4. *Insights are malleable.* They can be further built on (i.e., contextualized), or they can change over time (i.e., they are not static and there may be a window in which these insights can be monetized).

3.2.2 Making the Results and Insights Easy to Find

Creating insights will make it easier for clients and stakeholders to understand and process the results of a study, but a marketing research team still needs to make insights easy to find (Vriens, Chen & Vidden, 2018). This will not be an issue for the client(s) who commissioned the research. They will be in contact with the internal research team during the execution of the project, and the marketing research team will make sure that they present the results to their client first. However, it is more difficult to make marketing research results and insights easy to find for decision makers in the firm who were not included throughout the project. There are several ways a marketing researcher or a team can involve decision makers during the research project. One, internal e-mails can be sent out to a broad internal audience, just to let decision makers know that this research has been completed and that results are available. In such e-mails, one can include the most striking insights. Two, marketing researchers can build and maintain what they call a marketing research portal (see Vriens, 2012, p. 24). This is an online repository where all the studies executed by the marketing research team are kept, including other study materials such as questionnaires, raw data, secondary data, and so on. The challenge with such repositories is that they can quickly become daunting, and it may become difficult to find anything that may be of use to you. So, a marketing research team needs to think about how to make the discoverability of existing insights easier. Three, a marketing research team can develop what we call a stakeholder communication strategy.

One possibility is to have a one-to-one, one-to-few, and one-to-many approach. There will be a few stakeholders that you can consider your tier-1 stakeholders. With these people you want to have regular one-to-one conversations, preferably in person. There may also be a tier-2 of stakeholders who are still important, but due to the size of this group, a single marketing researcher cannot meet all of them in person. So, an alternative is to meet with them in larger groups. In other words, you are not meeting with one person, but you may be meeting with 5 to 10 people at once. One of the things we started doing at LinkedIn is to send e-mail summaries to 50-plus key decision makers across Product, Sales, and Marketing departments summarizing the most important insights of the month in the form of headlines. The e-mail digest has links to PPT reports with further detail and market researchers' contact information. The advantage of this approach is three-fold: (a) by casting a wide net of known decision makers we ensure everyone is aware of the most salient and recent findings; (b) it invites dialogue and prompts the organization to ask for follow-ups, which leads to other interesting research and problems to solve; and (c) it elevates the market research function and value it delivers. On a quarterly basis we also release a "State of the Union"-type update to the executives with an overview of the most provocative findings and the extent to which we believe we are sufficiently addressing them.

This is an important job for the marketing research team: When companies have lots of research (and often analytical insights) to choose from, then decision makers may refrain from using anything at all or may only use those results that are most easily accessible or available (Glazer et al., 1992). This presentation should be discouraged as it has the risk of making things worse.

3.2.3 Perceived Credibility of the Results

Using marketing research results or insights to make a specific decision carries what Grover and Vriens (2006) call information usage risk. This refers to the risk the decision maker takes if they act on your recommendation. What if you were wrong? Recall the New Coke debacle: a decision that was based on tons of research (however, the research had flaws). To minimize the perceived degree of information usage risk we need to be transparent of the methodology, and if feasible present any validating evidence (see Vriens, 2012, p. 85). We may or may not include the methodology information in the core PPT deck (e.g., the methodological details can be included in an appendix), but they need to be shared. This can include information on sample size, sampling approach, the composition of the sample, non-response, if and how data were cleaned, if new variables were created, types of analyses (e.g., regression, factor analysis, etc.), and some detail about such analyses. The key is to communicate the quality of the results and insights and to state the limitations of the insights (Menon & Varadarajan, 1992; Vriens, 2013). In almost all market and customer intelligence projects we often need to accept limitations, be it a low response rate, incomplete customer data, and so on. Smith and Fletcher (2001) state, "We are beginning to accept the notion of fitting together evidence much of which falls short of scientific purity" (p. 62). This is often referred to as triangulation. (For a more extensive discussion of this topic see Vriens, 2012.)

3.3 QUALITY OF COMMUNICATION

Today, a PPT deck is still a core deliverable for a marketing research project, but we want to avoid creating boring PPT decks that are too long. How do we do that? We start with thinking about how to create a story.

3.3.1 Creating an Inspiring Story

We have been reading and writing great stories since we were children. Figure 3.2 shows an example of how kindergarten students at a New York City (NYC) school are learning about story structures.

FIGURE 3.2 Story Structure

Our challenge is to start writing strategic stories, not research reports. Great stories have a *structure* and a *context* (i.e., data in the story to make it come alive), and they *inspire* us to act. In this section, we will discuss these elements in more detail and how we can apply these three rules to our market research reports.

3.3.2 Structure: The Pyramid Principle

All great novels have a story structure. *The Wonderful Wizard of Oz* doesn't end when Dorothy kills the Wicked Witch of the West. It ends when Dorothy leaves Oz and goes home to Kansas. It follows a simple narrative structure; an observer who sees things the way we'd see them gets to the strange place, observes things that interest him, is transformed by what he sees, and then comes back a new person. Most mysteries follow another simple structure. The story begins when a crime takes place. The question we ask is, "Who did it and why?" The story ends when the identity and motive of the criminal are revealed. *The Lord of the Rings* begins when Frodo discovers that the ring Bilbo gave him is the key to the overthrow of Sauron, the great adversary of the world's order; it ends not with the destruction of Sauron, but with the complete reestablishment of the new order—which includes the departure of Frodo and all other magical people from middle-earth. This story follows an event structure: Something is wrong in the fabric of the universe; the world is out of order. The event story ends at the point when a new order is established or, more rarely, when the old order is restored (Card, 2010).

As mentioned, a common problem is overloading the report with data, insights, information, and more. When you have spent days or weeks looking at interesting data tables and analyses, you will have found many interesting insights. When you start writing your report and have your structure, the most difficult part begins: You have to decide what to put in the report (critical for your story) and what to put in your appendix (nice to know). Remember, less is more. The sharper and more to the point your report is, it is more likely the client will read it and be interested and inspired to follow your argument.

In marketing research, we use another structure, the pyramid principle (similar to the hypothesis tree mentioned in Chapter 2). Developed by Barbara Minto (2010), the **pyramid principle** puts the key message at the top of the pyramid, with the supporting insights following it. These supporting insights are then broken down into sub-insights (see Figure 3.3).

FIGURE 3.3 Story Structure

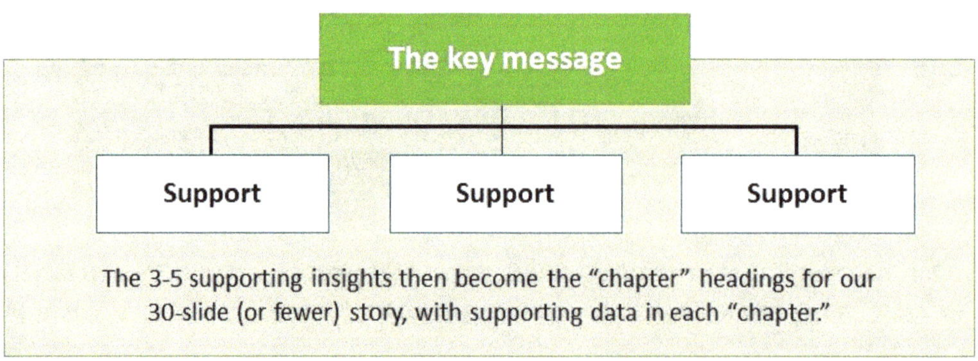

Carefully select which data pages you really need to support your insights from your pyramid page. Any data pages that do not directly support your insights should be moved to the appendix. This will force you to only use the most important data slides in your main report. It's important to review which hypotheses in your issue tree tested true and which ones were false. Your report should focus on the ones that tested true and had a significant impact on answering your why or how problem statement.

A very useful principle is the rule of three. We don't believe it has to be exactly three, though we have found that to work well (some research suggests that short-term memory can contain seven-plus or minus-two items, e.g., Miller, 1956). Most people will only remember three things. Aristotle already wrote about this in his book *Rhetoric*. Remember when you were sent to the store when you were young? By the time you got to the store, you could only remember three things. That is a great example of the rule of three. You can use this rule when you structure your insights. As a general rule, if you have more than three insights try to cluster the insights back to three. If you have two insights, then go back to the data and see if you can find a third insight.

In other words, you start your story with the main answer to the business question or the main recommendation. This is then followed by three to seven supporting insights. Any insight that does not directly support the main recommendation is nice to know and needs to be moved to the appendix. Also, if you have more than seven supporting insights, then try to cluster them further. Ideally, you end up with three to seven supporting insights. Then you add facts from the research to showcase each of the insights. Facts that do not help highlight any of the supporting insights should be moved to the book of tables or the appendix.

You want to develop the structure (the pyramid) before writing the report. Figure 3.4 shows an example of a pyramid structure narrative.

FIGURE 3.4 Example Pyramid Storyline

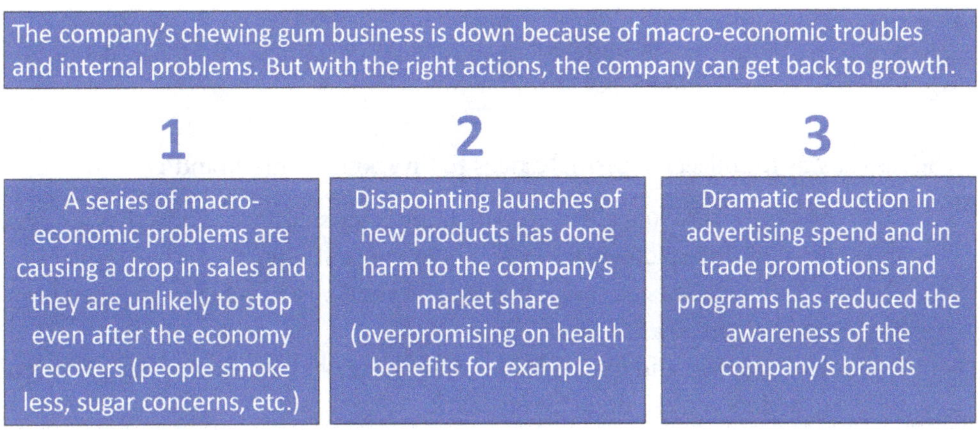

Once you are comfortable with the pyramid, you can start writing the report, structure where each node in the pyramid is a separate chapter.

3.3.3 Context

Now that you have a story structure and have decided what data to use from the research, think about how you can add contextual insights in your report to further support your story. Contextual insights are insights gained from **everything** around you that is *not* the primary study you are conducting for your client. Relevant contextual insights are insights that do not come from the marketing research but from other trustworthy sources (e.g., data from competitive products or competitive advertising, market shares, sales data, retail information, trend data, relevant demographic information, etc). (See Figure 3.5 for inspiration.)

FIGURE 3.5 Contextual Data Sources

- Academic Journals
- Company information
- Financial News and reports
- Friends and family
- Google search trends
- Available statistics
- Colleagues
- Management consultants
- Marketing associations
- Online behavioral data
- Other research
- Population statistics
- Retail tours (visit a store)
- Search engines and other social data
- Syndicated data
- Videos and ads

The easiest way to collect contextual data is to "live your clients' brand":

- Go to the store where your client's products are being sold and see how they are priced and promoted. Take pictures that you can use in your report.
- Check out your clients advertising in magazines and on YouTube; review their brands on Google, Facebook, and Pinterest.
- If possible, purchase and try out the products yourself; have your family and friends try the products and ask them for feedback.
- Read the brand and its competitor's websites and financial reports to better understand their business strategy.

All of these "living the brand" examples will bring the report to life. There are different ways you can integrate this data into your report.

You can use it to set up your story. Use financial data, competitive information, and industry data in your introduction where you describe the business problem. Or, use shelf pictures, competitive ads, and personal product experiences to strengthen your insights. You can also use the data to provide case studies.

3.3.4 Inspiration to Act

And finally, inspire your audience to act. There are many ways to inspire your stakeholders, which is ultimately the definition of success of your market research project. There are some key elements that a story needs to capture for it to become effective and for your insights to be accepted. These elements are commonly found in most great stories (Snow & Lazouskas, 2018):

1. **Tension.** Tension is a powerful element to frame your main insights in a way that demonstrates an evolution or revolution: "What we used to think is no longer true or outdated and now we need to think differently" suggests that there is a concerning gap between where we are now, which isn't working well or describes concerning market dynamics, and where we need to go to reverse negative trends and what we need to do to continue to grow our business. It creates urgency and tension. The objective with tension is to describe a situation that is dissatisfying or disconcerting to your listeners (e.g., revenue is declining because a new competitor is grabbing shares or customer have a pain point with a product). Similarly, in organizations for an insight to be effectively presented it needs to highlight a gap between "what is" and "what could" with the insights leading the way to "what could be" if acted on.
2. **Relatability.** For insights and stories to grab attention, there needs to be an element of relatability. Our brains are conditioned to like things that are familiar, which is an evolutionary trait that helped us survive and make quick decisions such as whether to flee or fight when something that we encountered was foreign. The implication for a research story is that if the insights are so different from the way an organization used to think, and so foreign, then they need to be grounded in something that is already accepted or familiar; they need to connect with what we already know and build off that. This can either be along the lines of "This is how other well-known companies dealt with this situation and this is what we need to do," or "This product is doing this well (a known fact) but with the following changes, it can overcome X, Y, or Z." If the insights are shocking or hard to believe but true, then you need to share these insights multiple times in different ways; describe in seven ways the what, when, and to whom. In psychology this is called the mere exposure theory, which basically means that just because you've experienced something before doesn't mean that you will be more inclined to like it later. The same is true for market research stories: You often need to tell the same story multiple times to multiple stakeholders before it takes root.

3. **Novelty.** Our brains also pay attention to new things that make us excited or scare us (see, for example, Ranganath & Rainer, 2003; and Schomaker, 2015). This is part of, again, how we survive, flee or fight, and our brains are very good at detecting what's new. A story and set of insights that is completely unoriginal and confirms what we already knew is going to get less attention from our brains, and it's going to get us less excited. Obviously if there is nothing new, we don't need to inspire the organization to make any changes, but if there are nuggets of information embedded in lots of things we already knew, it's important to highlight these. We will discuss information overload a little later, but it's important to tease out the pockets that are novel first.
4. **Fluency.** The insights and stories need be written in a way that they are easy to understand; write at a fourth-grade reading level. The greatest authors of our time write for a lower grade level, such as Ernest Hemingway and J.K. Rowling. The simpler you keep it, the more fluent it is. Great writing speeds you along, so great stories need to be written in a way that people don't have to think about the vocabulary. Reports need to be written in this manner so that your reader can speed through it quickly and get the main points and key takeaways. Write short sentences with words that are easy to process. Expect to rewrite your sentences and cut out clutter and go with shorter rather than longer words.

What else can you do to inspire your audience instead of a simply presenting a PPT report? Emotion is an important element in connecting with your audience in a creative way. Following are a few examples of what Ipsos has done to inspire their audiences. Remember, these are just examples. Anything that you can think of to make sure your client remembers your story is fair game. The client is likely not going to remember exactly what you tell them, but they will surely remember how you made them feel.

- For a large consumer study in Africa for a global consumer goods company, videos of people drinking beverages at breakfast, in the street, during dinner, in bars, and so forth were inserted in the online version of the report.
- For an Italian sauce producer, the product test report was delivered in the form of a restaurant menu, laminated and folded, instead of in a PPT report.
- For an appliances company, an interactive website was created to report the results of a segmentation study where the client could delve into any of the segments at will.
- The results of another large segmentation study for a large consumer goods company were delivered in the form of a pop-up show in a large building, where each room was decorated in the atmosphere of one of the segments, including actors, food, drinks, and so on. The client could walk through the rooms, engage with the actors and delve into each segment. The rooms were also recorded using a virtual reality camera so that client teams across the globe could interact with the different rooms at their own offices afterward.

3.3.5 Recommendations and Power Page

There are a few more things to consider when preparing your report. First, different from your insights, recommendations are subjective. Insights are the outcome from your marketing research. And, assuming the sample was large enough and the analysis was robust, your quantitative insights are statistically correct. A client can be pleased or disappointed with the insights and can even see an insight that you have missed. Recommendations, however, are your interpretation of the insights. How do you think the client should react to, or capitalize on, these insights? A client can, and often will, challenge you on your recommendations. Clients have more background information on the topic than you, and they have more experience in the industry than you, and as a result, they may have a different opinion on how to act on the recommendations.

It does not mean you should not give recommendations. Clients expect you to advise on what to do, even if you have limited information about the company or do not have all the background information to determine what is possible.

For all these reasons, it is important to keep the recommendations on a separate page in your report, where you clearly state that these recommendations are based on your personal judgement and with your limited knowledge of the company and what is possible. In many marketing research reports, recommendations start with phrases such as "If I were in your shoes ... "; "One possible way to capitalize on these insights is ... "; or "These insights lead to many possible growth opportunities. One way to start thinking of these opportunities, is ... "

Another way to deal with this ambiguity is to have a workshop at the end of the marketing research, but before you write the final report, where you discuss the recommendations with the client and get their input (we will discuss workshops later in this chapter). When you have client input, you can finalize the report. This way, you have already the clients input and alignment on the recommendations before you issue your report.

And finally, if you really want to push yourself and truly want to excite the client, you can try to hypothesize the monetary impact of your recommendations. This is what management consultants often do in their recommendations. This is what we call the power page, which has three elements:

1. A picture of the framework or key insight that drove your thinking
2. A numbered list of two to four recommendations for growing the client's future business that follows the "MECE" principle: mutually exclusive and collectively exhaustive
3. A graph summarizing the expected potential financial impact of each of the individual growth initiatives we've recommended

In Figures 3.6 and 3.7 you see two examples of power pages.

FIGURE 3.6 The Layout of a Power Page

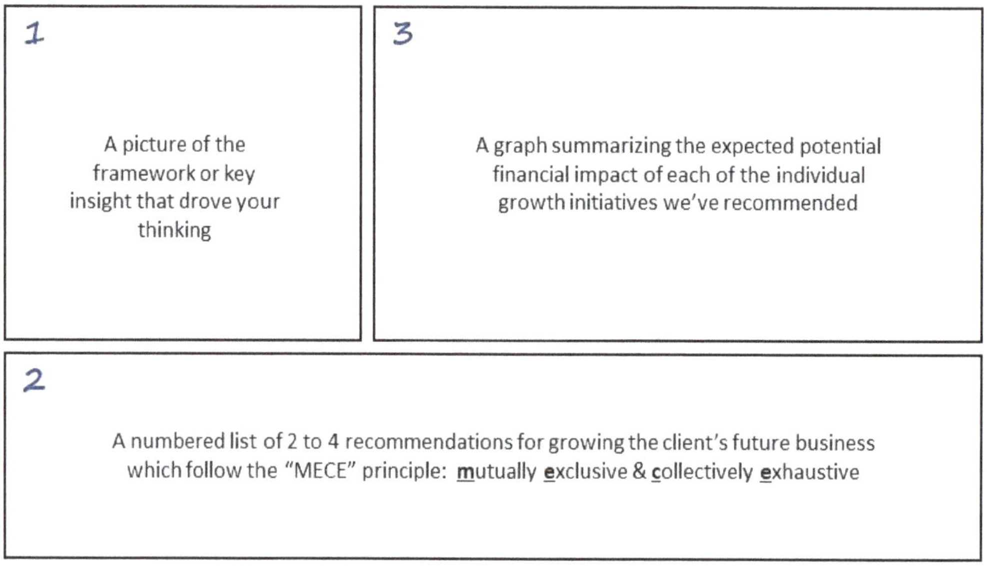

FIGURE 3.7 Power Page Example

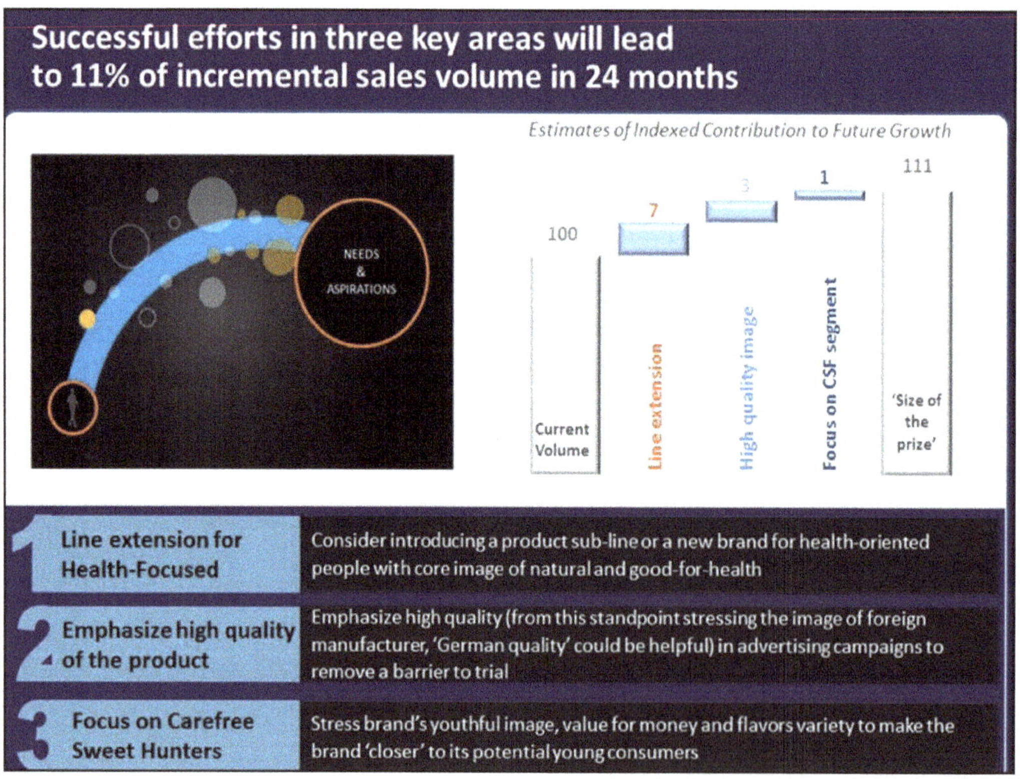

It is not widely used in the marketing research industry, but it is very highly appreciated by many clients and a great way to beat your clients' expectations.

> Example:
>
> One of your recommendations is for the client to launch a new product extension in an interesting consumer segment. For example, a candy company decides to create a new chewing gum positioned as a stress reliever for the businessperson on the go. The research shows that this segment is large (15%) and enjoys candy on the go to relieve stress but does not have many options to choose from. They think most candies are too sugary. This is the undisputable insight. We also know that the total size of the chewing gum market is 150 million (we got this information from an industry report). Our hypothesis (from previous successful launches the company has done) is that a new successful launch could give the client a 25% market share within the first year. We can now quickly calculate the monetary value of our recommendations. The segment is worth 15% of the total market (150 million), equal to $22.5 million. And, our hypothesis is that the new product will get a 25% market share in the first year, which is equal to $5.6 million. Therefore, we predict that our recommendation will lead to a $5.6 million incremental value for the client.

If you decide to use a power page in your report, it is important to clearly state the hypothesis you made in your calculations. And if your client challenges you on your hypothesis, then have a discussion, change your hypothesis if necessary, and update the power page.

> Example
>
> In the previous example, the marketing manager challenges you on your hypothesis and tells you that their largest retailer will probably not put this new product on the shelves, and as a result the marketing manager does not believe in the 25% market share in the first year. She believes 15% is a much more reasonable hypothesis. You can now simply change the 25% to 15% in your calculation and change your predicted incremental value for the company from $5.6 to 3.4 million.

3.3.6 Executive Summary

The executive summary is one of the most important parts of your report. Most stakeholders don't have time to read lengthy PPT reports, so if they see only one page or slide in your report, which one should it be? What is the one slide that provides them with the essence of all they need to know? That is the purpose of the executive summary, to quickly answer the main gist of your findings: the so what and now what. Unfortunately, the executive summary is often an afterthought, whereas it should be the forethought and receive a significant amount of time of writing and rewriting. It shouldn't take more than 15 seconds of scanning to get at the heart of the takeaways. A useful technique is to write the executive summary first, before producing the report, using the issue tree as your structure. Each bullet in the executive summary refers to a future headline of your slides. Ideally limit it to three or five main bullets with two to three sub-bullets:

- The main bullet should clearly highlight the "so what," and the sub-bullet should include the supporting data point or argument for why
- The executive summary should have the minimum number of words possible to convey the key message. (See Zinsser (1976) who provides useful tips on how to declutter sentences, improve readability, and be concise.)
- Use the exit principle to put the key reason up front, followed by further supporting arguments.
- Don't wrap lines; keep sentences on one line.

Following are some examples of a structure for an effective executive summary:
Example 1:
Our recommendation is X. We believe this is true because of the following:

- Finding A
- Finding B
- Finding C

Example 2:

- Headline: Investments in site navigation are paying off:
    - 54% of our customers are very satisfied, a significant increase of 6 points, year over year
- The increase of satisfaction is driven by the following:
    - Improved ease of use
    - Customers citing that is easier to find relevant features
- We expect an additional 6-point increase in satisfaction once we improve the site speed by 0.05 seconds in June

And here is an example of the exit principle, before and after applying it and reducing clutter in the sentences:

Before:

We are getting feedback from customers that it's harder to justify the price they pay for our products. There are several issues that may explain this. We're playing in an increasingly crowded space where value differentiation is harder than before and some customers struggle to get adequate results; customers cite declining product performance and lack of quantifiable results as reasons for dissatisfaction. Twenty-five percent of customers believe that we are "far too expensive;" however, 80% say they would pay a premium for a solution that delivers quality. Also, many reps are unable to explain the value, exacerbating poor customer perceptions.

After:

Twenty-five percent of customers perceive us to deliver poor value for the money. This is driven by the following:

1. **Increased competition:** An increasingly crowded space with aggressive pricing practices
2. **Product performance:** Customers struggle to get adequate results
    a. Customers cite declining product performance and lack of quantifiable results
    b. Reps are unable to explain the value of the product
3. **Price not always commensurate with quality:** 80% say they would pay a premium if quality was guaranteed

This example shows how you can greatly improve the readability by putting the key principle up front in each bullet in bold and structuring the main findings and sticking with the thinking in three principles, allowing the reader to grasp in less than 10 seconds what is driving poor value perceptions. Go ahead and compare it to the previous example and try and boil down the key points; you will find that it will take more time to process. A visual can often further improve the readability as humans are very visually oriented. We process visuals much faster than words. For example, the use of chevrons in PPT are a helpful aid in grouping the main themes on the left and supporting arguments on the right, following each chevron. Executive summaries with a strong visual aid are an important part of how you communicate your findings, and they need to be tailored to your audience depending on what area they have decision making authority over. Getting really good at writing executive summaries improves how you communicate your findings from the report and enhances both how you are being perceived and the confidence you exude. We will elaborate on this in the next section.

3.3.7 Attention to Detail

Remember, your client has seen many, many PPT presentations before and will not easily be inspired by yet another boring PPT presentation. You don't need to be extremely creative to add inspiration to a page, story, or presentation; just keep the elements presented in mind.

Format wise, there are also some things you can do to make your slides more inspiring:

- Attention to detail matters (use the right colors, fonts, and alignments).
- Maximize the amount of white space on the slide (simpler is always better).
- Pictures, flags, maps, and other visual objects make slides more interesting.
- Titles should be headlines or action titles, not descriptive titles.
- Display data in more interesting ways (fewer bar charts and tables).
- Data charts should be sorted so that the patterns and story are easy to see.
- The graphics (and pictures) must be relevant to clients; it's about them, not us.

- Make sure you have only one insight per page.
- The title should not spill over in two lines.
- Add page numbers.

3.3.8 Advisor Credibility

We know that the medium (the messenger) and the message go hand in hand. There are several qualities of a marketing researcher that affect his or her effectiveness in communicating marketing research results:

- Expertise: The more a person is seen as an expert in an area the more likely their suggestions (insights and recommendations) will be accepted (e.g., Bonaccio & Dalal, 2006).
- Confidence: The more confident a person delivers the message the more likely it is it will be accepted (e.g., Van Swol & Sniezek, 2005).
- Similarity: When a person (messenger) is perceived to be similar to the receiver they will be perceived more trustworthy (Sniezek & Van Swol, 2001; Perloff, 2008).

Trust is also key in identifying the right business problems (e.g., Grover & Vriens, 2006; Mayer et al., 1995; Zand, 1972) and in influencing stakeholders to use generated insights. Whenever there is an ongoing formal or informal engagement, the role of individual-level trust is critical for two reasons:

- Open communication helps with gaining an in-depth understanding of your stakeholders' business and facilitates dialogue between the two parties. It helps in getting vital information about the business and the associated problems that need to be tackled or further understood. This also helps when translating the insights into actionable and acceptable recommendations.
- It helps get the insights accepted. The likelihood of accepting an insight is influenced by information usage risk. Trust will lower the risk that comes from using information that may not be correct or from using insights that may not be valid (e.g., Grover & Vriens, 2006; Vriens, 2013).

Trust needs to be built over time and is a function of expertise, dependability, integrity, and one's ability to deliver on promises, be them explicit or implicit (Grover & Vriens, 2006).

The person who does the analytics may not necessarily be the best person to present the analytical insights. The person who communicates needs to be trusted and persuasive, especially when presenting to senior executives. In addition, the more the person who communicates is liked or is similar to the recipient of the advice, the higher the likelihood that advice is accepted (Tzioti, 2010; Vriens, 2012). The Greeks discovered that to understand your audience and to make presentations effective, three factors are needed: (a) ethos, (b) pathos, and (c) logos (e.g., see Moore & Parker, 2007). Ethos is your personal integrity and competency; it's the trust that you as the presenter have the knowledge and experience to share information that is credible and believable. Often, it's important that the person presenting has the gravitas, domain knowledge, and respect to make your audience accept the findings. Pathos is the emphatic side, how well you are in alignment with the emotions of your audience and in tune with the feelings toward the topic. Logic is the reasoning part, how well you structure and make your arguments so that people believe them to be true (Covey, 2013).

3.3.9 Understanding Your Audience: Intuitive Versus Analytical Decision Making

In the last chapter we discussed how to present to an executive audience. You prepare differently depending on who you present to. As a general rule, the higher up someone is in the organization, the less and less detail needs to be shared to be effective. In fact, for the highest-ranking executive you often don't need more than a one-page summary (executive summary); less is more has to be the mantra: saying the same thing in as few words as possible. We note that the marketing research team doesn't always have access to the CEO. This is a challenge and should be addressed. Some communication with the CEO and their direct reports is vital for a marketing research team to be successful. This senior management team typically receives "insights" via several layers of middle management. Crossing several layers of management may result in a distortion, and what gets to the top may be an incorrect version of the original insights. Some results may be left out if they don't support middle management's aspirations of if they don't understand them well enough (see Vriens, 2012, p. 75, for more details).

Over the years we have observed that as much as we believe that business decision makers are highly analytical and logical, the reality is that most decisions are made based on a high degree of intuition too. Emotion plays a key role in making decisions. There are numerous behavioral science examples across both the business and government landscape that illustrate this. Despite our best intentions to be as rational as possible, most decisions are irrational (Thaler, 2015). Hastings and Shapiro (2013) demonstrate this with how humans think about budgets. The economic principle dictates that money is fungible, meaning it has no labels restricting what it can be spent on. Contrary to this very rational idea, research has demonstrated that people have mental budgets and have a hard time shifting money around. In 2008, gasoline prices fell 50%. Rather than taking the savings and spending it on something else, research showed that people spent it on higher-grade gasoline, using up the mental gasoline budget for that sole purpose. There is really no benefit to higher-grade gasoline; this was an intuitive but rather irrational decision, which shows that audiences may not react in a rational way to facts and logic. Therefore, a good presentation needs to hit on both the rational and emotional aspects to influence decisions. We experienced this firsthand at LinkedIn when we presented our small business findings to the executive team and received a lukewarm response. The report was highly analytical, using lots of facts and logic, but it failed to inspire and land an effective message. To quote one of the leaders afterward, "I still feel like I don't really understand this segment." It wasn't until we took the executive team on a field trip to talk to some of the respondents from our study that it became clear how they needed to act and why. They were able to connect in a much more emotional way by experiencing and listening to small business owners and relating it back to the key insights from the research.

There are four key aspects one needs to consider when understanding your audience:

1. *What does your audience actually care about?* In general, most stakeholders care about understanding three things. First is feedback from customers on what's working well and what is not working and the extent to which action plans need to be put in place and adjusted. Second are opportunities that can help them grow the business, either from new suggestions to innovate, expansions into new markets, or altering an existing go-to market strategy (i.e., the way in which a product or service is marketed and sold). Third are external threats, disruptions from existing and new competitors, or shifts in customer behavior. Often a competitive forces analysis (e.g., Porter, 2008) or a SWOT analysis, summarizing the strengths, weaknesses, opportunities, and threats, is a good framework to characterize the different dynamics in the business and marketplace and is a way to integrate research findings with business dynamics. Covering these dimensions will hit topics that your audience cares about. It is always wise to bring stakeholders along at each step of the process, from problem definition and issue tree to analysis and report drafts so that it's clear what areas should be focused on. You make your stakeholders part of the problem and process.
2. *What's already on their mind? What are they expecting?* Every decision maker has a set of annual objectives (sometimes called commitments); these are accomplishments they agreed to with their manager for a given fiscal year. Sometimes decision makers have quarterly objectives too. These short-term objectives will motivate them. So, the more you can link the insights to these short-term objectives, the higher the likelihood they get acted on. Every business has a set of priorities they are operating against, so it's important that researchers and suppliers are aware of what these are. That way, the insights and stories can build to overarching priorities. Using that lens makes it easier to grab their attention in an area they already care about. For example, at LinkedIn we generally have priorities that are related to (a) team and talent, (b) operational excellence, and (c) product and monetization. Within each of these priorities there are questions and challenges the business is trying to address. How can we expand our offering to different segments? Should we raise our prices? What's the impact of reduced service levels on customer sentiment? How strong is employee engagement? Stakeholders expect answers to these questions. Research needs to address the why and provide an assessment of how it will impact the business. For example, suppose customer satisfaction has been declining because the website is becoming harder to navigate (that's the why part, and it's causal); therefore, we expect sales to go down by 20% (the impact piece). That last part leverages the power page and, as we demonstrated earlier, is a critical piece for getting traction. Often market research is too descriptive and doesn't go deep enough into building the business case for action by leveraging financial and sales data. Building a template report in advance of having

the data guarantees that the right areas will be covered in a visual way. Before you present the findings, it's important to have a clear agenda and a statement upfront that says, "This meeting will be successful if we agree that we need to act on X, Y, or Z."

3. *What level of detail would be most effective?* The higher up your audience is in the organization, the less detail you need to share. If your stakeholder is responsible for execution, the findings need to be very specific and tangible. For example, a recommendation from a market researcher to a product manager can be, "Remove asking location and company in the registration flow to improve the experience." If the stakeholder is a vice president (VP) of a business unit, the research needs to highlight strategic implications; for example, "The registration flow needs to be adjusted because its blocking growth."
4. *What decisions are they responsible for?* What are their preferences for how to consume research? You should always try and put yourself in the shoes of the audience and factor in the decisions they are responsible for and the tradeoffs that need to be made. A VP of sales will often want to know the one thing to drive sales, the area to focus the most energy on that can be directly influenced. For example, the research may suggest that product and account management drive customer satisfaction, but product has more weight. The report can elaborate on product, but a VP of sales will have little influence over it unless there is a clear connection to how the account teams are operating. The report instead should highlight what is directly in the VP's circle of influence and how his or her actions factor into the overall scheme of things. PowerPoint is still the common format in which results get shared, but it's worth getting an upfront idea of whether your audience appreciates a pre-read send in advance to have a discussion versus a presentation.

3.4 QUALITY OF IMPACT

With our quality deliverables in hand, now begins the task to make sure our client(s) and stakeholders do something with the insights. In our experience, embedding insights into the organization can take as much time as it took to produce the insights. Following, we discuss how to make insights actionable and so that they lead to good decisions.

3.4.1 Translating Insights into Business Growth Ideas

We previously discussed the idea of a power page to call out the expected monetary value of your recommendations. To do this, you need some basic understanding of how companies grow and how they make money. Understanding basic financial principles are key for a marketing researcher.

The number of people times the number of times they purchase the product in a month, times the number of products they purchase each time, times the price gives you client revenues per month. When you subtract the costs of the product and the overhead costs (staff, building, etc.) you get the profit. This means that there are four basic revenue drivers for a company:

1. How many people buy your client's product: A company can increase the number of people by targeting new consumer segments or new markets altogether.
2. How many times they purchase the product: A company can increase the number of times by finding more purchase occasions or more locations to sell the products (online, mobile, for example).
3. How many products they buy each time: A company can offer promotions in store, like buy two, get the third free.
4. The price they pay: By offering new features to a product, companies can increase the price.

For each of your insights, think how it could help your client drive revenues using the four revenue drivers. This will help translate your insights into business growth ideas.

3.4.2 From Insights to Action Through Workshops

Many marketing research suppliers use client workshops to bring insights to life, come up with new product ideas, or activate recommendations. In this section, we discuss how to run a productive and effective workshop and review a few typical types of workshops.

> Running a workshop is like being both the chef AND the host of an important meal. Like any good chef, you wouldn't turn up to a kitchen and hope to find the right ingredients. Good meals, like workshops, involve careful planning and preparation, skill in the cooking of the meal on the day as well as timely delivery of all the courses (nice and hot!) to keep your demanding guests satisfied! (Hamilton, 2016, p. 1)

In any successful workshop you define its purpose, you plan and prepare, and you execute and follow up. It is important to define the purpose before you start, because if you don't know where you are going, how will you know when you have gotten there? Define your purpose in a way that is specific (in what you are trying to achieve), clear (so everyone can understand what to expect), and relevant (so the participants think it is worth their time). It is critical to identify, discuss, and agree on this with your key stakeholders. It can be hard to establish clear, simple, and relevant objectives, but try to be as explicit as possible. For example, an objective can be to "develop strategies to grow the business," but it is better to be more explicit: "identify three key opportunities for growth for XYZ and specific point of purchase activities to capitalize on them."

Before you start your workshop, make sure you are well prepared. That means think about the structure of the session and about an inspiring venue and who should be invited. Think about what stimuli you can bring to the workshop and how to make the day special.

It is not easy to manage a workshop; it requires skills and expertise to be a workshop facilitator. A great workshop facilitator understands the business objective, has a great relationship with the client, is in control of the room, and has a charismatic and inspiring personality. Most importantly, a great facilitator makes sure that the team delivers on objectives. A few tips for a great workshop are as follows:

- Be very clear in your instructions. Keep it clear, simple, and visual.
- Don't be scared of constructive conflict because polarized views are part of a healthy process in creating ideas.
- Boost energy levels by changing seating and groups, moving the room around, making people stand, playing energizing games during the session, and so on. In general, you get as much energy from the group as you put in. A passive facilitator creates a passive group and vice versa.
- Create an inspiring ambiance with visuals, sensorials, and musical impact.
- End the workshop by discussing next steps and considering how the takeaways from the session can be applied to the future.

There are different types of workshops in marketing research. One type is the "bringing insights to life" workshop. The goal of this workshop is to energize the audience behind the insights and make them truly understand and experience them. These types of workshops are often used in segmentation studies where the research finds several interesting consumer segments. See Figure 3.8 for a few examples from a workshop where clients were asked to use pictures from magazines and brainstorm to develop a one-page report of a persona to describe a segment.

FIGURE 3.8 Bringing Segments to Life

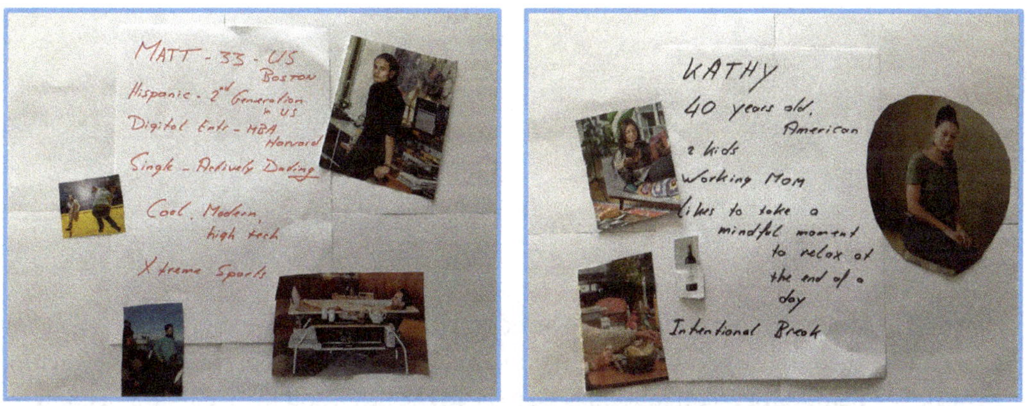

Another type of workshop is an ideation workshop, where the goal is to develop exciting new product ideas or concepts based on the consumer insights your marketing research found. Figure 3.9 gives an example of the kind of concepts that are created by a visual sketch artist in an ideation workshop. An ideation workshop is a specialized workshop and needs trained and skilled facilitators to deliver impact. There are specialized ideation companies who offer these kinds of workshops, but some large marketing research companies, like Ipsos, have trained and specialized ideation teams who can deliver these workshops.

FIGURE 3.9 Ideation Workshop

And, finally, there are activation workshops, where the goal is to agree and decide on how to activate the recommendations in the organization. This is a more business-oriented workshop where key decision makers need to be in the room and the facilitator needs to be more business oriented.

3.4.3 Driving Decision Quality

After decision makers have shown the intent to use the results and insights, we still need to ensure the actual and the correct usage of the results and insights. There are several factors that affect decision quality:

1. Outcome and insights uncertainty and how it is managed
2. Having "making good decisions" processes
3. Leveraging decision support tools

3.4.4 Outcome and Insights Uncertainty

Mistakes can still be made even when decision makers use the results or insights. There are two types of uncertainty that, if not recognized, can cause mistakes: outcome uncertainty and insights uncertainty (Vriens & Rademaker, 2016). Outcome uncertainty is defined as the confidence that a decision maker can have in either the statistical results of the data or in the analytic methods used (Vriens & Rademaker, 2015). Statistical uncertainty can be caused by low-quality (unreliable) data or by a model being used.

Insights uncertainty exists when insights are incomplete. There are still unanswered questions that are needed (e.g., the insight is open to interpretation or the results are not validated). For example, consider the marketing director of a financial services bank who is responsible for making the decision to go forward with a new financial service. Initial focus groups seemed to support the firm's gut feeling that consumers want this new service. Even though the new product was initially suggested by a senior executive, the marketing director commissions a concept test study to verify that it indeed is a product that consumers would buy and that it's a good idea to launch this new service and justify the infrastructure and marketing investments. The marketing team also expects a discrete choice conjoint test to tell them exactly how big the demand for this new product is so that it can set expectations and ask for the required budget. The results indicate that 25% of the sample would be willing to buy this service at a price of $15 per month. After the service gets introduced, the uptake is slow—much slower than expected. The result is that the internal decision maker's faith in marketing research is reduced. Consumers are known to overstate their intention to buy something and known to overstate the price they are willing to pay for it. To avoid insight uncertainty mistakes, one can articulate the assumptions, increase the likelihood that the assumptions are holding up in the market, or quantify how the predicted outcome might change if assumptions are not holding up in the market.

3.4.5 Making Good Decisions Processes

Insights may not reach all decision makers and may remain unused. So, in addition to presenting and disseminating the insights, we should also try to use processes (e.g., a process that requires decision makers and executives to follow certain steps leading up to the decision). There can be a process for planning and review (this section is based on Vriens, 2012, pp. 93–100).

Any manager or executive setting their annual goals and articulating their operational plans is required to have a plan or playbook. In that document, they need to articulate the consumer facts, trends, and insights that form the foundation of their program. For example, any chief marketing officer (CMO) is required to have a marketing plan that contains relevant insights that support their specific programs.

We need to make sure plans are reviewed in terms of how well they are supported by data and insights (Vriens, 2012). Part of a review process could also be a commitment to do, wherever feasible, a small-scale field test to see whether the new approach works. It is very possible that an organization takes an incorrect action either because the insights weren't complete enough and/or were misinterpreted.

An additional benefit of a planning process is consistency. It is entirely possible that decision makers do the right thing in one situation but then drop the ball in another situation. An example is given in a case described in the *Harvard Business Review* on Henkel's global branding decisions (Kashani, 1989). For one of their brands, they ensured that a decision was backed by data and insights, and this decision was successful. They made also made a similar decision for a different brand without checking if this decision was warranted by data and insights, and this decision was not successful.

Leveraging Decision Support Tools

It will help to have a tool (e.g., an Excel file) that embeds the insights in an interactive decision support tool (DST). A DST tool can help make decisions more easily and effectively. Marketing DST tools have been proposed and used for resource allocation decisions, sales force optimization decisions, pricing and branding decisions, and so on. DST can offer several benefits:

- It enables easy access to vast amounts of data. Easy access to a relevant subset of the data helps the decision makers ask the right questions and narrows the set of possible directions in which a decision needs to be pursued.
- It reduces mistakes and creates efficiency. If all the data is in one place, then all decision makers will access the same data and will see the same numbers.
- It allows simulations of hypothetical decisions. A DST can calculate many different hypothetical scenarios in a way that helps the decision maker quickly home in on those most likely to succeed, leading to the best decisions. An underlying statistical model that predicts the outcomes of various hypothetical scenarios is needed for this type of use.

Samsung used a DST when they were transitioning from a behind-the-scenes brand to a fully recognized by consumer brand. One of the executive vice presidents in charge of this, Eric Kim, wanted to understand where the organization was wasting money and under-spending. The challenge was to get insights from data on 14 product categories in more than 200 countries. A detailed description of this case is described in a *Harvard Business Review* article (Corstjens & Merrihue, 2003).

A DST tool can improve both the efficiency and effectiveness of decisions (Sharda et al., 1988). However, getting decision makers to use a computer-based tool and its recommendations is not a given. Four factors have been found to affect the adoption of DST: ease of use, training, feedback on upside potential, and feedback on how to improve one's own mental model (Lai et al., 2006). Even if one develops a system that seems very easy to use, one will still find that for some it is not as intuitive. Hence, training of the target user group is typically a requirement (Lai et al., 2006).

In addition to building a system that is very easy to use, one should try to make the system transparent and aim for not only helping the user make better decisions but to help the user learn while using the system. Providing feedback on the upside potential (i.e., the gain from following the system's recommendation) and feedback on corrective actions (i.e., guidance on how one's "mental model" should be corrected) helps in getting users to accept and use the DST) (Kayande, 2008). The latter finding also applies to insights that are being used outside a DST. A second component of guidance, therefore, is outlining the various gains and risks that can be conceptualized from the insights (Vriens & Verhulst, 2008).

3.4.6 Follow-Up

The final report, presentation, or workshop is often used by market research suppliers as an opportunity to strengthen the client relationship and start a new marketing research project. It could lead to a workshop to help maximize actionability of research findings and the impact of marketing decisions. Or, it could lead to new research to track brand equity, positioning, or the performance of the latest innovation launches (more about this later in the book). Many suppliers make a point of recommending such follow-up research in their list of recommendations.

Even if there is no immediate follow-up research, as a market researcher, you should stay in touch with the user of the research to understand the impact of your recommendations. It is easier said than done. When a project is completed, the market researcher is likely to start working on another project and has little time to think of following up on a finished project. But, in many cases, a follow-up can be as simple as a quick e-mail, text message, or phone call a few months after the completion of a study to understand what was implemented and how it impacted the client's business. Or, send your client a relevant article you read, a thought you have on one of the insights you presented, or an example of a competitive product or advertisement you've seen related to your recommendations.

And finally, many companies, marketing research suppliers, as well as consultancies create a simple one-page business case study at some point after they complete the research. This business case can be used to capture and catalogue the learnings, to use as an inspiring example in proposals, or to inspire the organization. A simple structure for a one-page business case is to show the business issue, the marketing research solutions that were used, and the impact the study had. In addition, you can use inspiring quotes to bring the case study to life (see Figure 3.10 for an example).

FIGURE 3.10 Example Business Case Study

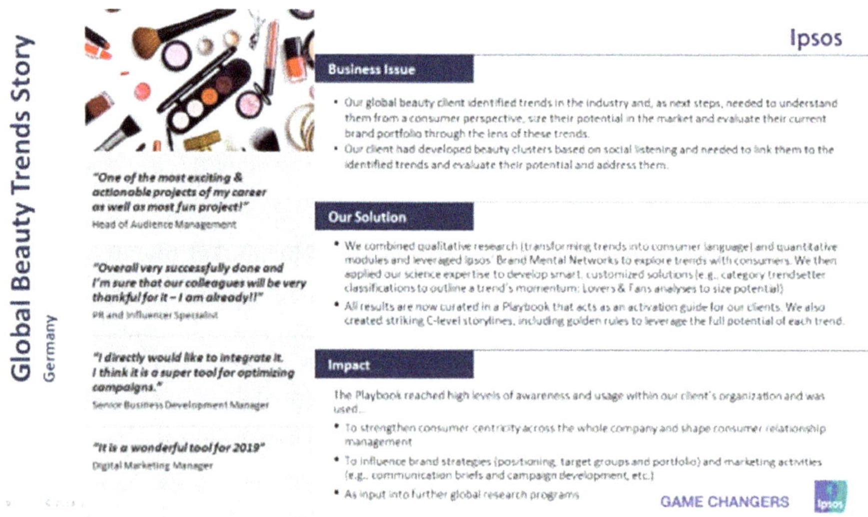

3.5 QUIZ AND EXERCISES

1. What factors drive whether clients will use marketing research results and insights?
2. How can you establish credibility?
3. What does the term "triangulation" refer to?
4. How can you drive good decisions?
5. What are the three elements of a story structure?
6. What are some of the reasons why internal stakeholders, or even your clients, may not act on the marketing research results and insights?
7. What are the four basic revenue drivers?
8. What four things do you need to know about your audience?
9. What is outcome and insights uncertainty?
10. What are some of the benefits of a decision support system?
11. You are the head of a financial services company. The audience you serve is both high-net personal investors and professional asset managers. Both use and pay for a variety of services (including special market reports, in-person market updates, etc.). You have tons of data on this audience. Recently, the global CMO shared the data that the marketing team has access to with you; it pertains to engagement data. Table 3.1 shows the engagements.

TABLE 3.1 The Effect of Engagements on Customer Satisfaction

Engagement options for customers	Percentage very satisfied customers if NOT using engagement	Percentage very satisfied customers if using engagement	Delta
Newsletters subscription	6%	7%	1%
Webinar attendance	4%	6%	2%
Blogs readers	5%	6%	1%
Online communities	3%	9%	6%
In-person training	2%	10%	8%
Life events attendance	1%	7%	6%

Table 3.1 also compares the percentage of satisfied customers across versus those who are not satisfied using the engagement. The table is based on results of a survey that asked customers to rate the satisfaction with the company on a five-point scale (1 = very dissatisfied, 2 = somewhat dissatisfied, 3 = neutral, 4 = somewhat satisfied, and 5 = very satisfied. In the table we show the percentage of the survey respondents who rated the firm a 5 (top-1 box score). For example, among all respondents who said they did not subscribe to newsletters, 6% are in the top-1 box whereas 7% of respondents who do subscribe fall in the top-1 box.

a. Is there anything the company should do immediately?
b. Is there information missing that you wish you had?

The CMO shares with you that this information is available at the international level. The company does business in 10 countries. For each engagement, the CMO receives monthly updates on (a) how many customers used the engagement, (b) how many in each country used the engagement, (c) the money spent on an engagement by country. Each country has a marketing manager who is responsible for trying to get as many customers to engage with the company as possible. Each engagement has a global engagement manager. This person is responsible for setting the global guidelines for this engagement and supporting the country's marketing managers. The CMO shares the challenges that she wants addressed. She feels overwhelmed with all this data that comes in on a monthly basis.

c. Is there a way for it to be presented to her in a more insightful way?
d. Can you think of any other data that will lead to better decisions?

REFERENCES

Bonaccio, S., & Dalal, R.S. (2006). Advice taking and decision-making: An integrative review of the literature. *Organizational Behavior and Human Decision Processes, 101*(2), 127–151.

Card, O. S. (2010). The 4 story structures that dominate novels. *Writers Digest*. https://www.writersdigest.com/writing-articles/by-writing-goal/write-first-chapter-get-started/4-story-structures-that-dominate-novels

Christensen, C., Hall, T., Dillon, K., & Duncan, D. (2016). *Competing against luck: The story of innovation and customer choice*. Harper Collins

Corstjens, M., & Merrihue, J. (2003). Optimal marketing. *Harvard Business Review*, 114–121.

Covey, S. (1989). *The 7 habits of highly effective people*. Simon & Schuster

Egan, M., Manfred, K., Bascle, I., Huet, E., & Marcil, S. (2009). *The consumer's voice—can your company hear it?* Center for Consumer Insights Benchmarking. https://www.bcg.com/documents/file35167.pdf

Gadiesh, O., & Gilbert, J. L. (1998). Profit pools: A fresh look at strategy. *Harvard Business Review*, 139–147.

Glazer, R., Steckel, J. H., & Winer, R. S. (1992). Locally rational decision-making: The distracting effect of information on managerial performance. *Management Science, 38*(2), 212–226.

Grover, R., & Vriens, M. (2006). Trusted advisor: How it helps lay the foundation for insights. In R. Grover & M. Vriens (Eds.), *Handbook of marketing research* (pp. 3–17). SAGE.

Hamilton, P. (2016). *The workshop book: How to design and lead successful workshops*. Pearson.

Hastings, J., & Shapiro, J. (2013). Fungibility and consumer choice: Evidence from commodity price shocks. *Quarterly Journal of Economics, 128*(4), 1449–1498.

Kayande, U., De Bruyn, A., Lilien, G. L., Rangaswamy, A., & Van Bruggen, G. H. (2008). How incorporating feedback mechanisms in a DSS affects DSS evaluations. Information Systems Research, 20, 4. 481–609.

Kashani, K. (1989). Beware the pitfalls of global marketing. *Harvard Business Review*, 91–98.

Lai, F., McMillan, J., Daudelin, D. H., & Kent, D. M. (2006). The potential of training to increase acceptance and use of computerized decision-support systems for medical diagnosis. *Human Factors*, *48*(1), 95–108.

Lavis, J. N., Robertson, D., Woodside, J. M., McLeod, C. B., & Abelson, J. (2003). How can research organizations transfer research knowledge to decision-makers. *Milbank Quarterly, 81*(2), 221–248.

Mayer, A. C., Davis, J. H., & Schoorman, E. D. (1995). An integrative model of organizational trust. *Academy of Management Review*, *20*(3), 709–734.

Menon, A., & Varadarajan, P. R. (1992). A model of marketing knowledge use within firms. *Journal of Marketing*, *56*(4), 53–71.

Miller, G. A. (1956). The magic number seven, plus or minus two: Some limits on our capacity for processing information. *The Psychological Review*, *63*(2), 81–97.

Minto, B. (2010). *The pyramid principle: Logic in writing and thinking*. Pearson.

Moore, B. N., & Parker, R. (2007). *Critical thinking*. McGraw-Hill.

Perloff, R. M. (2008). *The dynamics of persuasion: Communication and attitudes in the 21st century*. Lawrence Erlbaum.

Porter, M. E. (2008). The five competitive forces that shape strategy. *Harvard Business Review*, *88*(1), 78–93.

Porter, M. E., & Miller, V. E. (1985). How information gives you competitive advantage. *Harvard Business Review*, *85*, 149–160.

Ranganath, C., & Rainer, G. (2003). Neural mechanisms for detecting and remembering novel events. *Nature Reviews Neuroscience, 4*(3), 193–202.

Schomaker, J. (2015). What's new: The interaction between novelty and cognition (Dissertation, University of Amsterdam).

Sharda, R. S., Barr, H., & McDonnell, J. C. (1988). Decision-support systems effectiveness: A review and an empirical test. *Management Science, 34*(2), 139–159.

Silver, N. (2012). The signal and the noise: Why so Many predictions fail—but some don't. Penguin.

Smith, D. V. L., & Fletcher, J. H. (2001). *Inside information: Making sense out of marketing data*. Wiley.

Sniezek, J. A., & Van Swol, L. M. (2001). Trust, confidence and expertise in a judge-advisor system. *Organizational Behavior and Human Decision Processes, 84*(2), 288–307.

Snow, S., & Lazouskas, J. (2018). *The storytelling edge: How to transform your business, stop screaming into the void, and make people love you*. Wiley.

Thaler, R. (2015). *Misbehaving: The making of behavioral economics*. Norton.

Tzioti, S. (2010). *Let me give you a piece of advice: Empirical papers on advice taking in marketing* (Doctoral dissertation, Erasmus University of Rotterdam, The Netherlands).

Van Swol, J. M., & Sniezek, J. M. (2005). Factors affecting the acceptance of expert advice. *British Journal of Social Psychology, 44*(3), 443–461.

Vriens, M. (2012). *The insights advantage: Knowing how to win*. iUniverse.

Vriens, M. (2013). The cure for infophobia. *Quirks*, 62–67.

Vriens, M., Chen, S. & Vidden, C. (2018). From data to decision: Handbook for the modern business analyst. Cognella academic publishers. San Diego, USA.

Vriens, M., & Rademaker, D. (2015). To be determined. *Marketing Insights*, 17–21.

Vriens, M., & Verhulst, R. (2008). Unleashing hidden insights. *Marketing Research Magazine,* 12–17.

Weiss, C. H. (1991). Policy research: Ideas or arguments? In P. Wagner, C. H. Weiss, B. Wittrock, & H. Wollmann (Eds.), *Social Sciences and Modern States: National experiences and theoretical crossroads* (pp. 307–332). Cambridge University Press.

Wikipedia. (n.d.). *New Coke*. https://en.wikipedia.org/wiki/New_Coke

Zand, D. E. (1972). Trust and managerial problem solving. *Administrative Science Quarterly, 17*(2), 229–239.

Zinsser, W. (1976). *On writing well: The classic guide to writing nonfiction*. HarperCollins.

Image Credits

Fig. 3.10: Copyright © 2018 by Ipsos. Reprinted with permission.

CHAPTER 4

MARKETING RESEARCH DATA

4.1 WHAT AM I GOING TO LEARN?

In this chapter we take a broad view of marketing research data. We discuss traditional marketing research types of data, such as quantitative survey data and qualitative data (e.g., focus group data, ethnographic research, etc.), secondary data sources, internal company data, online consumer-generated data (e.g., discussion on consumer review forums, social media data, etc.), and other types of Big Data.

In section two we preview various general features of data. In sections three and four we discuss qualitative and quantitative data. In section three we discuss focus groups, individual interviews, ethnographic research and online research communities, whereas in section four we discuss briefly surveys, transactional, and experimental data. There are many market research textbooks where you can find more elaborate discussion of these methods (e.g., Babin & Zikmund, 2016). There are also specialized books and papers, some of which we will refer to in this chapter. In section five we introduce the topic of data governance, an increasingly important topic, and section six covers the topic of ethics.

4.2 FEATURES OF DATA[1]

There are many types of data that can be described along several features. See the following examples:

1. *External versus internal.* Some are collected by firms as a byproduct of operating their business (e.g., sales data, customer complaints, service calls, etc.). Internal data is, in most cases, just the byproduct of operating the business (Ferguson et al., 2005). Data can also be collected externally, often with a specific business objective in mind. Examples of external data are (a) marketing research reports based on primary market research surveys, focus groups, and observational research and experiments (discussed in the next sections, but also see Babin & Zikmund, 2016); (b) syndicated commercial research reports (i.e., you have to pay for this data); (c) syndicated free data (e.g., see Marr, 2016); (d) data that can be scraped from the internet; and (e) public data that may give information on demographics, economic and consumer trends, government

1 This section is based on Chapter 2 from the book by Vriens, Chen & Vidden (2018).

regulations, unsolicited comments on your brand or product, and so on. For example, if I want to find out what houses in my area have sold for, then I can request this data from City Hall.

2 *Levels of aggregation.* An important distinction is the level of aggregation. We distinguish between individual-level and aggregate-level data. For example, if we collect data via surveys, we typically obtain data from individual respondents. If we collect or use scanner data, that level of detail may be lost. We may get the aggregate level of sales of a given store without the detail of what an individual customer may have bought. Figure 4.1 shows some examples of different levels of aggregation.

FIGURE 4.1 Example of Levels of Aggregation

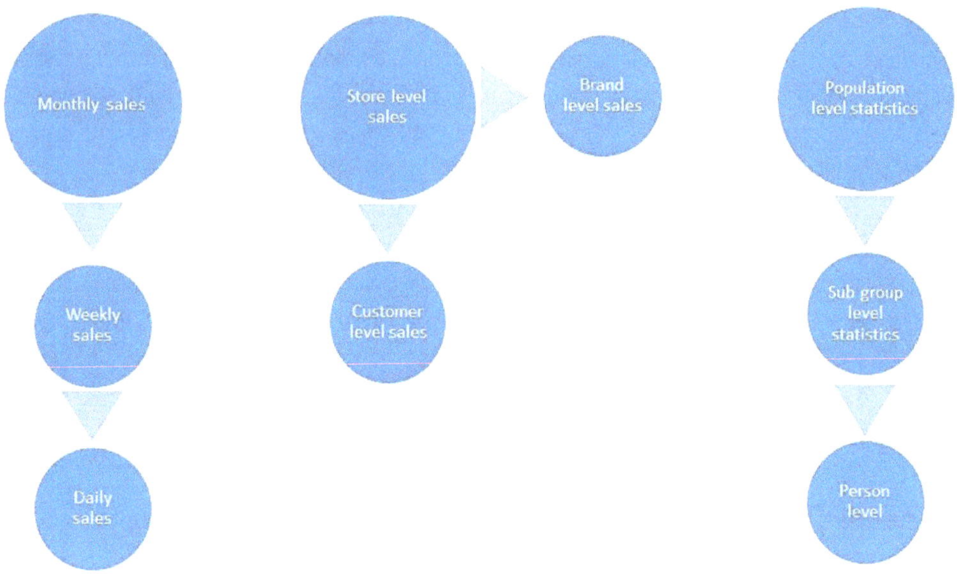

3 *Cross-sectional versus longitudinal versus time-series.* Cross-sectional data refer to data that is collected in a (somewhat specific) point in time (e.g., within the span of say 1 or 2 weeks, though it can be longer than that), but is treated as a "snapshot" (i.e., the data points are not differentiated by a time variable). Examples include one-time surveys and focus group data. Surveys can be repeated over time. For example, a brand tracking study design may be set up in such a way that 500 people are interviewed every quarter (referred to as a wave) to keep a pulse on how the brand is doing. Different samples of N = 500 are typically used for each quarter. If we attempt to interview the same sample of N = 500, then we consider this to be *longitudinal data.* Time series data typically has a larger number of data points, say, daily sales data over the course of a year.

4. *Hard data versus soft data.* Hard data pertains to metrics that can in most cases be observed without response-style bias, for example, the temperature in the room, the sales of a product in the store, how much venture capital a start-up firm has acquired, questions on age and gender, and so on. Soft data is data that is less readily available and may be subject to bias, such as consumer attitude (may be subject to response bias, perceived strength of a brand, how many units of a given brand a respondent bought over the past 3 months, may be subject to memory effects). See the example:

   Please indicate which of the statements you associate (Y = yes, N = No) with brand [X]:

   - Offers high-quality products
   - Has excellent customer service
   - Is widely available
   - Has a good price
   - Offers what I need

   One can see that responses to such questions are subject to how the respondent "defines" things like "high quality" and "excellent customer service."

   Sometimes, marketing researchers will create scales that are intended to represent a certain concept they believe is useful for the business problem at hand. This concept is captured using multiple questions. The analytical question then becomes, "Do these variables indeed point to one underlying construct and is this construct measured in a reliable and valid way?" (See Chapter 10 for details of how to assess whether a series of variables can be represented by one [latent] variable.) For details on how scale reliability and validity can be determined, we refer to standard market research books (e.g., Babin & Zikmund, 2016).

5. *The information value of data: measurement scales.* There are four different types of data measurement scales. These scales help classify and clarify how the data can be used and what type of calculations can be applied. The psychologist Stanley Stevens (1946) came up with four classifications that are widely used in many statistical software packages. They help guide these programs on the kinds of computations you can do with the data. For example, they help us understand for what data you can calculate a mean, median, or mode or what data can be added, subtracted, multiplied, or divided. The four measurement scales are nominal, ordinal, interval, and ratio and can be best explained with some examples:

   a. *Nominal.* Nominal scales are labeling variables or simply "labels" and don't have a quantitative value. For example, gender ("male" or "female") or country ("U.S.," "U.K.," etc.) are examples of nominal data. The scales of nominal data are mutually exclusive. There is no overlap, and each record in a data set has one unique label, but each label has no quantitative significance. "Nominal" sounds like "name" to easily remember that names simply *describe* a characteristic, but you cannot do any computations on them. If a variable such as gender has two designations, it's often referred to as a dichotomous variable.

You can't do much with nominal scales other than to count the number of instances of each label, but you cannot say females have a higher value than males.

b. *Ordinal.* With ordinal scales, the order of the values matters, but the differences between each one is not relevant. For example, you can arbitrarily assign #1, #2, #3 for a certain order to your data but the distance between 1 and 2 has no meaning and is arbitrary; 1 ranks higher than 2 in the results of a race, for example. We could have also assigned 10 and 20, but it's rather arbitrary, and the difference of 1 versus 2 or 10 versus 20 has no quantitative significance. Many Likert scales used in surveys are ordinal. For example, we cannot determine if the difference between "happy" and "unhappy" is the same as the difference between "very happy" and "happy," although you can say that "very happy" is better than "happy" when asked about the experience of shopping at a store. Moreover, with ordinal data we can only determine that a master's degree is of a higher order than a bachelor's degree. Ordinal scales are typically measuring non-numeric concepts like satisfaction or happiness. What you can do with the data is limited. Often when we conduct surveys we ask respondents to rate their agreement on a scale from 1 to 7 or 0 to 10, and because values are assigned, we make it clear what the unit difference is between each; these scales therefore classify as an interval or ratio. However, the purists may disagree with this practice.

c. *Interval.* Interval scales are numeric scales; we know the order and the exact differences between the values. A typical example of an interval scale is Celsius temperature because the difference between each value is the same. For example, the difference between 30 and 40 degrees is a measurable 10 degrees, which is the same difference between 50 and 60 degrees. Interval scales open a lot more opportunities for analysis. For example, you can determine the central tendency of the mode, median, or mean. You can also calculate the deviation between the highest and lowest measured value, the variance. "Interval" means "the space in between," which is important to remember, here. Interval scales not only describe the order, but they also provide the value between each measurement point. The problem with interval scales is that they don't have a "true zero." For example, there is no "no temperature" value: Temperature can be as high or low as can be measured. In the case of Celsius temperature and interval scales in general, zero is not a true zero but rather a number used on a scale to determine the freezing point, but when the temperature drops below zero it doesn't mean there is no temperature. Height or age, for example, have a true zero. Without a true zero, it is impossible to compute ratios. With interval data, we can add and subtract numbers but cannot multiply or divide.

d. *Ratio.* Ratio scales, on the other hand, allow analysts to perform all mathematical computations available to them. Ratio scales provide the order and the exact value between units, and they have an absolute zero. Other examples of ratio variables are duration and price, along with age and height. These variables can be meaningfully added, subtracted, multiplied, and divided. The fact that ratio scales can be divided into a ratio helps you remember what it is that sets ratios apart from all other measurement scales. With ratio-scaled data you can measure the central tendency of the mode, median, or mean, and you can calculate measures of dispersion, such as standard deviation and variation.

6 *Structured versus unstructured data.* Structured data is anything that has been coded prior to collection. An example is the following satisfaction question: "How likely would you recommend our hotel, using a 10-point rating scale where a 1 means not very likely at all and a 10 means very likely?" This data is structured because all respondents answer the same questions and choose between the same preset response options. This has the benefit of directly assigning numbers to each type of response, and the data can almost instantaneously be analyzed. Unstructured data is usually completely free format. For example, after we ask the recommendation question (typically used to calculate an NPS score), we may ask, "Why did you give this rating to the recommendation question? Respondents can answer any way they see fit. It is a free-format response. These responses cannot immediately be aggregated across respondents. Typically, they need to be cleaner and preprocessed and coded before any tabulation or further analysis can be done.

Increasingly, data is scraped from the internet, and text is analyzed and coded for further analyses and insights. For example, Netzer et al. (2012) scraped car conversations from Edmunds.com (a car website). Using text analytics, they determined which car brands were being perceived as similar.

7 *Observational data.* Observational data is any data that we obtain by observation without asking any questions (and hence without the risk of biasing the response). Here, we distinguish the following:

a. *Scanner data* (e.g., Neslin et al., 1994). Scanner data is an important source of hard data (e.g., Rossi et al., 2000) and is captured in store when items (SKUs) are being scanned at the checkout counter. Such data can tell us how much was purchased in a given category, how much was sold of each brand, at what price items were sold, whether items were on promotion, and so on. The downside of typical Nielsen-style scanner data is that it is store-level data (i.e., the data is aggregated: We cannot link or relate it to individual customer-level characteristics). Such data may be used for category, product, and brand tracking (e.g., Andrews et al., 2011). Some stores have loyalty cards, and this enables them to get panel data. The actual purchases of individual customers are captured and integrated with survey-based information (by sending these loyal customers surveys). This is behavioral and attitudinal data at the individual level. Quite a lot has been published on the use of scanner data to understand the effects of, for example, evaluating the effectiveness of in-store coupon promotions, pricing (Natter et al., 2007), and a marketing plan for a new product (Neslin et al., 1994).

b. *Unstructured online data*. Anything that consumers tweet, blog about, comment on, like and so on happens without any questions. We can then scrape information from the internet. Though we analyze individual comments, this data is often analyzed as if it were aggregate-level data, as information about the individuals who posted the content is lacking.
c. *Consumer interest tracking data*. Google search data is one example of this type of data. We can extract, from Google, the volume of search queries for certain key words or combinations of key words (e.g., wine, red wine; see Du & Kamakura, 2012, who used this data to identify trends in wine consumption).
d. *Clickstream data* (e.g., Montgomery et al., 2004). This refers to data that captures consumers online "clickstream." Firms operating online website(s) usually make use of aggregate-level metrics such as number of (unique) visitors on a given day or week, duration of visits, number of page views, and so on. What pages did they visit before they came to your website? Did they click on any ads? When did they leave the page? How long did they stay on each page? Studies have now shown that looking at this data more dynamically, and at individual visitor's behavior, may give insight about who is most likely to buy (Moe & Fader, 2004).
e. *Ethnography*. This is the art of observing people (consumers) and is a popular methodology in marketing research. Increasingly, technology is used, such as in-home cameras and smart devices, to capture consumer behavior (see section three).
f. *RFID data*. We discuss this next.

8 *RFID data*. Brazeal (2012) provides a summary of what this technology entails and describes the four components of it. The first component is a (possibly very) small chip radio receiver (a tag) that can be attached to a product or shipment you wish to track. These tags are always "on," meaning they can always be detected. The second part is a reader (which can also be a chip-sized device). The third part is the software to analyze and sort through the potentially millions of readings. The fourth part can be additional sensors on the tag that can observe and capture some part of the condition of whatever is tracked (e.g., if food is it still fresh, the temperature of ice cream, etc.). Brazeal (2012) also describes various applications for both marketing and operational efficiency. For example, a study by Sorenson (2009) describes a study where RFID tags were put on shopper shopping carts to trace how they move through a supermarket, where and how often they stop, and so on. One of the insights from that study was that the width of the isle was very important. Narrow isles were only used if they contained must-have items. Brazeal (2012) also describes the use of RFID tags on

pills prescribed by physicians. These (digestible) tags can let the physician know if the medication was taken. He also describes keeping track of freshness by batch. If we know which batch was contaminated, we can throw away just that batch; instead of throwing away a $1 million in food, we only throw away $100,000.

9 *MtM SIM card data.* Machine-to-machine (MtM) SIM is part of the Internet of Things (IoT). IoT refers to machines, devices, products, and so on that have chips embedded so they can communicate with other devices, products, and machines. For example, a chip in your refrigerator may communicate with your iPad or your watch with your phone; trucks with chips can automatically track stops, average speed, and so on. MtM SIM cards collect and aggregate data from machines continuously, then transmit this information back to the manufacturer. MtM SIM cards can collect data about how various machines in the network are being used. Say that John Deere sells tractors to clients all over the world. By having MtM SIM cards installed they will know how long the machine was operating, under what conditions, what type of malfunctions it had, how often it was serviced, and so on. This could allow them, for example, to offer better service contracts and predict when a machine is likely to break down. These cards can also be permanently embedded in the machine to avoid human tampering.

10 *Spatial data.* These are situations where a concrete spatial aspect (i.e., spatial as in geographic distance) of the data can play a role:

- Do the locations of a store matter? For example, it might be that female consumers in the New York area prefer a different type of bra than female consumers in Florida.
- Do different countries have different patterns of innovation? Helsen et al. (1993), for example, segment countries based on innovation diffusion patterns.
- What path does a shopper take through a store? (This is also considered path data.)
- The analysis of spatial data is still in an emerging state, but we will increasingly see spatial data becoming available to marketers due to technologies such as RFID, Wi-Fi, and scanning.

11 *Path data.* Technology has enabled more granular observations of consumer behavior, an area now referred to as tracking data. Hui et al. (2009) discuss several examples:

a. Using RFID (radio frequency identification) tags (attached to a grocery cart) to observe how shoppers move through a physical store. This may help in optimizing store layouts.
b. Wi-Fi and Bluetooth to track event participant by asking participants to download an event app or embed a Bluetooth chip in their badge (see Ungerboeck, 2019).
c. Eye-tracking methodology to capture how consumers view a print advertising, where their attention goes first, and how long their view lingers on certain spots. Zhang et al. (2009), for example, use eye tracking and find that the duration of consumers' attention to a print ad correlates with sales and how eye tracking analysis can be used to test the expected effectiveness of print ads.

d. Web browsing and clickstream data captures what websites (or website pages) consumers visit prior to coming to a firm's website before going to the checkout page.

12 *Big Data.* Big Data matters can be described in terms of size or volume, variety, velocity, and veracity (Wedel & Kannan, 2016). Size refers to data getting too big to be stored or analyzed by standard software, though "size" and what is considered too big to be handled by standard software is a somewhat moving target. Zwitter (2014) illustrates how data volume has changed over time (e.g. in 2011, 5 Billion Gigabytes every two days, in 2013, 5 Billion Gigabytes every 10 minutes, in 2015, every 10 seconds, see Zwitter, p. 2). The size feature also has two components: large *n* and large *p* (see Buhlmann et al., 2016). Large *n* refers to a large number of observations. Survey sample sizes vary from a few hundred to a few thousand, in most cases; occasionally there are some in the, say, 10k, 2k range. Though large this is still not considered Big Data. Compare this with, for example, Twitter data: If we collect Twitter data, we may easily get millions of data points (Twitter activity). Large p refers to a large set of possible "predictors" (the independent variables in a regression model). See, for an example, Sadilek et al. (2012) who use Twitter data to predict the spread of the flu; they identified several million features in tweets that could potentially predict the flu. There are ways to deal with large n (e.g., software alchemy; Matloff, 2014, 2016): breaking the data up into various equal-sized subgroups, running the analyses on each subgroup, and averaging the results. To deal with large p we can utilize factor analysis or principal components analysis.

Variety refers to having more diverse data available. Increasingly, we have more than just surveys. See the following examples:

- Firms are using in-house data (e.g., transactions data, complaint data, service records, financial data, etc.).
- Data that can be pulled from the internet has now become ubiquitous. Think of information contained in blogs, online forum discussions, Twitter comments, Facebook postings and likes, and so on.
- As a result of the Internet of Things, penetration of mobile phones, and the increase of video-capturing technology, we now can have video data, physical personal data, and so on.

The variety of data available nowadays makes it easier to determine if certain insights are consistent with data from multiple sources (triangulation) using triangulation, replication, and in-market prediction.

Real-timeliness refers to data being available, at the moment, or shortly after, it becomes available (e.g., Vriens, 2013). See Table 4.1 for some examples of data firms now likely have access to.

Velocity refers to how fast data is available. For example, a survey is typically a snapshot in time, and the time between commissioning a survey study and getting the data can take

TABLE 4.1 Examples of Data Sources

A lot more variety	Uncommon size
• Tons of survey data • Tons of secondary data • Scanner data • Marketing spent • Complaint data • Sales & transactional data • Financial data • Customer service data • Word-of-mouth (e.g., TalkTrack, etc.)	• Google search insights & other online trend sources • Online requests for information or quotes (e.g., Edmunds.com) • Blog data & insights • Tweets (Mood states, key phrases) • Facebook/Twitter brand mentions • Click Stream data • Text Data

anywhere from several weeks to several months. Online consumer-generated data, on the other hand, is a continuous stream. There is always somebody posting a Twitter comment, writing a blog, and posting something on Facebook.

Veracity involves reliability and validity (Wedel & Kannan, 2016) and pertains to all kinds of data. For example, with online consumer-generated data we may know very little about who posted the comment. Evaluating and assessing reliability and validity of Big Data is still in the early stages.

4.3 QUALITATIVE RESEARCH DATA

A major distinction in commercial market research is between qualitative and quantitative research. It is useful to understand the pros and cons of both approaches. Qualitative research includes approaches such as focus groups, individual depth interviews, ethnographic research, and more recently unstructured online data, something that is referred to as "social listening," where market researchers will scrape consumer-generated online content from the internet. Quantitative research includes the use of surveys, scanner data, experiments, and consumer-generated data.

Quantitative research usually involves larger samples compared to qualitative research. For example, a typical survey study may yield a sample of 500 respondents. But focus groups are smaller. Three focus groups may be done in three different cities but may only involve 30 respondents. Qualitative data allows for interaction between the interviewee and the interviewer, or between the focus group participants (i.e., if a respondent gives an answer to a question, the researcher [often called moderator] can easily probe a bit further if the answer isn't fully clear or if the answer introduced a new issue not previously thought of).

The flexible interview style used in a qualitative research also means that "resulting data is not fully accessible by those who only listened or only read the transcripts" (Gordon & Langmaid, 1989, p. 2).

Recall from Chapter 1 that qualitative research approaches are well suited for situations where we have few if any hypotheses (i.e., have little to no prior knowledge) and where we expect a significant chunk of "what we don't know that we don't know." Note that almost all situations will have some part of "what we don't know that we don't know," so it becomes a bit of a judgment call whether to use qualitative research, and timing and budget will then have to be weighed as well.

In our view there are three distinct situations where and how we recommend using qualitative research:

1. *As a standalone project*. When we need to identify what possible the problems are of why sales are going down, a standalone project may sufficiently work. For example, Cox, Higginbotham, and Burton (1976) describe a case study where a firm discovered in focus groups that there was a problem with the product's packaging that was affecting sales and shelf space. There are situations where there is not enough time or money to execute a full-scale quantitative survey, and one decides to do a less expensive qualitative study. In our view this is risky. Situations that are best for standalone qualitative approaches include (a) when quantitative data is just not feasible or would be cost prohibitive, (b) when the main objective is to identify issues with a product, and (c) to get some initial reactions to product or ad concepts with the goal of narrowing down the list.
2. *As a pre-step to quantitative survey research* (e.g., Calder, 1977; Cox et al., 1976). In this situation, a qualitative research project is used to provide input in survey research. This can happen for two reasons. One, if there is too little knowledge about the business issue (e.g., product category, market, etc.) one wants to know about all possible topics that should be addressed in the quantitative survey. Two, one wants to check the wording of questions (e.g., Calder, 1977), or understand the way in which people talk about a topic, product, or issue, as this then can be used to frame the questions in the survey in the best way.
3. *After a quantitative research project*. Surveys and quantitative analyses are great tools to analyze large samples and perform multivariate analyses that give us insight into relationships between variables, especially segmentation studies, where various segments are described on many variables and are hard for managers to comprehend. Some argue (Calder, 1978) that surveys can be used to make focus groups better. This is in line with using focus groups after survey research.

Qualitative research has become a specialty in and of itself, and most commercial market researchers on the supplier side specialize either in quantitative or qualitative research. Large market research supply firms such as Ipsos usually have a separate qualitative research business unit. In the remainder of this section we briefly outline the key qualitative research approaches that you are most likely to encounter: (a) focus groups, (b) unstructured individual depth interviews, (c) the laddering interview approach, (d) ethnographic research, (e) Social listening (i.e., online market research communities (MROCs) and online consumer generated data.

4.3.1 Focus Groups

In a focus group research project (e.g., Calder, 1977; Yuhas Byers & Wilcox, 1991), participants are invited to a focus group facility. The size of a focus group is around 6 to 10 people. There are companies that manage office space and offer the use of focus groups interview rooms; these are spacious rooms where participants can sit comfortably around a table. A focus group also needs the following:

1. *A moderator.* A person who asks the group questions, has them do certain exercises, and so on. Moderators are market researchers who specialize in running focus groups, and this may be all, or mostly, what they do.
2. *A discussion guide.* A discussion guide is a list of topics that the client who commissioned the research wants to cover. Hence, a focus group is considered a semi-standard interview, meaning the topics and initial questions are determined but the direction in which a focus group evolves is not (e.g., one focus group may end up talking a lot about topic A while another focus group may spend more time discussing topic B). Moderators ensure that the topics on the discussion guide are being covered, but they can be flexible in terms of how much time is spent on each topic.
3. *Recording equipment.* Focus group discussion are (video) recorded, and after the focus groups are completed the moderator listens back to the discussions or views the video recording, interprets the discussion, and writes a summary of what they think came out of the focus group.

Note that to some degree interpretation already takes place during the focus group (e.g., the moderator decides on the spot what topics to pursue further and which to leave). This feature, where data collection and interpretation of results go hand in hand is a key feature of qualitative research (we note that this also happens in quantitative data analysis but not so in quantitative data collection).

Often, focus groups are conducted in person, though it is also possible to conduct focus groups online (Stewart & Shamdasani, 2017). Focus groups are great for topics that lend themselves to group discussion and being explorative. The participants are supposed to feed off each other and to encourage group thinking. Focus groups must be carefully recruited, and it's the role of the moderator to make sure everyone gets a chance to speak and to avoid one person dominating the conversation (the alpha) with everyone else simply following along. Often, during the screening, you want to screen for a person's ability and comfort to speak in a group setting. If a deeper conversation on a complex, sensitive, or personal topic is being sought after, it's better to consider doing depth interviews, especially if we expect a variety of responses based on a large variety of backgrounds.

4.3.2 Individual Depth Interviews

If the topics of discussion are likely to be influenced by social desirability bias or stigma then focus groups may not be the best option (e.g., political preferences [expressing extreme left or right positions], abortion, racial and gender equality, consumption of luxury goods, etc.). Respondents may be unwilling to express how they really feel in the presence of other people. Individual depth interviews may be a better choice, though here too we need to be aware that respondents may give socially desirable answers. With individual-depth interviews we can choose to use a semi-structured interview approach or an unstructured interview approach. In a semi-structured interview, we predetermine the topics and questions beforehand, but after an initial question, any follow-up question will be dependent on the initial response the respondent gives. In an unstructured interview, only the topics (or topic) are predetermined. The interview style is open, and the interviewer aims to impose as few biases as possible. He or she can do this by using silence, open-ended questions, and so on (e.g., Corbin & Morse, 2003).

4.3.3 The Laddering Interview Technique

Laddering is a special type of individual-depth interviewing. This interviewing technique makes use of what is called the "means-end-chain" framework (e.g., Gutman, 1982; Reynolds & Gutman, 1988; Vriens & ter Hofstede, 2001). The notion behind the means-end chain framework and the laddering interviewing technique is to gain insight into how people connect with products (i.e., it attempts to bridge features of the product with "features" of people). Features of the product are attributes. For example, a car has features such as brand, price, engine HP, and color. We also know that people have values. Research (Kahle, 1986) shows that people may differ on a limited set of values. Examples of values are sense of accomplishment, fun and enjoyment, security, control, warm relationships with others, sense of belonging, excitement, and so on. A laddering interview aims to identify how product feature preferences are connected to people's values. The underlying idea is that consumers will buy products that align with their values. For example, if I value security, I am more likely to prefer a Volvo over a BMW, but if I value fun and enjoyment the reverse may be true.

A laddering interview has the following steps:

- It starts with identifying the product attributes that are important to consumers.
- For each attribute we ask what the most attractive level is.
- For each attribute we then do a laddering interview. For example, say, a respondent has indicated they prefer a strong car engine (this is a product attribute); we then ask, "Why do you prefer a strong car engine? The respondent may say, "Because it allows me to pass other cars on the freeway fast" (this is a product benefit; it is the result of using a product attribute). We then again ask, "Why is passing other cars fast on the freeway important to you?" The respondent may say, "Because it makes me feel that I am less likely get into an accident." Again, we ask, "Why is reducing your chance of getting into an accident important to you?" A respondent may say, "Because I feel more responsible because I need to take care of my family." Now we have reached a consumer end value or "sense of belonging."

This laddering interview is repeated for all attributes. Once completed, we have the ladders for one consumer. Across respondents these ladders can be integrated into a hierarchical value map.

4.3.4 Ethnographic Research

The ethnographic approach is a foundational research approach in anthropology. Researchers spend time in a new cultural setting (e.g., a tribe, or a country, and they may live among this culture for an extended period of time). There is no specific set of questions that have been identified beforehand. Instead the goal is to immerse oneself in the different culture and gain an in-depth understanding of it. It is common for such a process to span several months or even close to or more than a year.

The same notion is applied when ethnography is applied in marketing research, except the duration is usually much shorter, a few days to maybe a few weeks, at most. An exception is the work done by Martin Lindstrom (2016) who spent several months in cultural settings. He wrote his observations in a notebook, anything that seemed unusual or different, even if it didn't immediately make sense. Over time, some of these notes start to make sense as they pointed to a broader theme. Mariampolski (1999) phrases it as follows "Ethnography relies upon entering a respondents' natural life worlds—at home, while shopping, at leisure or in the workplace. The researcher, in essence, becomes a naïve visitor in that world by engaging respondents during realistic product usage situations in the course of daily life" (p. 4).

4.3.5 Social Listening

There several online qualitative approaches: (a) online focus groups, (b) online research communities (sometimes referred to as market research online communities [MROC]), and (c) online consumer-generated data. Online focus groups, in principle, are fairly similar to in-person focus groups.

Market Research Online Communities (MROCs)

Online communities are groups of consumers, sometimes customers, who have agreed to fill out (usually very short) surveys or quick questions for a firm. However, this takes place in an online community (think of it as a private Facebook group). The firm may post ideas, new product concepts, and so on, and members of the community can respond to this by commenting on the post and on each other's comments. These communities can exist for a few weeks but can also last several months. The benefit of an online community is that a firm gets feedback fast and that iteration is possible (i.e., if members don't like an idea, the firm can tweak it and ask again). A drawback is that the number of members is usually relatively small. At LinkedIn, we have created several online communities who have agreed to participate in ongoing ad-hoc studies and online discussion forums. These communities range in size from a thousand to several thousands of members and are grouped by function. This allows us to conduct agile and tactical research and turn around a research question in a matter of days. The speed of product development is high and being able to conduct quick research is key. Because these communities are set up in advance, we have to sacrifice a little on representativeness given a particular topic. We have also found that the members who agree to participate in these LinkedIn-branded communities tend to be more highly engaged and not always representative of the entire LinkedIn population at large. However, with some adjustments, these communities are effective and drive many valuable insights for the product development teams.

Online consumer generated data

Online consumer-generated data is data we scrape from the internet. These can include product ratings and consumer discussions of a specific category (e.g., cars, skincare) or brand. This is fully observational data and can be both quantitatively and qualitatively analyzed (e.g., Vriens et al., 2017; Vriens et al., 2019). Note that if we scrape consumer discussions, we have unstructured text data, and this needs to be cleaned and analyzed before we can do anything useful with it.

Online consumer-generated data has several distinct benefits. First, it is an online version of ethnography, sometimes referred to as netnography (e.g., Kozinets, 2002). This means it is an unobtrusive method (i.e., the researcher has no influence over how consumers might respond). Two, online data has a timestamp, and we can go back in time. This, obviously, is not feasible with surveys or other qualitative methods (but there are more benefits, e.g., see Vriens et al., 2017).

As an example, Vriens et al. (2017) analyzed online consumer-generated data pertaining to the VW Diesel emission crisis. See Figure 4.2 for a simple comparison of associations derived from online discussions prior to the crisis versus after the crisis.

FIGURE 4.2 Brand-Concept Network

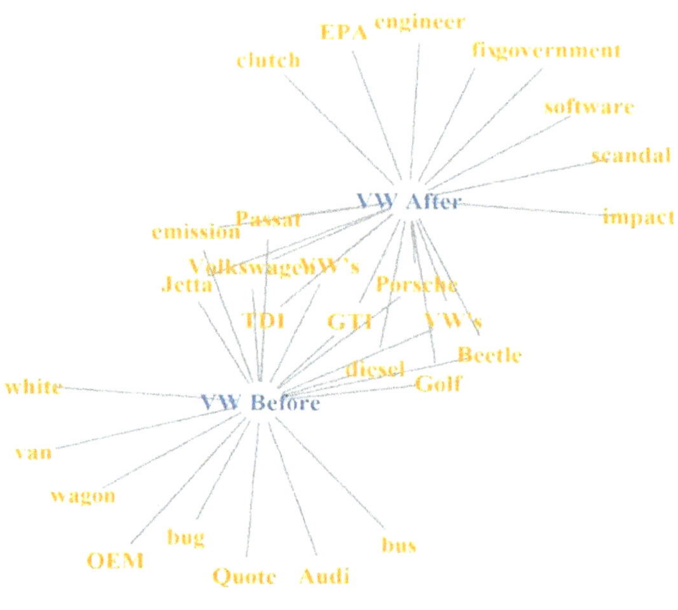

4.4 QUANTITATIVE RESEARCH DATA

Quantitative research lends itself best in situations where "we know what we don't know." In this section we discuss surveys, transactional data, and experimental data.

4.4.1 Surveys

A survey is a set of standard questions, most of which are structured, meaning the question and the answer options are the same for all respondents. They can be executed in person or via phone or be self-administered via an online link and, most recently, via a device-agnostic link. Device agnostic means respondents can self-take the survey via their desktop, but also via their smartphone or tablet. Device-agnostic surveys have pros and cons. An advantage of device-agnostic surveys is that they better capture a younger audience. A downside is that responding to surveys on smartphone can be tedious.

A survey data collection has several advantages over qualitative data collection. One, a survey is an efficient way to collect data over large samples and hence possibly get (at least to some degree) representative results. Two, because all questions are the same for everyone, results across respondents or groups of respondents can now be compared. For example, 70% of the male respondents said they preferred our brand whereas only 56% of the female respondent said they preferred our brand. Three, quantitative survey data allows us to look at interrelationships between variables (as we will discuss in more detail in the next chapter).

Surveys need to be well designed if they are to yield valid data. The characteristics of the sample used for the survey have implications for the types of inferences we can make from the results. (Sampling is a big topic, and the interested reader can find more in-depth information about sampling in Babin & Zikmund, 2015, and Valliant et al., 2013.)

The survey itself, however, can also be a source of response-style bias (e.g., social desirability bias, extreme responses, etc.). Some can be avoided, while others may not be fully controlled for. An entire chapter, or even book, can be dedicated to this topic, which is beyond the purpose of this book. Here, we limit ourselves to a few simple recommendations:

- Avoid leading questions (e.g., "To what extent do you agree with the notion that ... ?")
- Avoid double-barreled questions (e.g., "Do you agree that this hotel's customer service was fast and solved your problems?").
- Keep language as simple as possible, especially when surveying a general population. If a respondent doesn't understand a question, we will not get the answer we were seeking.
- Pre-test any survey you roll out. It is very easy to make mistakes, even for seasoned market researchers. We also want to make sure the survey isn't too long and flows well. Pretesting can help with avoiding mistakes and improve your survey.
- When respondents are being asked to rate the importance of a set of statements or attributes, it is usually a good idea to randomize the order in which these statements are shown across respondents to avoid order effects.
- When designing a survey, keep in mind the original purpose of the study. Ask yourself,

"What am I going to do with the data to this question or this set of questions?" If you can clearly articulate that, maybe the question does not belong in the survey.

- Ask yourself, "Can respondents realistically answer this question?" For example, if you ask someone "What brands of coffee did you buy 6 months ago?" chances are they won't recall.
- Be aware of response-style bias, for example, social desirability biases and halo effects. (For more details on survey design see Bradburn & Sudman, 1991.)

There are different types of surveys. The most popular surveys used in marketing research are usage and attitude surveys, customer satisfaction surveys, brand surveys, tracking surveys, and market segmentation surveys. These will be discussed in more detail later in the book.

4.4.2 Transactional Data

Transactional data is the result of transactions (e.g., sales). An example of transactional data is scanner data (described earlier in the chapter). When Microsoft sells its Microsoft Office suite, either via the brick-and-mortar retail channel (e.g., Best Buy, product is scanned) or via the online retail channel (product is bought via clicks), they will have an overall sales number for each version of their Office Suite products. A big benefit of transactional data is that it represents behavior. In marketing research such data is used in the estimation of marketing mix models; such models give us insight into whether the firm's marketing is working.

4.4.3 Experiments

Experimental data is the result of an experimental set-up. This use of this type of marketing research data has really exploded over the past few decades because experiments are relatively easy to conduct in an online environment. For example, if Amazon would like to know whether showing no reviews, up to five reviews, or up to ten reviews for a given product helps drive more sales, some weeks they could show zero reviews, some weeks up to five reviews, and some weeks up to 10 reviews. Then, it is just matter of comparing the sales during these periods to know what format of showing reviews yields the highest sales.

4.5 BRINGING IT ALL TOGETHER

Today, we rarely consider analyzing one data set from one source at a time. We typically want to look at multiple data sources to derive deeper insights and more actionable product or marketing implications. When a qualitative research phase precedes a quantitative one, we want to report from both sources in an integrated way. The qualitative research often brings the hard facts from the quantitative research to life, so the combined reporting becomes more effective as the qualitative findings help connect at a more emotional level with readers through surfacing salient verbatim quotes. These quotes often resonate more with your stakeholders than simply reporting the cold facts. One framework for how to think about integrating different sources is to apply the Trinity strategy (Kaushik, 2006), which is a way of thinking in terms of behavior, outcomes, and experiences and describes how these three are related—a customer's experience with a company and their underlying motivations leads to certain behaviors that lead to certain business outcomes (sales, clicks). Looking at the data from only one source at a time (outcomes, behaviors, or experiences) limits the opportunity to find deep insights and offer a holistic picture for how to address a business problem. For example, a company may only be looking at click stream data (behavior), and one such popular metric is the bounce rate (outcome), which is the number of visitors who land on a home page but didn't take any action (they bounced) relative to the total visitors who did take action. If the bounce rate is high, you may conclude that the home page is not well designed or assume that the call to actions aren't clear enough. Without measuring the experience in the product through a survey there could be all kinds of reasons for the bounce rate; some may have nothing to do with the site or the UEX at all. At LinkedIn we had an issue where the bounce rate for guests was really high; many didn't take an action to subscribe as a member, and the product team concluded that something was wrong with the guest page. When we conducted the research, we discovered that many were not guests but in fact members who had lapsed. They were already members but somehow got locked out of their accounts and landed on a guest page. Without a pop-up survey on the site, we would have ended up drawing a false conclusion. Taking a step back and thinking through how customers flow through a product, site, or store and what "breadcrumbs" they leave along the way is a useful exercise, as is trying to identify where all the breadcrumbs are landing.

Another way to think about what data to integrate is to think about data that helps answer the "what," the observations, and what data helps answer the "why," the motivations for what is being observed. Bringing these two together will help analysts develop a deeper understanding of the relationships among two seemingly disparate sources. A third useful framework for organizing data and uncovering insights is the funnel approach. The marketing funnel is one such funnel and captures data of awareness, interest, consideration, intent, evaluation, and purchase for a product. The data for each layer in the funnel can come from different sources; brought together in this way it helps illuminate the bottlenecks. It is very useful to understand where the breaks or conversions are, as you go down the funnel, and how they are related, which can be seen by looking at data across each step and how customers flow through this. The adoption funnel is another funnel that looks at how existing customers use and adopt features or a set of features to help identify whether issues are related to feature awareness, discoverability, usability, or satisfaction and pinpoint which features are causing relative low conversion at what stage in the funnel. Essentially, it is a way of thinking and a data strategy that helps the analyst identify where the "leaky" buckets are that are often jumping off points for other research. For example, at LinkedIn we have many features on the site, and with this type of funnel approach we were able to establish norms around each step in the funnel by looking at all features in the aggregate and determining which features were underperforming at what stage in the adoption funnel. For example, some features had less of an awareness issue and more of a usability issue; this became evident by looking at the ratio of people who are aware to the total people who could have seen a feature and by looking at those who used the feature. At LinkedIn we always encourage researchers to take a broad versus narrow view of the data instead of only considering the data that they are most comfortable with.

4.6 DATA GOVERNANCE

Firms will need to think about data strategy (Adelman et al., 2005) and governance, specifically the following:

- Data management. What data does the firm have across all departments? Who is able to access, change, or update data? How are errors corrected?, and so on.
- What are the opportunities to integrate data across different datasets?
- Who will ensure privacy rules are adhered to and how? How long should data be kept? Sensitive data?

4.6.1 Management

Data management starts with creating a data inventory and refers to identifying all key data a firm has access to, who collects the data or has it (owns or manages it), what data is ready to be used, and, if not ready to be used, what needs to be done to make it ready for use. A data inventory also enables eliminating data redundancy (i.e., the same type of data lives in different places in the organization). There are two types of redundancy: (a) multiple versions of the truth and (b) data that is unnecessarily purchased by multiple departments.

For example, in a firm the global marketing team can have an Excel file with their best estimates of the market shares of the firm's brands, but so does the global sales team, and so do the various geographical subsidiaries. Each department may have defined "market share" slightly differently, used different data sources, or adjusted their data-based estimates (which may happen because of political reasons or simply because they think they know something about the data that is not represented in it). This leads to unproductive discussions about whose estimate is correct, and it is also inefficient from a data management point of view. Creating one single version of the truth eliminates this and ensures everyone works with the same numbers. Ideally, where feasible, data integration also should aim to achieve a comprehensive view of the customer in one database. For example, what did this customer buy from us? Were there ever any complaints filed? How satisfied is this customer? For some of the advanced analytics (e.g., marketing mix modeling, customer lifetime value, etc.), such integration is required. Hence, we recommend that any analytics department builds an inventory of the data that should be or is available in the firm.

It is also possible, in case of syndicated data, that multiple departments buy the same report or the same dataset. Identifying this and only buying what is needed can be a significant cost saver (see Vriens, 2012).

Once a firm knows what data it has, it can start thinking about if there is any data that it should have and then decide which gaps should be closed.

Redman (2008; 2016) recommends that firms get in front of their data. Getting in front of data means we have to fix data quality problems at the source, not just fix one analysis when someone realizes there is a problem with the data. For example, we have seen situations where quarterly market share data for a geographical region was adjusted four times over the course of one quarter by an individual regional marketing manager without anybody knowing why and how. The market share numbers lacked internal credibility when viewed by other stakeholders (global marketing, finance, etc.). Redman (2016) calls this the hidden data factory. In firms, departments have or get data, and before they present them further in the organization they adjust this data, possible. because they discovered and fixed an error or because they feel they have additional information that justifies changing the data. For example, data may get adjusted based on assessments of how to make numbers representative. When this happens, a firm should ensure that key stakeholders and consumers of this data agree with the adjustment process and sign off on it. Especially for key business metrics such as market size and market share, there needs to be a single version of the truth. Data needs to be evaluated on quality, readiness, and credibility.

Data quality can be comprised if the data is not complete or contains errors. Completeness refers to the extent to which the data represents the domain it ideally should represent. Data can be incomplete for various reasons: (a) incomplete coverage and (b) missing data. A data source that reliably captures a few key competitors in the markets may account for 80% of the market. The data may have good quality for the part of the market it covers, but it is important to point out that the data does not cover the entire market. If this data is adjusted internally so it supposedly represents 100% of the market, then this adjustment process needs to be fully transparent and agreed on by all key stakeholders. Another source of incompleteness is missing data (e.g., Allison, 2010). In the context of survey data missing data issues arise if respondents are unwilling or unable to answer a question (Vriens & Sinhara, 2006). In the context of internal transactional data (purchase histories, client/customer information, engagement data, etc.) we may encounter missing or incorrect fields (for a business example see Lakshminarayan et al., 1999): e.g., a customer did not give their phone number and hence that data point is missing; or the salesperson forgot to ask how big the customer firm is (in business-to-business cases). There are several procedures available to fill in the missing data, some better than others. We recommend a regression-based imputation (in Chapter 5 we discuss this topic in more detail; see also Allison, 2010, and Vriens & Sinhara, 2006).

Errors are a second source of compromising data quality. We can encounter numerous errors in surveys, spreadsheets and so on (e.g., Panko, 2005). Redman (2008) states that 10 to 25% of all data contain inaccuracies. In surveys, we can look for logical inconsistencies, typos, or intentional misrepresentations. For example, someone indicated they were born in 1898, or they indicated they were male but reportedly took anti-pregnancy pills. Sometimes (e.g., with financial and insurance services) members of the same household are in the database yet are not indicated as such. The latter would obviously have implications for sales strategies and CLV strategies.

Data readiness means that data is ready for consumption and usage and for further analysis and is easily accessed. To be ready for consumption and usage the data must be transparent and credible. For data to be ready there should also be a shared and communicated definition of what the data represents, what the underlying data sources are, and whether manipulations have been done on the data, when, and by who. Data that is ready for analysis may also be prepared so that analytics across several datasets can be done. Especially for marketing mix modeling projects, integration across multiple datasets is quite common.

Credibility is a function of data quality and timeliness.

4.6.2 Data Integration

The data used for individual projects may be stored in a single location, or if the project may involve combining the data from different sources. The data is stored by whoever "owns" the data in the organization. For example, if we want to use marketing data to estimate a marketing mix model, the Finance or Procurement departments most likely have that data.

In some projects data from different sources needs to be combined. In the case of marketing models, for example, we may encounter datasets with different levels of aggregation. We may have daily sales data and monthly advertising expenditure data. To align these two datasets, we need to convert one of two datasets so that both datasets are at the same level of aggregation. In this example, we could roll up sales to the monthly level or come up with a rule that breaks the monthly spent data down in "likely" weekly numbers (maybe by just dividing the monthly number by four). Now we can perform a statistical time series analysis to see if ad spending correlates or precedes sales.

Data fusion refers to the process of merging two or more datasets together so that we can perform multivariate analyses across the variables across the different datasets. If we have a unique customer/respondent ID, then this is straightforward. For example, a firm may have completed an internal customer satisfaction study where respondents agreed to be identified, and this survey data could be merged with the internal customer transaction database. Once these datasets are merged, we can research if customer satisfaction is related to certain customer characteristics (e.g., if customer satisfaction is related to certain purchases).

4.6.3 Privacy and Ethical Considerations

Anytime we collect data from people, be it for marketing intelligence purposes or otherwise, we have to go about it in an ethical way. This topic has legal, moral, technological, and branding angles. It is beyond the scope of this book to fully discuss this topic, but we aim to summarize the key issues at stake.

The definition of what ethics entails varies, but in the practice of marketing research, customer analytics, Big Data, and data science one needs to be aware and be prepared with (a) privacy protection of individual data, (b) people's consent to collect and use the information, and (c) consent (possibly) from who owns the data (see Royal Statistical Society, 2015).

In marketing research organizations, these issues have been in place for a long time, but the more recent customer analytics and Big Data disciplines are catching up. In the marketing research discipline, professional industry organizations exist that have taken ownership of ethical issues (e.g., privacy and consent). For example, in the United States we have the Market Research Society (MRS), and in Europe we have the European Society of Opinion and Market Research (ESOMAR). These organizations have developed a set of guidelines that the industry, as a whole, should abide by; some of these may be legal requirements, and others may not be enforced legally. Instead they are stated as ethical standards to strive for or abide by (see Babin & Zikmund, 2016, for an extensive discussion). See, for example, the following guidelines:

- *Informed consent*. This refers to the individual's consent to participate in a survey and understanding what the researcher may want. This is sometimes referred to as active research because before we collect any data (e.g., via a survey) we ask for permission, and the respondent has a right to refuse. In passive research where we may observe consumers (e.g., in a mall, a store, or online), such explicit permission and explaining the purpose of the study may be much harder if not impossible to obtain. As long as it pertains to say the "undifferentiated public," it is okay to assume implicit consent (Babin & Zikmund, 2016).
- *The right to privacy*. In the United States there is legislation that states consumers who are on the "Do-Not-Call" list cannot be called for sales purposes, but in some U.S. states this is extended to "information purposes" (e.g., Babin & Zikmund, 2016).
- *The right to anonymity*. This refers to anonymous responses in surveys (i.e., specific responses cannot be tracked to detail individual data such as who this respondent is).
- *Not mixing sales and marketing research*. No research firm is expected to disguise or mix a sales call as a marketing research call.

The emergence of the internet, social media platforms, and increasingly the Internet of Things (IoT) has given rise to an explosion of data. Firms quickly realized that such data (a) is less expensive compared to surveys, (b) sometimes allows firms to study problems at a much larger scope than surveys (e.g., Vriens et al., 2017), and (c) can contain many valuable, unexpected insights. Even better, some firms are realizing that the data they collect may have resale value. All this has given firms an incentive to collect such data; some argue without carefully considering the privacy implications (Boyd, 2010; see Nunan & Domenico, 2013 for examples). These developments also resulted in new ethical challenges, such as in the following examples:

- The data may be misused or fall in the wrong hands. For example, Facebook collected data from their users via apps and quizzes. This data was given to Cambridge Analytica under the unchecked assumption that it would be used for academic purposes. It turned out Cambridge Analytica used the data for the Trump campaign. (See also Christiansen, 2011.)
- Data may be collected from consumers that they would never expect to be shared (e.g., Facebook collects (a) everything that is typed even if not published (Sorenson,

2016), and (b) call and text history (Langone, 2018).

- Big Data may include information that the firm never intended to collect and that may infringe on people's privacy (Herschel & Miori, 2017).
- People (consumers) may not be aware of what data they are sharing and how this data is being moved.
- Several studies have shown that by combining multiple datasets (recall one of the features of Big Data, variety), combined with the use of advanced analytics, individuals could be re-identified (e.g., Herald, 2016). Gartner asserts that Big Data subjected to advanced analytics capabilities will mean new risks (i.e., they predict that by 2015 50% of the business ethics violations will occur through improper use of Big Data analytics).
- Lots of personal information is held by firms, and internet exchanges have enabled hacking and security breaches at an unprecedented scale (e.g., breaches at Target, Ashley Madison, etc.).
- New phenomena arise, such as group privacy and predictive policing, each of which may have unintended consequences for individuals (e.g., Boyd, 2010).

Legal guidelines exist but may not always be clear, and they may vary across regions. The European Union is making progress to define regulations about how personal information and meta data can be collected and used for marketing (General Data Protection Regulation). Not abiding by such guidelines may result in steep fines. Hence, firms need to be conscious when entering the Big Data domain.

4.7 QUIZ AND EXERCISES

1. Describe the difference between internal and external data.
2. Give an example of different levels of aggregation.
3. What are the key benefits of survey data? What are the key benefits of transactional data?
4. Describe three features of Big Data.
5. What are the three ways qualitative research can be used?
6. What are two types of social listening?
7. Think about the restaurant example. Where could you find restaurant inspection results data?
8. How would you go about creating a data inventory for your firm? Lay out some steps and a possible project approach.
9. What is data integration about?
10. What are the components of data quality? Which component is most important and why?
11. What does it mean "Getting in front of data"?
12. Why is it important to have "a single version of the truth"?

13 You just got hired by Tesla, the electric car manufacturer. The CMO comes to you and wants to know the key complaints and issues with Tesla's model S. What publicly available data sources can you think of that you would be able to acquire? What type of data might Tesla have from its customers that you could get access to? Design a dataset, using as many examples from real data as possible, that is set up in a way that you could analyze. Make a recommendation as to what type of data would be useful (actionable). Assume that Tesla does not have that data and develop a plan for where and how to get it.

14 Your IT department has figured out how to link customers that visit the company's website to their survey data. Are there any ethical or privacy issues they should be concerned about?

REFERENCES

Adelman, S., Moss, L., & Abai, M. (2005). *Data strategy*. Pearson.

Allison, P. (2010). Missing data. In: P. V. Marsden & J. D. Wright (Eds.), *Handbook of survey research* (2nd ed.) (pp. 631–657). Emerald Group Publishing Limited.

Andrews, R. L., Currim, I. S., & Leeflang, P. S. H. (2012). A comparison of sales response predictions from demand models applied to store-level versus panel data. *Journal of Business and Economic Statistics, 29*(2), 319–326.

Babin, B., & Zikmund, W. (2016). *Exploring marketing research* (11th ed.). Cengage.

Bradburn, N. M., & Sudman, S. (1991). The current status of questionnaire design. In P. P. Biemer, R. M. Groves, L. E. Lyberg, N. A. Mathiowetz, & S. Sudman (Eds.), *Measurement errors in surveys* (pp. 29–40). J. Wiley & Sons Inc.

Boyd, D. (2010). Privacy and publicity in the context of Big Data. Paper presented at the World Wide Web Conference, Raleigh, NC. http://www.danah.org/papers/talks/2010/WWW2010.html

Brazeal, M. (2012). RFID in research: 19 things you can do with RFID that you couldn't do before. In R. J. Kaden, G. Linda, & M. Prince (Eds.), *Leading edge market research* (pp. 365–378. SAGE.

Buhlmann, P., Drineas, P., Kane, M., & van der Laan, M. (2016). *Handbook of Big Data*. Chapman & Hall.

Calder, B. (1977). Focus groups and the nature of market research. *Journal of Marketing Research, 14*(3), 353–364.

Calder, B. (1978). Surveys' objective: To improve focus group studies. *Marketing News, 12*(8), 1.

Christiansen, L. (2011). Personal privacy and internet marketing: An impossible conflict or a marriage made in heaven. *Business Horizons, 54,* 509–514.

Corbin, J., & Morse, J. M. (2003). The unstructured interactive interview: Issues of reciprocity and risks when dealing with sensitive topics. *Qualitative Inquiry, 9*(3), 335–354.

Corstjens, M., & Merrihue, J. (2003). Optimal marketing. *Harvard Business Review,* 114–121.

Cox, K. K., Higginbotham, H. B., & Burton, K. (1976). Applications of focus groups in marketing. *Journal of Marketing, 40*(1), 77–80.

Du, R., & Kamakura, W. A. (2012). Quantitative trendspotting. *Journal of Marketing Research, 49,* 514–536.

Ferguson, G., S. Mathur, and B. Shah. 2005. "Evolving from Information to Insight," *MIT Sloan Management Review* 46, no. 2, 51–58.

Fern, E.F. (1982). The use of focus groups for idea generation: The effects of group size, acquaintanceship, and moderator on response quantity and quality. *Journal of Marketing Research*, XIX, 1–13.

Gordon, W., & Landmaid, R. (1989). *Qualitative market research*. Gower.

Gutman, J. (1982). A means-end model based on consumer categorization processes. *Journal of Marketing*, *46*(2), 60–72.

Helsen, K., Jedidi, K., & DeSarbo, W. S. (1993). A new approach to country segmentation utilizing multinational diffusion patterns. *Journal of Marketing, 57*(4), 60–71.

Herald, R. (2016). *10 Big Data privacy problems*. https://www.secureworldexpo.com/industry-news/10-big-data-analytics-privacy-problems

Herschel, R., & Miori, V. M. (2017). Ethics and Big Data. *Technology in Society, 49,* 31–36.

Hui, S. K., Fader, P. S., & Bradlow, E. T. (2009). Path data in marketing: An integrative framework and prospectus for model building. *Marketing Science, 28*(2), 320–335.

Kahle, L. R. (1986). The nine nations of North America and the value basis of geographic segmentation. *Journal of Marketing*, *50*(2), 37–47.

Kang, J. S., Kuznetsova, P., Choi, Y., & Luca, M. (2013). Using text analytics to target government inspections: Evidence from restaurants hygiene inspections and online reviews. *Harvard Business School Working Paper, No. 14–007.*

Kaushik, A. (2006, August 10). *Trinity: A mindset and strategic approach.* Occam's Razor. https://www.kaushik.net/avinash/trinity-a-mindset-strategic-approach/

Kirti, M. P. (2015), Database for Unstructured, Semistructured data-NoSQL, "International Journal of Advanced Research in Computer Engineering & Technology", Vol. 4, Issue 2, pp. 466–469.

Kozinets, R.V. (2002). The field behind the screen: Using netnography for marketing research in online communities. *Journal of Marketing Research*, *39*(1), 61–72.

Lakshminarayan, K., Harp, S. A., & Samad, T. (1999). Imputation of missing data in industrial databases. *Applied Intelligence, 11,* 259–275.

Langone, A. (2018, March 26). Facebook admits it may collect data about your call and text messages: Here is how to turn it off. *Time*, http://time.com/5215274/facebook-messenger-android-call-text-message-data/

Lindstrom, M. (2016). *Small data: The tiny clues that uncover huge trends*. St. Martin's.

Mariampolski, H. (1999). The power of ethnography. *International Journal of Market Research*, *41*(1), 75–86.

Marr, B. (2016, February 12). Data strategy. *Forbes*, https://www.forbes.com/sites/bernardmarr/2016/02/12/big-data-35-brilliant-and-free-data-sources-for-2016/#7c5e810bb54d

Matloff, N. (2014). Software alchemy: Turning complex statistical computations into embarrassingly parallel ones. arXiv: 1409.5827.

Matloff, N. (2016). Big-n versus big-p in Big Data. In: Bulmann, P., Drineas, P., Kane, M., Van der Laan, M. (Eds.), *Handbook of big data* (pp. 21–32). Chapman & Hall.

Moe, W., & Fader, P. (2004). Capturing evolving visit behavior in clickstream data. *Journal of Interactive Marketing, 18*(1), 5–19.

Montgomery, A. L., Li, S., Srinivasan, K., & Liechty, J. C. (2004). Modeling online browsing and path analysis using clickstream data. *Marketing Science*, 24, 4, 579–595.

Natter, M., Reutterer, T., Mild, A., & Taudes, A. (2007). An assortment-wide decision-support system for dynamic pricing and promotion in DIY retailing. *Marketing Science, 26*(4), 576–583.

Neslin, S., Allenby, G., Ehrenberg, A., Hoch, S., Laurent, G., Leone, R., Little, J., Lodish, L., Schormsker, R. & Wittink, D.R. (1994). A Research Agenda for Making Scanner Data More Useful to Managers. Marketing Letters, 5, 4, 395–411.

Netzer, O., Feldman, R., Goldenberg, J., & Fresko, M. (2012). Mind your own business: Market structure surveillance through text mining. *Marketing Science, 31*(3), 521–543.

Nunan, D., & Domenico, M. D. (2012). Market research and the ethics of big data. *International Journal of Market Research, 55*(4), 505–520.

Panko, R. R. (2000). Spreadsheets errors: What we know. What we think we can do. *Proceedings of the Spreadsheet Risk Symposium,* 1–9.

Redman, T. C. (2008). *Data driven: Profiting from your most important business asset.* Harvard Business Press.

Redman, T.C. (2016). Getting in front of data: Who does what? Technics Publications, Baskins Ridge, NJ, USA.

Reynolds, T. J., & Gutman, J. (1988). Laddering theory, method, analysis and interpretation. *Journal of Advertising, 28*(1), 11–31.

Rossi, P., deLurgio, P., & Kantor, D. (2000). Making sense of scanner data. *Harvard Business Review,* 78, 2, page 24.

Royal Statistical Society. (2015). *The opportunities and ethics of big data* [Workshop report]. https://royalsocietypublishing.org/doi/10.1098/rsta.2016.0116 (https://doi.org/10.1098/rsta.2016.0116).

Sadilek, A., Kautz, H., & Silenzio, V. (2012). *Predicting disease transmissions from geo-tagged micro-blog data.* Association for the Advancement of Artificial Intelligence.

Schoemaker, R., & Wittink, D. (1994). A research agenda for making scanner data more useful to managers. *Marketing Letters, 5*(4), 395–412.

Sorenson, E. J. B. (2016). The post that wasn't: Facebook monitors everything users type and not publish. *Computer Law and Security Review, 32*(1), 146–151.

Sorenson, H. (2009). *Inside the mind of the shopper.* Wharton.

Stevens, S. (1946). On the theory of scales of measurement. *Science, 103*(2684), 677–680.

Stewart, D. W., & Shamdasani, P. (2017). Online focus groups. *Journal of Advertising, 46*(1), 48–60.

Ungerboeck. (2019, November 19). *Monitoring and tracking attendees: New methods.* https://ungerboeck.com/resources/monitoring-and-tracking-attendees-new-methods

Valliant, R., Dever, J. A., & Kreuter, F. (2013). *Practical tools for designing and weighting survey samples.* Springer.

Vriens, M. (2013, July 30). 3 Reasons Big-Data Has Big Relevance. *ECornell.* http://blog.ecornell.com/3-reasons-big-data-has-big-relevance/

Vriens, M., Chen, S., Kaularz, S., & Vidden, C. (2017). Assessing the impact of a brand crisis using Big Data: The case of the VW Diesel emission crisis. *DMA Annual Analytics Journal,* 107–118.

Vriens, M., Chen, S., & Vidden, C. (2019). Mapping brand similarities: Comparing consumer online comments versus survey data. *International Journal of Market Research, 61*(2), 130–139.

Vriens, M., & Sinhara, S. (2006). Dealing with missing data in surveys and databases. In R. Grover & M. Vriens (Eds.), *Handbook of marketing research* (pp. 178–191). SAGE.

Vriens, M., & ter Hofstede, F. (2000). Linking attributes, benefits, and values: A powerful approach to market segmentation, brand positioning and advertising strategy development. *Marketing Research Magazine*, 3–8.

Wedel, M., & Kannan, P. K. (2016). Marketing analytics for data-rich Environments. *Journal of Marketing, 80*(6), 97–121.

Yuhas Byers, P., & Wilcox, J. R. (1991). Focus groups: A qualitative opportunity for researchers. *Journal of Business Communication, 28*(1), 63–78.

Zhang, J., Wedel, M., & Pieters, R. (2009). Sales effects of attention to feature advertisements: A Bayesian mediation analysis. *Journal of Marketing Research, 46*(5), 669–681.

Zwitter, A. (2014). Big Data ethics. *Big Data and Society*, 1, 2, 1–6.

CHAPTER 5
INTRODUCTION TO ANALYTICS

5.1 WHAT AM I GOING TO LEARN?

Business in general, and the marketing function surely, is increasingly run and managed by numbers. For example, CMOs and their marketing teams will typically look at many numbers (e.g., sales data, market share data, share-of-wallet data, etc.). They will look at consumer online discussions and at how many visitors their website attracted and if they bought something and, if not, where they dropped off. They will keep track of how satisfied their customers are, and then they will want to know what is driving (read: causing) this satisfaction; they will quantify the image of their brand, try to identify market segments, predict whether a new product idea will be successful, or at the very least want to narrow the number of new product ideas they want to pursue. They will try to quantify the relative importance of product attributes, measure multidimensional constructs such as brand loyalty, forecast the uptake of a newly introduced product, and want to know what ad concept is most likely going to resonate with their audience (i.e., quantitatively they will want to know what the lift in intention to buy is); in general they will want to know if their advertising is working, and maybe even more importantly, what changes in their advertising mix are going to give better results. All these questions involve numbers. Many numbers will come straight from survey data. However, many will come from other sources (such as the ones discussed in the previous chapter).

Numbers can be raw data, minimally processed data, or the result of analyzed data (using statistical modeling or machine learning (e.g., Vriens et al., 2018). In this chapter we will cover the principles of numbers and how to read them, how to interpret them so you understand and convey exactly what the number means and what one can infer from the numbers. We will also discuss analysis techniques that can be used to uncover meaning or insights from the data in cases where a visual inspect just can't do that.

This chapter is structured as follows. First, we start with how to read numbers and with visualization. This section is not meant to be comprehensive, but it highlights the importance of looking at numbers and how to get a read on them. Next, we outline briefly the process we recommend for analyses, followed by a brief discussion of some basic analyses and an introduction to some multivariate analyses.

5.2 HOW TO READ NUMBERS

In business, many reports will come to your desk. These reports will have data, tables, and figures (coming from various types of data). You need to process the numbers and decide what, if anything, it means for the things you need to accomplish in your job. It may be that you decide valuable insights might be extracted from that data. Alternatively, it may be that you won't have to further analyze the data; you just need to interpret the data, be it a table, a figure, or the result from an analysis. Strange as it sounds, this is an area where we see many people struggle. In this section, we discuss some basics to keep in mind when looking at numbers. The following list is not comprehensive; it is based on commonly encountered factors you need to be aware of. You should ask yourself the following questions: Are you looking at absolute numbers or relative numbers? What was the sample on which the numbers were based? What was the measurement approach?

5.2.1 Relative Versus Absolute

Imagine your firm offers a newsletter to its customers, say a financial advice newsletter. There are three sales regions in the United States, each with its own sales director who needs to help the customer engagement representatives sell these newsletters. You receive an update from two regions: California and Wisconsin. In California the sales directors claims success because of 750 net new subscriptions, while Wisconsin only added 500 net new subscriptions. Is this a fair comparison? Not quite. For one, the total population of adults in California is roughly 24 million, and the total population in Wisconsin is roughly 4.5 million. Even that doesn't give us quite the whole picture. Let's say the total number of customers the financial services firm has in California is 24,000, and in Wisconsin it is 15,000. So, now we have two ways to calculate relative numbers. Let's compare the three sets of numbers.

Absolute numbers net new customers:
California: 750
Wisconsin: 500
Potential conclusion: The performance of the sales director in California is better.
Relative to population size:
California: 750/24 million = 0.003%
Wisconsin: 500/4.5 million = 0.01%
Potential conclusion: The performance of the sales director in Wisconsin is better.
Relative to the current customer base:
California: 750/24,000 = 3.1%
Wisconsin: 500/15,000 = 3.3%
Potential conclusion: The performance of both sales directors is roughly equal.

Now, we can better compare the relative performance of the sales directors. The most meaningful comparison seems to be the comparison based on the current client base, and we see that the Wisconsin director does better. We now also see that California, overall, isn't doing that well.

5.2.2 Sample Size

It is important for researchers to determine upfront the right sampling approach and the size and to understand how the sample was pulled and who is responding. In survey research, we never have the luxury of talking to all the customers in a population; at best you get anywhere between a 1–5% response rate. This poses some real challenges for the researcher and for how the data coming back can be interpreted. A researcher needs to decide on three things: who the target population is, what sampling method to use, and what margin of error is acceptable. The reason for conducting a sample survey is to estimate the value of some attribute of a population. The sample needs to be sufficiently large and representative so that we can approximate the true value that exists in the population so that our findings are statistically representative. The sampling method refers to the way that respondents are selected from a population to be in the sample. The most common approaches are random sampling and stratified sampling.

Random sampling is quite rare. First, we need to have a sampling frame from which we select our initial sample. We could draw from a list of U.S. telephone numbers. However, even if that list was easy to get, some people are on the "Do Not Call" list, some people may only have cell phones, and some people may have more than one number. So, that initial sampling frame already creates issues. The second challenge is that in most commercial projects the response rate is likely to be 10% or less (i.e., 90% of your initial sample does not respond). So, even if your initial sample was random, the final sample most likely isn't.

Stratified sampling sets quotas for certain cohorts, usually based on a demographic or product behavior. The quotas are sufficiently large so that we can find statistically meaningful results within each stratified sample group. You keep sampling until each quota group is filled.

Often there is bias in the sample due to how it is selected (sample bias) or because some of the cohorts within the target sample respond at a higher or lower rate (response bias), skewing the overall representation. We will discuss this topic in more detail in Chapter 9 when we look at satisfaction data among a customer data set. We will demonstrate with an example that response and sample selection bias can have a dramatic impact on your findings and its' important that before you analyze the data you compare your sample to the universe on certain variables such as product engagement levels or certain demographics such as age, industry and education. The universe defined as in how your population is represented in your customer database. It's important to pay close attention to how the distributions in demographic or firmographic variables compares to the universe. If there are large discrepancies in your distributions in your sample compared to what the distribution should be in the universe, you may need to make an adjustment and weight the data to correct for imbalances. Especially if they significantly impact some of the core metrics such as overall satisfaction or some other key metric. We will come back to this topic in Chapter 9.

Sometimes you may see charts or tables and you see what seems to be an interesting pattern or an interesting statistic. For example, someone in your firm e-mails you an interesting table (see Table 5.1a). They mention that this table was part of a recent survey among customers and claim that in-person training is the key to building customer satisfaction because it yields the highest increase in very satisfied customers between those who use it and those who don't.

TABLE 5.1A Interpreting Numbers

Engagement options for customers	Percentage very satisfied customers who do NOT use this engagement	Percentage very satisfied customers who DO use this engagement
Newsletter subscriptions	6%	7%
Webinar attending	4%	6%
Blogs	5%	6%
Online communities	3%	9%
In-person training	2%	12%
Life events attendance	1%	7%

Note, that in Table 5.1a there is no mention of sample size specifically. I don't know how large the overall sample size was and I don't know what the relative number of customers are who use or don't use an engagement. In Table 5.1b we added that information.

TABLE 5.1B Interpreting Numbers

Engagement options for customers (Sample size study, N=600)	Percentage very satisfied customers who do NOT use this engagement	Percentage very satisfied customers who DO use this engagement	Lift
Newsletter subscriptions	6% (n=300)	7% (n=300)	1%
Webinar attending	4% (n=200)	6% (n=400)	2%
Blogs	5% (n=50)	6% (n=550)	1%
Online communities	3% (n=46)	9% (n=554)	6%
In-person training	2% (n=595)	12% (n=5)	10%
Lift Life events attendance	1% (n=6)	7% (n=130)	6%

5.2.3 Measurement

Say, someone in your firm has done an ad copy test. These are market research studies that assess whether an advertising that is in the works is likely to work once it is aired on television or goes online. They used a survey approach. Respondents were asked how likely they were to buy the Green Mountain coffee brand (to calibrate, this question was asked for up to three coffee brands, and possibly a non-coffee brand, but more about that later). To measure likelihood a 10-point rating scale was used. The higher the number the more likely the respondent says they will buy your brand. Then respondents were shown an advertisement. After seeing the advertisement respondents were again asked if they would buy the brand (see Figure 5.1).

FIGURE 5.1 Survey Flow Ad Testing

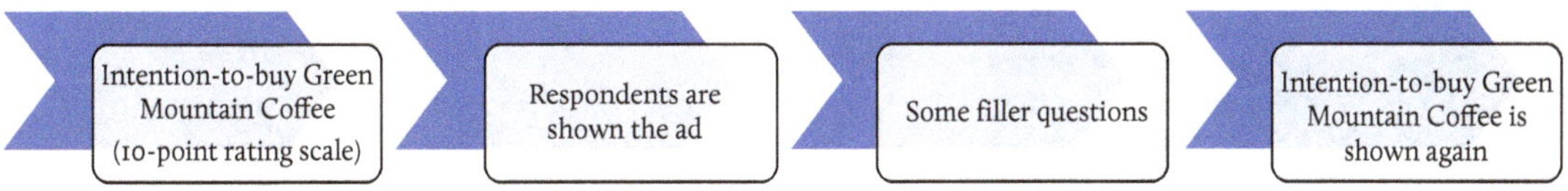

Your colleague shows you a table (see Table 5.2a), and it shows that the average likelihood to buy Green Mountain coffee is 6.5 and the average likelihood to buy after seeing the advertisement is 7.5.

TABLE 5.2A Average Pre- and Post-test Intention-to-Buy Ratings

	PRE-TEST	POST-TEST
Mean	6.5	7.5

This is proof that this ad is working. They even did a statistical test and it showed that the difference between 6.5 and 7.5 is statistically significant. However, consider the following (see Table 5.2b):

A closer inspection of the data shows that out of the overall sample of 100 respondents that those who scored very low on the pre-test scored a bit better on the post-test. Respondents who had a high score on the pre-test had an even higher score on the post-test (say they went from 9 to 10). However, respondents in the middle (those who scores a 7 on the pre-test) went down (to 6 on the post-test). The result is that yes, the average score went up, but the median score went down from 7 to 6. What does this mean? One way to interpret this is that respondents who were very unlikely to buy the brand still are unlikely to buy the brand, maybe a little bit less so. Those who were already very likely to buy the brand became even more likely, but they were going to buy the brand (most likely) anyway. Those in the middle, the ones we should really have convinced, went down.

TABLE 5.2B Pre- and Post-test Intention-to-Buy Numbers

	PRE-TEST	POST-TEST
Respondent 1	3	5
Respondent 2	3	6
Respondent 3	4	6
Respondent 4	4	6
Respondent 5	7	6
Respondent 6	7	6
Respondent 7	9	10
Respondent 8	9	10
Respondent 9	9	10
Respondent 10	10	10
Mean	6.5	7.5
Median	7	6

5.2.4 Visualization and Revisualization

Reading numbers and seeing possibilities might sometimes require a reorganization or visualization of the original numbers. A key challenge is to pick the right chart to support a finding or insight, making sure everyone is clear on what the data is telling us and inspiring an organization to act. A good chart can be interpreted at a quick glance and makes the complex more accessible and understandable. A series of charts shown in a presentation tells a story and doesn't need much explaining. "A picture is worth a thousand words" is like saying that a good chart is worth a thousand words. There are many excellent charting solutions in PowerPoint, Tableau, Power BI, Excel, SPSS (SPSS stands for Statistical Package for the Social Sciences) but researchers need to build some intuition into what chart to use when. This is part art and part science. Visualization software has evolved to a stage where, based on the underlying data, Tableau or Power BI will offer suggestions on how to present the data most effectively. Tufte, Abela, and others have published extensively on best practices for how to create effective visualizations. Here, we will summarize the basics of what you need to know (see Figure 5.2 for how to decide on the right chart, a model from Abela [2008] that we have found to work well).

We follow up with some tips on the do's and don'ts of formatting charts so that they most clearly convey the insights. Also see Tufte (1990), Reynolds (2011), Few (2012), and Knaflic (2015) for a more comprehensive overview.

When you have collected your data there are several questions to ask that can help guide you on what type of chart or visual to use for each insight. Abela identified four factors to guide you in this process—four basic presentation types to choose from based on your intent.

FIGURE 5.2 The Analytical Process

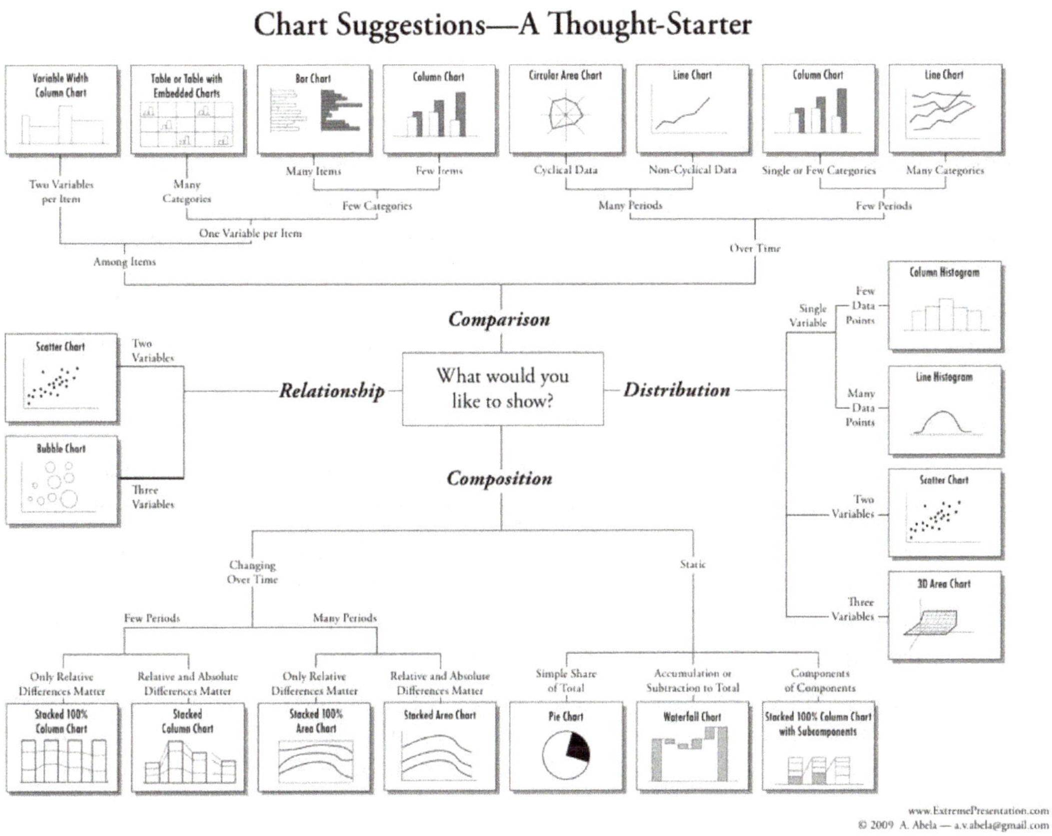

1 *Comparison.* In this case you want to compare values to make a point. For example, if you find that there is a large difference between certain subgroups or between time periods, you may want to highlight these differences in lower and higher values, whether they are absolutes or percentages.

2 *Composition.* Use this type of chart to show how individual parts make up the whole of something, such as the composition of types of users visiting your website or how cases from customer support break down across multiple categories of types of feedback.

3 *Distribution.* In this scenario you want to understand how the data is distributed, how the responses to a question vary across the different values, and to quickly identify the most or least common response, the spread, normal tendency (whether the data follows a normal distribution or is skewed) and whether there are outliers. Bar chart histograms are often used for this.

4 *Relationship.* Relationship charts show how one variable relates to other variables. You can use this to demonstrate how variables move together or not—whether they are correlated and a pattern that suggests there is more than a simple correlation but

perhaps causation. You are looking to see whether a high value for one variable corresponds to a high value on the other variable or whether a low value corresponds to a low value or variable. This can be for two variables at a time or for multiple variables in a multidimensional space.

Once you have decided on the type of presentation format of the data, you need to determine how many variables you want to show in a single chart: one, two, three, or many, for example, age and gender or age, gender, and income? That drives the options with the presentation type, as shown in Abela's decision framework. You also need to decide how many items (data points) you want to display for each variable and whether they are categorical or continuous. Only a few or many? Number of categories or scaled continuously? Display values over a period? Show absolutes or percentages? All that impacts what chart best represents your data and makes the point you are trying to highlight. A good chart has the following characteristics:

1. *Clean and simple*. The chart is clean without any redundant information, lines, colors, and text that do not add value to the point you are trying to make. Reduce the information to the essence of what your headline is saying. If necessary, split the data into multiple charts and highlight what areas are directly connected to the point you are trying to make. Add a legend for clarity, add labels directly on the chart, and avoid making the reader look up what the lines or bars mean.
2. *Logical*. Humans like to see things organized in logical ways as it is easier to know what to focus on. For column, pie, and bar charts, sort the data in ascending or descending order by value, not alphabetically. For time interval charts, set time periods on the horizontal axis running from left to right. Do not skip time periods, even if there are no values. Percentages in a chart should be directly proportional to the numerical quantities presented and add up to 100%.
3. *Consistent*. Use a clear and consistent scale, especially if you want to compare two or more graphs. You cannot have one chart start at a different numerical value unless you want to show proportional changes.
4. *Use colors and fonts smartly*. Colors in graphs are key, but use them sparingly as they can be distracting. Don't use more than a few colors; otherwise, the chart gets too busy. Keep the same color palette and style for all charts across your presentation. For comparing the same value at different time intervals, use the same color in a different intensity, going from dark (most recent) to light (oldest), or vice versa. For different categories for example occupation or title, use different colors. The most widely used colors are black, white, red, green, blue, and yellow. Check how your charts would look when printed out in grayscale. If you cannot distinguish color differences, you should change them. Some people are color-blind. Keep that in mind when creating charts, ensuring they are readable and that color palettes are friendly to color-blind people. Try to use a font size greater than 14 so that people in the back of a typical classroom-sized room can see the chart well enough to follow the point you are making.

5.3 AN ANALYTICAL PROCESS

To analyze a dataset, we recommend starting with cleaning and preprocessing, univariate analysis, and bivariate analysis to review data quality and to glean initial insights. Only then continue with multivariate analysis, and then evaluation (which assess the stability and validity of the results), and possible assessment of causality. Figure 5.3 shows a simple overview of the basic steps we propose.

FIGURE 5.3 The Analytical Process

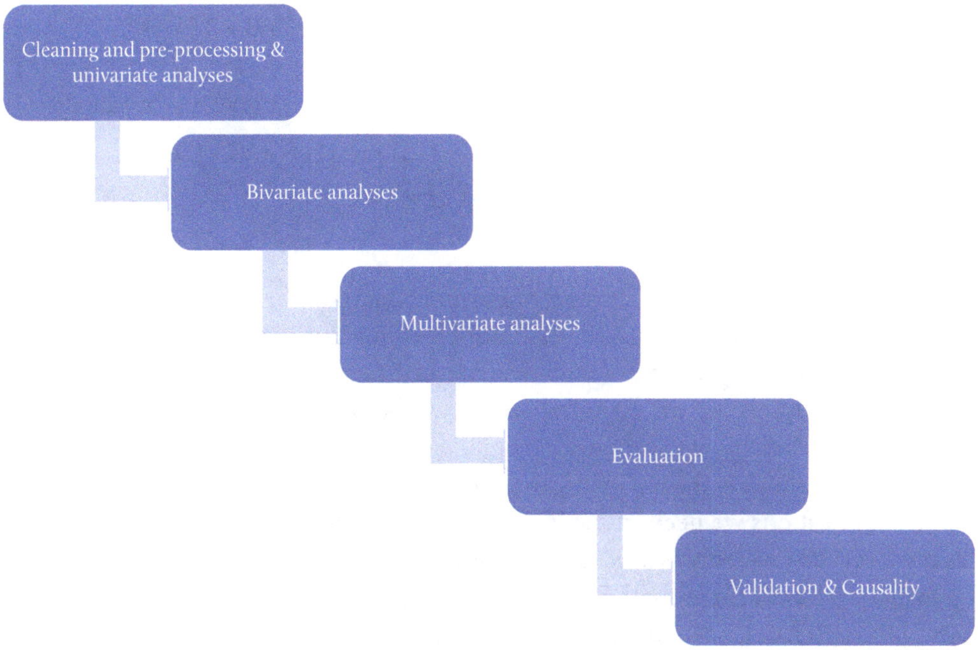

In the section below, we outline the various steps in the process briefly, and then in subsequent sections we discuss several steps more in-depth.

Data cleaning and preprocessing is an important step in the process. It includes finding mistakes, errors that have been made by the respondent or the data collection agency. It also includes evaluating whether missing data is an issue that should be dealt with.

The reasons we want to univariate analyses are threefold. One, it allows us to get a feeling for the data. Two, this initial exploration allows detection of possible errors and inconsistencies and assesses the degree of missing data. Questions to be asked here include (a) Are there any errors in the data? For example, do data points from a single respondent contradict each other? (b) Is the extent of missing data an issue we need to correct? (c) In case of survey data, do we suspect response style biases (e.g., halo responses, extreme responses, etc.)? (d) How do responses to our questions look (e.g., skewed, normal, etc.)? (e) Do we need to transform or convert certain variables (i.e., create new variables by combining several variables [in data mining this is referred to as feature engineering])? (f) Do some of the results look surprising?

and (g) What are appropriate statistics and analyses given the measurement levels of the variables? Three, it may already give us actionable insights.

Bivariate analyses aim to quantify the relationship between two variables. The statistical approaches you can select for this purpose depend on the measurement level of the two involved variables. Table 5.3 shows some options.

TABLE 5.3 Bivariate Analyses

Both interval scale	Both ordinal scale	Interval & nominal	Both nominal
• Correlations (Pearson)	• Spearman's rank correlation	• T-Test (if comparing means) • One sample t-test • Two-sample t-test • ANOVA	• Chi-squared test • Adjusted residuals • Eta coefficient

Multivariate analyses refer to analyses where more than two variables are analyzed simultaneously. We look at relationships across multiple (sometimes many) variables. There can be several reasons why we want to do multivariate analysis: one, to understand relationships and patterns based on several/many variables; two, because we want to get insights into trade-offs; three, because we want prioritization among multiple variables. Lastly, we may at times want to simplify the reporting, and multivariate analysis can help with that.

Some of questions we need to ask include the following: Do we need to consider any data reduction or pre-analysis (e.g., factor analysis, principal component analysis, etc.)? For example, if we have a survey with a set of attitudinal questions around a certain topic, we may want to check if this set can be reduced to a few principal factors (see Chapter 10). What (statistical) models are appropriate given the characteristics of the data and variables and given the business question at hand? Should we consider looking at more complicated relationships? For example, one might want to look for interaction effects or nonlinear effects or see whether heterogeneity across respondents should be considered. More strategic insights are often the result of deeper analyses (e.g., multilayer analyses, digging deeper on certain aspects, making it more difficult for the competition to replicate what you did).

The next step is evaluation. If multivariate analysis results are used for recommendations, we should assess stability and, in the case of predictive models, predictive accuracy. The specific ways to evaluate an analytical result depends on the specific analyses. However, in general we would consider (a) the stability of the results under various bootstrap samples and (b) how well the model fits the data. Fit measures vary by technique. For linear regression, the standard fit measure is R-squared and adjusted R-squared. Can we triangulate the results with other studies? Additional data and analyses can contextualize an insight and reinforce the validation of the insight (Smith & Fletcher, 2004). Andrew Ehrenberg, one of the early writers about the importance of looking at validation from a broader perspective, made the case for using multiple sets of data to validate insights (Ehrenberg & Bound, 2000).

Lastly, we need to think about causality. Does listening to music to reduce stress affect a students' GPA score? Imagine we have done a survey, and we measure how many hours students listen to music to reduce stress (this can be asked, and students just give their own estimate). We also ask their average GPA. Say we find a high correlation. Does that mean that listening to music to reduce stress causes a higher GPA? Of course not. Does increased ice cream consumption cause homicide rates to go up? There is a close relationship between these two variables. The notion that ice cream causes murders is obviously ridiculous and illustrates that correlation is not causation. It is just that as temperatures rise, people are more likely to be out on the street and drinking alcohol, and the chance that people will get upset or seek violence increases, resulting in higher murder rates. This is an example of spurious correlation or covariance with another factor; there is a third variable that explains increased murder rates. And it just so happens that when temperatures go up, ice cream sales go up too. We see this mistake being made all the time in the news media and next we suggest how to get around this and find true causality.

Multivariate analyses that are not based on (quasi-) experimental designs are the result of correlational analyses. There are analytical applications where we don't care much about causation. For example, if I simply want to forecast whether the market is growing or declining a good forecast can be useful even if we don't understand what is causing the growth/decline. However, there are applications where one needs the causality feature. Say a firm has a dataset derived from a customer survey containing several hundred variables. One of these variables may be purchase intent. The question becomes, "What variables in the dataset are most predictive of purchase intent?" The analyst can start analyzing the data using linear regression (discussed in more detail later in this chapter). The analyst keeps working on the dataset until a good model is found, and his stakeholders are happy with the results. The real question that the business needs to answer is "If the results are being used to make changes to the product or service, will this really lead to more prospective customers with a higher intention to buy, and will it lead to more prospective customers that will actually buy the product?" Here, we do care about causality.

In non-experimental analytics (e.g., regression models, time series analysis, etc.) we can assess the likelihood that we have truly uncovered causal factors via the following steps:

1. Evaluate hold-out predictive accuracy. This is a good first step. If we cannot predict a hold-out sample. the likelihood of truly having uncovered a causal factor is low.
2. Are the effects consistent across a variety of studies (triangulation)? See previous step (assessing predictive validity).
3. Are the results consistent with theory? The degree that our results fit within a theoretical framework can provide some credibility to causality claims.
4. Where feasible the most robust validation is via in-market testing. This can be implemented using a field experiment or via stepwise implementation. When using a field

experiment approach, a firm defines an action based on the insights and sets up a field experiment. In the field experiment, part of the market will continue to see the status quo and another will be subjected to the new marketing approach, namely those based on the insights. For example, in the case of Inofec, they created four experimental conditions and showed that the condition that fully made use of the insights resulted in the highest profits. In the case of Baumax, they rolled out their pricing strategy stepwise, starting with only a small number of stores and gradually increase this.

5.4 CLEANING, PREPROCESSING, AND UNIVARIATE ANALYSES

Part of data cleaning involves looking for outliers and errors. Look at Table 5.4 for two examples of mistakes we might encounter.

TABLE 5.4 Two Examples of Errors in the Data

Part of data set—variable: What was your graduation year	Part of data set—variable: What was your graduation year
2017	
2016	2013
2012	2017
2000	
2012	
1996	2016
Economics	2096
2011	
2013	2011
2014	
2012	

Such mistakes should clearly be fixed (cleaned) before interpreting any analyses. Outliers can be observations that in some way are extreme or very different from the other observations. Outliers can be valid data points, but they can also be mistakes. Sometimes it is hard to tell. For example, if one of our questions was asking about someone's annual income, and one response is $10 million, this most likely is an error, but it is not an impossible observation. If someone states their age is 400 years, then this is an error; maybe they meant 40; maybe they just did not want to give you that information.

For the next section, consider that the dataset contains 1,436 sales records of used Toyota Corollas. See Table 5.5 for a list of all variables in this dataset and see Table 5.6 for the first 10 rows of the dataset.

TABLE 5.5 Variables in the Car Sales Dataset

Variable Name	Variable Type	Variable Description
Price	Continuous	Price at which the car was sold
Age	Continuous	Age of the car in months
KM	Continuous	Mileage driven in kilometers
Fuel Type	Categorical	Fuel type including diesel, petrol, and compressed natural gas (CNG)
HP	Continuous	Horse power
Met Color	Categorical	If the car color matches what buyer requested (0 = unmatched, 1 = matched)
Transmission	Categorical	0 = manual, 1 = automatic
Engine size in CC	Continuous	Displacement volume of a cylinder in cubic centimeters
Number of doors	Ordinal	Number of doors ranging from 2-5
Weight	Continuous	How much the car weighs in kilograms

TABLE 5.6 First 10 Lines of the Car Sales Dataset

Car ID	Price	Age	KM	Fuel Type	HP	MetColor	Automatic	CC	Doors	Weight
1	13,500	23	46,986	Diesel	90	1	0	2,000	3	1,165
2	13,750	23	72,937	Diesel	90	1	0	2,000	3	1,165
3	13,950	24	41,711	Diesel	90	1	0	2,000	3	1,165
4	14,950	26	48,000	Diesel	90	0	0	2,000	3	1,165
5	13,750	30	38,500	Diesel	90	0	0	2,000	3	1,170
6	12,950	32	61,000	Diesel	90	0	0	2,000	3	1,170
7	16,900	27	94,612	Diesel	90	1	0	2,000	3	1,245
8	18,600	30	75,889	Diesel	90	1	0	2,000	3	1,245
9	21,500	27	19,700	Petrol	192	0	0	1,800	3	1,185
10	12,950	23	71,138	Diesel	69	0	0	1,900	3	1,105

5.4.1 Missing Data

Part of correcting and preprocessing involves evaluating and dealing with missing data.

In both customer survey data as well as transactional or other internal database information (see Chapter 2), there is usually missing data. In some techniques, discussed later in this book, we don't have to worry about missing data because the technique or algorithmic approach takes care of it more or less automatically (e.g., decision trees, neural network analysis, and any time we use maximum likelihood via the EM algorithm; see Dempster et al., 1977). In others, this is not the case (e.g., linear and logit regression, MDS, cluster analysis with the exception of latent class). For some introductions, mostly non-technical introductions, in the topic, we refer to Vriens and Melton (2002) and Vriens and Sinhara (2006). In this section, we summarize the key points from those two papers.

Recognizing missing data is important, as it can have dramatic effects on the results of your analysis:

- It may lead to biased parameter estimates (e.g., over- or underestimations of the regression coefficients in a regression model) (Ramaswamy et al., 2001; Schafer, 1997).
- It may lead to increases in types I and II errors and reduce statistical power (Schafer & Graham, 2002).

It is also important to realize that these negative effects do not disappear with just any method that is available in popular software packages. There are various methods to deal with missing data. The pros and cons of these methods depend on the nature of missing data. There are three types of missing data: (a) MCAR, MAR, and MNAR. MCAR is "missing completely at random." Say we have data with 10 variables, x1–x10. The missing data on x1 is said to be MCAR if the missing data does not depend on the values of x1 and does not depend on the values of x2–x10. MAR is "missing at random." Missing data on x1 is said to be MAR if the missing values in x1 do not depend on the values of x1 itself. Say, x1 = income stated, x2 = education level. If the missing data does not depend on income levels but could be a function of x2 (e.g., more educated people are less likely to report their income) (Vriens & Sinhara, 2006). MNAR is "missing not at random. If the missing data in x1 is a function of the values of the values of x1 itself.

Unfortunately, it is impossible to test whether missing data is MAR. Let's consider a few missing data approaches:

1. The complete case method (or list-wise deletion): We only use respondents who have no missing values. If the missing data are not MCAR, this approach will result in biased estimates.
2. The available case method (pair-wise deletion): In general, this method is less preferred than the complete case method (Allison, 2001).
3. Mean substitution: We replace each missing value by the mean of that variable. This method results in biased estimates regardless of the type of missing data, except when estimating the mean (Peugh & Enders, 2004). We note that we often see this method applied in practice, but we would really caution against using it.
4. Regression substitution method: For the variable that has missing data and the regression model is estimated using the available case method, we aim to predict the values of x1 based on the values of x2 - x10. Then, we use this regression equation to predict the missing values and impute these predictions in the dataset. If the missing data is MAR, this method can result in unbiased estimates.
5. Model-based multiple imputation: A popular well-perming approach is the Bayesian model-based multiple imputation approach. In essence, in this modeling approach

we produce multiple estimates for each missing value (see, for more details, Schafer, 1997; and Vriens & Sinhara, 2006).

We recommend the following practices. The likelihood that the missing data is MAR becomes larger the more variables we have in our dataset (Sinhara et al., 2001). If we assume MAR, the ML and Bayesian model-based multiple imputation approaches are recommended. The list-wise and pairwise deletion methods are not recommended. This recommendation was made by the American Psychological Association Task Force on Statistical Inference (Wilkinson & Taskforce on Statistical Inference, 1999). If the missing data becomes very high, say more than 30%, the likelihood that the missing data is MNAR becomes larger as well, and it may be better not to use this variable in subsequent analyses (Vriens & Sinhara, 2006).

5.4.2 Basic Univariate Analyses

We define basic analyses as analyses that pertain to one or two variables. Many reports and charts you will encounter are univariate or bivariate. Basic, univariate, and bivariate analyses can sometimes be sufficient to support a decision, in which case no further multivariate analyses are needed. Univariate (analyses pertaining to one variable) and bivariate analyses (analyses pertaining to two variables) help us develop intuition for the data.

5.4.3 Types of Variables

Variables come in different types and can be described in various ways (e.g., Babin & Zikmund, 2016). Here, we review two typologies we believe are useful: the distinction between nominal, ordinal, and interval ratio measured variables and the distinction between single versus composite variables.

Looking at Tables 5.2 and 5.3, the first thing we notice is that price is a continuous range of numbers, while automatic is a yes/no option (i.e., categorical) and number of doors is a range of integers. While exploring and eventually further analyzing this data, we need to keep in mind these differences among variables: Variables have certain measurement qualities.

1. Categorical: Nominal or ordinal variables give a qualitative classification. Nominal variables cannot be ranked or ordered. For example, the color of a car (blue, red, white) has no order. Common examples of nominal variables are gender, race, occupation, or yes/no responses. Ordinal variables can be ranked but cannot be quantified in terms of the distance between successive values. For example, in a survey we may ask respondents "How often do you smoke?" and we provide three answer options: never, sometimes, and often. We know that sometimes is more than never, and we know that often is more than sometimes. However, we cannot say anything about the differences other than greater than/lesser than. Other examples include ratings/rankings on a Likert scale (strongly disagree, disagree, neutral, agree, strongly agree), although such scales are quite often treated as interval-level scaled.
2. Interval-scaled variables have ranking as well as quantifiable spacing between values. Interval variables have quantifiable spacing between values, but there is no "true

zero." Because no zero exists, one cannot multiply or divide by values. An example of an interval-scaled variable could be something such as safety rating, ranging from 0–100, but as a composed variable (i.e., an average of five safety criteria, each worth a maximum 20 points).

3 Ratio-scaled variables contain even more information. For the car dataset, price is an example of a ratio-scaled variable. The first car in Table 5.1 sold for $250 less than the second car. Common examples of continuous variables include age, income, and time. Within continuous variables, these are often separated into either interval or ratio variables. An example of a ratio variable is temperature. Zero degrees does not imply no heat. Similarly, 20 degrees is not twice 10 degrees. Ratio variables have a zero and thus allow for multiplication and division. Our car price variable has a zero (free car!). We can say a $1,000 car is half the price of a $2,000 car.

These distinctions are especially important to consider when designing surveys.

Most statistical software considers variable type when loading a dataset, though the terminology may differ. The measurement level of a set of variables has implications for the type of statistics and analyses we should use. For example, to "best" summarize nominal data, we use the mode; to "best" summarize ordinal data, we use the median; and to "best" summarize interval and ratio data, the average/mean is the best summary statistic.

A second typology is the distinction between single and composite variables. Imagine you want to get an understanding of how loyal a customer is to your brand. You come up with several yes/no questions (e.g., Are you willing to postpone your purchase if your preferred brand is out of stock? Are you willing to pay more for your preferred brand? and Are you willing to recommend your preferred brand to a friend?). We can analyze each variable separately, or we can count the number of times a respondent has said yes to these three questions. This count variable now is a measure of "brand loyalty." We call such variables composite variables as they are composed of several component variables.

5.4.4 Univariate Exploration

Now that we understand the structure of our data, let's summarize and explore the information it contains. We will do this via descriptive statistics (such as mean, variance, frequency, and others) as well as visualizations (bar plot, box plot, scatterplot, and others). This data exploration step is a crucial first step to perform before any analysis begins.

Let's start with some of our categorical variables, say fuel type. Table 5.7 gives a simple frequency and percentage frequency for the three types of fuel.

TABLE 5.7 Frequency of Fuel Types

Fuel Type	Frequency	Frequency Percentage
CNG	17	0.01
Diesel	155	0.11
Petrol	1264	0.88

These frequencies are easily visualized via a bar graph (Figure 5.4).

FIGURE 5.4 Bar Plot of Fuel Type Frequencies

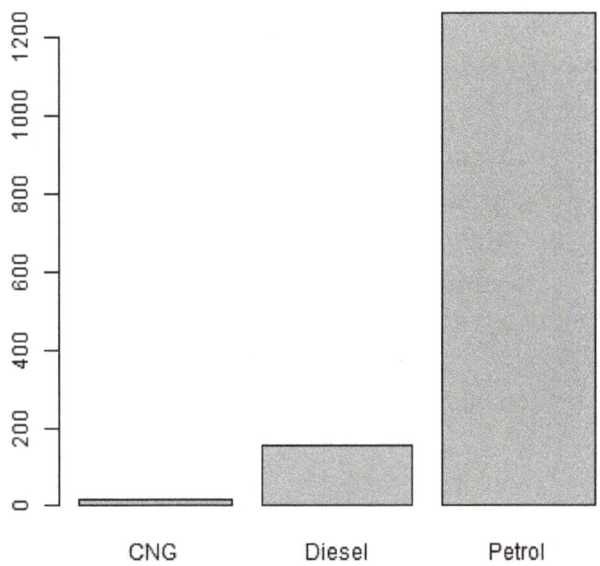

With numeric variables, our goal is to summarize each variable in terms of its distribution, including its mean, standard deviation, range, and points of interest, such as outliers. Let's examine the price variable in our car dataset. Figure 5.5 gives a histogram of the sales price values, which is known as the distribution of our sales price values.

FIGURE 5.5 Histogram of Car Prices

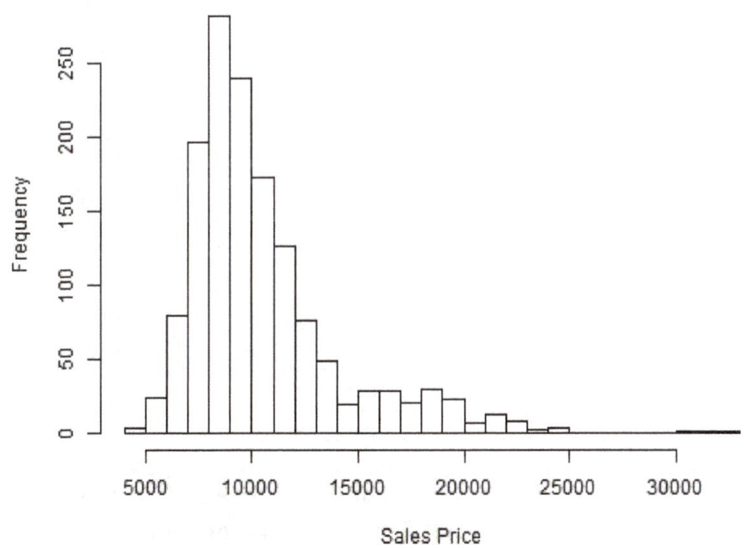

How do we completely describe this sales price distribution? There are several statistical measurements that collectively provide a wealth of insight (see Table 5.8). Let's calculate these values for our sales prices (see Table 5.9. For the actual formulas see Vriens et al., 2018).

TABLE 5.8 Descriptions of Distribution Metrics

Distribution Information	Statistical Measurement	Description
Extremes	Maximum	Largest value
	Minimum	Smallest value
Center	Mean	Arithmetic average
	Median	Middle value
Spread	Variance	Average squared distances from the mean
	Standard Deviation	Square root of variance (same units as original data)
	Interquartile range	Difference between the 75th and 25th percentile
Values	Percentiles	99 intermediate values resulting from dividing the data into 100 groups according to median.
	Quartiles	3 intermediate values resulting from dividing the data into 4 groups according to median.

TABLE 5.9 Statistics for Car Sale Prices

Statistical Measurement	Value
Maximum	32,500
Minimum	4,350
Mean	10,730.82
Median	9,900
Variance	13,154,872.1
Standard Deviation	3,626.96
Interquartile Range	3,500
1st Quartile	8,450
3rd Quartile	11,950

To find quartiles, the data distribution is divided into equal groups according to the median. That is, since the median of our price data was 9,900, this value divides the data into two groups: the lower half and upper half. Taking the median of the lower half, divide again. The first quartile (8,450) is the median of the lower half. The third quartile (11,950) is the median of the upper half. The same division process used for quartiles is used for any general percentile of the distribution.

Note that there are multiple options for measuring the distribution center and spread. Because our sale price data is skewed to the left, the median gives a better indication of the distribution's center than the mean does since the mean can be heavily influenced by outliers. Likewise, the interquartile range can give a better indication of the spread of skewed data than standard deviation.

Distributions are very important in marketing analytics, but here we limit our discussion to the normal distribution. Statistically, the normal distribution is significant because of the central limit theorem, which states that as the number of samples increases, the shape sample distribution becomes normal (of course, if the metric of interest sampled is normal in the population).

A key characteristic of the normal distribution is the 68-95-99.7 rule (also known as the three-sigma rule). That is, about 68% of data is within one standard deviation of the mean, 95% is within two standard deviations, and 99.7% is within three. One standard deviation is defined as the inflection point of the bell-shaped curve (point where curve changes from concave up to down). This rule is illustrated in Figures 5.6 and 5.7.

FIGURE 5.6 Normal Distribution Examples

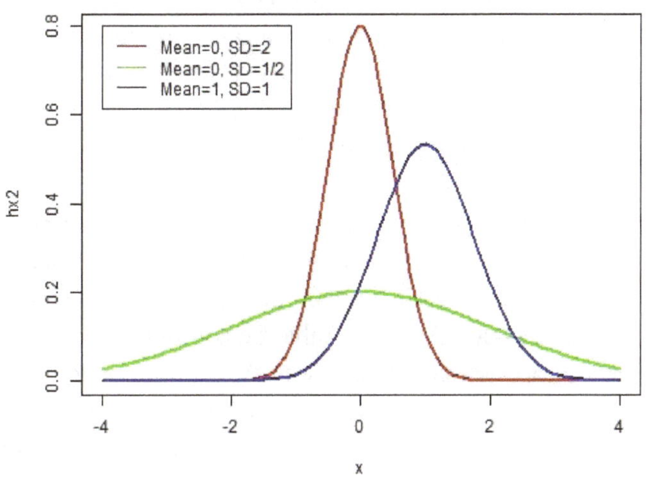

In Figure 5.6 we show the sample normal distributions with various combinations of mean and standard deviations. In Figure 5.7 we illustrate the 68-99-99.7 rule on normal distribution with mean 0 and standard deviation 1. The blue line indicates the range of the distribution 1 standard deviation from the mean; 68% of the samples (area under the curve) lie within this range; and, likewise, for 95% (red) and 99.7% (green) ranges.

FIGURE 5.7 Normal Distribution: 68-95-99.7 Rule

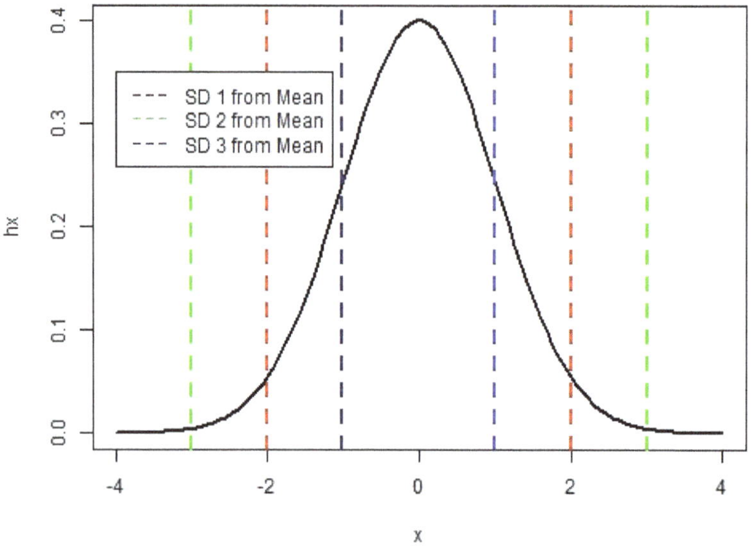

In short, if one is wondering how the distribution of their data compares to a normal distribution, the best method is to plot the actual distribution and examine visually. Measures like skewness and kurtosis help flagging skewness when the number of variables is large, but visualizing is most important. Further, there are formal statistical tests for normality of data (see Vriens et al., 2018). Note that when discussing distributions, there is a distinction to be made. A distribution, such as the normal distribution, ambitions to model an entire population. The distribution for the car sale price data is a sample distribution formed from a (hopefully) random sample of the entire population. Because the entire population of car sale prices is not known, we use the sample to formulate judgments on the entire population. This process is known as statistical inference. Because the true statistics such as mean and standard deviation of the entire population cannot be known, we can estimate them within some confidence interval. The size of our random sample does play a role. The larger the sample, the more confidently we can estimate parameters of the entire population. Let's illustrate this concept with our sale price data. Table 5.9 computed the mean of our price sample ($10,730.82). How sure are we that this is close to the true population mean? Assuming the prices follow a normal distribution, we calculate a 95% confidence interval around our sample mean as 95% confidence interval = Mean ± 2 * standard error. The standard error is calculated from the standard deviation (of the sample) as Standard error = (Standard deviation)/$\sqrt{n}$. For our data, we then have Standard error = 3626.96/$\sqrt{1436}$ = 95.71. Hence, the 95% confidence interval = 10730.82±2(95.71) = [10539.40,10922.25]. Then we are 95% certain that the true population mean lies in the interval [10539.40,10922.25]. Note that division by $\sqrt{n}$ in the standard error ensures that as we have a larger sample (n gets large), our confidence interval gets smaller.

5.4.5 Data Transformations

When comparing pairs of variables, sometimes the scaling and distribution shape of each variable can create complications. For example, the mean sale price is $10,730.82 and the mean age is 55.95 months. If we see two different cars for sale, one with a sales price of $15,000 (about $5,000 more than the mean) and one 80 months old (25 months more than the mean), which is more unusual? The trouble is the scale of these two variables differs, making it difficult to tell. A simple idea is to *rescale* both variables to have mean zero and standard deviation 1. That is, if our original variable is x, the new variable X would be the standardized version of x:

$$X(standardized) = (x - mean(x))/s$$

where mean(x) is the variable mean and s the standard deviation. It is easy to see that positive values of x are greater than the mean while negative values of X are less than the mean. This rescaling is known as standardizing the data. Recall the standard deviation for the sale price is $3,626.96, while the standard deviation of age is 18.6 months. By computing the number of standard deviations from the mean (known as the z-score), we now have a fair comparison. Let's do this for the previous discussion: The z-score of the $15,000-priced car is z = (15000 − 10730.82)/3626.96 = 1.18, while the z-score of the 80-month old car is z = (80 − 55.95)/18.6 = 1.29. So, the $15,000 priced car is 1.18 standard deviations above the mean while the 80-month old car is 1.29 standard deviations from the mean. This implies that the age of the 80-month old car is more unusual (relatively farther from the mean) than the $15,000-priced car. Rescaling to mean zero and standard deviation helps make fair comparisons across variables.

Figure 5.8 shows the relations between price of the car and age of the car. We can see that many of the data points are concentrated in the upper left-hand corner of the plot. To create a better comparison, let's see if we can correct for this skewedness by transforming our sales price data. There are many options for transforming variables (log, powers, etc.). For right skewed data, log transformations are a good choice. That is, for our sales price, we will create a new variable as

$$X(\text{log-transformed}) = \log(x + 1)$$

where x is the original variable and X is the transformed variable. We add one inside the logarithm to avoid possible zero values of x (log(0) is undefined). Figure 5.9 gives the new distribution of the log-transformed sales price.

In Figure 5.8 each dot represents a car. The red line is a LOESS smoothing of the plotted points. In Figure 5.9, after taking the log transform of sale price, the distribution looks more normal than in Figure 5.7.

Note the resulting distribution of Figure 5.9 is now centered and looks more normal. Let's use our new log-transformed sales prices to update the scatterplot (Figure 5.10).

FIGURE 5.8 Scatterplot of Car Price Versus Age

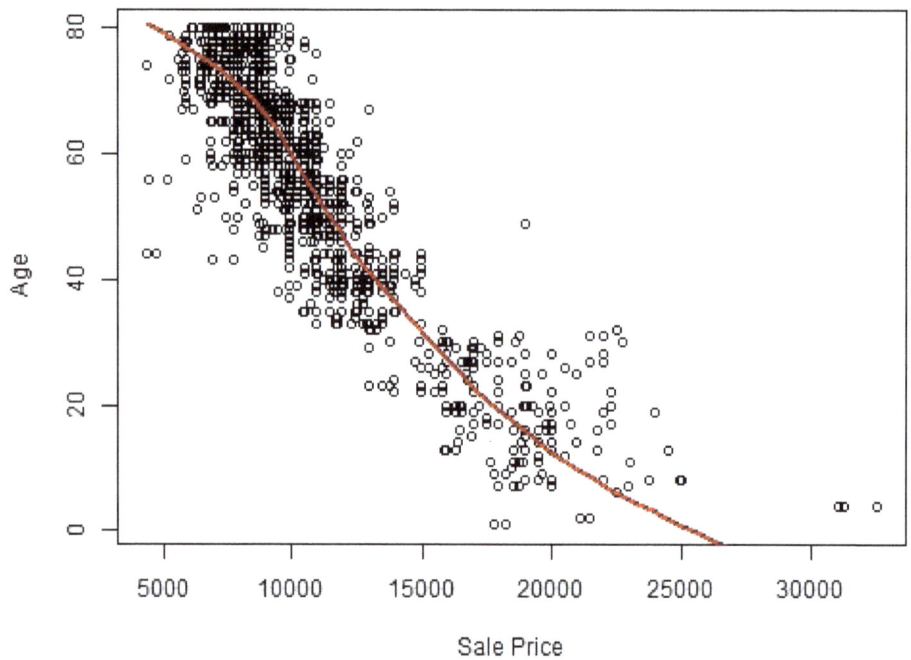

FIGURE 5.9 Distribution of Log Transformed Sales Prices

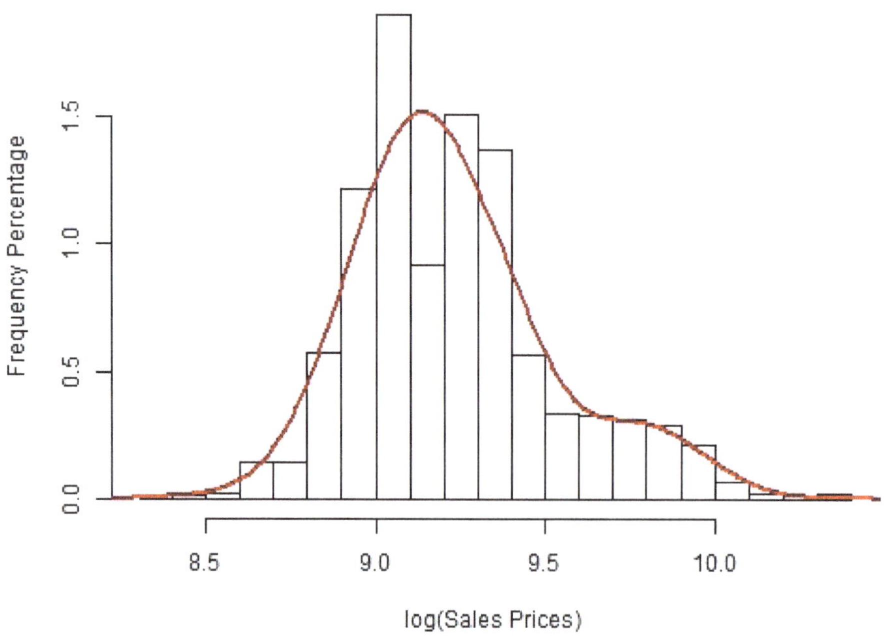

FIGURE 5.10 Scatterplot of Log Transformed Sales Prices Versus Age

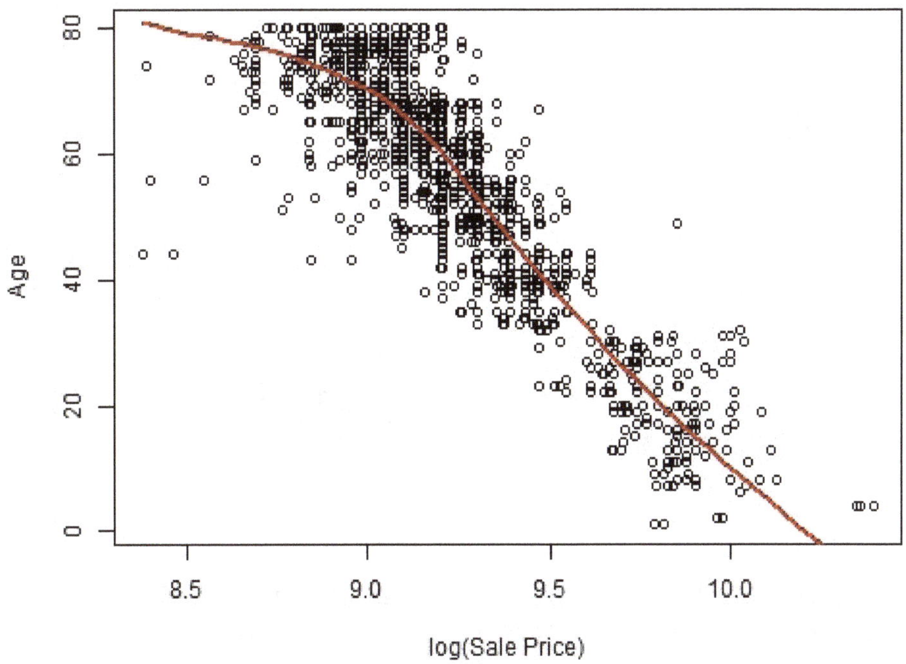

In Figure 5.10, after taking the log transform of sale price, the scatterplot against age is clearer.

There are multiple options when transforming data to correct for skew and best fit the data to a normal distribution (see for more details Vriens et al., 2018).

5.5 BIVARIATE ANALYSES

If we have two interval or ratio-scaled variables we call that the Pearson correlation coefficient (Pearson, 1900; see also Rodgers & Nicewander, 1988). If we have two ordinal variables, we can use the Spearman rank correlation coefficient (there are other association statistics as well). If we have two nominal variables, then we can use the chi-square analysis to find out if there is a relationship between the two variables. If we have two nominal variables, we use the chi-square to find out if there is a relationship between the two variables. If one of the variables is interval or ratio and the other is categorical then we can apply either t-tests or an analysis of variance. We discuss these methods briefly next.

5.5.1 Correlation

Scatterplots are a nice way to visualize the relationships between pairs of variables. For example, Figure 5.11 illustrates two different variable relationships.

FIGURE 5.11 Different Relationships Between Pairs of Variables

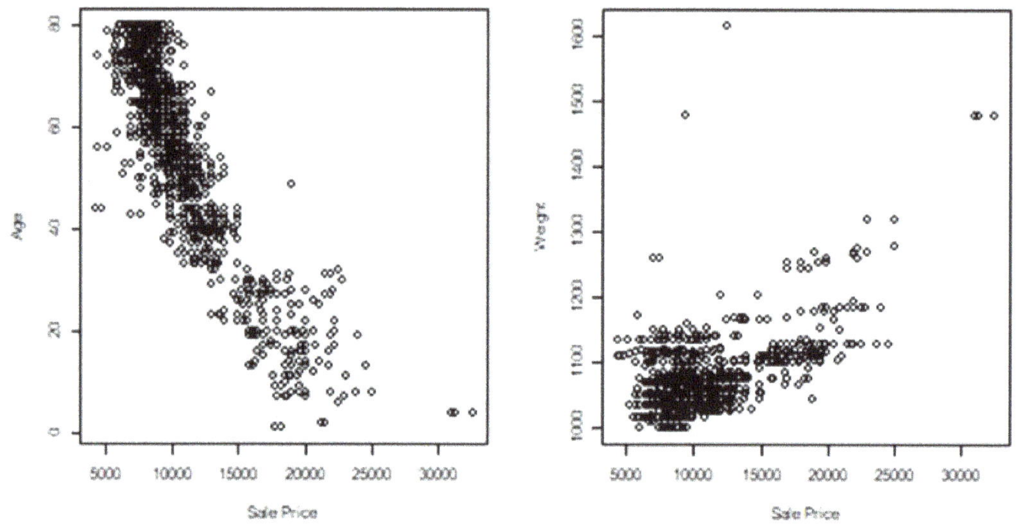

The left plot in Figure 5.11 shows variables that are negatively related. That is, as age increases, price decreases. The right plot has positively related variables. As weight increases, price also increases.

Correlation gives a way to measure the relationship between pairs of variables. The Pearson correlation (Pearson, 1900) can be used with interval and ratio variables, and there is a rank-order correlation used with ordinal data (the Spearman [1904] correlation coefficient). Correlation coefficients range from −1 to +1, where −1 represents a negative correlation, 1 represents a perfect positive correlation, a negative 1 a perfect negative correlation, and 0 represents no correlation. The *Pearson r* correlation (also known as a linear correlation) is the most common choice. This measure is used when we have two variables interval scaled or higher. Pearson r measures the extent to which two variables are proportional (linear relationship) to each other. That is, if the scatterplot of two variables is exactly on a straight line with positive slope, the correlation will be exactly 1. Likewise, if the scatterplot is a straight line with negative slope, correlation will be −1.

Looking at the three plots of Figure 5.11, we see the price-age plot has a linear relationship (negative slope) and expect these to have a negative correlation close to −1. The price-weight relationship is positive and somewhat linear, so we expect a positive correlation. Figure 5.12 gives a pairwise comparison of all our continuous variables.

The correlation coefficients are listed in the lower left triangle. These coefficients are visualized in the upper right triangle. Note our price-age correlation is −0.88. In the upper half, −0.88 is visualized as a strong negative relation (red) where the relation is visualized with an ellipse. Overall, we see that the strongest negative correlations are price with age and mileage, while the strongest positive correlations are age/mileage and CC/weight.

FIGURE 5.12 Correlation of Continuous Variables

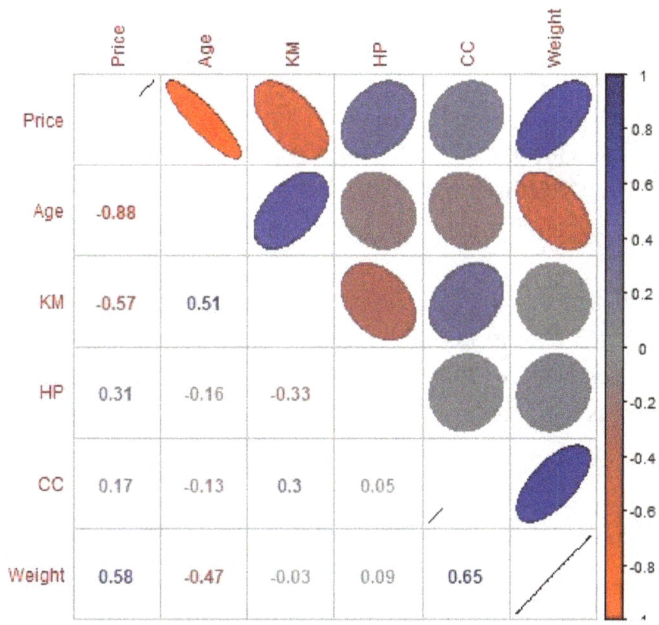

It is important to keep in mind that correlation measures the linear relationship between two variables. Because of this assumption, there are a few pitfalls to be weary of:

1. Outliers: Outliers can skew the correlation calculations. Imagine fitting a straight line to the price-weight plots of Figure 5.11. The outliers on the top left of this graph will most certainly influence the correlation coefficient between the two variables. Even one extreme outlier could lead to a different correlation value than expected. Removing outliers is an option, but one should consider that every data point has validity, which needs to be considered. Overall, one should view a scatterplot whenever considering correlation coefficients to gain a more complete understanding.
2. Non-linear relationships: As we saw with our price data, distributions can be skewed. Comparing two skewed variables can result in seeing a strong relationship that is not linear. In this case, a data transformation before measuring correlation may be appropriate. Again, visualizing scatterplots is the best way to detect situations such as this.
3. Non-homogeneous groups: It is possible that data can contain hidden groups, which can skew correlation results. For example, men and women may fill out a survey in very different ways. For a certain pair of variables, men may positively correlate while women negatively correlate. If these groups are considered together, a correlation of zero may be seen even though the underlying groups have strong correlation. Likewise, it is possible that the groups show no correlation, but combined correlation is nonzero. In the end, visualizing variable relationships via scatterplot is an essential tool here.

The fact that the Pearson correlation can be used for interval and ratio variables means that the metric is invariant under linear transformations. However, if we have two ordinal scaled variables, we need to use a different coefficient (e.g., Spearman's (1904) rank correlation or Kendall's τ, Kendall, 1938). These metrics capture the monotone association between ordinal variables (i.e., the relationship can be nonlinear). Ordinal scales are invariant under monotone transformations. A positive value between two variables X and Y means if X increases so does Y. If there is a perfect monotone relationship the metric will be 1.

5.5.2 The χ^2-Test

The χ^2-Test (e.g., Cochran, 1952, although its original is often attributed to Pearson, 1900; see also Plackett, 1983) is the most common test for testing for a relationship between a pair of categorical variables. Here, we will be using Pearson's chi-square. As an example, consider Table 5.10, which cross tabulates fuel type against number of doors in the car data.

TABLE 5.10 Chi-Square Cross Tabulation for Comparing Fuel Types and Doors

	Diesel	Petrol	Sum Rows
3 Doors	61	555	616
4 Doors	14	121	135
5 Doors	79	587	666
Sum columns	154	1263	1714

In Table 5.10 we see cross-tabulated frequencies; comparing categorical variables fuel type and number of doors. Since CNG is a rare fuel type and two doors are unusual, we leave these out for now. The chi-square test aims to answer the question of whether fuel types are independent of number of car doors.

The chi-square test is built on the idea that we can compute expected frequencies in a cross-tabulation table. That is, if we have 100 cars (50 gas and 50 diesel), each car can have either two or four doors. If there is no relationship between fuel type and number of doors, we would expect an equal number of two- and four-door cars for each fuel type. Assuming no relationship between variables is known as the *null hypothesis* for the chi-square test. The further our fuel-door cross tabulation gets away from this null hypothesis, the more significant the chi-square result becomes. If this significance is beyond a certain threshold, the null hypothesis is rejected, and we conclude that the variables are indeed significantly related. Let's put this idea to action.

Consider three door diesel cars (61 cars in our case) as in Table 5.10. There are 154 total diesel cars and 616 total three-door cars. If these two groups are independent of the 154 diesel cars, we would expect

$$e = 154.\frac{616}{1714} = 55.35.$$

Many cars should be both diesel and three doors. In reality there were 61 cars. The chi-square statistic sums all the differences from the observed values and the expected values as

$$\chi^2 = \sum \frac{(o - e)^2}{e}$$

where the expected value is computed as

$$e = \frac{\text{(row sum)(column sum)}}{\text{population sum}}.$$

Note that the chi-square statistic is the sum of squares of the difference between the observed and expected values scaled by the expected value. Comparing fuel type and number of doors, our chi-squared statistic ends up being 1.3063. The probability measurement of the chi-square statistic against the chi-square distribution is known as the -value. In practice a -value less than 0.05 is considered significant. In our case. P > 0.10 (actually 0.52), so we safely accept the null hypothesis that fuel type is independent of number of doors.

While the -value is a convenient way to measure statistic significance, use of the -value should be done with caution. There are many cases in which -values are misused or misinterpreted. To guard against such situations, it is important to consider other evidence as well, such as study design, confidence intervals, measurement quality, and so on (Wasserstein & Lazar, 2016). The American Statistical Association (Wasserstein & Lazar, 2016) published some principles, recommendations regarding the use of p-values. A few are worth repeating here (these are direct quotes from the ASA statement):

1. P-values can indicate how incompatible the data are with a specific statistical model.
2. Business and policy decisions should not be based only on whether a *p*-value passes a specific threshold.
3. A *p*-value or statistical significance does not measure the size of an effect.

Note: These guidelines pertain to the use of *p*-values in statistics and science in general, not just for chi-square tests.

The cross tabulation between number of doors and fuel type was maybe a little bit silly. Why would we expect there to be a relationship? And even if there is, what would we do with that information? Let's consider another hypothetical example. Say you are the marketer for the Mountain Dew brand, and you are about to launch a campaign to raise the awareness of a new flavor among college students. Your goal is to maximize reach, so you need to select two television programs that don't overlap in terms of viewership. Eight hundred respondents filled out a survey about their favorite TV shows that they watched over the past month. They were shown 10 TV shows and had to indicate whether they had watched it. The cross-tabulation results for two shows are shown in Table 5.11.

You will find that if you calculate the χ^2-value it is highly significant, and if you look at Table 5.11 you will see that we are dealing with a highly significant negative relationship (i.e., anyone who watches *Game of Thrones* is very unlikely to watch the *700 Club*).

TABLE 5.11 Chi-Square Cross Tabulation for Comparing Viewers of Different TV Programs

		Watch "Game of Thrones"		
		Yes	No	Marginal frequencies
Watch "The 700 Club"	Yes	93	197	290
	No	417	93	510
	Marginal frequencies	510	290	800

5.5.3 Student's t-Test

The student's t-test aims to test if a sample mean has a significant deviation from the population mean. There are multiple types of t-tests. First, there is the *one-sample t-test*; we use this to test whether the mean of a population is significantly different from a hypothesized mean. For example, is the average awareness of our brand still 20%? Second, there is an *independent two sample t-test*, which compares the means of two unrelated groups in a sample. For example, is beer consumption different for males versus females? We can test this with an independent paired samples t-test (see Table 5.12 for an example).

The results in the table show that the difference between male/female consumption is statistically significantly different. Third, we have the *dependent two sample t-test*; we use this test to compare the means of two related samples (say before and after some treatment). For example, is awareness of our brand higher after we ran an ad for week, and what were our awareness numbers prior to the ad and after the ad ran?

Note, as discussed, it is important sometimes to transform the data prior to applying the test (i.e., box-cox transformation). This scaling is essential for a t-test since it is assumed that variables are close to normally distributed.

5.5.4 Analysis of Variance (ANOVA)

The one-way ANOVA is an extension of the independent two sample t-test to more than two groups. As with the t-test, the null hypothesis states that the group means are the same while the alternative hypothesis is that *at least one* group mean differs from the rest. Again, we assume our data is normally distributed with common variance across groups (although we can relax this assumption if needed). Let's illustrate the idea of ANOVA using an example, derived from a commercial project. In this study, we asked respondents about their activities,

TABLE 5.12 An Example of an Independent Paired Sample T-Test

	Average amount beer consumed weekly	F-statistic = 66.7 P < 00.1 Hence the difference ids statistically significant
Male	2.30	
Female	2.80	

specifically how often they attended live performances. Activity level was measured on a 5-point scale (from never, rarely, sometimes, regularly, very frequently). Table 5.13 shows the results.

TABLE 5.13 How Often Do You Go to Live Performances?

	City	Suburb	Rural
Average age (in years)	4.30	4.5	4.5

When we run a one-way analysis of variance, statistical testing happens in two steps. The first step is to assess whether the results are overall significant. For this, the F-test is used. In this example, the F-value is 6 and is statistically significant ($P < 0.05$). This is a simple ANOVA (only three groups), but we need to assess whether the overall statistical difference was driven by differences between groups 1 and 2, group s1 and 3, groups 2 and 3, or maybe several of these pairs. There are several statistical tests that we can use. A common test is the least significant difference (LSD). This test looks at pair-wise difference (e.g., city versus suburb, city versus rural, suburb versus rural. It turns out that if we test city versus suburb and city versus rural, then these two are statistically significant but suburb versus rural is not).

5.6 MULTIVARIATE ANALYSES

In this section, we introduce briefly (a) linear regression analysis, (b) factor analysis, and (c) cluster analysis. These are probably the three most used techniques in marketing research. There are many other multivariate techniques (e.g. see Vriens et al., 2018).

5.6.1 Linear Regression

Linear regression and its variations can be used to quantify how changes on one or more variables might affect a variable of interest; it can also be used to make predictions when used in appropriate situations. For example, if I increase the price of my product, how much will demand drop? This may lead to potential business actions, which will be shown throughout this chapter. Several books have been written on this topic (see, for example, Belsey et al., 1980; Chatterjee & Price, 1977; and Draper & Smith, 1996).

The basic idea behind linear regression is "Can I predict the value of one variable if I know the value of another variable? Imagine, you have just moved to a new city; maybe you started a new job and hope to buy your first house. You look at what is available, but you don't know if the houses that are currently listed are priced reasonably. Maybe some houses are worth more than they are listed at; maybe some are worth less. This is a problem we can tackle with linear regression. We will start with a very simple example. Consider first, though, the terminology we use in linear regression (see Table 5.14).

The variable we want to predict is usually referred to as a dependent variable. The variables we are using to make the prediction are usually referred to as independent variables. So, in

TABLE 5.14 Some Terminology Used in Linear Regression

Term	Meaning
Dependent variable	The variable you are trying to predict
Independent variables	The variables that you want to use to make the prediction
Coefficient or regression coefficient	Weight given to a variable to make the prediction
Statistical significance	Whether the coefficient statistically speaking is not zero—i.e., is significant
Fit of the model or R-square	The amount of explained variance in the dependent variable

our first example, imagine you are selling your house and are wondering how much you should price it for. First, you probably want to collect information on your house such as the square footage, number of bedrooms, number of bathrooms, quality of materials used, whether the house needs any updating, and so on. In the United States this data can typically be acquired by asking City Hall. Let's start with looking at the scatterplot between square footage and price for which the houses were sold (see Figure 5.13).

FIGURE 5.13 Sales Prices of Houses by Square Footage

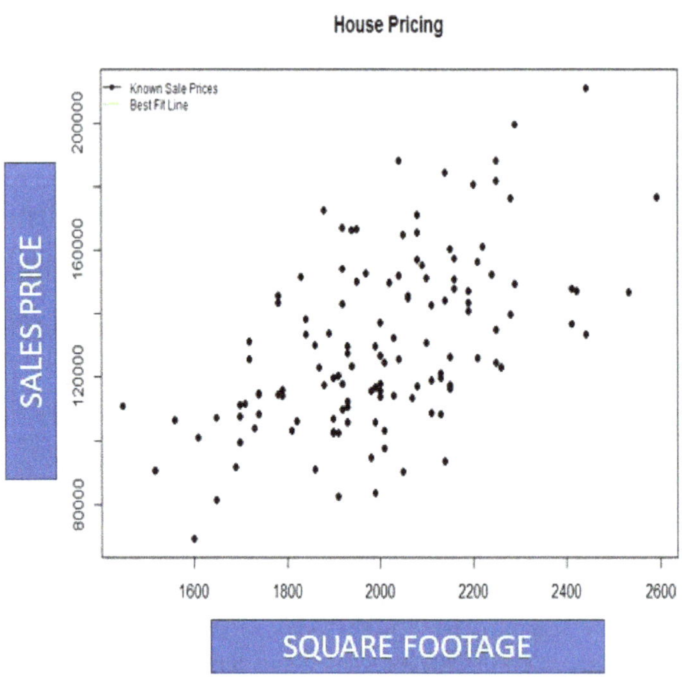

In Figure 5.13 each dot represents a house in the dataset. We can see that knowing the square footage of a house will not give us a perfect prediction of the price this house is sold for. For example, if we look at houses that are approximately 2,000 square feet, we can see that prices for which these various houses sold for vary quite substantially. Nevertheless, let's assume for now that square footage is all we have, and we want to find a "model" that will give us the best prediction. Using linear regression, this means finding a line (i.e., the model, this line will be our model) through this cloud of data points. See Figure 5.14 for an example.

FIGURE 5.14 Predicting with Linear Regression

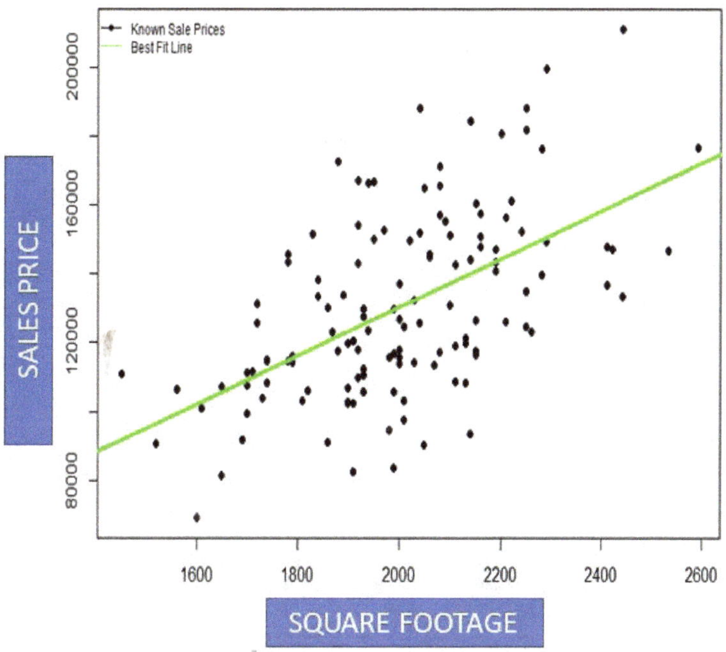

As you can see by just eyeballing the scatterplot (see beginning of this chapter, "reading the numbers"), as square footage goes up so does price. Now, you may ask, why this line and not a line that is maybe a little bit steeper, or a little bit less steep? The answer is that linear regression will find the line that minimizes the sum of squared errors.

Now, for the sum of squared errors, take for each data point the difference between the actual price and the predicted price and calculate the square of that difference. Then we sum, over all data points, these squared differences. A linear regression model will find a line that minimizes that number.

A linear regression model has the following form:

$$\text{Sales price of house} = \text{constant} + \beta^{*}\ \text{SQFT} + \text{error}$$

where the constant is called the intercept and represents the point where the line crosses the y-axis (i.e., what the expected price would be if the square footage was zero). The β represents the regression coefficient. Think of it as the weight I need to give to the square footage variable to arrive at my prediction. And, because my prediction will not be 100% accurate, there is an error term. It is also clear from the scatterplot that though square footage gives me information about the price of a house, it is not a perfect predictor.

This model can now be used for prediction, both for existing houses and houses that were not part of the data. If we look at Figure 5.14 we can see that using this line, for any given square footage, we can go up to see where we intersect with the line. From there we can go to the y-axis and find the price that our line (model) predicts for that footage (see Figure 5.15).

FIGURE 5.15 The Idea Behind Linear Regression Analysis

So, if I run into a house that is on the market, has a square footage of 2,000 square feet, I look where I intersect with the regression line and find the matching price. For predictions of houses that were not part of our dataset, but that square footage wise fall within the range of square footage observed in the data, we call this interpolation.

Of course, other factors may impact the value of a house (e.g., number of bedrooms, number of bathrooms, overall state and quality of the interior, lot size, etc.). Let's look at the linear regression model that predicts the sales price of a house (dependent variable) as a function of (a) square footage, (b) number of bedrooms, (c) number of bathrooms, and (d) overall state (let's use two levels for this variable: outdated or updated). In Table 5.15 we show the (hypothetical) results of a simple linear regression model.

TABLE 5.15 A Linear Regression Model for House Prices (In $s)

Independent variables	Scale of the variable	Coefficient	Significance
Square footage (x1000s)	Ratio	80	Yes
Number of rooms	Ratio	24000	Yes
Number of bathrooms	Ratio	16000	Yes
Overall state	0=outdated, 1=updated	89000	Yes

Table 5.15 has several pieces of information. Let's start with the third and fourth columns: the coefficients and whether they are statistically significant. Note that in this table we have only included the independent variables that were found to be statistically significant. When you run a regression model (using SPSS, Excel, R, etc.) the raw output will show the results of all variables you included in the model, both those that were statistically significant and those that were statistically not significant. To interpret a coefficient, I need to know the scale that was used to measure the independent variable. For example, were the levels of square footage in square foots or per thousand? The table indicates that the variable is expressed as per thousand square foot. Thus, increasing the square footage of a house by 1 unit of the square footage variable, my predicted house value goes up by $80,000. Number of bathrooms and number of bedrooms is expressed as simple numbers (1, 2, 3, etc.). Hence, if I compare two houses that are identical, but one has one additional bedroom, then this model will predict a value that is $24,000 more expensive.

Evaluating Models

In typical marketing datasets, we can estimate different types of models—each model having slightly different variables and different coefficients—and these models will differ in terms of how well they fit the data and their overall appeal. So, how can you evaluate and compare models? You can use the following criteria to do this: fit measures, average size of the regression coefficients, the presence of counter-intuitive effects, and inspecting the errors.

Evaluating Fit

There are three approaches that are used in practice to help with evaluating whether a model is good enough for the purpose.

First, a standard way of evaluating the fit is via the R^2-value and the adjusted R^2-value. The R^2-value is basically a measure for how close the data points are to the regression line, and this statistic lies between 0 and 100% and is referred to as the "explained variance" or "predictive accuracy." By adding variables to the model, I can increase this value, and in some cases can get close to 100%. However, we should not "over-fit" the data. To protect ourselves against overfitting we often also use the adjusted R^2-value and calculate an R^2-value using "hold-out" data. The R^2-value and the adjusted R^2-value are both calculated using the same observations that were used to estimate the model. For example, the regression line shown in Figure 5.14, is based on the observations in that scatterplot. I can now calculate how big the error is using the regression line predictions and comparing these with the actual values; I can compute the R^2-value. The adjusted R^2-value is computed from these same observations. The difference between the regular and the adjusted R^2-value is that now there is a penalty based on the number of variables in the model. For example, say I have two models, one having three independent variables and the other six independent variables. They both fit the data equally well, say R^2-value = 75%. Now if we would calculate the adjusted R^2-value, then the adjusted R^2-value for the model with six variables will be smaller than the one with three variables. Often, the differences between regular and adjust R^2-values are not very big, so the adjusted statistic is not all that helpful. A better measure is "hold-out predictive accuracy" or "hold-out" predictive fit. If we want to calculate hold-out predictive fit, we go about it differently. Before we estimate a regression model on a set of observations, we are going to take some observations out of the dataset and set these aside. We can, for example, randomly select 10% of the data and put this in a separate data file. Next, we use the 90% of the original dataset to estimate our regression line. Once this regression line is estimated, we use the model to predict the observations of the 10% of the original sample that was "held-out" (i.e., was set aside). This measure will typically be much lower than the regular R^2-value values, and especially if we compare different models, we can see huge differences. In statistics and data science this is a standard way of evaluating the performance of models.

Second, we look at the coefficients. Which coefficients are statistically significant? If a model has no statistically significant variables it is not very interesting. If it does have statistically significant variables, then we recommend evaluating both the sign and the size. It is quite common in practical situations to see in regression coefficients that a sign that is counterintuitive. For example, the regression may show if we reduce waiting time in our bank branch that overall satisfaction with the bank will go up. That is counter-intuitive and most likely the result of undesirable properties of the data rather than a real component of the data-generating mechanism. Our recommendation is that when one encounters counter-intuitive coefficients to take these variables out of the model and re-run the model. (See Vriens et al., 2018 for more details). The size of the coefficients can also be a consideration. In general, when comparing alternative regression models, we prefer the models with the biggest average coefficients. The reason for this is more managerial than statistical. If we make recommendations based on a regression model, we often do this based on simulations. For example, how much would my house increase in value if I add another bedroom and another bathroom? The bigger the coefficients for these two variables, the more value increase my model will predict. The same is true in business situations. If a marketing researcher predicts that the upside profit of decreasing waiting time in my bank branches is a net increase of

$1.5 million in net profits, the executive team will be more inspired to take action than if I predict $150k in net new profits.

A third approach to evaluate a model is by inspecting the errors. If we look at Figure 5.16 we can see the left model is much better than the right model.

FIGURE 5.16 Linear Regression with Small and Big R Squared Value

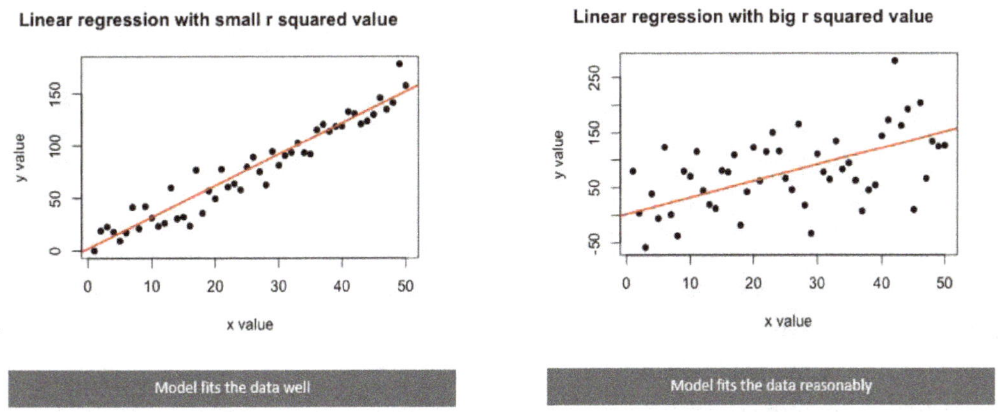

However, it is feasible to have a model that has a high explained variance (good fit), and most observations are predicted very accurately, except when we get to the high end of the scale (higher values of the X variable); then the errors suddenly become much larger. That doesn't mean we have a bad model. It does mean that predicting in this range is risky and should probably not be done.

Applications of Linear Regression

Linear regression can be used for prediction, what-if analyses, and prioritization.

Say you are in the housing market looking for houses. You are new to the area and are not yet in tune with what roughly reasonable home prices are. You have several homes that looked like good options, but you don't want to overpay. Say that we gave you a regression model. All you needed to do was tell the model the square footage of the house, the number of bedrooms, and the number of bathrooms, and the model would predict the home's value. You realize the model is not perfect. Yet, you quickly get at least an idea. If the home is priced much higher than the model predicts, you may ask yourself why that might be. Does it have a lot of recent updates? Is it in a particularly desirable neighborhood? If no reason can be identified that justified why it is higher priced, then the model predicts than maybe it truly is overpriced.

Now, you bought your house, but you wish it had a bathroom in the basement. You call some contractors, and they say they can add a bathroom for $9,000. You look at the model and see that by adding that bathroom your home will increase in value by $16,000. So, that seems like a good investment.

Now, imagine, you are the manager of online sales product. The chief marketing officer (CMO) has come to you to help the marketing team identify those areas of their service that will lead to highest increase in overall satisfaction. They don't have the budget to improve everything. So, you commission a survey and measure how customers perceive the components of the service (see Table 5.16a) and ask them how overall satisfied they are. Next, you run a regression model with overall satisfaction as dependent variable and the components as independent variables. The results are shown in Tables 5.16a and 5.16b.

TABLE 5.16A Components of a Sales Software Product

How overall satisfied are you with the following components of the sales software product?
Ability to reach target audience
Increase awareness of the company's services
Ability to target the right content to your customers
Ability to analyze customers comments
Interface ease of use
The ability to generate leads for the business
Satisfaction with the text ads
Generate sign-ups for newsletter
Increase sales
The ease of managing content

TABLE 5.16B Linear Regression Results

Driver Variable	Coefficient	Average Rating	
		Us	Best competitor
The ability to generate leads for the business	0.18	7.0	8.5
Ability to analyze customer comments	0.26	7.6	6.6
The ability to reach your target audience	0.10	5	8
Overall ease of managing content	0.03	7	5

Model fit: 77% (r-squared—percentage explained variance: This is a metric that falls between 0 and 1).

Table 5.16a shows the business problem. There are many components of this service, and for each there could be room for improvement, but you and the marketing team won't have enough time to work on improving all components and even if you did, some improvements may not have a positive return on investment. The regression model in Table 5.16b gives us two pieces of information that can help us prioritize those components that will most likely have the highest impact on overall satisfaction. One, the table shows those components whose performance levels are predictive of overall satisfaction, so these are natural candidates to focus the team's improvement work on. Note that just by looking at which components have a significant regression coefficient, we can already prioritize, because instead of having to worry about ten components, I am only focusing on five. Second, even within these five, I can further prioritize if I wanted and can decide to only focus on those components with the highest regression coefficient.

There is one other piece of information that researchers typically take into account when translating regression results into business recommendations: the current performance levels on the components (and sometimes vis-à-vis the competition). The last two columns of Table 5.16b give that information. We can see that on the most important component we are already better that the best competitor. So, would it really be best to prioritize improving that component first? Maybe not. Maybe we should first focus on the second most important component on which we are behind the best competitor.

5.6.2 Other Multivariate Techniques

There is vast arsenal of multivariate techniques. Even regression analyses come in many different varieties (we refer to Vriens et al., 2018 for those students who want to become proficient in analytics). From a practical point of view (i.e., what you are most likely going to encounter in a commercial marketing research project), we believe there are two techniques that you should at least have some familiarity with: factor analysis and cluster analysis.

5.6.3 Factor Analysis

Factor analysis (FA), and a related technique, principal components analysis (PCA) are among the most used techniques in commercial marketing research. We note here that FA and PCA are different techniques, and quite a bit has been written about the similarities and differences (e.g. Gorsuch, 1990). From a practical, applied point of view they are very similar (e.g., Arrindell & van der Ende, 1985). Differences are most likely when commonalities are low, though FA might be preferred: Snook and Gorsuch (1989) found in a simulation study that factor loadings in FA are unbiased.

It is often applied in brand studies, segmentation studies, and customer satisfaction studies. Its general purpose is to determine if a set of variables (most often survey variables) can be represented by a smaller number of factors (also referred to as latent variables). Practically, these techniques are used in three situations (see also Stewart, 1981): (a) measurement and scaling, because we think a number of variables are all indicators, are all measuring a construct or concept that we want to measure; (2) data reduction and simplification purposes; and (c) a pre-step to a subsequent analysis, most often a cluster analysis or a regression analysis.

1. FA is heavily used in measurement and scaling. Recall that earlier we talked about composite variables; these were variables constructed from several "component" variables. For example, we could ask in a survey what types of exercise activities

somebody engages in (e.g., tennis, golf, biking, hiking, swimming, etc.); each activity is answered with a yes/no format. Now we could decide to create a new composite variable where we count the number of activities a respondent engages in and we may call this variable activity intensity. This new variable can now be analyzed further. However, there are situations where we want to construct a composite variable, but we are not sure whether (a) the set of variables could or should be represented by one composite variable and/or (b) that each of the component variables should we weighted equally. Sometimes this is done in an exploratory fashion (i.e., we may not have a theory about how many latent factors to expect). For example, in commercial marketing research, we may encounter a large battery of brand attributes that are intended to capture several distinct components of a brand (e.g., if we want to identify brand personality dimensions, for example). In other cases, we may have a good idea of what to expect. For example, we want to measure a specific construct such as brand loyalty, brand love, and so on. Such constructs often are operationalized via several survey questions, and factor analysis is then used to assess whether this set of questions can indeed be represented by one or (sometimes two) latent variables (we discuss the concept of latent variables next. For an example see Segars and Grover (1993), who investigated psychological constructs such as ease of use and usefulness.

2. In some cases, we may simply want to reduce a large set of variables to a smaller number of factors. The idea is then to use this smaller number of factors in the marketing research report instead of the larger set of original variables.
3. FA is often used as a pre-step to other types of analyses such as segmentation analysis (i.e., cluster analysis). Segmentation studies often involve lengthy surveys. The clients who commission them may want to know about what types of needs the consumers have in a given category, they may want to ask about behaviors (how often they consume the category, where, with whom, etc.), and segmentation studies typically involve a set of attitudinal questions that ask about how consumers feel about certain aspects of consumption (e.g., Do you agree that coffee drinking is healthy? Coffee drinking keeps me up at night, etc.) or a brand. To make the cluster analysis more manageable researchers often, as a first step, analyze these various batteries of questions with FA (or PCA) to find out if the larger set of variables can be represented by a smaller number of factors. A small number of components or factors make analysis and reporting more manageable.

How Does It Work?

Say we collected survey data on N = 500, among retired consumers to whom we want to market a health tracking device that they can carry with them all the time. As part of the survey we asked the respondents their attitudes about health and technology. We have 14 statements and asked respondents, using a 10-point scale, to what extent they agreed with the statements. We want to use these variables in a regression analysis but would like to see if we can represent these 14 variables by a smaller number of factors. Our initial "theory" is that all 14 questions are to some extent an indicator of how overall positive/negative a consumer feels about technology. We want to find out if this is indeed the case: Do all these variables point to an underlying construct (variable)? For this we use factor analysis.

Let's start with terminology. The starting point of a factor analysis is a set of observed variables, also referred to as manifest variables. In our example, these are the 14 survey questions. In factor analysis, we also have what is referred to as latent variables or factors. These are not directly observed and, actually, do not exist yet at the start of the analysis. Look at Figure 5.17, the variable on the right, "consumer technology attitude," is our hypothesized latent variable or factor. So, what we are showing in Figure 5.17 is a one-factor model.

FIGURE 5.17 The Idea Behind Factor Analysis

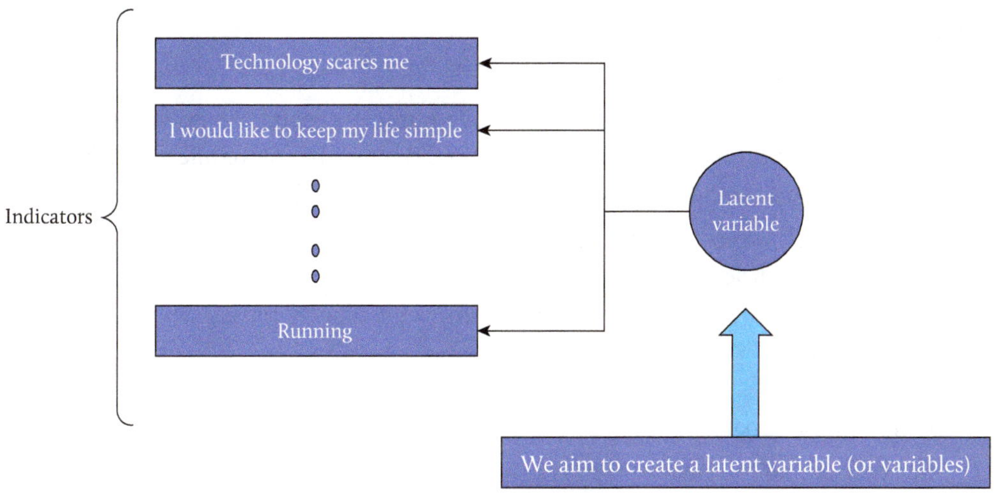

When we run or estimate the factor analysis model, shown in Figure 5.17, the analysis procedure will create the latent variable, and because it is a variable, the procedure will create values for each respondent in our sample on the latent variable (we refer to these scores as factor scores). This will also create weights for the observed variables. Here is where it gets a little confusing. Let's explain this step by step. Let's first look at the underlying model in factor analysis. Let X(1), X(2), X(3), … , X(14) be the observed variables. We denote this as X(i) for I = 1, 2, 3, … ,14. Let F1 be the one (in this initial example) factor (or latent variable). The one-factor factor model (somewhat simplified) is defined as

$$X(i) = \beta(i) * F1 + \varepsilon.$$

For i = 1, … ,14 (referring to 14 variables; see e.g., Meerling, 1981). In other words, this looks like a regression; except in this case, the latent variable is the independent variable and the observed variables are the dependent variables. In standard linear regression all variables are observed, and we typically have multiple independent variables and one dependent variable.

Here, it is the other way around. The underlying factor is also sometimes called a common factor because it is a common independent variable used to explain all the observed variables. A model such as this will try to find β's and F1 values in such a way that the values of the X-variables and their inter-correlations can reproduced. In other words, the analysis will look for F1 values that capture what the X-variables have in common. The β's in this model are called the factor loadings. These factor loadings are estimated as well, and they can be viewed as how important the latent variable is in explaining the observed variables, but also the other way around. The β's also indicate how much an observed variable is a part of the underlying latent variable.

When we run factor analysis we have to go through several steps, and it typically involves making a number of analytical decisions. We will illustrate the key elements of a factor analysis via the previous example where we have 14 activities. A factor analysis typically is comprised of the following steps:

1. Select an estimation method.
2. Run a one- to five-factor solution (the exact number depends on how many factors you would expect maximally). Cannot exceed the number of manifest variables.
3. Evaluate solutions. Solutions are evaluated on the following:
    a. How well we can interpret the factors in the various solutions
    b. Communalities
    c. Eigenvalues (Kaiser criterion, eigenvalue > 1; Gorsuch, 1983) and explained variance
    d. Scree plot
    e. Model comparison
4. Select "optimal" number of factors
5. Re-run the model with optimal number of factors
6. Select a rotation method and interpret the final factor loadings
7. Calculate, if needed, the factor scores for further analysis

We discuss each of these steps briefly; for some steps we will use the previous example to illustrate.

There are various estimation methods analysts can choose from (e.g., unweighted least squares, weighted least squares, principal axis factoring, maximum likelihood, etc.). From a practical point of view, it probably doesn't make a big difference. Some studies (e.g., Fabrigar et al., 1999) favor maximum likelihood (ML) because it enables formally comparing different factor models via the likelihood ratio statistic (which is a common approach for all models estimated with ML). In Fabrigar et al.'s study (1999) they found that this approach worked better than others in terms of selecting the optimal number of factors (in our example, we used the maximum likelihood method). The next step is to run a factor solution. Say that we don't think we need more than five factors, so we estimate a five-factors model. To evaluate whether such a five-factors models represents and fits our data, we look first at the factor loadings and see if the five factors have an intuitive interpretation (step 3a). Look at

Table 5.17, where we show the factor loadings of the initial solution along with the communalities. Look at the factor loadings first; these can be interpreted as the correlation between the factor and the observed variable.

TABLE 5.17 Factor Loading and Communalities for the 5 Factor Solution

Variable	VARIABLE DESCRIPTIONS	Factor Loadings					Communalities
		F1	F2	F3	F4	F5	
V1	Technology scares me	0.73	0.28	−0.23	0.00	−0.07	0.66
V2	I can't keep up with all the technological innovations in healthcare	0.78	0.27	−0.30	0.09	−0.04	0.78
V3	I would like to keep my life simple	0.65	0.15	0.05	−0.04	0.17	0.48
V4	I prefer calling someone instead of texting them	0.54	−0.15	0.09	0.31	0.11	0.43
V5	I am not a fan of social media websites	0.40	0.08	0.07	0.65	0.02	0.59
V6	I don't trust websites with my data	0.60	0.25	0.10	−0.13	0.19	0.48
V7	I do not like online banking	0.63	0.08	0.00	0.11	−0.14	0.44
V8	I use email but only very occasionally	0.50	0.20	0.45	−0.09	−0.14	0.51
V9	I have trouble keeping track of passwords for online websites	0.54	0.21	0.26	−0.13	0.26	0.48
V10	If there is a problem with my PC I do not know how to troubleshoot the problem	0.47	0.19	0.46	−0.10	−0.20	0.52
V11	Managing my health is complex	-0.42	0.65	-0.03	0.10	-0.03	0.60
V12	I feel always nervous about my health	-0.38	0.63	0.08	-0.07	0.07	0.55
V13	It is difficult to get an appointment with a healthcare professional	0.40	0.65	-0.05	0.08	-0.03	0.58
V14	I would like to stay independent	0.40	0.70	0.00	0.05	0.02	0.65

First, it looks like all observed variables load on factor 1, with loadings anywhere from a high loading (< 0.60) to a moderately high loading (> 0.40 but < 0.60). This might suggest that a one-factor solution might work. However, items 11 and 12 have negative loadings, and the loadings are not very high. These two items load stronger on factor 2, so maybe we should consider a two-factor solution. The third factor does not seem to be determined by any specific variable; it doesn't seem to have a clear interpretation. Factor 4 is very similar to factor 3 except we have this one variable, item 5, that loads heavy on it. Factor 5 does not seem to be relevant. The communalities indicate the percentage of variance in an observed variable that is explained by the factors. These values all look decent, but since we are likely not going to go with the five-factor solution, we need to review these numbers again in the final solution. Next, let's look at the explained variance by factor via explained variance and eigenvalue numbers (step 3c). In FA the first factor always explains the most variance (compared to the other factors). The second extracted factor is always perpendicular to the first factor and will explain the second-most amount of variance (see Table 5.18).

TABLE 5.18 Eigenvalues and Explained Variance

Factors	Eigenvalue	% Explained Variance	Cumulative Explained Variance
1	4.2	30%	30.0%
2	2.1	15%	45.0%
3	0.65	4.60%	49.6%
4	0.61	4.30%	53.9%
5	0.24	1.70%	55.6%

Eigenvalues can be thought of as standardized explained variance. Since we have 14 variables the total amount of standardized variance is 14. It is recommended to not retain any factors with an eigenvalue of less than 1 because that factor would explain less than any of the observed variables. There are two factors with an eigenvalue larger than 1, so we should probably choose either a one-factor model or a two-factor model. We can visualize these eigenvalues in what is called a scree plot (step 3d) (see Figure 5.18).

Typical advice is to look where the plot makes a sharp drop and use that point as the choice for what number of factors to retain. In this case that would be one factor. However, in addition to statistical criteria, we also use interpretation and whether retaining a factor might be useful for later analyses and insights. So, in this case, let's say we decide to retain the two-factor model (step 4), and we now rerun the model retaining only two factors. In some applications, especially when using FA for academic research, we might want to do a more formal model comparison using likelihood ratio tests, but in practical applications this is rarely done (step 3e) (see Farbigar et al., 1999 for details). Now that we have selected the, for us, optimal number of factors, we rerun a two-factor solution. There is one more step we need to do. A factor solution is indeterminate; this means if we would plot the factor loadings

FIGURE 5.18 A Scree Plot

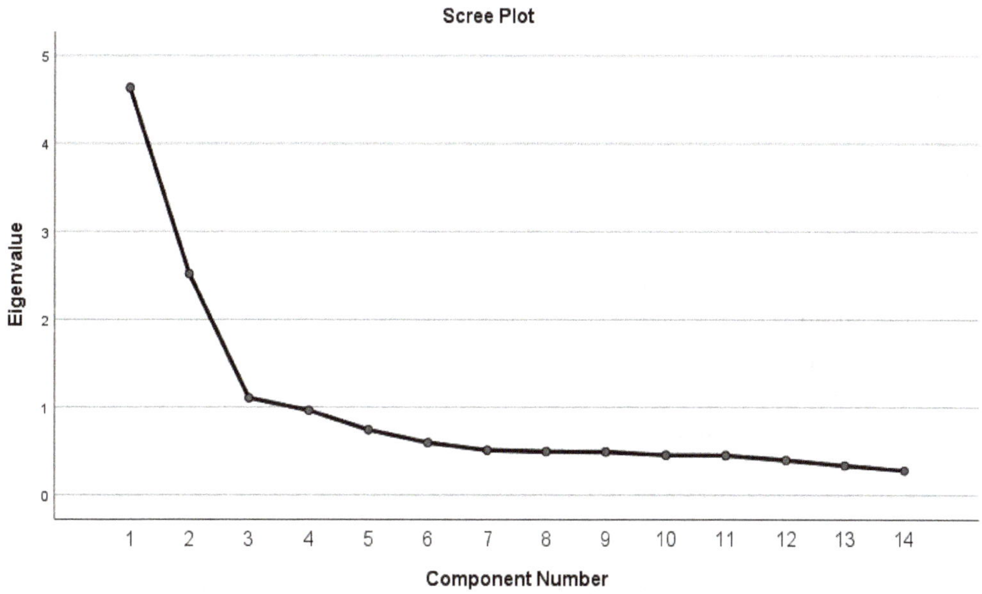

in a two-dimensional graph, we would be able to rotate these axes, and thereby the factor loadings. It would leave the percentage of unexplained variance unchanged. The benefit of looking at rotated solutions is that we may get a solution that has a better interpretation. In general, rotation methods (there are several) will maximize the factor loadings that are highest and minimize the one that are lowest. Look at Table 5.19, where we show the initial, final two-factor solution (left side of the table) and the rotated two-factor solution (using varimax rotation (for a discussion of rotation methods see Osborne, 2014).

As Table 5.19 shows, the rotated solution is easier to interpret. Factor 1 now seems to be a general technology readiness factor that measures consumers' proficiency and comfort with technology. Factor2 seems to be a health management factor. When we look at the specific items underlying these factors, the solution makes sense.

Three final notes on FA: One, the extracted factors are now actually variables (i.e., each respondent will have a value on each of the two factors). We call these scores factor scores. Two, factors are extracted (in most cases) in such a way that that the factor scores between different factors are uncorrelated. Three, factor scores are often used in subsequent analyses, most often in cluster analysis (used for market segmentation) and regression.

TABLE 5.19 The Final Two Factor Solution (Unrotated and Rotated)

		Factor Loadings			
		Final Unrotated		Final Rotated (Varimax)	
Variable	Variable Descripotions	F1	F2	F1	F2
V1	Technology scares me	0.63	0.43	0.76	-0.06
V2	I can't keep up with all the technological innovations in healthcare	0.67	0.40	0.78	-0.10
V3	I would like to keep my life simple	0.61	0.30	0.66	-0.14
V4	I prefer calling someone instead of texting them	0.55	-0.12	0.42	-0.35
V5	I am not a fan of social media websites	0.34	0.16	0.36	-0.09
V6	I don't trust websites with my data	0.53	0.39	0.66	-0.03
V7	I do not like online banking	0.59	0.22	0.60	-0.20
V8	I use email but only very occasionally	0.43	0.30	0.52	-0.03
V9	I have trouble keeping track of passwords for online websites	0.48	0.33	0.58	-0.04
V10	I there is a problem with my PC I do not know how to troubleshoot the problem	0.41	0.28	0.49	-0.04
V11	Managing my health is complex	-0.55	0.54	-0.10	0.77
V12	I feel always nervous about my health	-0.51	0.52	-0.08	0.72
V13	It is difficult to get an appointment with a healthcare professional	-0.53	0.54	-0.09	0.75
V14	I would like to stay independent	-0.56	0.59	-0.07	0.80

5.6.4 Cluster Analysis

The main application of cluster analysis in marketing is market segmentation. Market segmentation refers to the identification of distinct consumer groups (segments) where consumers within a specific group are homogeneous on some set of variables (e.g., Smith, 1956). In most cases such variables pertain to needs (unmet or met; e.g., I prefer decaf coffee), attitudes (how consumers feel about the category; e.g., "I believe drinking coffee is healthy") or customer behaviors (e.g., light user, heavy user). Consumers across groups are different on such aspects. Overviews of cluster analysis and market segmentation can be found in Wedel and Kamakura (1997) and Punj and Stewart (1983).

We discuss one commonly used clustering method: K-means clustering. Note that there are many alternative methods. In this short section we aim to cover just the basics. For a more in-depth discussion see Vriens et al. (2018) and Vidden et al. (2016).

Market segmentation can be done *a priori* and *posteriori* depending on the situation. As an example of a priori segmentation, a firm could decide ahead of time to market to Midwest college students or the California middle class. This means that the firm could define a segment before any analysis is performed. In commercial marketing research most research is a posteriori segmentation. Given data on a sample of consumers, we would like to know if we can identify groups that differ in a meaningful way that helps us better market our products and services. The major challenge with posteriori segmentation is the unstructured nature of the problem at hand. How many clusters should I expect? What kinds of consumers are in each cluster? Which variables should I use? Note that a clustering problem is much more unstructured than, for example, linear regression or even factor analysis. In linear regression we can evaluate how well the model can predict a dependent variable. There isn't really that much to argue: A regression model fits the data or it does not. In clustering analysis, we have to evaluate how big and meaningful the differences between groups (segments) really are and determine if those differences are meaningful. It is rather difficult to do this, even more so because it is not uncommon to have multiple solutions that are very similar in their ability to differentiate between segments. We will have to balance statistical measures with business insight to overcome this challenge.

How Does It Work?

Searching for useful market segments with cluster analysis requires first deciding which variables to use to identify the segments. We use an example to illustrate the basics of cluster analysis. Your marketing research firm has just received an assignment from the Mall of America in Minneapolis. The mall has steadily seen their average weekly visitors decline. The marketing director of the mall decides she wants to run a short survey among visitors of the mall. She intends to ask a few questions to determine the main motivations for customers to come to the mall. The survey is kept very short, as she imagines mall visitors come to the mall to have fun and shop, not to answer surveys. The following questions are included in the survey:

Ratings (scale 1–10, with 1 being strongly disagree and 10 stronger agree):

- Fun: I think shopping is fun.
- Eat: I combine shopping with eating out.
- Quality: I try to get the best quality while shopping.

- Saving: I save money by comparing prices.
- A demographic variable: i.e., Income: This is the customer's household income in dollars.
- Monthly visits: This is the frequency customers often visit the mall.

She asked the marketing research agency to collect a sample of N = 1,000. She used the mall-intercept method. Over about 2 weeks the data is collected. One of the questions she is interested in is "Are their segments of consumers that differ in their reasons or overall customer profile?" The reason she wants to know that is because she imagines if she has a deeper understanding of the different reasons why customers visit, she might be better able to make changes to the mall or she might be better able to communicate or advertise by highlighting the things the customers are looking for. Let's look at the first seven respondents in Table 5.20. In Table 5.20 we show the respondent ratings: the categories fun, eat, quality, and saving from 0–10, where 0 is strongly disagree and 10 is strongly agree. The income and number of visits were also recorded. Can you identify who are similar customers and how many segments are among the seven respondents?

TABLE 5.20 Respondent Ratings for Each Category

Respondent	Fun	Eat	Quality	Saving	Income	Visits Monthly
Respondent 1	8	8	4	3	49000	4
Respondent 2	2	3	4	10	19000	8
Respondent 3	7	7	9	4	70000	1
Respondent 4	1	3	1	8	20000	8
Respondent 5	1	2	5	10	36000	7
Respondent 6	5	3	8	6	65000	3
Respondent 7	10	7	4	4	46000	4

Eyeballing the results of these first seven respondents we might determine that there are, roughly speaking, three groups: group 1 (respondent 1 and 7), group 2 (respondents 2, 4, and 5), and group 3 (respondents 3 & 6). We can call group 1 the "Mall Enthusiasts," perhaps young people who have a stable income. They go to mall every week for entertainment such as movies and are somewhat neutral on purchasing. Group 2 are the "window shoppers." They care about price over quality of product and go to the mall frequently for sale events and price comparison. Group 3 are more like the "middle-class buyers," perhaps mid-aged people with kids. They have higher income and are willing to pay more for better quality. They visit the mall less often but are not against some entertainment. With this we are starting to understand our customers better.

However, remember the marketing director wanted a sample of N = 1,000. Eyeballing 1,000 respondents is not feasible anymore. It would take too long, and most of us wouldn't be able to do it even if we have time. We need to do using data analysis techniques (e.g., a cluster analysis algorithm).

One of the most used analysis techniques for cluster analysis is the K-means method (MacQueen, 1967; Steinley, 2006; see Wedel & Kamakura [1998] for a more comprehensive discussion on analysis techniques for market segmentation). K-means starts with a specific classification of the sample in a predetermined number of segments (either based on a random allocation procedure or based on a user-specified initial clustering). Subsequently, respondents are "moved around," from one segment to another. If the solution improves the transfer is kept; otherwise, the respondent goes back to his or her initial segment. K-means is easy to understand, fast to implement, and works well in most of the cases. Let's assume that we want K-means to find a three-cluster solution for the mall survey data. We start by generating three random cluster centers, as noted in Figure 5.19 (left graph). Figure 5.19 in (a) we can see that three random centers are put on the graph.

FIGURE 5.19 K-Means Analysis First Iteration

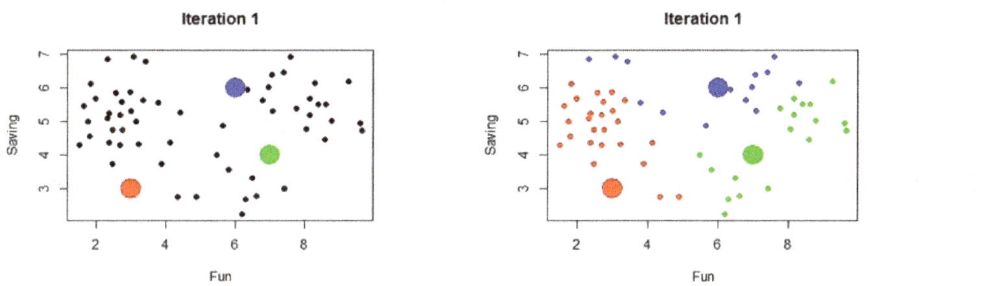

(a) Three main centers are assigned

(b) After k-means analysis all points are assigned

From there each point is assigned a color until the graph looks like (b). Now, for each data point we compute its distance to the three centers and color it the same color as the nearest center (Figure 5.19b). This is the first guess of our three-cluster solution, represented by different colors of points. This is certainly not the best solution because we can see that the centers we picked are not actually the center of the clusters we found. Let's assign new centers by simply taking the center of each cluster. Now, since we got new centers, let's erase the color of all the samples points and recolor them, this time using the new centers. In Figure 5.20 we show the second iteration of our clustering solution.

This is still not perfect, but we certainly improved a bit. Now we just need to let the computer take over and repeat the process until the algorithm converges.

FIGURE 5.20 K-Means Analysis Second Iteration

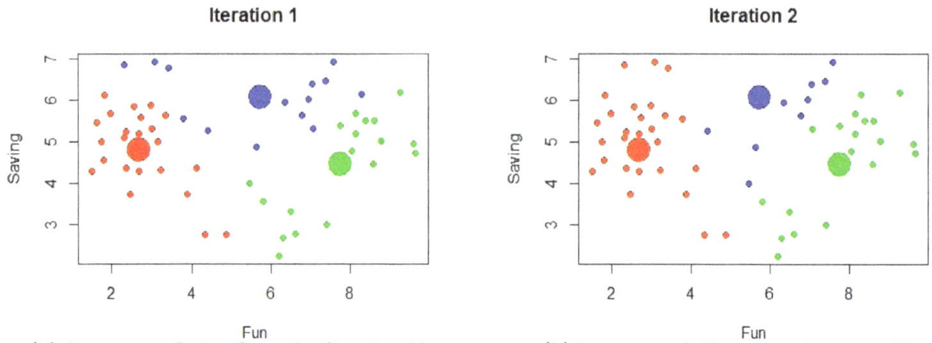

(a) K-means solution from the first iteration (b) K-means solution after the second iteration

Let's summarize the process:

- Pick random initial centers depending on the number of clusters.
- Assign each data point to the closest center and take all points assigned to the center to be the temporary cluster solution.
- Update the centers to be the center of each temporary cluster.
- Repeat steps 2 and 3 until the centers don't change any more. This indicates that the new centers and the previous centers are the same. Therefore, the centers are the true centers of the data, and this leaves nothing to improve.

The result of the K-means analysis is shown in Figure 5.21 and shows good clusters!

FIGURE 5.21 The Final K-Means Solution

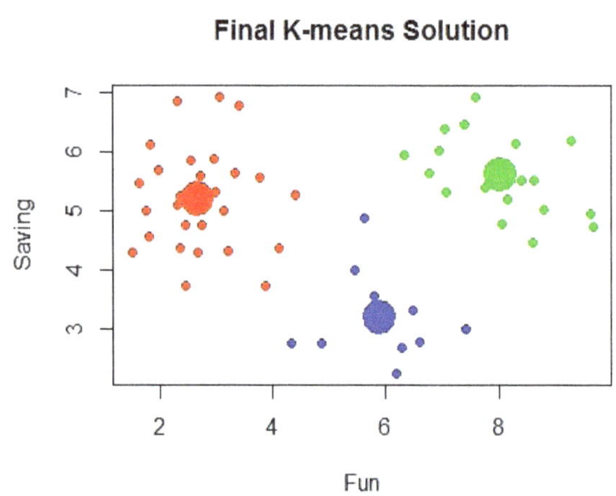

K-means helped us to identify three customer segments from the mall survey. This matches the manual results we had before, with the red group being the window shoppers, blue being the middle-class buyers, and green the mall enthusiasts.

5.6.5 Evaluating Clustering Solutions

How can we tell which solution is the best? This is the most challenging part for clustering analysis in practice. People usually run several (actually, often many) different clustering methods on the same data; they review and compare the solutions and pick the ones that work best for them from a *business application point of view*. Statistical criteria are often used secondary, just to weed out the bad solutions. There are many metrics and statistics available to evaluate cluster solutions, but it always best to combine statistical insight with business intuition. Here, we mention two metrics that are common: silhouette scores and the BIC criterion.

Silhouette score is a number ranging between −1 and 1, which combines two important measurements of the quality of a clustering solution: how compact each cluster is and how separate (between different clusters) the clusters are. A high positive silhouette score indicates a better cluster solution. A negative score indicates we likely have a bad solution. The Bayesian Information Criterion (BIC) is a statistical measurement used to assess the qualities of a variety of models. The idea of BIC is to quantify the likelihood of the tested cluster solution being the true solution based on the data information. We should pick the model with the smallest BIC number.

5.6 QUIZ AND EXERCISES

1. You just received an e-mail from a colleague, and it has an intriguing table attached to it. It might come up in a meeting you have this afternoon. You look at the table, and you see several sales numbers from several districts. You also see some numbers as to how many complaints there were in each region. What questions do you ask yourself?
2. What are elements of visualization?
3. What steps are recommended in the analytic process?
4. What is the difference between correlation and causality?
5. Look at Table 5E.1

   TABLE 5E.1 The Brand Funnel: Comparing Univariate Results Across Brands

	Toyota Corolla	Toyota Camry
Awareness	85%	85%
Consideration	76%	44%
Preference	24%	24%
Total	N=100	N=100

   Interpret the numbers in this table and write down your conclusions.
6. Why is an F-test in an analysis of variance not sufficient?

7. In your own words, explain regression analysis and for what type of business problems is it useful.
8. What does it mean if a regression coefficient is not statistically significant?
9. Your peer in the market research team has come up with several regression models. They all seem good. How would you evaluate these various models and what criterion would be most important in selecting the model you like best?
10. What is interpolation and what is extrapolation?
11. What is the difference between regression analysis and factor analysis? Are there any similarities?
12. In what situations is factor analysis a useful technique?
13. What is the primary application of cluster analysis in business?

REFERENCES

Abela, A. (2008). *Advanced presentations by design: Creating communications that drive action*. Pfeiffer.

Allison, P. D. (2001). *Missing data*. SAGE.

Arrindell, W. A., & van der Ende, J. (1985). An empirical test of the utility of the observations-to-variables ratio in factor and components analysis. Applied Psychological Measurement, *9*(2), 165–178.

Babin, B. J., & Zikmund, G.J. (2016). *Exploring market research* (11th ed.). Cengage.

Belsey, D. A., Kuh, E., & Welsch, R. E. (1980). *Regression diagnostics*. Wiley.

Chatterjee, S. & Price, B. (1977). Regression analysis by example. Wiley & Sons, Hoboken, NJ.

Cochran, W. G. (1952). The $\chi 2$ test of goodness of fit. *Annals of Mathematical Statistics*, *25*(3), 315–345.

Dempster, A. P., Laird, N. M., & Rubin, D. B. (1977). Maximum likelihood from incomplete data via the EM algorithm. *Journal of the Royal Statistical Society, 39*(1), 1–22.

Draper, N., & Smith, H. (1981). *Applied regression analysis*. Wiley.

Ehrenberg, A. S. C., & Bound, J. A. (2000). Turning data in to knowledge. In C. Chakrapani (Ed.), *Marketing research: State-of-the-art perspectives* (pp. 23–46). American Marketing Association.

Fabrigar, L. R., Wegener, D. T., MacCallum, R. C., & Strahan, E. J. (1999). Evaluating the use of exploratory factor analysis in psychological research. *Psychological Methods, 4*(3), 272–299.

Few, S. (2012). *Show me the numbers: Designing tables and graphs to enlighten*. Analytics Press.

Gorsuch, R. L. (1983). *Factor analysis* (2nd ed.). Erlbaum.

Gorsuch, R. L. (1990). Common factor analysis versus component analysis: Some well-known and little-known facts. *Multivariate Behavioral Research, 25*(1), 33–39.

Kendall, M. (1938). A new measure of rank correlation. *Biometrika, 30*(1–2), 81–89.

Knaflic, N. C. (2015). *Storytelling with data. A data visualization guide for business professionals.* Wiley.

MacQueen, J. (1967). Some methods for classification and analysis of multivariate observations. In: Le Cam, L.M. & Neyman, J. (Eds.), *Proceedings of the 5th Berkeley Symposium* (Vol. 1) (pp. 281–297). University of California Press.

Meerling, X. (1981). Methoden en teachnieken van psychologisch onderzoek. Boom, Meppel, the Netherlands.

Osborne, J. W. (2014). *Best practices in exploratory factor analysis.*

Pearson, K. (1900). On the criterion that a given system of deviations from the probable in the case of a correlated system of variables is such that it can be reasonably supposed to have arisen from random sampling. *Philosophic Magazine, 50*, 157–175.

Peugh, J. L., & Enders, C. K. (2004). Missing data in educational research: Review of reporting practices and suggestions for improvement. *Review of Educational Research, 74*(4), 525–556.

Plackett, R. L. (1983). Karl Pearson and the chi-squared test. *International Statistical Review, 51*(1), 59–72.

Punj, G., & Stewart, D. W. (1983). Cluster analysis in marketing research: Review and suggestions for improvement. *Journal of Marketing Research, 20*(2), 134–148.

Ramaswamy, V., Raghunathan, T. E., Cohen, S. H., & Ozcan, K. (2001). *A multiple imputation approach for the analysis of missing data in marketing research* [Unpublished working paper, University of Michigan].

Reynolds, G. (2011). *Presentation Zen: Simple ideas on presentation design and delivery (voices that matter)*. Peachpit.

Rodgers, J. L., & Nicewander, W.A. (1988). Thirteen ways to look at the correlation coefficient. *American Statistician, 42*(1), 59–66.

Segars, A. H., & Grover, V. (1993). Re-examining perceived ease of use and usefulness: A confirmatory factor analysis. *MIS Quarterly, 17*(4), 517–525.

Schafer, J. L. (1997). *Analysis of incomplete multivariate data*. Chapman & Hall.

Schafer, J.L. & Graham, J. W. (2002). Missing data: Our view of the State of the Art. Psychological Methods, 7, 2, 147–177.

Sinhara, S., Stern, H. S., & Russell, D. (2001). The use of multiple imputation for the analysis of missing data. *Psychological Methods*, 6(4), 317–329.

Smith, D. V. L., & Fletcher, J. H. (2001). *Inside information: Making sense out of marketing data*. Wiley.

Snook, S. C., & Gorsuch, R. L. (1989). Component analysis and common factor analysis: A Monte Carlo study. Psychological Bulletin, *106*(1), 148–154

Spearman C. (1904). The proof and measurement of association between two things. *American Journal of Psychology, 15*(1), 72–101.

Smith, W. (1956). Product differentiation and market segmentation as alternative marketing strategies. *Journal of Marketing*, *21*(1), 3–8.

Steinley, D. (2006). K-means clustering: A half century synthesis. British Journal of Mathematical and Statistical Psychology, *59*(1), 1–34.

Stewart, D. W. (1981). The application and misapplication of factor analysis inn marketing research. *Journal of Marketing Research, 18*(1), 51–62.

Tufte, E. R. (1990). *Envisioning information* (2nd ed.). Graphics Press

Vidden, C., Vriens, M., & Chen, S. (2016). Comparing clustering methods for market segmentation: A simulation study. *Applied Marketing Analytics, 2*(3), 225–238.

Vriens, M., & Melton, E. (2002). Managing missing data. *Marketing Research Magazine,* 12–17.

Vriens, M., & Rademaker, D. (2015, September). To be determined. *Marketing Insights,* 16–21.

Vriens, M., & Sinhara, S. (2006). Dealing with missing data in surveys and databases. In R. Grover & M. Vriens (Eds.), *Handbook of marketing research: Uses and misuses* (pp. 178–191). SAGE.

Vriens, M., Chen, S., & Vidden, C. (2018). *From data to decision: Handbook for the modern business analyst*. Cognella.

Wasserstein, R. L., & Lazar, N. A. (2016). The ASA's statement on *p*-values: Context, process, and purpose. *American Statistician, 70*(2), 129–133.

Wedel, M., & W. A. Kamakura (1998). Market segmentation: Conceptual and methodological foundations. *International Series in Quantitative Marketing.* Kluwer Academic Publishers.

Wilkinson, L., & the Task Force on Statistical Inference. (1999). Statistical methods in psychology journals: Guidelines and explanations. *American Psychologist, 54*(8), 594–604.

Image Credits

Fig. 5.2: Copyright © by A. Abela.

CHAPTER 6

PRODUCT AND ADVERTISING RESEARCH

6.1 WHAT AM I GOING TO LEARN?

Improving and developing new products is hard. According to Christensen et al. (2016), each year more than 30,000 new consumer products are launched and 80% of them fail. This rate is consistent regardless of what category you look at. For example, the failure rate for new products launched in the grocery sector is 70% to 80%, according to Inez Blackburn (n.d.) of the University of Toronto (see also Blackburn & Deeter, 2010). The capital investment required to launch a new product varies greatly; this cost is higher for manufactured or tangible products than for intangible products. Roughly, worldwide firms spent more than $1 trillion on R&D (Congressional Research Service, 2020), some reports even project more than $2 trillion (Heney, 2020). Firms invest in advertising globally more than $560 billion (Statista, n.d.; Gutman, 2020).

For companies investing in developing new products or improving existing products (e.g., by adding new features or entering a new market), there is a strong desire to know whether the investments will be successful. A whole range of questions need to be answered, such as "Is the product going to make money? Are people willing to purchase the product? Is it addressing an unmet need? Will it be able to compete effectively? How should it be best promoted and advertised? Is it consistent with our brand(s)?" These are the types of questions any organization would like to get ahead of before significant investments are made in building or improving a product.

Marketing research departments are often organized around product development research and go-to-market research.[1] Product development research entails all types of research needed to help the company improve their current products or develop new products that consumers need or want. Go-to-market research entails developing promotional activities, advertisements, and content that will help sell the products. Product development research can include various types of marketing research such as identifying consumer needs and wants, idea generation, concept development and evaluation, benchmarking to the competition, cost reduction, and forecasting.

Advertising research includes research such as ad copy testing and marketing mix modeling. In this chapter, we review these types of marketing research briefly. Note that this chapter is not intended to be a

1 We note that marketing research departments usually also include brand research and customer satisfaction research (discussed later in this book) that don't neatly fall in these two types of marketing research. Brand is both part of product development and go to market, and customer satisfaction is considered more in-market monitoring.

comprehensive discussion. Both product research and advertising research are highly specialized areas and not without debate as to the right methodologies. Hence, the chapter should be viewed as a concise introduction.

In the first part of this chapter we will discuss approaches and methods of product testing to minimize the risks of making the wrong call on what to build and in the second half we will address how to effectively advertise products, two areas companies spend a significant amount of money on trying to get right.

6.2 PRODUCT RESEARCH

Here, we will discuss product research, starting with a commonly used framework for product development: the Ansoff matrix, followed by an overview of the (new) product development marketing research process and a discussion of a few commonly used marketing research approaches.

In (new) product development, it is useful to differentiate between the types of "new" products. To this effect, Ansoff (1958) developed a matrix, a strategic planning tool to help a company develop strategies for future growth. (Many companies still use this framework or derivatives of it such as the three horizons framework by McKinsey & Company, n.d.; see also Baghai et al., 2000.)

Ansoff discussed that products are either extensions of existing products or net new products. He also distinguishes between products built for new markets or existing markets; this results in four different types of "new product situations," as shown in Figure 6.1.

In a market penetration strategy, the organization tries to grow its existing offerings (products and services) in existing markets and increase its market share. This can be accomplished through reducing its price, incremental product improvements, expanding product placements, increased advertising promotions, or acquiring other companies. Sometimes this is referred to as the marketing mix decision framework. A company can influence the marketing mix through the four P's: product, price, place, and promotion, with research centering around these four key dimensions. In market development strategy, an organization tries to expand into new markets (geographies, countries, etc.) using its existing offerings, often with minimal development.

In a product development strategy, a company tries to create new products and services targeted at its existing markets to achieve growth. This involves extending the product range available to the organization's existing markets.

In a diversification strategy, an organization tries to grow its market share by introducing new offerings in new markets. It is the riskiest strategy because both investments in product and market development are required. For example, LinkedIn acquired Lynda, an online learning platform in 2015 to help accelerate its development of its online learning courses, with the goal of targeting new customers and tapping into new growth opportunity while building a new learning platform. This is an example of diversification.

With the Ansoff framework in mind, a company tries to determine the fastest and most sustainable path to growth. Another framework is the three-horizon framework, which is built on the premise that companies need to continuously invest in their core businesses

FIGURE 6.1 The Ansoff Matrix

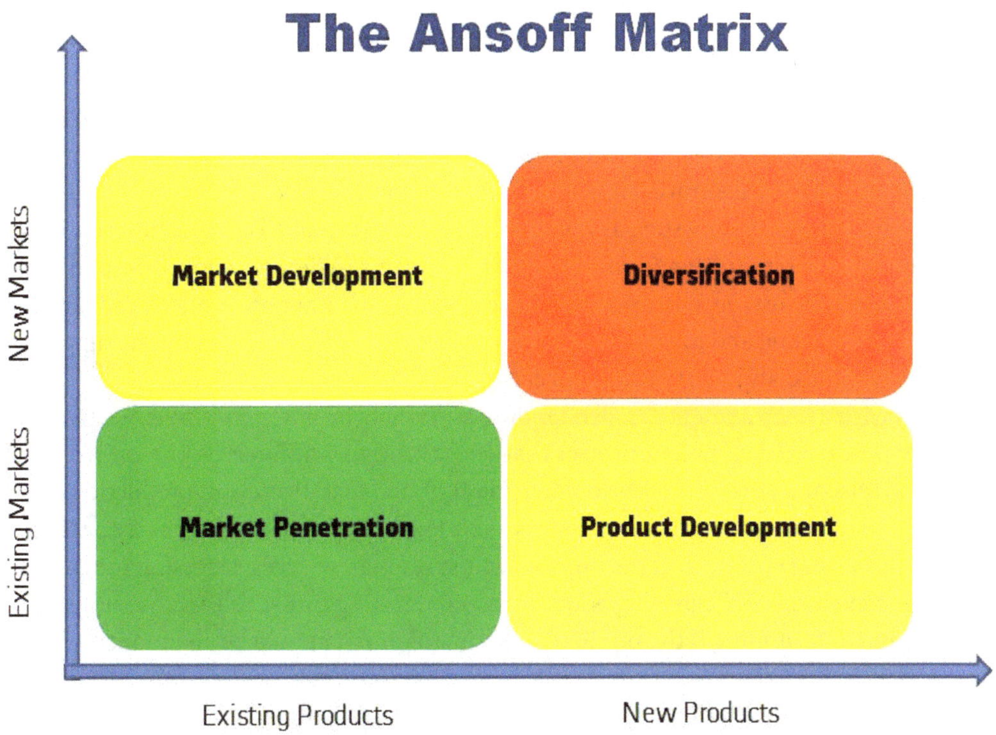

to strengthen a competitive position in a 0–1 year horizon while also investing significant capital in emerging businesses 1–2 years out and seeding many small embryonic businesses with a 3–5 year horizon (McKinsey & Company, n.d.). Regardless of the time horizon, when you design and build a product you need to have some sense of whether your product will be successful and why your company is best suited to achieve success. Market research plays a critical role in addressing that.

At LinkedIn, the objective of scaling and growing is not to create a new product for every country but to customize certain aspects to allow some level of localization while staying true to the overall value the company delivers: to be a place where people can advance their career. Uber has grown from a U.S.-based application to a worldwide phenomenon operating in over 60 countries in only a few years. For companies that are more heavily reliant on manufacturing, such a feat would be difficult to replicate; think of the challenges of scaling manufacturing and distribution or regulatory complexities. It took Coca-Cola roughly 25 years to cover every country in the world by opening bottling plants everywhere between the mid-1940s and 1960. The McDonald's franchise has grown fast, but it took a while to get to global scale; it went from operating only in the United States in 1948 to operating in 118 countries by 2008. For companies that operate in a largely digital world, it's less about understanding how to build a new product for new markets and more about how to take the existing product and localize it to different countries and then slightly alter the functionalities to operate successfully. For example, Uber offers a slightly different app experience for riders and drivers in New York, where regulations mandate more transparency on pricing. The LinkedIn app in Japan doesn't ask for a title when new members sign up because in Japanese culture it's not common to have a title until you reach manager status. Instead, most workers go by a description of their occupation. In Germany, many workers go through an apprenticeship period and want to be able to express that on their profile. The core needs of being able to network, build a reputation, and share information are universal, but the tactics of how the product strategy gets executed are different. For a company such as Intuit, it's difficult to expand TurboTax internationally due to regulatory complexities in the different tax systems. When companies need to decide what to build, they also need to understand the existing landscape and understand how they are going to add value and in what way. All these factors have an impact of what supporting research is required and what problems need to be solved for.

Armed with a deep audience understanding and what the potential size is, we then kick off a new product development project that goes through a number of phases, from idea generation (discovery), concept development (design), and manufacturing/production (development) to launching the product (delivery) (see Figure 6.2), followed up by a continuous cycle of measuring success and the impact against set market goals, assessing the product, listening to customers, diagnosing issues early on, iterating future releases/versions of the product, and determining if the product is successful or if it should be abandoned.

FIGURE 6.2 Product Development Lifecycle

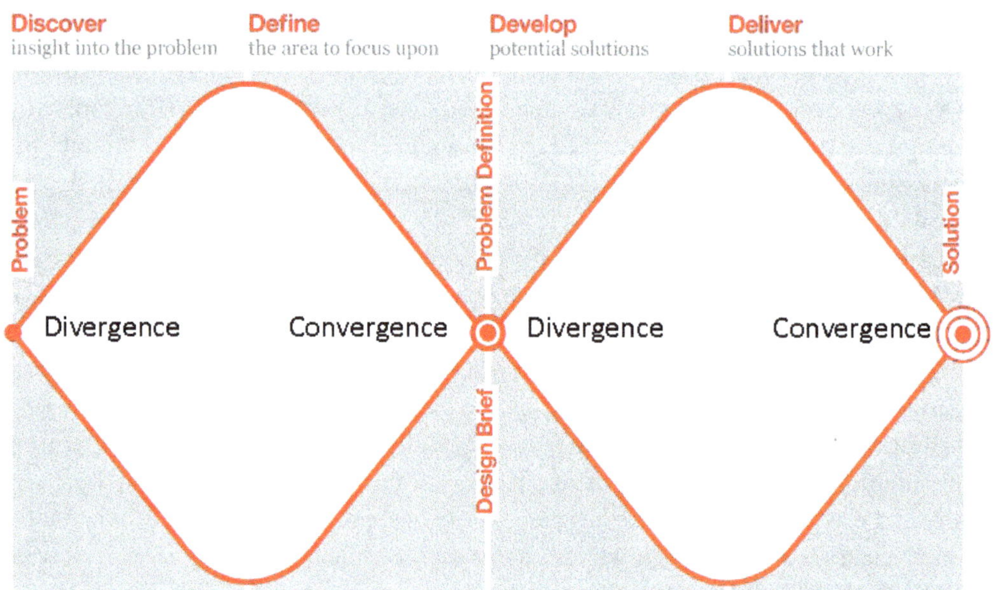

In a digital world the mantra is to fail fast, fail often, and to iterate fast through multiple pivots of the product. This poses significant challenges for market researchers that we will discuss in more detail later in the chapter. Ipsos is working with companies to kick off the product development lifecycle much earlier. They start with future casting (i.e., a qualitative analysis of current trends and an assessment what these trends may mean for future consumption needs), then finding growth domains, and only then addressing idea generation within a growth domain. This ensures companies come up with solutions/value propositions/ products that are futureproof.

When companies want to develop new products, or improve existing products, they are faced with a series of questions they will have to address, with or without marketing research, through several different stages (see Figure 6.3).

FIGURE 6.3 The Phases in the New Product Development Process

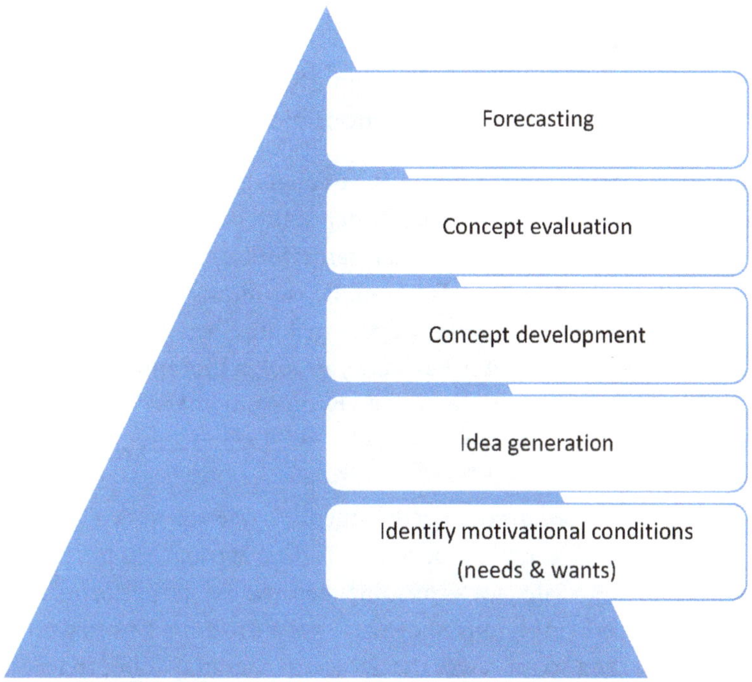

6.2.1 Uncovering Customer Needs and Wants

As a first step in the (new) product development process it is useful to think about what consumers may need or want. In the discovery phase, the objective is to find pain points or needs that current products are not or are poorly addressing, suggesting there is an opportunity to innovate and unlock greater value. The other objective is to determine how to define your target market—which customers will be in the sweet spot. The process is a collaboration across design, data sciences, product, engineering, business operations, and marketing, and the goal is to understand as many of the possible pain points that exist within a certain target audience for a specific use or task. The goal is to go broad and wide through a process of divergent thinking. Once all the issues are on the table, teams then decide which ones are worth solving, through a process called convergence, to converge on the one or two that are most plausible or present the biggest opportunity (see Figure 6.2). There are several research approaches typically applied in this phase.

First, it is argued we need to understand what Fennell and Allenby (2014) refer to as motivational conditions, which cause the consumer to search for benefits and attributes. Consumers have goals (e.g., I need a toothbrush), but according to Fennell and Allenby (2014) we also need to understand what is giving rise to this need. For example, I may wish to prevent cavities by brushing my teeth. Fennel and Allenby (2014) describe different classes of motivational conditions that can give rise to specific needs. Here, we just give a few examples.

1. *Solving or preventing a problem*. For example, I want to prevent cavities, or I have a headache and want to get rid of it.
2. *Sensory opportunity*. I may ask my friend out to go see a movie hoping for a nice evening that will result in some pleasant conversations.

To gain insight into motivational conditions we can use a variety of qualitative research techniques, such as focus groups, individual in-depth interviews, online communities, or user-generated online content. There are other frameworks that can give insight into what motivates a consumer to perceive a need. For example, the means-end chain framework aims to understand the relationship between product attributes, benefits, and end values (e.g., Reynolds & Gutman, 1988; Vriens & ter Hofstede, 2000). In this approach, one starts with individual depth interviews by asking a series of why questions. (See Table 6.1 for an outline of the laddering methodology.) This approach, as we will see, is also used in the process of advertising strategy development.

A third framework that is used in commercial practice is referred to as the outcome-driven innovation approach (Ulwick & Bettencourt, 2008). This approach is based on two ideas: one, that a product provides a value for a consumer because the job performs a job for them. For example, my laptop stores my family photos, allows me to e-mail, use a word-processing program, watch Netflix, and so on. Two, these various jobs may differ in how important they are for the consumer and how satisfied that consumer currently is with how much the existing products in the market can satisfactorily do these jobs. Practically, this approach is implemented in two steps: a qualitative step where one aims to identify all the jobs consumers may want a certain product category to perform, and a quantitative step where for each job we ask the respondent how important this job is to them and how satisfied they are currently with the products performing this job. It is not unusual to have between 50–100 jobs (or outcomes) in the study. The notion is that those jobs consumers have indicated as being very important, and at the same time cannot be done satisfactorily with the current products, constitute areas where innovation can lead to successful new products.

TABLE 6.1 The Laddering Approach

Brief description:

The laddering method was originally developed in psychology and then adopted in marketing. Methodologically, this approach starts with a qualitative phase and can after a qualitative phase be expanded in a quantitative survey study. Qualitative approach proceeds via several steps:

1. For a given product category, we first ask the respondent what the key, important, attributes which they use to make a specific choice or which they use to decide which product or brand is preferred.
2. Then, we ask them, for each attribute, what is the most preferred level, and what is the least preferred level.
3. Then, for each attribute, we go through a series of why questions. We start with a first attribute, and we ask the respondent why their stated preferred attribute is important to them.
4. Then, after they provide an answer, we will ask them again why this is important.

By conducting the interview this way we intend to discover what attributes will lead to which benefits, and which benefits lead to motivational values. This is the ladder: attributes lead to benefits, benefits lead to values. According Kahle (1986) there are about 10 consumer values that have been found across all cultures: e.g., security, accomplishment, sense of belonging, need for excitement, need for control, etc. The values that are being identified from respondents tell us what the motivations are that steer consumers brand choices. For example, a BMW driver may show a need for excitement, a Mercedes driver a need for accomplishment.

Example:

The following example is derived from Reynolds & Rochon (1991). Say we want to understand the underlying motivations of airline brand choices, and we have identified on-time record as being an important attribute. We may ask respondents as to why an on-time record is important. Some respondents may say "Because then I will waste less time." Why is that important? Well. If I waste less time, I will get more done (sense of accomplishment, end value). Another respondent may say (or even the same, as multiple answers are allowed): Well. A good on-time record is a sign that the airline have their act together. Why is that important? Well, if they have their act together then it is likely that they also are professional in other areas such as safety and not cut any corners (end value: security).

6.2.2 Idea and Concept Generation

The generation of new product ideas or new product concepts can come from various sources (e.g., Toubia & Florès, 2007; Urban & Hauser, 1993). Ideas can arise within the firm (e.g., brainstorming with employees from the firm, such as senior executives, those from marketing or R&D, salespeople, and so on). Ideas can also come from marketing research. We use both qualitative and quantitative approaches for this. Qualitative approaches include focus groups (e.g., Calder, 1977; Durgee, 1987; Fern, 1982; Gordon & Langmaid, 1988), individual-depth interviews (e.g., Fern, 1982), online pop-up communities (e.g., Xie & Jia, 2016), ethnography, and social listening. See Table 6.2 for a short description of what a focus group entails.

TABLE 6.2 A Brief Description of What a Focus Group Entails

Focus groups are led by a moderator who asks semi-structured questions to a group of usually between 8-10 people. A number of Focus Group participants are invited (commonly) to a focus group facility to meet at a certain date and time for roughly one or two hours. The moderator and his/her client have prepared the Focus Group by deciding what the general topic(s) of the Focus Group are. To prepare for the Focus Group discussion, the moderator usually prepares a discussion guide. A discussion guide is a document that outlines what topics the moderator should attempt to cover during the group discussion, and it identifies possibly areas where the client would like the moderator to probe more deeply if feasible.

During the group discussion, the moderator will ask a series of open-ended questions, around various defined topics. The moderator may direct a question to a specific participant or pose it to the group. Participants are then allowed to weigh in by responding to the original question or comment or elaborate on what others in the group said. The entire discussion is typically video recorded and transcribed and afterwards the results from the focus group discussion are interpreted and summarized.

The analysis of the group discussion is qualitative: i.e., the moderator reviews the video and the transcript often multiple times and extracts what he/she believes are the main insights than came out of the Focus Group.

Ethnography is a qualitative method where researchers completely immerse themselves in the lives, culture, or situation they are studying. Ethnographic methods are research approaches that look at people in their cultural setting, language, and the symbols, rituals, and shared meanings that populate their world, with the object of producing a narrative account of that particular culture against a theoretical backdrop, and often this technique is used to understand the job someone is trying to get done, as we described earlier. For example, a global toothpaste company wanted to increase its penetration in India. It sent a team of its most senior marketers to India to live with families in various social classes in India for a few weeks to observe how they live. These in-home observations were organized and supported by ethnographic specialists from Ipsos, but the observations were done by managers from the toothpaste company. After 2 weeks, the team got together and used their observations for an ideation session. One of the insights from these observations was that many people in India still used wooden sticks to pick their teeth in the morning; they were never trained to use a brush. However, their kids learned how to use a toothbrush. As a solution, the kids trained their parents on the advantages of using a brush. This training program helped the company become the leading choice of toothbrushes in India.

Online pop-up communities are also a qualitative research alternative. Market research companies like Ipsos have a specialized community platform and the expertise to recruit people to participate in a community and then and engage with them. Think of these community platforms as small versions of Facebook. Participants can log on to an online virtual space where they may be asked questions directly (just like in focus groups), but the community moderator can also pose a question to the community, and anybody can respond "publicly" if they want. Participants can also respond to each other. A benefit of pop-up communities is that researchers can follow up on responses, over time. Not everything needs to be discovered in one meeting session. Pop-up communities often last anywhere from several weeks to several months (or longer).

Social listening amounts to scraping consumer comments from the internet (e.g., blogs, consumer discussion forums, social media platforms, etc.; e.g., see Christensen et al., 2017). For example, Intuit could scrape Twitter comments that pertain to their tax preparation or financial management products, and specific issues or problems mentioned in these tweets may give them ideas for product improvement. Online consumer-generated comment data can be quite large, and it is unstructured data, which means it must be text analyzed (e.g., Netzer et al., 2012). For example, at LinkedIn, we used Social Intelligence to extract new ideas by mining the web to uncover "hidden" needs among Small Business Owners. Advances in machine learning, Natural Language Processing (NLP), and the growing stream of unstructured data make it possible to build audience understanding, create empathy and discover pain points that can lead to new product ideas more effectively than traditional market research approaches can. Ethnographic or "Jobs-to-be done" type research can suffer from various issues such as interviewer bias, recall bias or response bias that make it less effective than listening to conversations that are happening organically on the web in real-time and at scale. By searching the web for certain key words and developing a list of sources where online conversations are happening in forums, articles and on social media, you can develop a deep understanding of an audience. At LinkedIn we didn't have a good grasp of what issues to probe on or what types of small businesses (SMBs) to include into a traditional research study given that it's such a broad and heterogeneous audience and it wasn't very active on the platform. Social listening allowed us to go broader and capture the diversity of SMBs while staying close to how people express themselves in an organic way in the moment without interviewer bias or recall bias. The process works as follows: 1) define the business challenge/opportunity audience or topic to investigate; 2) identify all the data sources where that audience/topic are engaged in forums, social media, blogs, traditional media, etc.; 3) ingest this data into an analytics platform and apply machine learning and natural language processing to identify narratives, topics of interest, degrees of sentiment, trends and other characteristics of the data; 4) use additional text analytics to identify examples of the specific language the audience is using, and excerpt verbatim quotes to provide stakeholders with a firsthand understanding of the audience's expressions; 5) determine the implications of those insights to the business challenge/opportunity; and 6) revisit the conversation on a regular basis to understand how people's opinions, priorities, attitudes and feelings are changing, and adjust strategies and tactics accordingly (Verhulst & Marshall, 2020).

Quantitative methods used to come up with new product ideas include U&A surveys (usage and attitudes surveys) and segmentation surveys (which will be discussed extensively in the next chapter).

The purpose of this stage is to develop initial rough ideas of what the new feature or the new product will like. An idea needs to be translated into some sort of statement that describes what the new product does and what benefits.

Many times, companies are looking for new solutions to address consumer trends. In these cases, they may not have a clear idea of what product/solution they are looking for. For example, a global beauty company realized that climate change may have an impact on their consumers. The thinning of the ozone layer is making women more afraid of sunburn, and sun-browned skin is not necessarily related to beauty anymore. What products can the company launch to address this trend? In these cases, companies start with brainstorming sessions, with or without consumers, moderated and facilitated by experienced market researchers. These brainstorming sessions can lead to hundreds of ideas. Quick online quantitative consumer feedback can assess these ideas and bring them down to a few that are ready for further investigation, prototyping, and testing. In this beauty case example, the company launched a necklace that users can wear when the skin experiences sunburn and needs protection. As this example shows, brainstorming sessions can be very effective to come up with creative solutions to consumer problems. But facilitating these sessions is not an easy task. Facilitating a brainstorming session needs a skillful facilitator. It is more than closing your eyes and waiting until great ideas spontaneously enter your brain. That could happen, but it is more likely that you will be asleep before that one great idea hits you. Like the discovery phase, it is recommended to go broad at first and think through all the possible solutions, and once that is determined, narrow it down and converge on one or two that address the pain points best. This process of divergence/convergence, followed by divergence and convergence, is called the double diamond approach, first introduced by Don Norman (2013). There are many research approaches for testing these designs; we cover a few in the next sections.

6.2.3 Initial Idea and Concept Screening

Once there is a clear understanding of the pain points and existing or potential needs that are that are unmet or partially met, it's time to determine what product, services, features, or brand promises would address these needs best. Many companies create a product spec using the needs and pain points as the starting point and develop the features of the product that deliver benefits against these needs. Often a supporting prototype or mock-up of what a minimal viable product (MVP) will look like is created, and the team describes the different persona involved in the delivery process along with a detailed description of the user flow.

If a firm has generated many ideas, it is common to reduce this set. The number of ideas can be quite substantial, sometimes over 100 (Cui et al., 2014). After reducing a large set to a smaller set, this smaller set is then evaluated more comprehensively. The product managers can reduce the set themselves, or one can interview consumers and ask them to evaluate each of the concepts on likelihood to purchase, uniqueness, believability, and so on. In this stage, the ideas or early new product concepts are described via factual statements without added "marketing" language to position the product or make the message persuasive (e.g., Lees & Wright, 2004).

6.2.4 Concept Development

For the initial concepts that survived the previous reduction phase, more comprehensive description are developed. According to Moore (1982), such statements can vary quite a bit in the degree of detail they provide and how much "marketing" is part of the description. Hence, in some cases the line between a concept evaluation and an ad copy evaluation becomes blurred, as concept descriptions may include objective information about the product and how information is superior to the competition (Moore, 1982). In this stage, though, especially when many ideas are generated, the concept statement may remain very basic (i.e., most if not all is just a basic description of the product). This is often done in focus groups (FGs) or individual depth interviews (IDIs). The reason for choosing FGs or IDIs over, for example, an online survey, have to do with concerns that new product ideas may be leaked to the competition. If the number of ideas is smaller, one can we more elaborate in the description. A concept description may include of four elements. The first element is a title, or a name for the concept. For example: "A more grown up tasting snack" The second element is a brief description of the insight. For example: "As my children grow up, I am proud to see them become individuals, but I still want to guide them and stay close to them." The third element is a brief description of the key functional and emotional benefits. And the fourth element is a picture, a drawing or a sketch of the concept. All of these elements are put on one page so that respondents can score and evaluate them against each other. Another, simpler way to write concepts is to use "Tweetable" concept descriptions. These are a very short description (no more than 200 characters) of a title and the key benefit of the concept. A Tweetable concept is used for mobile surveys where there is less.

6.2.5 Concept Evaluation and Test

The next step is the concept evaluation and test (in some cases an actual product may be developed, and consumers may be asked to test this product; this would be called a product test). At this stage, usually, feedback is sought from larger samples. Regarding the concept representation, we have to decide whether to use only a basic verbal description (sometimes referred to as the pure idea), a more visual representation (e.g., Holbrook & Moore, 1981; Vriens et al., 1998), or verbal/pictorial representation with added persuasive "advertising" language. Lees and Wright (2004) found no significant differences between the various options.

In a digital world, there are many options for quickly creating a mock-up of a solution. Companies such as Invision provide easy-to-use software that help designers build high-fidelity prototypes that have a great amount of interactivity so that user experience researchers can test the product in real-world scenarios for different use cases. With 3D printing, companies operating in a tangible world can create a close to real-life replica of what the form factor may look like.

Methodologically, two types of decisions need to be made (ADD) when testing different concepts.

Monadic Design

In a monadic research design, each respondent only evaluates one concept. Say the firm wants to evaluate four alternative new product concepts; then for a given sample of respondents, each respondent is allocated to one concept. If the firm decides on a total sample of 800, then 200 will evaluate concept A, 200 will evaluate concept B, 200 will evaluate concept C, and 200 will evaluate concept D. In each sample/concept combination the respondent is shown the corresponding concept statement and asked a series of questions regarding this concept (e.g., "On a scale from 1 to 5, 1 meaning you are very unlikely to buy this product, 2 meaning you are somewhat unlikely to buy this product, 3 meaning you are neither likely nor unlikely to buy this product, 4 meaning you are somewhat likely to buy this product, and 5 meaning you are very likely buy this product, how likely are you to buy this product?"). Using a similar scale, additional questions can include "How relevant is this product for you? How unique is this product? Do you believe this product will be able to do what it promises to do? Does this product meet your needs?"

Competitive Design

In a competitive set design, the new product concepts can be evaluated in choice sets with multiple choice alternatives via a methodology referred to as conjoint analysis (e.g., Vriens et al., 1998). One of the key benefits of the conjoint approach to concept testing is that the new product can be evaluated in the presence of already existing alternatives and the researcher can get some idea as to how likely it is that consumers will choose the new product over something that already exists; they can even include brand and price as factors in these multiple-choice scenarios. A full discussion of the conjoint analysis approach is beyond the scope of this book. Here, we outline some key concepts of this methodology.

New feature testing for digital offerings can also be done with A/B testing. Regardless of whether your company or client is predominantly focused on a tangible or intangible product, every company needs to understand the needs its product tries to fulfill. For technology companies that produce software products, the cycle of development is short, and the tools are such that new features can be deployed (pushing new code) as fast as a typical traditional research project takes, often within 4 weeks. The cost and risk of failure is relatively small, with only the time of a product manager, engineer, and designer working on it. Many tech companies therefore do not spend enough time understanding needs and pain points and instead build new products and features based on gut feelings and internal opinions in short cycles without much market research as input and prefer to pivot often. Success is often determined by engagement and revenue metrics, and if they do not meet a certain target, the feature is abandoned.

In theory, this creates agility, but there are risks. First, there is a risk that a company can go through many cycles before succeeding or too quickly abandoning a feature that with a few tweaks would have been successful. Often teams experiment using A/B, testing where a random proportion of customers gets exposed to the new experience (B) and the experience for a control group (A) is held constant. At LinkedIn many tests run at a given time to measure if new features are helping to significantly lift a key metric such as sessions (like the number of visits to a site) or make members more engaged, liking, commenting, or sharing content. For the key metrics we calculate the difference between control and exposed, the A and B group, and calculate a p-value, with a defined confidence interval to determine statistically significant lift. If the lift in the metric has a p-value less than 0.05, the typical cut-off to determine significance, the experiment is considered a success and the feature is rolled out to more customers with the idea that it will drive more sessions and engagement, the product goal. Taking p-values less than 0.05 is rather arbitrary, and many product teams may pursue a path of what is called "p-hacking": selectively reporting only the experiments that showed a significant difference and/or did not demonstrate the absolute impact from a baseline. The other challenge is that the test only shows whether a feature is successful for the average customer and ignores whether certain groups or cohorts are potentially negatively affected. The averages cancel out these effects and hide potential success or failure down to different cohorts such as countries or heavy and light users. Data science teams can offset this by alternating showing customers the treatment of B and the status quo of A in subsequent sessions but it's difficult to understand what all the relevant cohorts are and how to best optimize for long term success, setting the correct duration of an experiment, particularly if the goal is to drive more engagement from light or inactive users (Bojinov, Sait-Jacques, & Tingley, 2020). Those inactive users are often less savvy in how to use new features and need a different treatment to properly understand if B is working. So, while the feature may have been a great idea, the test comes back negative not because the feature is bad but because light users did not receive enough education or had difficulties discovering the feature. Market research can effectively shed light on that and support a more successful experiment.

The second risk with extensive experimentation is that a company can lose its reputation and erode trust if it continues to experiment without understanding user sentiment or how the feature will get used, even with a small number of users. For example, at LinkedIn, when we first launched the Endorsement feature to allow members to give and receive skills endorsements that are shown on the profile, we saw engagement sky-rocket but people weren't using it the way it was intended so we knew we had to rebuild it and put guardrails in place. Now when you must accept an endorsement before it shows on your profile, skills are ranked based on whether someone who endorsed you also has that skill so they can more accurately assess you. While the absolute number of engagements between members went down, it created a higher quality engagement. It's temping for product teams to develop a product based on trial and error, but without research up front around universal needs and pain points and considering the unintended consequences, trust can be tarnished. There are also many combinations and permutations, and it could take a long time to land on the right thing to develop that serves long term goals of driving engagement while creating a trusted brand. A better process that we are promoting at LinkedIn, and one that would work for the digital world, is to take stock of all the pain points that customers face in getting a particular task accomplished, or job done, followed by a process to determine all the ways in which these problems can be solved. Building a library or fact base of all known pain points and solutions ranked by severity or impact on a business outcome allows product teams to be more focused and prioritized in the experimentation phase, kick-starting and seeding what ideas should be experimented with as starting points and using market research effectively to understand the sentiments and emotions and what guardrails need to be put in place to minimize risks of failure. In a tangible world, where products are consumed and its more of a zero-sum game, the risk of getting it wrong is much higher. Teams often follow a very rigorous process of understanding paint points and needs, followed by ideation sessions on the right features to address these needs, feature prioritization, messaging and testing, followed with prototype testing sessions before the actual product is built and extensive user experience research is conducted. In product testing, the goal is to measure the product's performance and quality on its own, against previous versions and against the status quo. It's important that the voice of the customer or member is embedded throughout all phases.

Forecasting

One challenge, and sometimes complaint, with concept tests is that they are not always predictive as to what really is going to happen if the concept is truly launched in the market. Some marketing research firms, like Ipsos, have over the many years that they are in business, built an extensive database with information on all concept tests they have done. These databases also include information on which concepts later turned out to be successful. Applying these databases with highly sophisticated modeling and including marketing input from the company enables these firms to accurately forecast in market sales for new concepts. These forecasts are used by companies to decide if they want to move forward with the product and how successful it will be in the market when they launch it. It will also give them information on where the sales are coming from. Is it coming from new consumers or from existing consumers? Will it cannibalize on existing products or deliver incremental sales? Once a firm decides to move forward with the new product it will want to get insight into what percentage of the target market will try the new product, if it is launched, and how successful it will likely be overall (i.e., how many will buy it again, the uptake going to be over time). This is the domain of forecasting.

Commercial Practice

It is not easy to get a comprehensive view on how commercial firms tackle the new product development process, and what, if any, specific marketing research techniques they might use. In one study that aimed to shed light on this, the researchers found that 77% of the firms they interviewed used concept tests in the NPD process, 66% used focus groups, 53% used limited roll-out, 36% used clinics and show tests, 36% used A&U studies (see next chapter), and 28% used competitive conjoint choice analysis (see Peng & Finn, 2008). Firms also test the finished physical products (we will not discuss that here).

Not all companies take a rigorous approach to product development. Especially for products with longer lifecycles, product developers need to balance speed to market with rigorous consumer testing. Let's look at an extreme example of such a speed to market. An Asian car manufacturer decided to get in the market of full electric cars. It built (from scratch) a manufacturing plant that was fully operational in 6 months. Within 1 year, they were producing more electric cars (for the Asian markets) than Tesla. The research firm was asked to come up with a brand strategy for their new car within 3 weeks *and* come back with a name for the car *and* a visual identity (with logo) within the timespan of a week. This example shows that rigorous consumer testing may reduce risk of failing in the market, but it also may allow your competitors to beat you to the market. As a marketer, you need to find this balance, even (and especially) for products where common knowledge is that product development normally takes a long time (e.g., cars).

In a business-to-business (B2B) setting where conducting robust validation research is limited, a qualitative approach using a series of depth interviews with 20–30 customers is often the only option. Some believe that the product development process for B2B should follow a sell, design, build order versus a design, build, sell order. Often B2B offerings are more complex; think of a Salesforce implementation or new disruptive technologies that are difficult to describe in a 5- to 10-minute survey. Researchers need to spend a fair amount of time explaining the product and its benefits. The goal of the research is to determine if a client would purchase the product as it is being described to them; this can include a lightweight prototype or mock-up and explanation of how the product works to see if there is enough interest. If you follow this approach, you can identify evidence of potential product-market fit, a clear understanding of your target audience, and highly confident MVP requirements.

Once the organization has a good sense of what product to design for whom, there are often some trade-offs to be made on what features to include in the first version versus later versions.

Companies also want to do a market sizing analysis to determine the total addressable market (TAM), the total market expressed in revenue that a company could address if no competitors existed and determining what proportion a company can realistically capture within a certain timeframe, its serviceable available market based on its existing distribution channels and brand. The target market is a subset of the serviceable market, the customers that are most likely going to purchase your product. In a top downsizing approach, one starts with the largest size, the TAM and work backward to reduce it down to what a company can most realistically sell based on a set of assumptions (current distribution channel, reach, brand, cost to scale, etc.). The key is to understand how many customers a company believes that it can reach. The types of questions we are trying to answer in a top down approach are usually as follows: How much do people spend on a product yearly? Who's buying streaming TV? What % of snacks are ice cream? What is the likelihood that our company will capture most of the market? Do we believe consumers will buy more if we make the product more accessible? A bottoms-up approach on the other hand tries to understand how many customers would be in a target market and interested in purchasing a certain product and how many units a company expects to sell based on purchase intent questions. It starts with the basic units of a business (e.g., the product, price, customers) and estimate how large a company can scale those units. Simply put, how can a company scale up a product. Questions that one tries to seek include: What's the price per unit? How many products does a consumer buy regularly? How many people can we reach via marketing/other channels if we start selling in the US. How many countries do we believe we can expand into? A top-down approach is quick and easy but may overestimate TAM & be misleading as it ignores feasibility of scaling. A bottoms-up approach provides a more realistic view of TAM, grounded in the business's demographics (e.g., the product / services, operating model, etc.). This is an important assessment that determines if a company should proceed to creating the product and often market research helps answer questions around propensity to purchase and conducts the sizing analysis.

6.3 ADVERTISING RESEARCH

In this section we will look at what research to conduct to effectively promote and advertise a (new or existing) product or re-launch an improved product. Advertising drives awareness and influences how customers think and feel about the product and encourages them to purchase and engage with the product. Note that this section, like the previous section, is not intended to be a comprehensive overview of the entire field of advertising research. Instead, it introduces advertising research and some key methodologies.

Advertising research is either used to develop the advertising strategy, to develop and test ad copy prior to running the ad, or measure whether your advertising investments paid off (marketing mix modeling). We start with a framework of advertising.

We begin with briefly outlining the AIDA model that is often used in the context of advertising research (note that there are several alternatives to this model, but here we just use the AIDA model). Then, we discuss advertising strategy research, ad copy testing (prior to full launch), and how to assess the ad and campaign effectiveness.

6.3.1 The AIDA Model

The AIDA model (Strong, 1925) states that consumers must first pay attention to a product (A), then must become interested in it (I), then start desiring the product (D), and finally they need to act (A). Practically attention is often equaled with awareness (e.g., see Baldinger & Cook, 2006; Vakratsas & Ambler, 1999), though these two concepts are not the same: Attention refers to whether consumers pay attention to the product or the ad when they see it. Awareness refers to whether consumers recognize (aided awareness) or recall (unaided awareness) the product or the ad. Interest can be viewed as consideration: Is the consumer considering this product or brand, which generally means, "Is the consumer interested in the product or brand enough so that they will actively start thinking about it?" Desire can be thought of as intent to purchase or in some cases preference to. Action is indicated by actual consumer choices (sales). Marketers need to decide what they are trying to achieve with their advertising (i.e., where in the funnel the ad needs to focus but also what creative to develop, who to target, the reach, through what channels and at what frequency, and for what duration). See Table 6.3 for the initial AIDA ad objectives and possible corresponding metrics.

TABLE 6.3 Advertising Objectives and Metrics

Advertising objectives	Metrics to measure objectives	Methodology/examples
Attention	• Gaze duration • Number of eye fixations	• Eye tracking
Advertising evaluation	• Unaided ad awareness • Ad liking • Ad believability	• Survey open-ended question; e.g., Do you recall seeing (or reading) any coffee advertisements?
Brand awareness	• Unaided awareness • Aided awareness	• Survey open-ended question (Thinking of the coffee category, what brands come to mind?) • Survey (check all that apply), which brands from the list below do you recognize?
Interest	• Brand consideration	• Survey question; e.g., what coffee brands do you consider
Desire	• Brand/product perceptions • Liking/overall evaluation	• Survey-based question; e.g., Overall, how well does this brand fits your needs?
Action	• Sales • Stated product or brand choice	• Survey-based question; e.g., What coffee brand did you purchase on your most recent shopping trip? • Actual sales data (e.g., derived from scanner data)

For example, does the marketing team decide to focus on building product or brand awareness, changing or reinforcing the brand positioning or its salience, or getting an immediate action (e.g., getting new users to try the product, achieving a bump in sales)?

We note, though, in the original AIDA model it was assumed that consumers must move through these stages in a linear fashion; we now know that this isn't strictly necessary. Digital and social media has upset the marketing funnel somewhat (consumers can go, with one click, from awareness to action, can purchase shoes online only to return them if they don't like the color, and so forth). Though as consumers will move through a decision funnel, digital solutions can change the speed and can make consumers move back and forth between phases. But it is helpful to keep the funnel in mind when trying to make sense of the consumer journey.

At LinkedIn, we try to convey that we have jobs, lots of jobs, without going into the specifics of how to search and apply for these jobs, aimed at the top of the funnel with a simple marketing message. The targeting is usually broad, and reach is high over an extended period and is always on because people are always looking for jobs. A middle-of-the-funnel campaign tries to move potential customers to the next step of driving interest and consideration for the product. These campaigns may run on the company's website or in store fronts but can also include callouts in grocery stores. The creative and messaging is more focused on education and informing and emphasizing the benefits. The bottom-of-the-funnel campaign tries to elicit a direct response and get a customer to make a purchase after seeing the ad. On digital platforms these ads, along with middle-of-the-funnel ads, run "in the product" or try and direct customers to the store or site. A full-funnel campaign tries to move customers in a coordinated fashion through each step. However, most marketing campaigns are designed to move top-of-the-funnel metrics, especially in a B2B context and for complex products that require further personal education once awareness is established. The goal is to drive awareness, interest, or inquiries and hand off leads to the sales organization for follow-up and closure. Marketing campaigns targeted at current customers and designed to help customers get more value out of their product experience on the dimensions that drive loyalty or repeat purchases are also likely to have an impact on metrics such as NPS and satisfaction. Sometimes, brand campaigns are used to target existing or light users to make them feel even better about the brand. A large-scale study conducted Sharp et al. (2001) found that users are more than twice as likely to recall a brand's advertising than non-users, and any brand's advertising recall score tends to be 20 percentage points higher for users than for non-users simply because they are already using and aware. Bottom-of-the-funnel campaigns are targeted at groups of customers who already have a certain level of awareness with a brand, and the goal is to get them to try out the new or existing product.

Ostlund (1978) distinguishes several stages, ranging from advertising strategy to copy guidance research, to testing a roughly finished ad, to testing a finished ad, to testing the effectiveness of an ad in market (i.e., the ad is running).We can do advertising research prior to launching a campaign or running an ad; the purpose is to help with go/no-go decisions or to choose the ad that is most likely to be successful. What ads should we develop? Specifically, what should the message be, and how should the message be translated into creative (we refer to this step as ad copy testing)? This phase also includes research on who the target audience (especially for new products) is or should be and includes deciding on what the advertising strategy is or should be. We can also do research after the ad or campaign ran or during its campaign. The goal then is to determine if a given ad or a campaign was effective.

6.3.2 Advertising Strategy Research

At the start of developing an advertising campaign, the marketing communications/advertising team may start with reviewing the general research that is available on the audience they want to reach with the campaign. For example, if you want to develop a campaign to market your new enterprise cloud security software product, you may want to find all the relevant research available on IT professionals (in the markets, read: countries) where you plan this campaign. In this phase we may also use focus groups to get some initial insights from our audience. A research methodology that has been especially useful in the development of an advertising strategy is the laddering approach (see Table 6.1), sometimes referred to as the means-end chain framework.

6.3.3 Ad Copy Research (Pre-Testing)

The messaging—a key aspect of a successful product launch—is making sure the ad highlights the right words and phrases that describe the product and leads to customers wanting to purchase the product. Research typically includes testing different versions of the messages using different trade-off techniques, depending on the number of messages being tested. Typically, the messages are also tested among competitors to determine the optimal positioning and reasons to believe (RTBs). Focus groups can be used in the copy guidance or copy development stage as well.

The creative is the most important aspect of advertising; it carries the brand and needs to stand out, to cut through the clutter. Before a campaign launches the creative team comes up with several versions of the campaign in different formats: static, audio, and video for different channels (radio, TV, out-of-home [billboards], and digital [for example, social media]). For campaigns where the stakes are high, a company wants to test all the creatives for appeal and whether they catch attention. Neuroscience is a very effective way to guide the creative process and determine which ads have the strongest appeal. (See more about neuroscience in Chapter 11.)

Ad copy testing research is done prior to launching a campaign (or prior to fully launching the campaign). First, we note that in the literature several "cognitive" measures have been proposed to evaluate consumers' responses to possible ads (ad copy alternatives) that are being considered (recognition, recall, persuasiveness, believability, and memory changes). Researchers and practitioners have also proposed to evaluate ads on emotional impact. For excellent and very thorough reviews see Krishnan and Chakravarti (1999) and Ostlund (1978).

Ostlund (1978) distinguishes between the day-after-recall and forced exposure tests. If the ad is finished, we can use the day-after-recall method: the "to-be-tested ad" is run (usually in a contained geographical area) during a commercial break. A sample of respondents from that area are then called the next day and are asked questions as to what ads they can recall seeing. Similarly, we can do this for print ads in magazines. A challenge with such a study design is that we may not be able to control what position in the commercial break the ad airs. This may make it hard to interpret the results. For that reason, Ostlund (1978) prefers the forced exposure method. In forced exposure, we interview respondents. We may, for example, ask them to read a magazine and then afterward ask them various questions about what ads they saw, brands they can remember, and so on. Questions asked can be about recognition, recall, or even about how persuasive the ads were. In some cases, firms can use eye-tracking methodology to assess how much respondents looked at the ads and its components (e.g., brand, pictorial, text; see Chapter 10).

6.3.4 Assessing Advertising Effectiveness

The cognitive impact of ads can be assessed in various ways (Krishnan & Chakravarti, 1999), and tests can differ on what aspect of the ad was tested, how long after the respondent has been exposed to the ad the test was conducted (e.g., immediately, day after recall, etc.), and if any cue is provided. Krishnan and Chakravarti (1999) distinguish between direct and indirect tests and whether a retrieval cue is given (we've simplified the ideas, here). We outline (simply) four different types of advertising copy tests:

1. Direct recognition test
2. Direct recall test
3. Indirect recognition test
4. Indirect recall tests

Let's use an example to illustrate. Say Heineken, a beer brand, wants to advertise a new organic beer. They developed two ads where you see consumers ordering an organic beer after coming back from a workout. In the ad viewers clearly see the beer bottle; the brand name Heineken is not printed very large, but large purple letters are used to indicate that this beer in organic. The tagline/voiceover reads, "You care about your health; we do too. Heineken." Heineken now wants to know whether the ad conveys the organic claim.

In a direct recognition test, the Heineken commercial could be shown in a commercial break among other ads (this can be done in a DAR approach or forced-exposure setting). Then, subsequently, the respondents would be shown a series of ads and asked which commercials they have seen. This test could be done right after or with some delay (say day after). The percentage of respondents who correctly identify the target ad is a measure for how effective the ad was. In a direct recall test, we may give respondents only a cue: "Do you recall having seen a beer commercial?" The interpretation here is complicated by the fact that respondents may say they saw a Heineken commercial, while others may say they saw a commercial about organic beer.

Once a campaign goes live a company wants to understand if the ads, or the campaign, are driving awareness, perceptions, or sales. There are several methods that can be used here, including control versus exposed experiments, A/B testing, and marketing mix modeling.

In an indirect measure, no reference to the ads are made. For example, respondents may be given a set of brand names, Heineken being one of them, but no reference to the ads are made.

Respondents are then asked to write down the benefits of each brand. Those respondents who saw and processed the Heineken ad should write down words like *healthy* and *organic*.

Another way ads or campaigns are evaluated is through surveys, either ad hoc or in a tracking format. For example, if a firm uses a tracking format, then the first survey would be executed just prior to the launch of the campaign. In this first campaign tracking survey, respondents are asked about whether they know the brand, and so on. Then, every month or quarter, the survey is repeated, but question ad recall, recognition, and ad liking questions can be added. Such a campaign tracker has several useful pieces of information. First, one can see if key brand metrics, such as brand awareness, consideration, and brand preference, are going up during the campaign. If they do, that is a sign the campaign is working. Second, one can see if respondents recall the ads (brand and message) and if they liked the ad.

Control Versus Exposed Experiments

Building on the indirect test, often a control versus exposed experiment is used to determine if there is "lift" in awareness, familiarity, consideration and brand perceptions. And secondary, to determine what the optimal number of impressions are, to generate the lift and what the optimal channel mix is (TV, Digital, Out of Home, etc.) if there are multiple channels used in the advertising. The control group is a random group of a target audience that is otherwise similar in characteristics to the exposed group, the group that will be exposed to the campaign. At LinkedIn we often run campaigns in certain cities and compare the "lift" to cities in which the campaign did not run, the dark cities being the control. Dark cities are selected carefully to make sure they mimic the population composition and key behaviors of the test cities. All else being equal, with this approach we can attribute how much the campaign is contributing to increased awareness and engagement on the site. It is important that we maintain exposed and control cities for a long period, up to a year to understand the full effect of seasonality. In a digital world using online panels, research providers can leverage cookie or pixel tracking (tagging) and smart TVs to determine which panelists have seen an ad (exposed group) and control for who hasn't seen the ad (control group), and making sure key demographic and other factors, such as purchase intent and media consumption behavior are similar between the two groups. For example, if one group tends to watch more media across more channels (TV, Internet) they will naturally have a higher propensity of seeing an ad and fall into the exposed group. A lift in a metric compared to control may not be due to the ad campaign but simply because that group has a higher propensity of seeing ads. At LinkedIn we noticed that members who are more likely to search for a job are more likely to be aware of LinkedIn, not because they saw an ad from LinkedIn but because they are in the market of searching for jobs. In our control and exposed group, we needed to make sure to adjust for that through weighting so that both groups have a similar proportion of active job seekers. There are significant issues with ensuring that control and exposed are pure, given that you cannot control for all variables. At minimum we recommend carefully weighing for a propensity for buying a product in the next few days, weeks, and months, depending on frequency of purchases and awareness of the brand and to control for media consumption behavior. Often, we ask a set of questions in the survey to determine these factors and adjust for it, if needed. See Figure 6.4 for what the typical research process looks like.

FIGURE 6.4 Typical Control and Exposed Survey Process

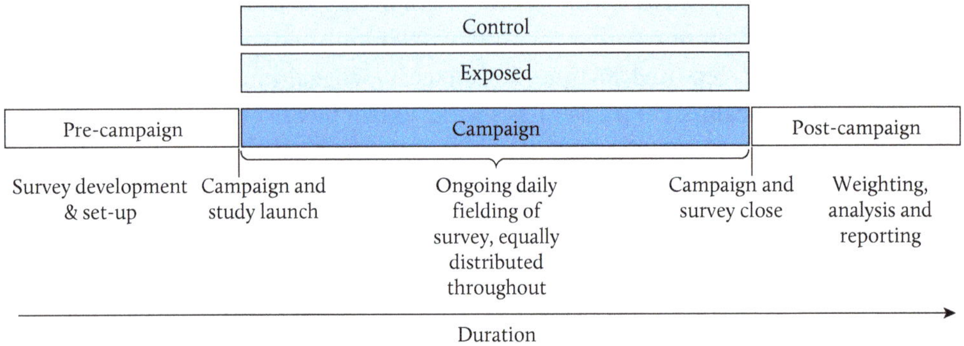

A more simplistic approach is to measure the effectiveness using a pre- and post-method–pre, to establish a baseline before the campaign launches and post, usually two weeks into the campaign to determine if there was a lift relative to the pre. The risk with this approach is that you cannot control for seasonality or external factors such as a media scandal or a sudden recession influencing perceptions of the company and its products. In a pre and post approach you also still need to monitor for differences in purchase intent; for example, you need to make sure that there is a similar distribution of people with a propensity for purchasing a certain product across pre- and post-campaign. At certain times of the year, people are more likely to search for jobs than at other times. We found that January is a much heavier job search month and that people are more predisposed to being aware of job boards and that varies by industry and country. Thus, to be extra safe, a control can also be set up during the campaign duration as a subset of the sample to account for these fluctuations. A pre- and post-method versus a running control group with ongoing survey fielding during the campaign has both pros and cons, and, in most studies, companies usually try a mix of both. The idea is to set up a control that is a subset during the campaign or part of the measurement after. The challenges with any of these approaches are that there can be a residual effect from prior campaigns affecting certain populations more than others. We will discuss one last approach that addresses this later.

In the case of digital media channels, exposure to an ad is commonly identified via tagging (but available for certain digital channels only), and the preferred method, or sometimes by asking respondents if they had the opportunity to see (OTS) the ads. These are two examples of "determined exposure" versus "forced exposure," which we will discuss later. The exposure can also be determined by whether someone was at a certain geo-fenced location when we want to test the effectiveness of out-of-home ads such as billboards, for example, a busy transfer station in metro areas, cinemas, or other physical and non-physical places. While you can achieve a reasonable control and exposure group, some caveats to keep in mind are the following: (a) opportunity to see (OTS) questions are dependent on a respondent's possible exposure to the ads in the past 7 days and whether we can accurately predict that they were in a place that they must have seen the ad (e.g., "Which of the following TV shows did you see in the past 7 days?"); and (b) if respondents may have been exposed to more than one campaign (if there are multiple campaigns running at the same time), which relies on respondent's memory that they visited a place or online site in a given time period. A well-constructed control group should adjust for that, but often there is a lagging effect or decay effect from prior campaigns that needs to be factored in.

As of this writing we cannot use social networks to get tags and determine who was exposed to an ad. Social networks are walled off due to data privacy, so researchers need to ask self-stated questions of what sites were visited, at what duration, and with what frequency to determine the opportunity to have seen the ad. The issues with Facebook, Instagram, and others is that visitation is high, making it hard to carve out a reliable control group, and often the results are underreported. For TV ads, companies such as Nielsen use technology to reliably track what TV shows the members of its panel are watching, which can be used to determine exposure along with self-stated OTS. The advantage of determined exposure is that we can also establish the number of exposures to an ad. Determined exposure works well if there is enough reach but harder when the reach is smaller. In forced exposure, we ask respondents at the end of the campaign effectiveness survey once we have collected all the key metrics, such as the funnel metrics and brand perception metrics. We either show them the ad and ask them if they saw it or we show the ad with the brand logo blocked off. While it does provide an unbiased control versus exposed group, it does not consider how many exposures to a brand are needed to see an increase in unaided recall. There is also a self-biasing effect happening, where respondents recognize the brand in the ad but may not have actually seen the ad, so the increase in brand perception metrics may not have been a result from the campaign, but simply due to customers who were already aware. Forced exposure (with the brand logo blocked off) does have the benefit that the results can be used to determine the effectiveness of the creative, and results can be compared to other campaigns. It also has the added benefit that we can assess the extent to which an ad was attributed to the wrong brand, and what the effect is of earned media (media from word of mouth or re-sharing of ads). The downside of forced exposure and OTS in general is that there is a heavy reliance on a respondent's memory, and the risk of recall bias is high. To execute the best adverting effectiveness research there are a lot of considerations and it's unclear what method is best. This is further compounded by the fact that it's getting harder and harder to track whether someone has been reliably exposed to an ad, across what channels and how many times due to increased data privacy considerations. At the same time, companies execute advertising that is infrequent and heavily dependent on discretionary spend levels. Given these two challenges, we have found that it's best to design an ongoing brand or advertising campaign tracker that tracks the key metrics such as unaided brand awareness and brand reputation metrics on an ongoing basis among a target audience. It has the added benefit that it factors in the residual effect from prior campaigns. In addition to the metrics companies want to improve with advertising, questions are added to understand the frequency and duration of media consumption ("what channels did you visit?" and "how many times during a given time period?") to gauge whether a respondent had an opportunity to see the ad and to the extent possible supplemented with impression data from cookie tracking. The advantage of ongoing measurement is that companies can understand what the effect is on brand metrics during periods of heavy, light and no advertising and what level of spend is desired to maintain high awareness and remain the preferred choice. Ongoing trackers also allow for better modeling and forecasting which we will discuss next.

Marketing Mix Modeling

Marketing mix modeling is used to assess overall effectiveness of a firm's advertising efforts and has grown in popularity. Marketing budgets are under scrutiny, and more and more CEOs are demanding a demonstration of the ROI on marketing. So, it is no wonder that chief marketing officers (CMOs) are looking to justify their spending and, if feasible, see more results out of their investments.

Marketing mix modeling is usually used for three purposes. The first is to answer the question of whether advertising investments (in dollars) have been effective (i.e. if it have a positive return on investment [ROI]). For example, say Microsoft spent $900 million to launch their new office productivity suite software. Did this investment return more than $900 million in additional profits that they otherwise wouldn't have had? The second purpose is to determine whether the firm has been overspending, underspending, or spent just the right amount of money. The third purpose is to determine the effectiveness of various advertising activities that have been used (e.g., T.V., radio, online ads, out-of-home advertising, etc.).

Marketing mix models are typically based on time series data and can get very complex from a statistical estimation perspective (e.g., for an illustration see Wiesel et al., 2011). A very basic scenario would be that we have sales data over time: say we have weekly sales data over a period of 5 years and have weekly expenditure data on what the firm spent on TV ads, radio ads, out-of-home advertising, digital advertising, and e-mail campaigns. In a situation such as this we can try to predict sales numbers from the spending levels on the various advertising vehicles. Let's say that we have run a time series regression model, and we have determined the ROI per dollar spent for each of the advertising vehicles. Table 6.4 shows the output in terms of ROI per advertising vehicle. It also shows the current spending (past year), and the range of spending over the 5 years.

TABLE 6.4 Return of Investment Marketing Mix Model

Marketing	Return on investment	Current spent (past year)	Range of spending (past 5 years)
TV Advertising	$ 1.15	$ 2 Million	$1.2 Million–$2.2 Millon
Billboards	$ 1.05	$ 500,000	$ 300,000–$ 600,000
Google ad words	2.20	$ 175,000	$ 75,000–$ 200,000
Radio	1.10	$ 200,000	$ 100,000–$ 220,000
Email campaign	0.90	$ 90,000	$ 50,000–$ 125,000

There are three pieces of information that need to be reviewed. First, we see in column 2 the ROI numbers per dollar spent (for each dollar that we spent on a given marketing activity, that column shows how much we get back in incremental profits). The table shows that all except e-mail campaigns have a positive return on investment. This is good news because it means the advertising is working. Now, we might say that e-mail campaigns are not profitable; let's stop wasting money on this activity, reduce that budget to zero, and move all funds to Google ad words, as that seems to be most profitable marketing activity. Before we do that, we must review column 3: the range of spending over the past 5 years. As Table 6.4 shows, the firm has never spent more than $200,000 on Google ad words in any given year. Hence, we really do not know how effective that channel is once we go over the $200,000 mark (recall the discussion of interpolation and extrapolation in the previous chapter). In this case, we would probably recommend reducing the e-mail campaign spending by $25,000 and putting that toward Google ad words. We could then reduce e-mail campaign spending even more, by $15,000, and put this $15,000 toward TV advertising, which is the next most effective channel. Both in reducing and increasing we want to make sure we stay within the range, because outside the range means we extrapolate our results, and this is risky.

Marketing mix models are complicated from a statistical perspective. They are also complicated from a "data-generating mechanism" perspective. If we think how advertising might affect the consumer, various effects may be encountered:

- We can have immediate effects: We advertise this week, consumers see the ad, and once in the supermarket that same week, they buy the product.
- We can have lagged effects: Consumers see the ad this week, say a coffee brand, but they still have coffee at home, so even they may have liked the ad, and the advertised brand, they won't buy it today or this week. However, 2 weeks later when they run out of coffee, they remember the ad and buy the coffee brand that week.
- Diminishing-returns effects: If we keep increasing the spending on this ad, and show/run it more and more, then at some point consumers will get sick of it or it will have reached all the consumers who were interested in the product, and hence further increasing spending doesn't help.

Marketing mix models can be very powerful because they may tell us if our advertising spending overall has been effective, which specific channels have been effective, and how we can possibly shift money from one channel to another to get a better return on investment. However, a downside of marketing mix models is that we need quite a lot of historical data to estimate our statistical models. In the example in Table 6.4, we had 5 years of data, which is not uncommon. However, this probably means the data represents several campaigns, likely with different ads (different creative, different messages, etc.) and different products. This means it is usually very hard to use marketing mix models to evaluate a specific campaign or ad.

6.4 COMMERCIAL PRACTICES

At LinkedIn we have been able to demonstrate a strong correlation between advertising spending and increased site engagement when looking at longitudinal data and unaided awareness; the unprompted, free-form responses to what products come to mind when thinking of job seeking, is a key metric for LinkedIn. There is a strong link between unaided awareness and increased site engagement and market share. We have found that unaided awareness is the most important metric and specifically first mentions relative to total mentions of the brand. We record separately, not only what brands come to mind but also which brand was the first one that was top of mind (ToM). Dividing first mentions (ToM) over total mentions and tracking that over time by different channels and spend gives us the best insight into how effective our advertising is, with what channel mix on a per impression or click basis. It is common for a company to report the advertising ROI during quarterly business reviews. Advertising ROI is the bookings a campaign generated divided by the advertising spending; a value greater than 1.0 suggests a positive contribution. The challenge with measuring ROI is that most companies are too short-term focused, struggle with attributing spending to bookings, and confuse cost per clicks (CPC) relative to bookings with ROI. Arguably, with advertising there is a delayed and cumulative effect on sales. There is also a threshold of saturation. Advertising is not linear to demand; at some point there are diminishing returns when more spending doesn't translate into more demand. The decay effect and saturation of advertising is called ad-stock, carry-over effects (see Vriens et al., 2002). The better metric, therefore, is calculating a cost per lead and compare that to bookings—the leads generated through the total advertising cycle, including the decay period following the advertising, compared to prior periods of the same ad spending. Advertising also has a positive impact on existing users and can help make more dormant, infrequent users more active. Advertising educates and makes users become more familiar of the product, which leads to users feeling even better about the products they purchased. It drives retention and repeat purchase and keeps your brand top of mind when a consumer has a need for your service or product assuming the product is widely available. There are many benefits of advertising beyond direct bookings that many companies struggle to measure. Does marketing/ad campaign investment drive Net Promotor Score (NPS) and generate more loyalty and therefore higher lifetime values? Assessing the impact of the campaign investments should be done by focusing on campaign objectives and measuring those relevant metrics before and after the investment period. These metrics are usually unaided awareness, familiarity, brand perceptions (among all aware, or even aware non-users), and finally consideration and usage. Companies also want to understand what channels are most effective and have the largest impact. Often prospects receive several touches, and a company wants to learn which touch was most significant. Attribution/marketing mix modeling delves deeper into this to better understand what the right mix is and how to distribute media spending across the different channels.

6.5 CONCLUDING REMARKS

There is still a debate on whether companies should pursue big, new innovations or gradual, incremental innovations that make existing products and brands better. Research by Corstjens et al. (2019) found that consumer goods firms pursuing smaller innovations, often iterating on an existing product, saw higher returns. Big innovations have the potential for big rewards but tend to result in big losses rather than big wins. The other question that a lot of companies struggle with is the cadence of launching new products, which varies by category, the competition, and the life of a product. It is an important consideration for how much money is set aside for R&D, and research can help understand upgrade cycles or usage patterns.

In the last 30 years, market research has seen a massive shift in how product testing gets done due to the digital transformation and new product development processes such as agile, scrum (e.g.,4 Pichler, 2010), 2D or 3D printing, and augmented reality. Agile product and software development is based on iterative and incremental development, where requirements and solutions evolve through collaboration between self-organizing, cross-functional teams spanning engineering, design, and marketing. Due to advances in technology, products can be developed much faster. Small teams break their work into actions that can be completed within timeboxed iterations, called sprints, usually divided into 2 weeks, then track progress and re-plan in 15-minute time-boxed stand-up meetings called daily scrums. Companies that are producing intangible products that require no manufacturing, think Amazon, Google, Facebook, LinkedIn, Microsoft, or any SaaS provider, follow such a process. These companies constitute the largest market caps in the world as of this writing and make up a significant part of the economy, so we have to look more closely at how product testing takes place relative to the rest of the economy. In an intangible world, new code for new features can be deployed within hours. This requires a different approach to product testing than what you encounter in traditional Consumer Packaged Goods (CPG), pharmaceuticals, or any industry that manufactures physical products where the tangible attributes such as touch, feel, taste, and smell play key roles in the purchase process and the distribution of products works differently. The pace of development in an intangible world demands insights faster than a typical research project can deliver. In physical product industries the development timeframe is much longer, and research gets executed differently. There are also differences between products built for businesses (B2B) versus consumers (B2C) that impact how to effectively design the right research approach. In a B2B environment, its often difficult to obtain a robust and representative sample of existing and prospective customers. In those instances, companies will rely on a more qualitative approach of product testing.

6.6 QUIZ AND EXERCISES

1. What are the stages of the new product development process? In what stage are qualitative approaches better suited, and in what stage is it better to prefer quantitative approaches?
2. Name three sources of new product ideas.
3. What is a monadic concept test? How would you analyze the data you collect from a monadic design study?
4. What are some disadvantages of a monadic concept test?
5. In the chapter we mention the A/B testing approach. What is the appropriate analysis for such data (Tip: review Chapter 5)?
6. What are the advantages of using a "competitive set" approach to concept testing?
7. If we do a monadic concept test, and we are testing three concepts in terms of the likelihood that the respondent would buy the product if it were available, what analysis approach could be used to analyze the data and decide what concept to move forward with?
8. Do a Google search on the term *p-hacking*: What is meant by this term?
9. What is the AIDA model?
10. What is the difference between a direct and an indirect ad copy test?
11. Which test is harder for respondents: recognition or recall? Are these good measures to evaluate the quality of ads?
12. What are some of the pros and cons of marketing mix models?
13. A marketing mix model shows the following output:

Marketing activity	Return on investment per dollar spent	Amount invested in past year	Range of spending over past 2 years
TV advertising	$3.0	$2.2 million	$950k–$ 2.2M
Billboards	$1.45	$880,000	$300,000–$ 900,000
Google ad words	$0.90	$50,000	$50,000–150,000
E-mail campaigns	$2	$15,000	$15,000–$190,000

14. Which of the following decisions would give you (most likely) the biggest increase in return on investment (ROI) for next year?
    a. Increase spending on e-mail by $150k
    b. Increase spending on billboards by $500k because the results show it is very effective
    c. Increase billboard spending by $40k and reduce TV spending a little, by say $40k
    d. Reduce TV spending by, say, $100k. Increase billboards by $40K, Google ad words by $20k, and e-mail campaigns by $40k
15. What is advertising decay? Is it the same as advertising wear-out?

REFERENCES

Ansoff, H. I. (1958). A model for diversification. *Management Science, 4*(4), 392–414.

Baghai, M., Coley, S., & White, D. (2000). *The alchemy of growth: Practical insights for building the enduring enterprise*. Basic Books.

Baldinger, A. L. & Cook, W. A. (2006). Ad testing. In R. Grover & M. Vriens (Eds.), *Handbook of marketing research* (pp. 487–505). SAGE.

Blackburn, I. (n.d.). *Speed to market: Capitalizing on demand.* http://www.markettechniques.com/assets/pdf/Speed2Market.pdf

Blackburn, I., & Deeter, M. (2010). *7 steps to category development*. Pride Passion Profit.

Bojinov, I., Sait-Jacques, G. & Tingley, M. (2020). Avoid the pitfalls of A/B testing. Harvard Business Review, 98, 2, 48–53.

Calder, B. J. (1977). Focus groups and the nature of qualitative marketing research. *Journal of Marketing Research, 14*(3), 353–364.

Christensen, C. M., Dillon, K. & Hall, T. (2016). *Competing against luck: The story of innovation and customer choice.* HarperCollins.

Christensen, K., Nørskov, S., Frederiksen, L., & Scholderer, J. (2017). In search of new product ideas: Identifying ideas in online communities by machine learning and text mining. *Creativity and Innovation Management, 26*(1), 17–29.

Congressional Research Service. (2020). Global research and development: Fact sheet. https://fas.org/sgp/crs/misc/R44283.pdf

Corstjens, M., Carpenter, G. S., & Hasan, T. M. (2019). The promise of targeted innovation. *MIT Sloan Management Review, 60*(2), 39–44.

Cui, G., Peng, L., & Florès, L.P. (2014). Selecting ideas for new product development. *European Journal of Innovation Management, 18*(3), 380–396.

Durgee, J. (1987). New product ideas from focus groups. *Journal of Consumer Marketing, 4*(4), 57–65.

Fennell, G., & Allenby, G. M. (2014). Conceptualizing and measuring prospect wants: Understanding the source of brand preference. *Customer Needs and Solutions, 1*(1), 23–39.

Fern, E. F. (1982). The use of focus groups for idea generation: The effects of group size, acquaintanceship, and moderator on response quantity and quality. *Journal of Marketing Research, 19*(1), 1–13.

Gordon W., & Langmaid, R. (1988). *Qualitative market research: A practitioner's and buyer's guide*. Routledge.

Guttmann, A. (2020). Global advertising spending 2010-2019. https://www.statista.com/statistics/236943/global-advertising-spending/

Heney, P. (2020). Global R&D investments unabated in spending growth. *R&D World*. https://www.rdworldonline.com/global-rd-investments-unabated-in-spending-growth/

Holbrook, M. B., & Moore, W. L. (1981). Feature interactions in consumer judgments of verbal versus pictorial presentations. *Journal of Consumer Research, 8*(1), 103–113.

Krishnan, H. S., & Chakravarti, D. (1999). Memory measures for pre-testing advertisements: An integrative conceptual framework and diagnostic template. *Journal of Consumer Psychology, 8*(1), 1–37.

Lees, G., & Wright, M. (2004). The effect of concept formulation on concept test scores. *Journal of Product Innovation Management, 21*(6), 389–400.

McKinsey & Company. (2009, December). Enduring ideas: The three horizons of growth. *McKinsey Quarterly*. https://www.mckinsey.com/business-functions/strategy-and-corporate-finance/our-insights/enduring-ideas-the-three-horizons-of-growth

Moore, W. L. (1982). Concept testing. *Journal of Business Research, 10*(3), 279–294.

Netzer, O., Feldman, R., Goldenberg, J., & Fresko, M. (2012). Mine your own business: Market structure surveillance through text-mining. *Marketing Science, 31*(3), 521–531.

Norman, D. (2013). *The design of everyday things*. Basic Books.

Ostlund, L. E. (1978). Advertising copy testing: A review of current practices. *Current Issues & Research in Advertising,* 87–106.

Peng, L., & Finn, A. (2008). Concept testing: The state of contemporary practice. *Marketing Intelligence & Planning, 26*(6), 649–674.

Pichler, R. (2010). Agile product development with Scrum. Addison-Wesley. Boston, USA.

Reynolds, T. J., & Gutman, J. (1988). Laddering: Theory, method, analysis and interpretation. *Journal of Advertising Research, 28*(1), 11–31.

Statista. (n.d.). *Global advertising spending from 2010 to 2019*. https://www.statista.com/statistics/236943/global-advertising-spending/

Sharp, B., Beal, V., & Romaniuk, J. (2001). First steps toward a marketing empirical generalization: brand usage and subsequent advertising recall. In Chetty, S. & Collins, B. (Eds), *Bridging marketing theory and practice [electronic resource]: Proceedings of ANZMAC 001 Conference*, Albany Campus, Auckland, New Zealand.

Strong, E. K. (1925). *The psychology of selling and advertising*. McGraw-Hill.

Toubia, O., & Florès, L. (2007). Adaptive idea screening using consumers. *Marketing Science, 26*(3), 342–360.

Ulwick, A. W., & Bettencourt, L. (2008). Giving customers a fair hearing. *MIT Sloan Management Review, 49*(3), 61–68.

Urban, G. L., & Hauser, J. R. (1993). *Design and marketing of new products*. Prentice Hall.

Vakratsas, D., & Ambler, T. (1999). How advertising works: What do we really know? *Journal of Marketing, 63*(1), 26–43.

Verhulst, R. & Marshall, J (2020, January 7). Uncovering "hidden" needs through mining the web. LinkedIn. https://www.linkedin.com/pulse/uncovering-hidden-needs-through-mining-web-rogier-verhulst/?published=t

Vriens, M., Grigsby, M., & Franses, P. H. (2002). Time series models for advertising tracking data. Canadian *Journal of Marketing Research, 20*(2), 62–71.

Vriens, M., Loosschilder, G., Rosbergen, E., & Wittink, D. R. (1998). Verbal versus realistic pictorial representations in conjoint analysis with design attributes. *Journal of Product Innovation Management, 15*(5), 455–467.

Vriens, M., & ter Hofstede, F. T. (2000). Linking attributes, benefits, and values: A powerful approach to market segmentation, brand positioning and advertising strategy development. *Marketing Research Magazine,* 3–8.

Wiesel, T., Pauwels, K., & Arts, J. (2011). Marketing's profit impact: Quantifying online and offline funnel progression. *Marketing Science, 30*(4), 604–611.

Xie, X., & Jia, Y. (2016). Consumer involvement in new product development: A case study from the online virtual community. *Psychology & Marketing, 33*(12), 1187–1194.

Image Credits

Fig. 6.1: Copyright © by JaisonAbeySabu (CC BY-SA 3.0) at https://commons.wikimedia.org/wiki/File:Ansoff_Matrix.JPG.

Fig. 6.2: Copyright © by Design Council.

CHAPTER 7
FOUNDATIONAL RESEARCH

7.1 WHAT AM I GOING TO LEARN?

Foundational research is done to understand a market or a category. Often, there is no immediate decision that needs to be made; the purpose of the research is to improve general understanding of a market or category. An overall motivation behind such research, sometimes articulated in the research brief (RFP), is to find ideas or insights that can spurn a new growth path for the company or the category. In this chapter, we cover three often used foundational research approaches: U&A studies, market segmentation studies, and market structure studies.

Usage and attitude research help the researcher understand their consumers. Who is the consumer? What do they buy and why? How much do they purchase? What do they think of the products available? Market segmentation helps find groups of consumers, of occasions, or of needs that are similar but still have some differences. With this research, a company can be more targeted and efficient in its marketing. Market structure helps a company better understand the market they are competing in. Who are their competitors and what areas can they address with new products or advertising?

7.2 U&A RESEARCH

If a company wants to better understand their category, or is looking for new growth opportunities, they conduct a usage and attitude study (U&A) (other names used for this type of research include habits and practices research or landscape studies). In this section we discuss the components of a typical U&A study (the type of questions that are asked and how it is analyzed), we discuss the pros and cons of using surveys versus diaries, and we comment on mobile, in-the-moment research.

Typical questions that may be asked by the stakeholders (the internal clients who will pay for the research) include: Who are your competitors? Who are your consumers? Who is using the category, who is using your products, your brands, and why? Answers to these questions will help companies build strategies to grow their business with new products and create targeted marketing campaigns and more precise brand positioning.

Results of a Usage and Attitude research are generally used to find new opportunities in the market for the brand to grow. This can be a consumer need that is not been serviced by any of the competitors, a direction to change the image of a brand to target a larger group of consumers, or an idea to remove a purchase barrier for consumers (either a real barrier, like the price or availability, or an emotional barrier, like an outdated image or a strong and well-positioned competitive brand). For example, a large coffee company wanted to understand coffee consumption occasions and product perception at each occasion to provide insights for product development and communication. A mobile consumption diary was used to collect reactions and perceptions at the exact moment and place of usage. The mobile consumption diary provided granular insights about product ratings, which varied according to time of day, location, and food accompanying the coffee. The client also uncovered the moods associated with drinking coffee and how moods change after consumption, leading to powerful input for the development of their brand communication. As another example, a global soft drink company conducts an annual foundational U&A study where they identify the full beverage landscape by market (read: country). The study includes claimed consumption and motivation for consumption as well as context (5 W's: who, what, when, where, and why) across the total population in nearly 60 countries. The results of this study are used across the organization to improve advertising, decide on new products, improve the shopper journey, and optimize the positioning of their brands.

7.2.1 The Typical U&A Study

Given the number of topics to be covered in a U&A survey, researchers often create lengthy questionnaires as they try to get as much information from the respondent as possible (when and where they bought the brand or competitors, why they bought it, what they thought of the brand and its competitors, etc.). It is not uncommon for U&A questionnaires to be over 45 minutes in length. There have been instances where it would take a respondent over 90 minutes to complete a questionnaire. The researcher has a very important role in balancing the need for respondent information with developing an effective questionnaire. Since most research nowadays is done through mobile phones, the maximum length of a mobile questionnaire is no longer than 20 minutes. Research has shown that longer questionnaires do not provide useful data; respondents are giving random answers to try to end the questionnaire.

The basic questions in a U&A study center around the five W's: who, what, where, when, and why. For example, a coffee brand wants to understand the coffee market. In a typical U&A study they would focus on who is drinking coffee (and who is not), what specifically they are drinking (e.g., brand, flavor, black or with sugar, etc.), when they are drinking coffee (e.g., morning, afternoon, evening, etc.), and why they drink it (e.g., to wake up, get more alert, for the taste, etc.). In Table 7.1 we show the types of survey questions that are often part of a U&A study.

A screener is, of course, a standard component of any survey: It is the first section in a survey: a number of questions are asked to determine if a respondent is the right audience for the study; i.e., to make sure we invite the right people to respond. A second component of a U&A study is a set of questions regarding their use of the category. For example, if we study the at-home coffee market, we may ask respondents if they drink coffee, how much,

TABLE 7.1 U&A Question Categories (Category Example Home Coffee Making)

U&A Survey question types	Examples
Screener questions/category screening	• Do you drink coffee? • What is your age?
Behavioral questions: Category usage & barriers	• How many times per week do you drink coffee? Where, when, what type of coffee, with whom? If you don't drink coffee, why not? If not coffee, what do you drink instead?
Brand usage and brand funnel	• What coffee brands come to mind? • Which of the coffee brands listed below are you familiar with
Brand perceptions	• On a scale from 1 to 10, how much do agree that the following statements apply to the <Insert brands?> Perceptions: (1) Is good value, (2) Is tasteful, (3) Is high-quality, etc.
Attribute importance	• Please rank (or rate) the following attributes in terms of how important they are to you
Category motivations & attitudes	• Reasons why you drink coffee (check all that apply: To wake up, as a break, to give me a midday energy boost, etc.) • Attitudes: Keeps you from sleeping well, Gives me bad breath, Is unhealthy, upsets my stomach, etc.
General demographics & media usage	• Age, household size, marital status, children, employment, etc.

when, with whom, and where. If they don't drink coffee, we may ask why not. In some cases, if respondents don't drink coffee and they have told us why they don't, we may terminate the survey. After general category usage, survey questions will become more specific through use of the following:

- Brand questions. Here, we ask brand funnel questions (unaided awareness, aided awareness, brand consideration, brand preference, and brand usage).
- Brand perceptions. For the brands that respondents are aware of and are considering for consumption, we may ask them to evaluate two to three brands on a set of brand perceptions.
- In some U&A studies there is a section that asks about the importance of product attributes. For example, in the coffee category there could be an attribute such as price, brand, packaging, whether it is organic, available flavors, whether there is a decaf option, whether it has added vitamins, and so on.

- Category usage and beverage consumptions questions. Some category usage questions are asked in the screening questionnaire because we need to determine if the respondent is the right person to interview. However, in the main survey we may ask additional, more detailed questions regarding their coffee drinking behavior, including what alternative beverages there are consuming when coffee is not available.
- Category motivations and attitudes. A section in the survey may delve into the reasons why the respondent drinks coffee. It may be to wake up, to get an energy boost, just to enjoy the taste, as a break, and so on. We may also ask about some general attitudes (e.g., Do they believe coffee drinking is healthy? Does it keep them awake/disturb their sleep? Does it lead to bad breath or upsets the stomach?, etc.).
- Additional demographic and media usage questions. Are they married/single/divorced? Do they have children? What is their estimate household income?

These U&A studies often cast a wide net of questions to try to find out as much as possible about what consumers purchase, why they purchase these items, and how they feel about the category or the different competitors in the market.

Consider a U&A study for a skincare product that the authors were involved in. The target audience were female consumers, between 18 years and 55 years. We asked a question about how they felt about their skin, relative to how they think the skin of their friends' looks. We also asked a question about how they see their ideal skin. See Figure 7.1 for how we could present the results.

FIGURE 7.1 Output Example U&A

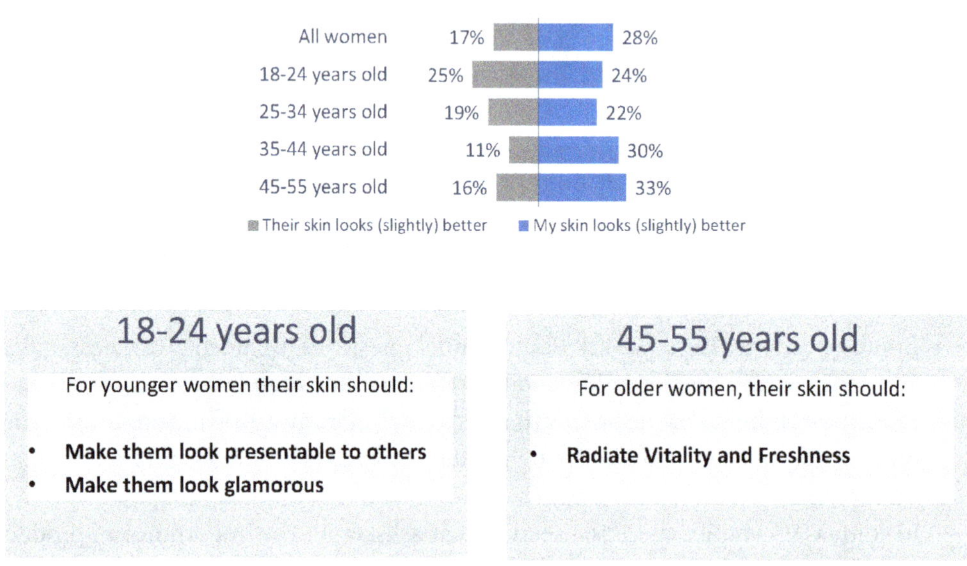

In the same skincare study, we wanted to know the importance of various skincare attributes. Attribute importance can be measured in various ways (rating, ranking, etc.). In this study, we first asked what attributes they cared about (a list of attributes was presented, and they could check all that apply). Then, in a following question, we asked them to indicate which were the three most important attributes. The results are presented in Figure 7.2.

FIGURE 7.2 The Importance of Skin Attributes

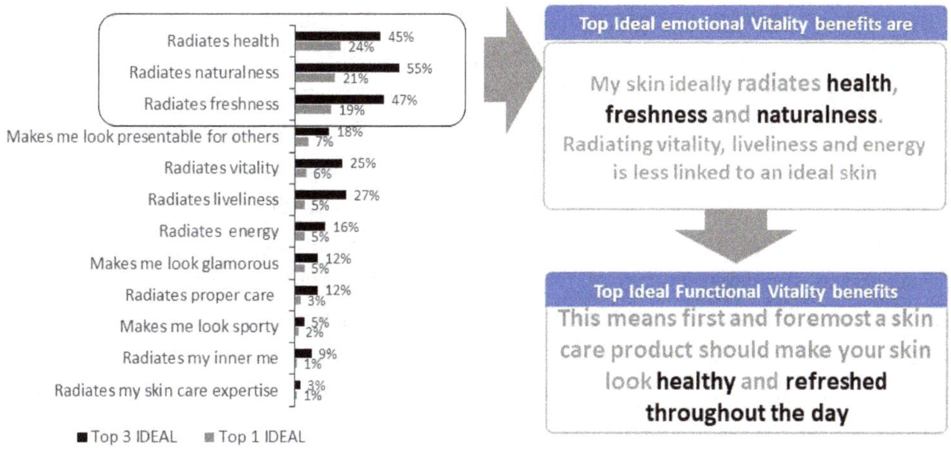

Question: Now we like to know more about your IDEAL skin. What would this be for you?
Question: And what is your top 3 of what skin care should ideally do for you? Ideally my skin...

In Figure 7.3 we show an example of an attitudinal- (beliefs) type of question. We asked respondents to tell us what factors contribute to their skin condition.

FIGURE 7.3 Attitudes and Beliefs About What Affects How Your Skin Looks

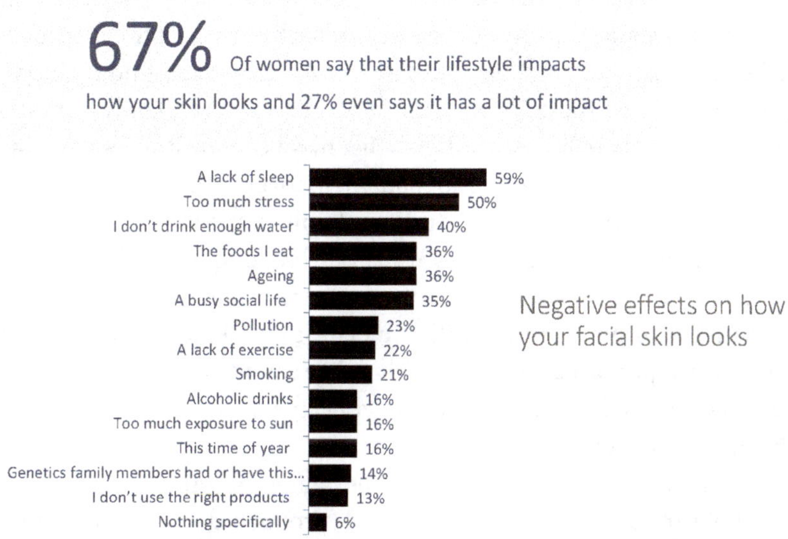

7.2.2 Surveys Versus Diaries

There are many smart tools in the researcher's toolkit to reduce the length of the questionnaire while increasing the accuracy of the data. The most used is combining a traditional survey with a diary. This reduces the size of the pre-survey. The downside is that some respondents may not complete the diary task. The researcher than ends up with a smaller sample size. We will discuss other behavioral tools later in this chapter.

Researchers, in general, prefer a diary over asking what was consumed in the past week or month. This recall is often not very accurate. As an illustration, can you remember precisely every occasion when you have drunk something in the past 2 weeks? And if you do, do you remember the brand and the amount for each moment? Or who were with you at that time? And how you felt about the product you used? Probably not. That's why researchers prefer to use a diary, where you log each consumption moment when it occurs. And with the use of a mobile app, this is a simple but accurate exercise for a respondent.

Accuracy in measuring usage is often an important factor in U&A research as the results are often used to calculate the total usage. And companies often compare the results with their sales data to see if the data from the research makes sense. This is another reason why researchers often use (mobile) diaries instead of recall questions in a traditional survey. If an accurate measurement of actual usage is an important element in the U&A research, then sampling becomes very important. If the researcher wants to predict actual sales, then the sample needs to be nationally representative.

7.2.3 Analysis

After completing the fieldwork, the researcher will tabulate the data and try to find interesting facts and insights. Given the lengthy questionnaire, U&A research often leads to a thick book of data tables. A common trap for researchers it the urge to translate each table in a PowerPoint (PPT) slide. As an example, many companies can recall examples where they received U&A reports with over 350 PPT slides without an executive summary. Instead, what researchers should do, when facing a thick pack of data tables, is to look for a story in the data before creating PPT slides. Go through the tables and find the key insights, then develop a story. Discuss the story with the key stakeholders and only then start developing slides to bring the story to life. Any insights that may be interesting but do not add anything to the story should be moved to the appendix. We covered this in more detail in chapter 3.

In most cases, the researcher will have to do more analysis than just looking at cross tables. This often includes a segmentation analysis, brand equity analysis, and category driver analysis. Figure 7.4 is an example where we compare the importance of skincare attributes with how satisfied respondents are with achieving these skincare attributes (this is a classic importance versus performance chart). A chart like this identifies, in an easy-to-understand way, those need areas that are important to consumers and, at the same time, are not well served by the market currently.

The attributes in the upper right-hand corner show opportunities for the company; these are important attributes, but currently available products do not solve these needs.

FIGURE 7.4 Importance Versus Fulfillment Consumer Needs

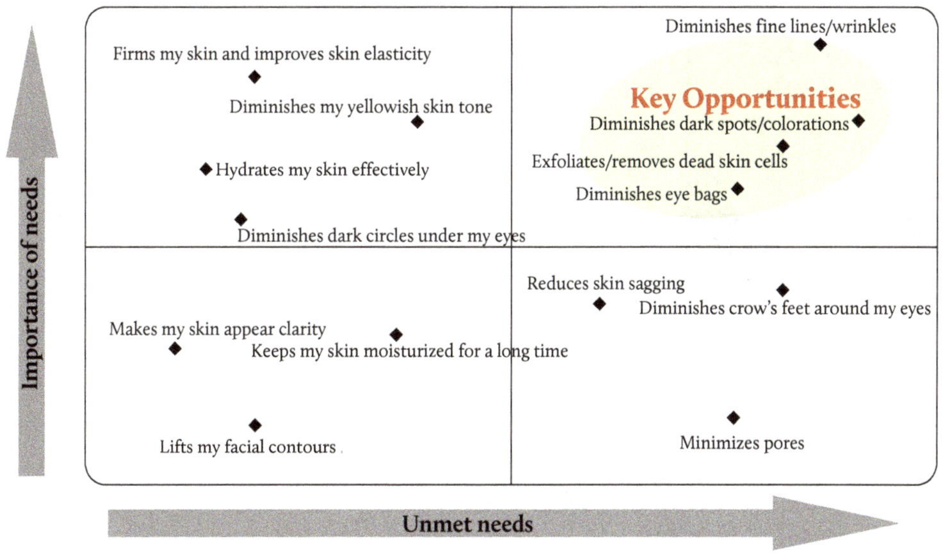

In Figure 7.5 we show a standard loyalty ladder; this is also sometimes called the *brand funnel*. It shows the percentage of people who are aware of the brand (total aided awareness), the percentage of people who have ever used the brand (ever use), the percentage people who have used it in the past 6 months (P6M), and the percentage of people who say that this is the brand that they use most often (BUMO).

FIGURE 7.5 Brand Funnel (Or Loyalty Ladder) to Monitor Brand Performance

Funnel Definition	How do brands perform?			
	BRAND A	BRAND B	BRAND C	BRAND D
Total Aided Awareness	79	74	48	56
Ever Use	24	21	9	15
P6M Use	12	11	4	4
BUMO	11	10	3	3

Figure 7.6 shows an example of a brand association map. This map shows how brands are associated with certain attributes. In this example, Brand C can be described as a brand associated with discounts, whereas Brand D is more associated with well-known, high-quality, attractive products. There are many more analyses possible, but these examples show the variety of analytical tools that can be used in U&A research.

FIGURE 7.6 Brand Association Mapping

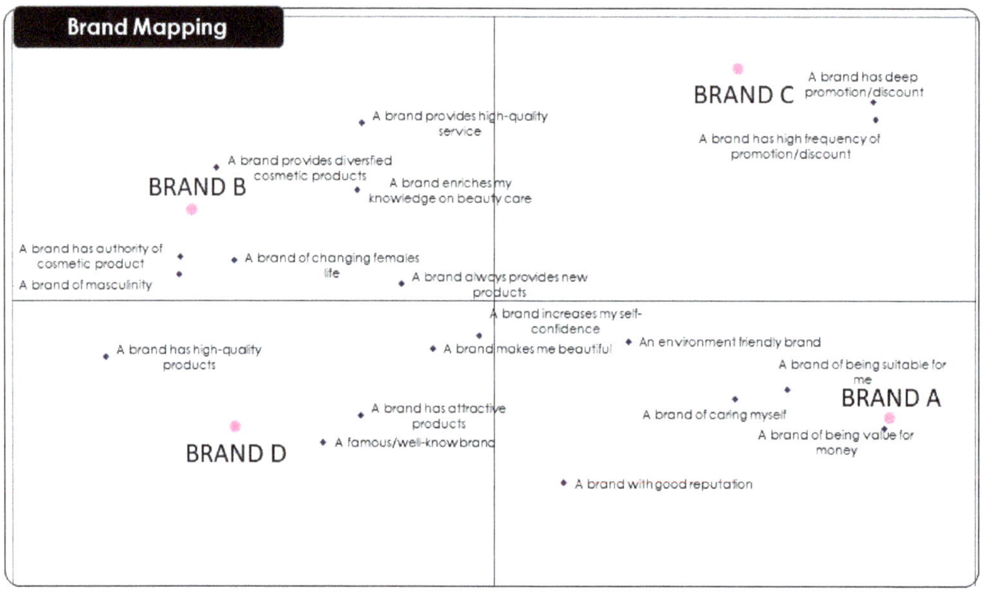

There are many pitfalls to such large and complex studies, as we can see from the following case study.

Case Study

A senior Unilever insights manager once told a story about a very large global U&A study in the laundry detergent market. It took the research agency months to do a qualitative pre-study to decide what topics to cover in the quantitative research. It then took a few months to design, test, and agree on a 60-minute questionnaire. Then it took more weeks to translate the questionnaires into local languages. Then was a long fieldwork process of trying to find many thousands of respondents in each market who fit the selection criterium and were willing to complete a 60-minute questionnaire. Then it took another few months to process and clean the data and create the data tables. And, finally, it took another 2 months to write and present a 1,000-page report.

When the agency finally was ready to present the results to the client, 12 months after the start of the project, the senior brand manager, the key stakeholder, said that she was not interested in the results for two reasons:

1. After 12 months, most of the markets changed so much that the results of the study were not so interesting anymore (new insurgent brands and innovative products had hit the markets and were not included in the research).
2. She did not believe that any respondent would be truthful answering a 60-minute questionnaire. She believed, and rightfully so, that respondents would have gotten bored at some point and started randomly clicking through the questionnaire

As a result, the client wasted over a million dollars and many, many hours of hard work on the research. For these reasons, many clients are changing the way they conduct U&A studies, as the next part of the case study illustrates.

Case Study, Part Two

In the example, the Unilever insights manager made some extreme changes to his next U&A study. He decided to ask zero questions, but instead, during the research, he had cameras installed in people's homes to capture real washing behavior. He asked respondents to wear camera's while they were doing laundry, and he analyzed social media to see what people post on the topic. The results were quickly analyzed and gave very interesting insights into people's real behavior instead of claimed behavior. For example, it showed that how women split white from colored laundry is very different from how men do this. This did not show up in previous survey questions.

This example shows how traditional U&As, with their lengthy and often tedious survey formats, are out of touch with today's digitally connected, visually obsessed, and time-deprived consumer. If people have shortened the phrase "thank you" to "ty" when texting and express themselves through images instead of words on Instagram, how much longer can we expect them to answer a 40-minute survey or write down candid details? With some of these tedious long questionnaires with many recall questions, the research can feel like driving backward while looking through your rearview mirror. When the road is straight, this approach may get you to your destination; but when the road is curvy, you will likely crash because you can't see all the twists and turns. In other words, a traditional U&A won't give powerful insights in today's changing markets. Moreover, when you depend on the rearview mirror, you are missing the scenery along the way: Respondent recall lacks the richness and emotion that help marketers discover true insights.

For this reason, researchers are increasingly changing the way they conduct U&As to capture real behaviors and actions, not stated responses. They prefer to connect with consumers in the moment, not through recall. New technologies have made it easier to connect with consumers in the moment more accurately, and to capture their real behaviors and actions. Technology can help lessen the burden for respondents by reducing or eliminating survey questions and, at the same time, provide marketers with more accurate information because they are behavior based and do not rely on respondent recall. Passive monitoring through a simple app on the respondent's phone can track respondents' online browsing and shopping behavior. Or, tracking respondents' movement through a GPS sensor app shows respondents' offline behavior (where they shop, how long they commute from home to work, etc.). Researchers are increasingly asking respondents to take a pictures or videos on their mobile phone and use advanced artificial analytics to get deep insights from these images. These new technologies can help the researcher further reduce the length of the questionnaire while getting more accurate data. These are truly exciting and inspiring times to be a market researcher.

In summary, U&As are a very important and strategic tool in the researcher's toolkit to help the company make strategic decisions on new product development, portfolio decisions, brand positioning, and much more. It is an exciting time to work on these studies. There is an abundance of available consumer behavioral data, we can use mobile for research, and there are new types of analytics to allow the researcher to shorten the questionnaires and get more accurate and deeper consumer insights.

7.3 MARKET SEGMENTATION STUDIES

If a company is looking for new growth opportunities, they can conduct a U&A study, but they may also decide to do a market segmentation study. The general business objective is the same for a U&A and a market segmentation study: find ways to grow your business. The difference is that in market segmentation we hypothesize or suspect that consumers may be heterogeneous. By understanding how consumer may be heterogeneous with respect to what they want or need from a category, or brand the firm hopes to offer more attractive products and services than the competition.

In a perfect world, a company would know consumers' individual needs at any given time and on any occasion. With this knowledge, companies would be able to offer a product (or a service) precisely targeted to you every time you are interested at precisely that price that you are willing pay. The internet and social media can help us to get close to this perfect marketing world, but for most companies it is not possible or not profitable to create a different product for each existing consumer. This creates a challenge: The more customers we can offer a (somewhat) customized product (or service) the more consumers are going like and buy our products. However, by doing this we lose efficiencies of scale. Imagine you are producing 1000 cars this month, and each car is painted with its own unique color palette. Maybe we would make 1,000 customers happy as they get exactly the color they want, but it would be very expensive to produce because after each car the coloring machine needs to be cleaned and re-filled with new paints. That would be time-consuming and hence costly. So, as an alternative, companies are looking for groups of people or occasions that they can target.

For this they need to know about consumers' heterogeneous needs, but instead of mass customization, they look to identify groups of consumers (segments) in such a way that the consumers within one segment are very similar in terms of what they need/want, how they may behave or buy, or attitudes with respect to the category or regarding issues related to the category and consumers from different segments are very different with respect to what they want/need, how they behave to identify segments where the consumers are homogeneous on these aspects. For example, beauty companies may look for young women interested in hair coloring, sports companies may look for active outdoor people, chocolate companies may be interested in holiday seasons, beer companies in people who like to go to bars because they seek to bond with friends while another "group" (segment) seeks to enjoy a special beer just for the taste. Marketers are looking for specific segments they can target with new products, segment-specific targeted advertising, different brands, with different distribution options (e.g., for the time-strapped worker there may be a drive-through window at Starbucks).

Segmentation research is aimed at finding these targetable segments, and in this section we will discuss the art and science of segmentation research.

7.3.1 Terminology and Concepts

Market segmentation is a useful marketing approach if we believe (hypothesize) that our target market is heterogeneous; in other words, different segments exist that are different in terms of want or need (e.g., Smith, 1956; Wedel, 2001), how consumers feel about the category or life in general (attitudes), or how they behave (e.g., heavy users versus light users).

To segment your target audience in different segments we need to decide what types of variables we are going to use to find possible segments. One distinction we need to think about is between active and passive variables. Active segmentation variables are those variables that we are actually using in our analysis (e.g., cluster analysis, see Chapter 5) to identify the number and nature of the different segments. We also have passive variables in a segmentation study. The average or median values of these variables will be calculated based on the identified segmentation solution, and as such these variables contribute to the interpretation of the segments but don't drive the composition and nature of the segments. There are various types of variables that can be used as *active* segmentation variables: (a) consumer needs and wants, (b) consumer attitudes and lifestyle, (c) consumer behaviors, (d) psychographics, and (e) demographics/firmographics. Sometimes active segmentation variables are referred to as segmentation bases (for an extensive discussion see Wedel & Kamakura, 1998). It is not uncommon to find all these types of questions in a segmentation survey, and the segmentation that is identified as best can easily include variables from each of these different variable types.

Types of Segmentation

With these variables different types of segmentation can be created:

1. Needs-based segments. For example, in our coffee example, we might find a segment of consumers who drink regular coffee but want high-quality, a second segment who drink a mixture of regular and decaf and want a reasonable price, and a third segment who prefer flavors and only drink coffee occasionally.
2. Behavior-based segments. For example, in the earlier used skincare product, we might find a segment where consumers use skincare for general purposes (i.e., they use skincare to keep the skin moisturized and protect against sunburn, and they use it on a daily basis). A second segment may look for a specific benefit (e.g., reducing redness, or wrinkles, or dark spots). For example, they may use a skincare product after they exercise to reduce the redness that results from heavy sweating. A third segment of consumers uses skincare products that add a layer of tanning to their skin.
3. Attitudinal and psychographic (lifestyle) segments (e.g., see Beane & Ennis, 1987; Ziff, 1971; and Van Auken, 1978). We typically ask a set of questions pertaining to the category, or pertaining to a person's view on life, technology, their values, activities, interests, opinions (AIOs), aspirations, and so on. Often respondents are shown a set of statements and are asked to what degree they agree with these statements, or, in some cases, how important these values or aspirations are to them.
4. "Attribute importance"–based segments. For example, as firm may want to find out if consumers attach to different product attributes. Attribute importance can be determined in a variety of ways, ranging from direct questioning (simply ask respondents to rate or rank a set of product attributes), or using methods where consumers have to tradeoff product attributes (e.g., methods such as conjoint analysis [e.g., Green & Srinivasan, 1978] and Maxdiff analysis (Louviere et al., 2013)). For example, in Vriens, Oppewal, and Wedel (1998), consumers were segmented based on how important attributes of coffeemakers were (e.g., brand, price, capacity, etc.). Related to attribute importance–based segmentation is benefit segmentation. For example, Haley (1968) segmented the toothpaste market using benefits.
5. Demographic/firmographic segments. In some cases, we have seen firms use basic demographics or firmographics to identify different segments. A very simple segmentation, if you are a business-to-business firm, could be small firms, mid-sized firms, and large firms. Such a segmentation is easy to understand, and the firm will easily know where to find these different segments. An assumption with such a segmentation is that small-sized companies have different needs than mid-sized companies or large firms. Unfortunately, that is not always the case. Another example could be cigarette brands: Some may be targeted to women, others to men; or vitamins: Some may be targeted to adults of 50; and so on. LinkedIn, as another example, determines where someone is in their career based on a number of demographics such as their derived

age from their graduation year, title, and seniority, and then groups members into career lifecycle stages. This helps LinkedIn better cater to members' needs. Demographics as the sole basis for segmentation is probably not recommended anymore (see Yankelovich & Meer, 2006).

6 Occasion-based segments. This is also based on behaviors (i.e., in what situations consumers use or consume a product). For example, a global ride-sharing company used an occasion-based segmentation to find targetable occasions when people use a ride-sharing service. They used a specific occasion, going out to for a quick snack, to launch a new, successful offer in partnership with a large fast-food restaurant where people could use the ride-sharing service to get snacks delivered to their house. Another example of an occasion-based segmentation can be found in the chocolate category. A global chocolate manufacturer was looking at a people-based segmentation research of the candy market. It could not find any differentiation among chocolate eaters. However, when it zoomed in on the different emotional needs in the chocolate market, it found eight very distinct needs-based segments. One day you want chocolate to keep you going (black segment), and another day you want to have a premium chocolate to show off (purple) or to share with your kids (brown). The reason why this is called an occasion-based segmentation is not because we group respondents in segments, but rather we group occasions or needs together, where any given occasion may or may not be relevant for any given respondent. This needs-based segmentation helped create a portfolio of products targeting a variety of needs-based segments and helped the chocolate company increase their sales as a result.

The choice of the right type of segmentation is not an easy one. It depends on the objectives and the business decisions. Is the objective to target people with specific campaigns or to understand specific shopping behaviors? Then the answer may be a demographic segmentation. If the purpose is to develop effective advertising strategies, then an attitudinal segmentation is preferred, and if the goal is to reposition different brands, an occasion- or needs-based segmentation may be better, and if it objective is to develop a new product, a needs-based segmentation may be better. There are no precise rules for which segmentation solution to use in which specific case. The better you understand the business objectives, the easier it will be to decide. Often, in practice, several types of segmentation bases are included in a study (e.g., Foudermayr & Diamantopoulos, 2008).

The Application of Segmentation

If a good segmentation is found, the insight can help firms in various ways; exactly how depends on the active segmentation variables used in the segmentation study.

One, segmentation insights can be used for category growth. For example, it may be that the firm identifies a segment with a specific need that has not been addressed in the market (we refer to such segments as white spaces). For example, a chocolate company identified a need for luxury indulgence. A moment for people to curl up on a couch after a long day at work and indulge on a high-calorie, luxurious bar of chocolate. There were no products available for such a moment. When they introduced a new premium bar in this market, it was an immediate success.

A second application is brand strategy (though there is some discussion about whether this is the right application for segmentation) (e.g., see Fennel & Allenby, 2002; Kennedy & Ehrenberg, 2001; Vriens et al., 2017). Specifically, at the segment level we can look at various segments and view how our brand compares with competing brands, and we can look at brand usage across segments. This will give us insight into who we are competing with and where we may fall short. The same chocolate company also noticed that all their other brands were targeting the same needs-based segment: sharing with friends. All their products came in bags of shareable small chocolate bites. They used the results to optimize their brand portfolio to target different segments, and the results were a significant increase in sales and market share across all brands.

Third is product development; many companies use segmentation research to develop products that are aligned with the needs of a target segments. The rise of a segment of beer drinkers worried about calories has resulted in the development of new low-calorie brands like Marston Resolution from the UK, with less than 2 grams of carbs and only 85 kilocalories.

Fourth is pricing strategy. Airlines have been very good at optimizing airfares according to price sensitivities of target segments. Business travelers pay different fares than tourists, prices are higher for last-minute bookers, consumers pay different prices if they buy direct versus through a travel agency, and so on.

Fifth is communications/media allocation. For example, a large pet food company personalized their direct communication to the kinds of pets people have. Cat owners get advertising for cat food, owners of puppies get food targeted to young dogs, and so forth. As an additional example, a beer company that did a segmentation study and found its most profitable segment to be young blue-collar males targeted this segment on television with a fun add during a Superbowl game.

Sixth is channel optimization. For example, a beauty company saw its fastest growing segment, young girls, mainly using YouTube and TikTok for beauty advice. With this information, they moved all their advertising and product placement to these channels and made ecommerce the main channel for their brands.

7.3.2 The Segmentation Marketing Research Process

Segmentation studies are very hard to implement successfully. There are several reasons for this. One, stakeholders may not be very familiar with how segmentation works. Two, the process itself is somewhat unstructured (i.e., there is not a very clear objective against which we can measure whether a segmentation is a good one). Three, developing segment-specific market approaches is not easy, and it takes resources to develop different value propositions for different segments (e.g., Dibb & Simkin, 2009). In this section, we discuss the steps typically done in a segmentation study, and we have found these to be vital in ensuring the study will yield robust results and will be acted on by the business stakeholders. In Table 7.2 we outline the various steps.

TABLE 7.2 Overview of a Market Segmentation Study

	Steps	Goal
1	Stakeholder interviews	• To ensure the business stakeholders are supportive of the project, they need the information and are willing to be engaged throughout the project.
2	Design of the study & data collection (e.g., qual, quant)	• There are various ways in which a market segmentation study can be set and this determines what types of questions we can answer and what type of segments we can identify. • This is closely related to the previous step, but here we need to determine how exactly we will ask the questions. This has implications for the analyses we can do after the data has been collected. In this step we also need to think carefully about the sample and sample size
3	Data collection	• This is the step where the actual interviews are being conducted or send out or in general where the data is collected.
4	Segmentation analysis, evaluation & selection optimal solution	• The analysis is a very substantial part of a segmentation study. See details in Table 7.3 • After a final segmentation solution has been selected—firms want to be able to identify a short list that will help them predict segment membership
5	Development of the typing tool	
6	Activation	

Stakeholder Interviews

A first step is, or should be, stakeholder interviews. In this phase you want to interview the people in the organization who will use, or are likely to use, the results of the segmentation research. Typically, stakeholders are people from a variety of teams such as marketing (brand managers, product managers, marketing communications), public relations, sales, R&D, and sometimes even the CEO him- or herself. The objective in these stakeholder interviews is to understand how the results of the segmentation research will be used. The final output of this phase is a decision on the specific segmentation tool to be used and, as a result, a more detailed outline of what is needed in the next phases.

Design of the Study

Next, we need to think about the best design for the study. Specifically, this means doing the following:

1. Considering whether qualitative research is needed as a first step. Qualitative research can help us understand "what we don't know we don't know" and can help as input for developing a survey. Types of qualitative research used include focus groups, online community research, one-on-one interviews.
2. Developing a survey. The researcher needs to understand the wide range of attitudes, emotions, behaviors, and needs and wants in the use of products in the category. The final output will be a quantitative questionnaire. The danger with segmentation research is that the questionnaire can become quite lengthy. The role of the researcher is to make sure the questionnaire includes the key questions but leaves out any non-relevant questions. The goal should be to keep the length under 20 minutes, especially when the fieldwork is done through mobile phones. There are new, exciting tools to reduce the length of questionnaires such as the use of pictures instead of attribute statements. It is the task of the researcher to reach out to research companies, like Ipsos, to get support in the development of an efficient and effective quantitative questionnaire using the newest and most innovative research techniques and to manage the fieldwork. A segmentation study questionnaire, in general, contains four topics:
    - Screener, demographics, and profiling metrics (e.g., age, gender, income, household size).
    - Behaviors and activities: What do consumers do in the context of the product category? In some segmentation studies we ask about occasion-specific behavior and needs (e.g., types of category usage occasions, emotional and functional needs). For example, if the product category is beer, we may want to know during what occasions consumers drink beer (e.g., at home while watching TV, in a bar while hanging out with friends, during a dinner date, etc.).
    - Needs and wants: What do consumers need or want? In some cases, we may ask about their aspirations.
    - Values and category attitudes: Questions pertaining to attitudes around general life and around the category.
    - Competitive landscape (e.g., awareness, consideration, and brand perception).

You may note that the question types are very similar to a U&A study. In this design stage, it is vital to think about how the segmentation insights are going to be used. For example, if the firm has considered developing different products for different segments, then we need to ensure we have specific enough questions in the survey that will help with such an objective. Most likely, the survey should contain detailed questions about consumer needs and wants. If the goal of the segmentation study is to support advertising and sales, then we should have detailed information from attitudes, maybe psychographics, and the purchase process.

Data Collection

In the fieldwork phase (when the actual data is being collected), a key issue to resolve is the sample size. A general rule of thumb is that the minimal sample size for a segmentation research is, at least, 800 to 1,000 respondents. The reason is that, on average, a researcher will find four to five segments. The segments can vary in size, but for a segment to be economically viable most firms would not accept segments that are not at least about 15% of the sample. This would give us a sub-sample of about 120–150, enough to get a read on the average values of the segmentation variables and make a robust comparison with the values in other segments (usually via one-way ANOVA, or the $\chi 2$ analysis sometimes followed by adjusted residuals; see Chapter 6; see also Lewis & Burke, 1950; and Sharpe, 2015).

Other decisions that may have to be made during data collection include (a) whether quotas need to be set for hard-to-reach groups (e.g., older consumers who may not be online much; high-income consumers, etc.), and (b) whether in the early stages of the data collection one needs to look at a small sample just to check if the respondents have filled out the survey properly (were too fast, took too long, straight-lining, etc.).

Analysis

The goal of the analysis is to identify market segments that are meaningfully similar to yet different between one other. This requires both analytical skills as well as creative skills. It is often referred to as a balancing act between art and science. The best segmentation research exhibits a balanced blend of marketing science, artful insight, and pragmatic usefulness. In Table 7.3 we outline the key steps in segmentation analysis. We briefly discuss these steps next.

As with any type of analysis, the analysis phase starts with data cleaning, preprocessing, and data exploration. We may look at the missing data at the variable level: variables with too many missing values may be left out of the segmentation analysis, while for other variables, with more acceptable levels of missing data, we may want to apply missing data imputation. In this step, we also look for suspicious survey completion metrics. For example, one of the authors conducted a segmentation study where we used a survey that was estimated (in pre-testing) to take around 25 minutes to complete. In addition, we had four question batteries, each consisting of roughly 20–25 items that each used the same five-point Likert agreement scale. For each battery we looked at how many items a given respondent gave the same score (e.g., on all 20 battery questions a 5, or a 1, etc.); those respondents were eliminated from subsequent analysis as it was highly likely they were not thinking about each item; they just wanted to get the survey done fast.

In most cases, a segmentation questionnaire includes many variables that can be used in the actual segmentation analysis (often a first analysis is K-means, see Chapter 5). As we mentioned in Chapter 5, cluster analysis may not work well with many variables. To deal with this problem, in commercial practice, we often use factor analysis to see if we can reduce a large set of items to a few latent factors. For example, in one of our segmentation projects, we had four question batteries; each battery was factor analyzed, and for each battery we reduced the set of items to between two to four latent factors, so instead of 80-plus variables,

TABLE 7.3 Overview of Segmentation Analysis

Steps	Key elements to keep in mind
Cleaning, pre-processing data, exploratory analyses	• See chapter 5. Researchers review the extent of missing data, outliers, suspicious response patterns such as straight-lining, etc.
Pre-analysis: e.g., factor analysis	• Factor analysis is commonly used in segmentation studies. It is recommended to use factor analysis, and not principal components analysis (see chapter 5). Be diligent on extracting optimal number of factors (don't just rely on scree plots). • Use factor scores for selected variables in the next analysis step or select a few variables per factor that can represent that factor.
Segmentation analyses	• Use K-means, K-modes, or latent class analyses to identify the market segments. • Typically, a large number of segmentation solutions are generated. At first, these solution are evaluated based on inter-segment differences on the active segmentation variables. The degree to which there is a difference between segments can be summarized and tested with the SMD-value. • Once, a few viable solutions have been identified show differences in passive segmentation variables.
Evaluation of possible solutions with stakeholders & selection optimal solution	• Segmentation solutions are not just selected based on statistical criteria. Often, they are reviewed in the context of a business situation.
Typing tool	• Once a final segmentation has been selected, a typing tool is developed: i.e. a predictive model is developed predicts segment membership based on a set of background.

we conducted the cluster analysis on 12 latent variables (review the section on factor analysis in Chapter 5). Factor analysis looks at responses to different questions. If some questions get similar responses from all respondents, they can be grouped together and replaced by a common factor.

With these factors, the researcher should conduct a clustering analysis to determine the optimal segment solution. There are many statistical algorithms available for this. In commercial practice the most commonly used methods are K-means (sometimes K-modes), hierarchical clustering (of which there are several varieties), and latent class analysis (see e.g., Vidden et al., 2016). There are many different clustering methods, some of which are used in specific situations. It is the choice of the researcher to choose one, or various, algorithms to run a clustering analysis.

With each algorithm the researcher will choose the number of clusters to be identified. In general, the researcher will ask for a two-, three-, four-, five-, and six-segment solution. These solutions are then compared on statistical criteria (e.g., silhouette score; e.g. Vriens et al., 2018). Often, in segmentation studies many possible segmentation solutions are generated (in a recent study we were involved in we produced over 100 solutions). These solutions are typically reviewed by the internal marketing research client and the external marketing supplier team and narrowed down to a few viable solutions. This is partially a subjective task. Yes, researchers will use statistical criteria, but these criteria will not be distinguishing enough across solutions. In none of the commercial applications the authors have worked on (we estimate collectively, we have been involved in probably 30-plus segmentation projects) was the optimal segmentation solution determined primarily by statistical criteria. Usually, statistical fit criteria are used to weed out the solutions that are not very good (i.e., they don't discriminate between market segments, and some or all of the market segments may not be homogeneous). Hence, researchers will assess the degree to which the results are interesting, and how likely each solution is going to be useful for their stakeholders. This results in one, sometimes two solutions that are being shared with internal stakeholders (usually the internal client who manages the project and the internal client who pays for the study). We might call this stage the art of segmentation. Once a preferred solution has been identified, it is shared and explained to the broader group of stakeholders.

Consider the following small example. Look at Table 7.4. This table shows two possible segmentation solutions: a two-segment solution and a three-segment solution. Note: This is a simplified example; in most cases we have more solutions and more variables, and we add more statistics to the table.

Imagine you are the chancellor of a regional college in the Midwest, and you want to try to grow the college. You decided to do a segmentation based on broad benefits students are seeking, and the marketing research supplier presents you with the two solutions shown in Table 7.4. Both solutions could be actionable, but the three-segment solution has more detail and the segments seem to be differentiated a bit better. Note that this is somewhat subjective (though we can quantify the degree to which segments are differentiated). However, in the three-segment solution the inter-segment differences are a little bigger, and the solution lends itself to a nice interpretation: Segment 1 seek the best college that they can get into. This may not be the right target for this regional college. Segment 2 looks to go to where their friends go. The marketing communication team can probably do something with this information. Segment 3 looks for a good price, wants to remain close to home, and wants a nice campus. This segment, of course, should be one of their main targets. They could find out what features make a campus attractive and decide, within budget, what they could do to make the college campus as appealing as possible. At the same time, they could look for sponsors/donors to offer more scholarships so that they can lower the actual cost for more students.

TABLE 7.4 Two Hypothetical Segmentation Solutions

Variable	Description	Stastitic	Segment 1	Segment 2		Segment 1	Segment 2	Segment 3
Cluster Size	Cluster Size (number of respondents in segment)	Number	1430	1120		750	550	1250
Cluster Percent	Cluster Percent	Percent	56%	44%		29%	22%	49%
ACTIVE SEGMENTATION VARIABLES (BENEFITS COLLEGES)								
1-10 agreement rating scale								
variable 1	The campus appealed to me	Mean (average)	4.5	8.9		2.5	5.1	9.3
variable 2	College is close to my home town	Mean	5.5	9.1		2.9	4.1	9
variable 3	The cost of college	Mean	6.5	9.5		3.1	5.5	8.5
variable 4	My friends plan to go to this college	Mean	6.7	8.8		3.02	9.5	3.48
variable 5	This college is strong in the area I am interested in	Mean	6.6	4.9		9.5	5.6	4.4
variable 6	The college has a good reputation	Mean	7.1	6.3		8.9	6.1	3.5

In general, a good segmentation solution should have the following features:

- **Measurable**: Market segments are usually measured in terms of sales value or volume (i.e., the number of customers in the segment). Reliable market research should be able to identify the size of a market segment to a reasonable degree of accuracy so that strategists can then decide whether, how, and to what extent they should focus their efforts on marketing to this segment.
- **Substantial**: Simply put, there would be no point in wasting marketing budget on a market segment that is insufficiently large or has negligible spending power. Longevity is also important here: No market segmentation expert would recommend focusing on an unstable customer group that is likely to disperse or change beyond recognition within a year or two.

- **Accessible**: When demarcating a market segment, it is important to consider how the group might be accessed and, crucially, whether this falls within the strengths and abilities of the company's marketing department.
- **Differentiable**: An ideal market segment should be internally homogeneous (i.e., all customers in the segment have similar preferences and characteristics) but externally heterogeneous. Differences between market segments should be clearly defined so that the campaigns, products, and marketing tools applied to them can be implemented without overlap. The researcher can use statistical measurements to measure the "distance" between the segments (e.g., Euclidean or angular distance) and will have to look at the segment profiles to see if they are different enough.
- **Actionable**: The market segment must have practical value; its characteristics must provide supporting data for a marketing position or sales approach, and this in turn must have outcomes that are easily quantified, ideally in relation to the existing measurements of the market segment as defined by initial market research.

The researcher should score each segment solution against these five measures and decide which is going to help the company best address their business questions. There is often more than one acceptable solution. It is best to profile the one or two acceptable segment solutions with all available information. This will help decide which segment solution to choose. It is best to involve key stakeholders in this final decision to make it easier for them to accept and embrace the final segmentation solution.

A great way to further enrich the segments is to add information that can be found on social media like Facebook. As an example, Synthesio, an Ipsos company, has a database with Facebook and other social media data from millions of people in many countries. As a researcher, you can use the database to find people similar to your segment profile and then add profiling data to your segment profile from over 10,000 categories with country-specific consumer interest. All you need to do is to add a few questions to your questionnaire so that you can link the data from your research to the data from this database.

Alternatively, you can link the data to other databases if you make sure that you can link the data in your questionnaire. For example, you can link it to the companies' CRM or user database. Or, you can link it to other external databases with massive consumer data. In today's digital world, there are increasingly more databases available to researchers with interesting consumer data. What people shop, where they shop, what they watch, how they move, what they consumer, who they meet, and what they search for is all available in some sort of database and available at a cost.

Development of the Typing Tool

There is one other analysis activity that needs to be done after the broader team of stakeholders has determined they can use the proposed segmentation solution: The development of a typing tool. A typing tool is a predictive model that predicts what segment a respondent belongs to (the idea is similar to linear regression, except in this case the dependent variable is categorical (A respondent belongs to either segment 1, segment 2, segment 3, and so on), and hence we use multinomial logistic regression, or alternative analysis techniques that might be suitable for this. Usually, two types of independent variables are being used: (1) the active segmentation variables or (2) demograhics, firmograhics, and media usage variables. The goal is often to find a small set of predictor variables that do a decent job in classifying the respondents in the right segments. There are three reasons why firms need this. One, if the segment-memberships can be predicted by media usage, demograhics and firmograhics variables then the firm will know how to reach these segments with advertising. Two, some firms have extensive customer databases, which thousands, sometimes tens of thousands of customers in there. If the predictor variables are part of this database then this means that for each customer in my database I can make a prediction as to what segment they belong too. For example, a mobile provider used the results of their segmentation research to identify consumers in their database and personalized their service. Sophisticated and premium users would get a free replacement if they came in the store with a broken smartphone, while casual users would have to pay a replacement fee. Three, if a small number of predictor variables have been identified, then these predictor variables can be included in future surveys and as a result, the respondents in these future surveys can be profiled on the segments. A typing tool is a very important part of ensuring the segmentation can be used by the stakeholders.

Activation of the Segmentation

The final step in segmentation research is the socialization phase. The goal of this socialization is to make the company aware of the segments, bring the segments to life, and ensure the results drive real action. Because, in the end, segmentation research is valuable only if it is actionable.

The first step is to present the segments to the stakeholders. As a researcher, it is your task to make sure the stakeholders really understand these segments. The better they understand the different segments and what makes them different, the more likely they will be to act on them. Showing them data on a page is often not enough. You can create more creative pages to bring these segments to life. But you can also get more creative. For example, when a company did a large dishwashing segmentation study, they rented a large house for the presentation of the results. In each room, they built a kitchen where actors acted out how that segment did the dishes. These actors were well briefed about the typical consumer in that specific segment so that they could play the role. The company marketing teams moved from room to room to watch the actors doing the dishes. Then, they were allowed to ask the actors questions to get an even deeper understanding of the segments.

For the segmentation research to have impact, the stakeholders in the company need to embed the segmentation in their business processes. Some examples we have encountered in our practice include the following:

- The chocolate manufacturer that was mentioned before launched a new product targeted at a specific growth segment and repositioned the other products in their portfolio to better target the other segments.

- An online retailer used segmentation research to target specific consumers with different marketing campaigns, each focusing on a different emotional need.
- A car-sharing company used the results of a segmentation research to target different potential users with different marketing campaigns.

In summary, the eight rules of a segmentation research are as follows:

- Don't start until you know what the business objectives are.
- Get the key company stakeholders involved in the research.
- Choose the right segmentation approach.
- Start with a qualitative understanding of the market.
- Develop a well-balanced questionnaire, not too long, but make sure to include questions that allow you to link the results back to a database or to develop a typing tool, if you plan to do so.
- Due your due diligence in the analytical phase to make sure you find the right segment solution and involve the key stakeholders in the process.
- Bring the segments to life in the final presentation of the results.
- Embed the results in the organization to make sure you have impact.

Market segmentation is a vast topic, with many different approaches, some highly specialized. More detailed information on market segmentation can be found in Wedel and Kamakura (1998), Weinstein (2004); Foedermayr & Diamantopolous (2008), and, for a more in-depth discussion of segmentation analytics, Vidden et al. (2016).

7.4 MARKET STRUCTURE ANALYSIS

In many markets there are more than a few competitors. In such cases, it would be very useful for firms to know which competitor they are competing with most (e.g., if their brand for some reason is out of stock or not part of the store's portfolio) and what other brand consumers would choose. When consumers get close to making a decision, what two or three brands do they look at most closely? Answering these questions is referred to as market structure analysis. However, it goes further than that. In today's market it is not always easy to know who your competitors are. Many companies like to think they play in a simple category. Heineken might think it competes in the beer market, Uber in the car-sharing market, Samsung in the mobile phone market, and Harley Davidson in the motorcycle market. But when you ask consumers what they would choose if their current choice was not available, their responses may surprise you. Instead of a Heineken, a consumer may choose a glass of wine, instead of an Uber someone may choose to walk, instead of a Harley Davidson someone may choose an expensive watch, and instead of a Samsung mobile phone someone may choose a tablet computer.

It is important for companies to understand the structure of their market. Who are their competitors? What are the needs of their consumers? What are the alternative options for consumers in the market? This knowledge will help them optimize their marketing and grow market share.

As a researcher, there are some interesting tools and techniques to answer these questions. A simple and effective approach is a technique called natural grouping. In this qualitative focus group approach, focus group respondents stand around a large table with all available competitive products randomly put in the middle of the table. The respondents are then asked to group the products together in any way they think they are similar. Then they are asked to draw a circle around the groups they have identified and give the group a name. This technique helps the researcher understand how consumers cluster available products in the market.

The same can be done in a quantitative setting, where respondents in a questionnaire are asked to rate various products. With a similarity analysis, the researcher can group the products together. See Figure 7.7 for an example.

FIGURE 7.7 Example Soft Drinks Market Structure Output (Based on Needs and Moments)

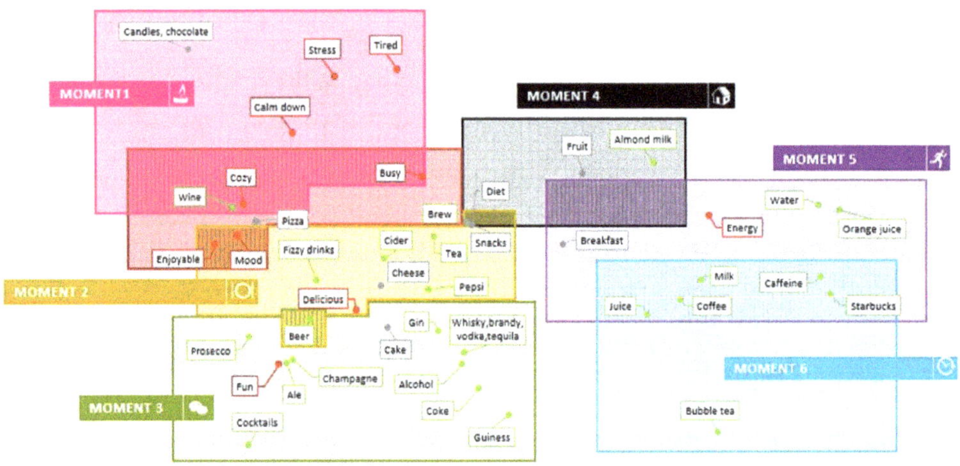

In this example, a market structure analysis is done for a soft drinks company. For example, one moment (moment 1) is all about calming down in stressful moments when you are tired. People in these situations prefer to grab chocolate or candies. In another, more fun moment (moment 3) people tend to gravitate toward cocktails, prosecco, beer, and champagne. And moments can overlap. For example, stressful can also mean busy and enjoyable (moment 2). In these moments, people tend to drink wine or cider but also tea or Pepsi. And they eat pizza and snacks.

Social media intelligence enables us to quickly, efficiently, and accurately identify consumers' mental associations relevant to brands. Co-mentioning of brands (i.e., brands being mentioned in online conversations near to each other) can be used to create a distance matrix, which feeds into structural mapping by incorporating how consumers talk about brands and how they make choices. This analysis of social data helps us derive a market structure from the consumer's perspective. Moreover, social data not only allows a static analysis of the market but also a dynamic reflection that captures how consumers' category and brand perceptions change with new product launches, competitive activity, and unforeseen events. In Figure 7.8, you can see an example where Ipsos has used artificial intelligence to codify online pet food conversations to map the pet food landscape

FIGURE 7.8 Using Humanized A.I. to Map the Pet Food Conversation Landscape

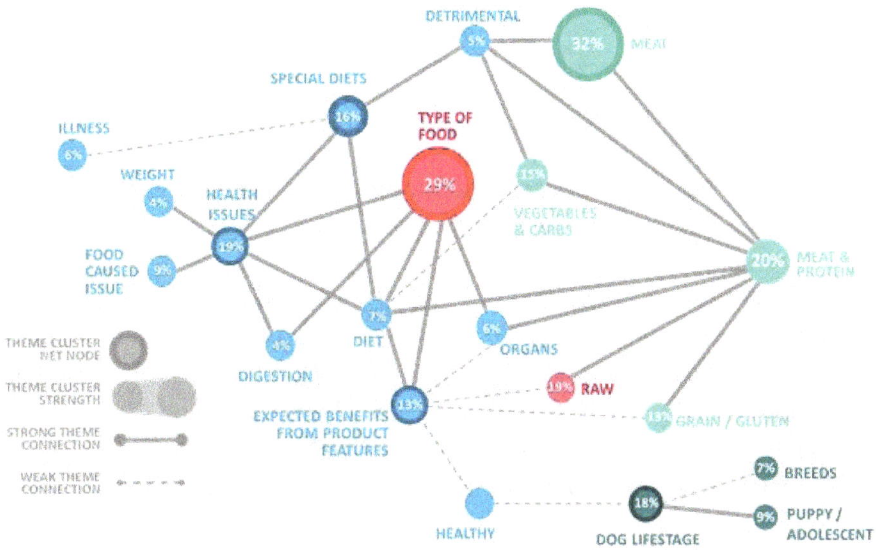

In another example, Ipsos gathered data by scraping more than 875,000 relevant comments for 15 brands from over 65,000 web sources in the United States (see Vriens et al., 2017). They used advanced text analytics to extract themes, associations, emotions, and, importantly, brand co-mentions. They then used the co-mentions to build a market structure map before and after the Volkswagen crisis occurred (see Figure 7.9).

FIGURE 7.9 Using Humanized A.I. to Map the Impact of the Diesel Crisis on the Car Brand Landscape

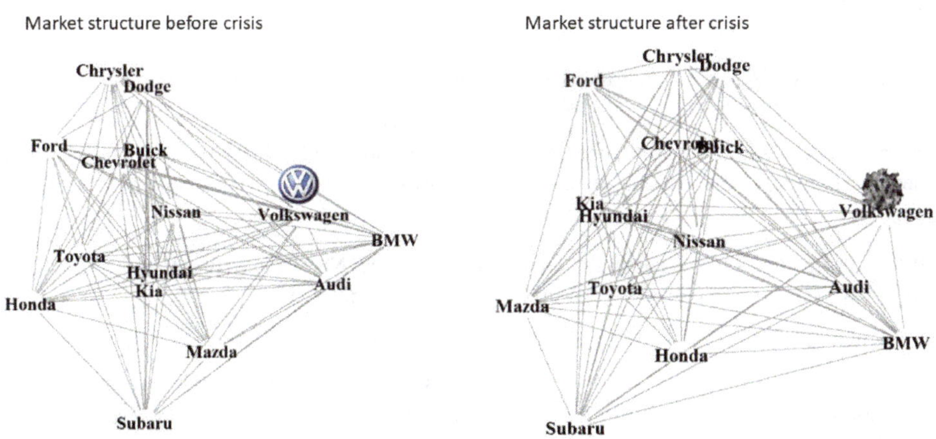

The maps that were formed showed how consumers viewed the auto market. Specifically, the market was segmented in terms of U.S. brands, European brands, and Japanese brands. However, after the crisis occurred, there was a slight shift as Volkswagen became more aligned with (lower-equity) U.S. brands and lost some connection to European brands.

7.5 QUIZ AND EXERCISES

1. Why do firms commission U&A studies?
2. What is a brand funnel?
3. Look at Figure 7.2. Critically evaluate the information in this figure. What would you conclude, if anything, from this slide? Is any information missing? What other analyses can you think of?
4. Why do firms commission market segmentation studies?
5. What is the difference between active and passive segmentation variables?
6. In the text we gave an example of a skincare behavior-based segmentation. Could this also have been an occasion-based segmentation?
7. What are the stages of a segmentation project?
8. Why is market segmentation considered both an art and a science?
9. What is a white space?
10. How do firms select the best segmentation solution for them?
11. What is the goal of market structure analysis?
12. What the relationship between market segmentation and market structure analysis?

REFERENCES

Beane, T. P., & Ennis, D. M. (1987). Market segmentation: A review. *European Journal of Marketing, 21*(5), 20–42.

Dibb, S., & Simkin, L. (2009). Implementation rules to bridge the theory/practice divide in market segmentation. *Journal of Marketing Management, 25*(3–4), 375–396.

Fennel, G., & Allenby, G. (2002). "No brand-level segmentation": Let's not rush to judgment. *Marketing Research Magazine,* 14–18.

Foudermayr, E. K., & Diamantopoulos (2008). Market segmentation in practice: Review of empirical studies, methodological assessment, and agenda for future research. *Journal of Strategic Marketing, 16*(3), 223–265.

Green, P. E., & Srinivasan, V. (1978). Conjoint analysis in marketing: New developments with implications for research and practice. *Journal of Marketing Research, 54*(4), 3–19.

Haley, R. I. (1968). Benefit segmentation: A decision-oriented tool. *Journal of Marketing, 32*(3), 30–35.

Kennedy, R., & Ehrenberg, A. S. (2001). There is no brand segmentation. *Marketing Research Magazine*, 4–7.

Lewis, D. & Burke, C.J. (1950). Further discussion of the use and misuse of the chi-square test. Psychological Bulletin, 47, 4, 347–355.

Louviere, J., Lings, I., Idslam, T., Gudergan, S., & Flynn, T. (2013). An introduction to the application of (case-1) best-worst scaling. *International Journal of Research in Marketing, 30*(3), 292–303.

Sharpe, D. (2015). Your chi-square is statistically significant, now what? Practical assessment, Research & Evaluation, 20, 8, 1–10.

Smith, W. R. (1956). Differentiation and market segmentation as alternative marketing strategies. *Journal of Marketing, 21*(1), 3–8.

Van Auken, S. (1978). General versus product-specific life-style segmentation. *Journal of Advertising Research, 7*(4), 31–35.

Vidden, C., Vriens, M., & Chen, S. (2016). Comparing clustering methods for market segmentation: A simulation study. *Applied Marketing Analytics, 2*(3), 225–238.

Vriens, M., Chen, S., & Vidden, C. (2018). *From data to decision: Handbook for the modern business analyst.* Cognella.

Vriens, M., Martins-Alves, A., & Chen, S. (2017). Brand segmentation using implicit measures. *Applied Marketing Analytics, 3*(2), 172–182.

Vriens, M., Oppewal H., & Wedel, M. (1998). Ratings-based versus ratings-based latent class conjoint analysis: An empirical comparison. *Journal of the Market Research Society, 40*(3), 237–248.

Vriens, M., Vidden, C., Chen, S., & Kaulartz, S. (2017). Assessing the impact of a brand crisis using Big Data: The case of the VW Diesel Emission Crisis. *DMA Annual Analytics Journal*, 107–118.

Wedel, M. (2001). Is segmentation history? *Marketing Research Magazine, 13*(4), 26–29.

Wedel, M., & Kamakura, W. A. (1998). *Market segmentation*. Kluwer.

Weinstein, A. (2004). *Handbook of market segmentation*. Haworth Press.

Yankelovich, D., & Meer, D. (2006). Rediscovering segmentation. *Harvard Business Review, 84*(2), 122–131.

Ziff, R. (1971). Psychographics for market segmentation. *Journal of Advertising Research, 11*, 3–9.

Image Credits

Fig. 7.9a: Source: https://www.motor1.com/features/369759/vw-logo-history/4347539/.

CHAPTER 8

BRAND RESEARCH

8.1 WHAT AM I GOING TO LEARN?

Brands play an important role in people's life. They simplify our choice process and communicate to others who we are or who we want to be. For example, think of Rolex owners, BMW drivers, shoppers at Whole Foods or Costco, or wearers of Armani. Most likely, you have an image in your mind of what types of people buy or consume these respective brands, and you probably have an idea what it is these brands have to offer.

Brands provide value to both consumers and companies. Having a strong brand has been linked to better stock returns (e.g., Mitzik & Jacobson, 2008), higher sales (e.g., Attaman & Ülengin, 2003), willingness to pay more (e.g., Yoo & Donthu, 2001), usage and share of wallet (e.g., Cobb-Wallgren et al., 1995; share of wallet is covered in Chapter 9), and higher market shares (e.g., Vriens et al., 2019), and consumers may wait if a specific brand is not available.

For this reason, brands have equity and appear in the valuation of companies. It is therefore important for companies to build and maintain strong brands; they are worth a lot of money. There are specialized brand consultancies who calculate the value of all global brands. For example, the brand valuation company Brand Finance determines the value of a company based on factors such as marketing investment, familiarity, loyalty, staff satisfaction and corporate reputation. Based on these factors, they determine what proportion of a business's revenue is contributed by the brand (see Brand Finance, 2019). Amazon is listed as the world's most valuable brand worth $187.9 billion; Shell is the most valuable oil and gas brand with a brand value of $37 billion.

In this chapter, we will discuss the role of brands for consumers and companies and how brand research can help companies strengthen their brands. But we will also briefly discuss challenges for global brands in today's disruptive world of e-commerce, mobile consumers, and technological innovations.

8.1.1 Scope

The academic literature on branding is vast. Entire journals are dedicated to this topic. In addition, marketing research suppliers often have their own brand models and theories. For example, Ipsos promotes their attitudinal brand equity approach (see Hofmeyr et al., 2007), and Kantar[1] promotes its meaningful, different, and irresistible brand approach (e.g., see Hollis, 2013). Manufacturers of brands sometimes also use their own frameworks. For

1 Kantar is one of the global marketing research firms. A competitor of Ipsos.

example, Nestlé has its House of Brands. It is beyond the scope of this chapter to cover the branding topic comprehensively, but we will cover key concepts.

The key theories and concepts that have been proposed in the academic literature and that we see applied in commercial research include (a) the law of double jeopardy (macro theory) and (b) memory theory about brand. Specific research approaches have been developed around brand equity research, brand associations and brand positioning research, brand personality, and brand architecture research. Even within some of these topics, multiple viewpoints and/or methodologies exist. What we present in this chapter is based on what we believe will be most valuable and essential to know. For those who want to go deeper we offer references to journal articles and books for further study.

8.1.2 Terminology

Brand equity research: Brand equity is often used in marketing to describe the value a company can charge for a product or a service, over and above the true value of the product or service. Brand equity research is used to calculate one score per brand to measure (and track) the brand's strength compared to other brands (and over time). These measures are often composite scores based on how well consumers like the brand, what the emotional connection is with the brand, how relevant the brand is to them and how different it is from other brands.

Brand funnel research: Brand funnel research measures and tracks how many people are aware of your brand—how many of these "brand-aware consumers" would consider purchasing your brand, how many have purchased your brand, how many have bought it more than once, how many are loyal to your brand, and finally how many of these brand loyalists really love the brand.

Brand associations and positioning research: For a brand to be considered, it needs to meet a consumer need, it needs to positively stand out from its competitors, and it needs to be emotionally relevant. Brand positioning research measures how the brand is positioned compared to its competitors and if the positioning is relevant to consumers. If it is not, brand positioning research should give precise insight into how to improve its positioning.

Brand architecture research: Brand architecture measures how a mother brand supports its sub-brands and vice versa. It helps a company better manage the value and positioning of its portfolio of brands.

Brand tracking research: To track the brand performance over time, companies use cost-efficient regular research to measure a few key brand metrics for their own brand and their key competitors at regular intervals. These metrics often include brand equity, brand funnel, and some key positioning attributes.

Next, we discuss the role that brands play in society and how important they are for firms and consumers. Then, we discuss the six brand research topics in more detail.

8.2 THE ROLE OF BRANDS

There are more than 7 billion brands globally, with new brands coming and going all the time. And brands are important assets for companies. For example, according to Brand Finance, the two best-known brands in the world are Amazon and Apple, each worth more than $150 billion. Together they are worth more than the gross domestic product (GDP) of Israel, South Africa, or Ireland. Companies spend a lot of time and money building and maintaining strong brands. Together they are projected to spend nearly $600 billion in 2019 on advertising, a growth of nearly 4% compared to 2018. Brands clearly are an important asset for companies. But why are brands so important? Why do consumers need brands? Before discussing brand research, we will discuss the role of brands in people's life and how brands impact sales.

People are always unconsciously looking for ways to simplify their life. Our brains are hardwired to use shortcuts or heuristics to simplify decision making. Heuristics can include the use of stereotypes, the rule of thumb, an educated guess, an intuitive judgement, a guesstimate or common sense. And the more complex people's life gets, the more they depend on such mental shortcuts. This is an evolutionary trait. Brains take up over 25% of our daily calorie consumption yet only make up 7% of our body mass. For the brain to function most efficiently its goal is to form habits, learned behaviors that are unconscious and conditioned over multiple experiences so that actions are automated to minimize energy consumption and so that the brain can redirect its spare energy to dealing with new experiences that require conscious processing.

Brands are a perfect tool for people to make mental shortcuts. "Brands are symbols that signal expectations of outcomes based upon our past beliefs and impressions" (van Praet, 2012, p. 21). Through the brand image, the brand unconsciously reminds people of their past experiences with the product, their feelings, their emotional connection to the advertising, past occasions they had when they used the product, and so forth. The color of Coca-Cola, McDonald's golden arches, the scent of Tide—these are brand properties anchored in our past experiences (van Praet, 2012). Brands elicit automated unconscious responses that companies want to connect to messages and value propositions that exist in people's minds and are carefully cultivated and made relevant through advertising, experiences with the product, services provided, or any repeated touchpoint between the company and the consumer. Brands engage, enlighten, and educate consumers about what to expect, both functionally and emotionally, when purchasing products and services. A Coca-Cola quenches our thirst, but it also gives us a sense of happiness and makes us feel we belong to a group of young, happy, outgoing people. It is therefore important for brands to decide what its image should be, what memories it wants to provide to its consumers. And this image should be uniquely different from its competitors but also be relevant to consumers. This is not an easy task. Brands are always looking for ways to improve their brand positioning as new competitive brands enter the market and competitors strengthen their brand positioning.

8.3 BRAND THEORY AND CONCEPTUAL FRAMEWORKS[2]

Many theories and conceptual frameworks have been proposed. Three of these, we believe, are generally accepted and are useful to keep in mind before studying and becoming familiar with specific marketing research approaches: (a) the law of double jeopardy (a macro theory), (b) memory-based theories of brands (micro theories), and (c) brand architecture (a conceptual framework).

8.3.1 The Law of Double Jeopardy (a Macro Theory)

The law of double jeopardy states that a small brand not only has fewer buyers, but that the buyers it attracts also buy the brand less often (Ehrenberg et al., 1990). So, a small brand has fewer buyers and has less loyal buyers, hence, the name double jeopardy. Ehrenberg et al.'s (1990) explanation involves mental availability: For everyone who considers the small brand, the large brand will come to mind as well, but for everyone who considers the large brand the smaller one likely won't.

Larger brands have an easier time attracting new customers because they are more familiar and a safer bet in the minds of consumers. They enjoy familiarity bias and mere exposure effect (Zajonc, 1968). Sharp (2010) refers to this as the "double jeopardy" law and has demonstrated that larger brands have a large halo effect and grow quicker simply because they tend to have stronger mental and physical availability. Brands should spark consideration and purchase when a consumer is ready to buy it and the brand is physically available.

For example, for Coca-Cola, when a consumer is thirsty and is close to a store, the first brand that should come to mind should be Coca-Cola. Coca-Cola should spark the right emotions, feelings, memories, and experiences to make the consumer pick up a Coca-Cola can and not a Pepsi can. Coca-Cola has therefore an easier time attracting customers than lesser-known brands and can capitalize on its strong brand recognition. But, as we will demonstrate later, the digital transformation is helping smaller, insurgent brands to challenge larger brands through targeting, reach, and authentic messaging at the same scale as larger brands.

8.3.2 Memory-Based Theories (Micro Theories)

Branding is memory based (e.g., Walvis, 2008). There are several "memory theories" that have been used and applied in the context of branding. Like branding, the theories on memory and the empirical literature are vast. The following is a short summary of some key memory concepts and terms that are useful in the context of brand research.

Memory is said to consist of declarative and implicit memory. Declarative is further split out in episodic and semantic memory. Briefly, episodic memory involves personal experiences, things you remember, things you have felt. Semantic memory is referred more to as things you know, a network of associations. For example, all the times you went to Starbucks may be remembered as events in time (episodic memory), but all these events translate into a network

2 Our discussion of the various theories is brief and meant as a simple introduction to these theories. We recommend reading some of the referenced papers to become more familiar with them.

of associations (semantic memory) (see, for example, Keller et al., 2016). Implicit memory refers to things that can't consciously be recalled because the act has become automatic. Following, we discuss the spreading activation theory (a more specific theory on semantic memory), and explicit versus implicit memory. Both have implications for brand research.

Spreading Activation Theory[3]

Spreading activation theory states that memory is an associative network of nodes (e.g., Anderson, 1983; Heckler et al., 2014; Quillian, 1967) in the context of branding refer to brand associations. When a buyer is cued by something associated with a brand, this then activates that brand. For example, "I need a good cup of coffee" may evoke the association Starbucks, and I may start looking for Starbuck signs. Consequently, the more attributes, occasions, needs, physical experiences, and events a person associates with a brand the more likely it is that this brand will be evoked at a relevant moment. The more associations a brand has in a consumer's mind, the easier it will be for a consumer to recall and consider the brand (Coates et al., 2004; Nedungadi, 1990). Brands that are evoked or recalled first are more likely to be chosen (e.g., Thelen & Woodside, 1997) and hence purchased. Associations can also be linked to each other. For example, "soy latte" and "healthy drink" can be linked to each other, and both or one of them may be linked to Starbucks. If only one of them is associated with Starbucks (say soy latte), then thinking of a healthy drink may still evoke Starbucks because "healthy drink" evokes "soy latte," and "soy latte" then subsequently evokes Starbucks.

The spreading activation theory is supported by brain research. Ison et al. (2015) show that single neurons in the hippocampus encode concept-to-concept associations. Positive brand associations (e.g., the logo of a favorite brand) can activate the reward system in the brain, including the striatum (Schaefer & Rotte, 2007; Schaefer et al., 2011), and Chen et al. (2015) show that firing of neurons can be specific (e.g., the association "soy latte" will have a different firing pattern than the association "healthy drink").

Explicit Versus Implicit Memory[4]

Behavioral economics show that humans rely on heuristics (Gigerenzer & Gaissmaier, 2011). The literature describes two "systems" (system 1 and 2; e.g., Evans & Stanovich, 2013), where system 1 is more automatic, autonomous, faster, and more intuitive; makes decisions and choices subconsciously (e.g., Bargh, 2002; Weinberg & Gottwald, 1982); and is affected more by emotional factors (Heath, 2009). This system is referred to as implicit memory. System 2 is more conscious and controlled and is slower and more rational. This is referred to as explicit conscious memory. Emotional connections to a brand are more important in creating brand favorability than is the transfer of rational cognitive reasons for why they should favor the brand (Heath et al., 2006). For example, I may buy Heinz ketchup because that's what my mother used to buy, and what I used to see in diners when I was a child. Buying Heinz may

---

3 Our discussion of this section is based on Vriens et al. (2019).
4 This section is based on Vriens and Martins Alves (2017).

have become a habit and may implicitly be associated with a brand. This association has been repeated so many times that it is not a conscious thought anymore, but an automatic one.

Brand Architecture

Before we discuss specific marketing research approaches that are used to understand brands it is important to take a higher-level view of how firms manage their brands. Unless you are a small firm, most likely you have several to many brands. Unilever, for example, has over 1,000 brands, and Google has over 20 brands. So, how do companies manage these brands? To build brand architecture, first the individual brands need to have a solid framework. These are the bricks of the brand architecture. This framework outlines the brands' strategy. It establishes a common language for the brand and can have different elements, but the most common elements are the brands' vision, mission, personality, and target group.

8.3.3 A Commonly Used Brand Framework: The Brand Key

The most common framework, developed by Unilever and used by many companies, is the brand key, as shown in Figure 8.1.

FIGURE 8.1 Brand Key

At the heart of the brand key sits the brand essence, the core of the brand. This brand essence is like the brand's DNA; it states, in one sentence, what the brand is all about, its value proposition. This brand essence is surrounded by the brand's values, the reasons to believe the brand can deliver on these values, functional and emotional benefits the brand delivers, and the one unique thing the brand has that other brands don't have. This is further supported by a key consumer insight on which the brand positioning is based. (We discussed insights in Chapter 2.) The insights should show a friction, a tension, or a consumer problem that the brand can solve. They also describe the competitive environment or the category a brand plays in, and often this extends beyond the obvious *direct* competitors. Knowing what the category is a brand plays in sounds trivial, but often it's not and should be an important first step to investigate. For example, for a brand like Nestle waters, who are its competitors in quenching thirst? Other waters, sports drinks, soft drinks, coffee, tea, beer, ice cream? Marketing research can help companies figure out what consumers consider the alternatives to quench thirst. Qualitative interviews with consumers are a great first step to get a deep understanding of the space a brand operates in and who the competitors are.

For LinkedIn, what's at its core is providing a product that helps its members navigate their professional life with confidence and support from their community. That is a broad value proposition and touches on many ways a consumer can go about fulfilling this goal. As such, LinkedIn plays in many different categories—think job searching, e-learning, networking, mentorship, staying up to date, and establishing a professional reputation. It competes with companies such as Google, Indeed, Skillsoft, Udemy, Facebook, and traditional educational institutions for different aspects of its value proposition. What's distinct about LinkedIn is its professionally oriented approach to networking and community building. As LinkedIn evolved from simply a digital "Rolodex" to a collection of resumes, to a site today that provides daily and industry-specific news, matches jobs, and fosters community discussions, it wanted to understand how members were perceiving the site and to what extent members use it to help navigate their professional life. One of the first things we tried to understand is what LinkedIn stands for, and asking an open-ended question to list everything that comes to mind when someone thinks of LinkedIn was a helpful technique to understand how well the value proposition, the brand essence, is ingrained in people's mind—the mental map of all the things that someone associates with LinkedIn, including the colors and physical and nonphysical assets. The brand key further describes the target group for the brand and the brand assets or its root strengths. Figure 8.2 shows an example for Dove.

Marketing research plays an important role in the development of this brand framework, as we will see later in this chapter. To develop this framework at LinkedIn we have done extensive research to understand the different needs that exist around someone's professional life, the challenges that someone encounters in their career, how well LinkedIn is positioned to address these challenges, and how much permission LinkedIn has to address current and future needs. A combination of depth interviews with existing members and non-members as well as active professionals in key geographies who are in different stages of their career and seniorities, followed by internal discussions with senior executives, helped inform and

FIGURE 8.2 Brand Key Dove Example

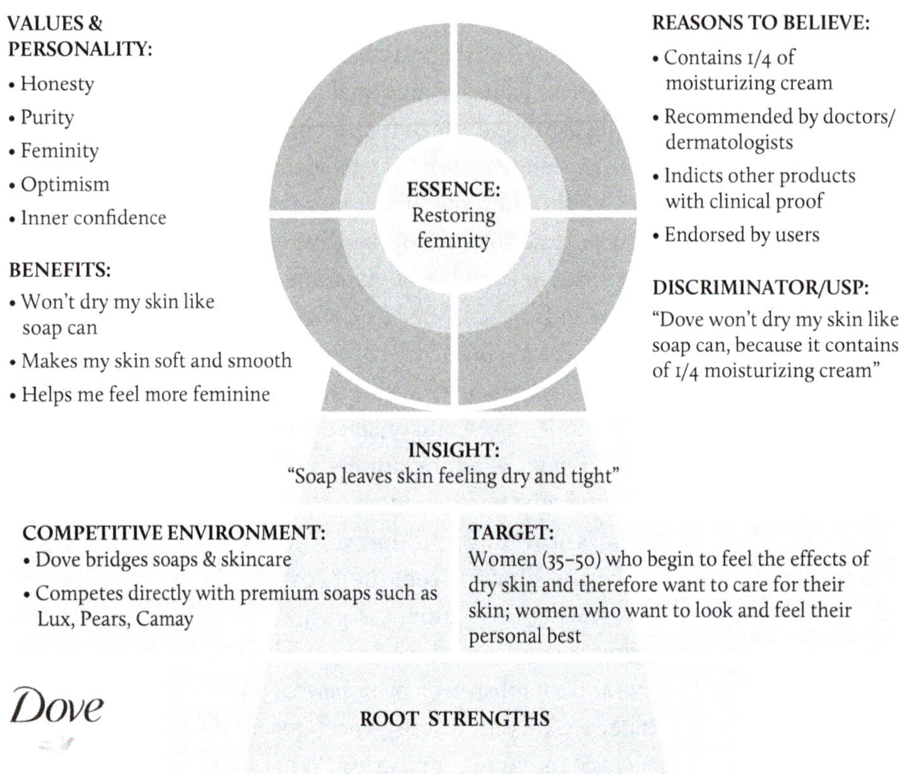

answer questions around what the brand stands for: Why do people join LinkedIn and what do we want the brand to be known for? It's important to carefully define the target population and ensure it is representative of current and future members. Subsequently, we wanted to understand where the gaps are between who we internally believe we are and how the market sees us. Do people come to LinkedIn simply to search for jobs, or do they come to LinkedIn to build relationships, establish a professional reputation, and stay informed? These are essential questions that are not immediately obvious, and it is not clear whether LinkedIn is more known for one or the other. From the feedback of the depth interviews we developed a battery of need statements such as "searching for jobs," "getting the latest industry-specific news," "building relationships," and so on. We ended up with roughly 25–30 statements and asked members, in a quantitative survey, to measure the importance of these needs, how challenging they are, and how strongly LinkedIn delivers on them, using a 7-point Likert scale. Once we collected the data we conducted a factor analysis and structural equation modeling to cluster different attributes together into meaningful themes or latent constructs—unobserved factors that we connected to overarching constructs in a hierarchical map using structural equation modeling, essentially doing a series of factor analyses to reduce the attributes down to overarching themes that are connected to higher-level value propositions such as "advancing career" with underlying constructs of "building meaningful relationships," "staying informed," and "finding and getting a job." Each latent construct explained the variance of the underlying attribute statements that were rated. Strong brands have a clear and singular value proposition, and the challenge with a brand such as LinkedIn is that it has many value propositions. It's therefore quite complex to define the brand essence and align the brand promise with what's expected through a single platform. For example, as soon as a consumer sees the golden arches, it elicits hunger, fries, and hamburgers including strong emotions that stem back from childhood, prompting people to pull over into McDonalds to satisfy their hunger. The value proposition is clear. LinkedIn's brand has broad appeal for many different types of segments and the value proposition is at a much higher level of abstraction to help connect people to economic opportunity.

8.3.4 Types of Brand Architectures

Each brand will have its own brand key. And in a perfect case, these individual brands should play together like the different instruments in an orchestra. Each brand plays a different tune, but together they make beautiful music.

Brand architecture (sometimes referred to as brand strategy or brand structure) refers to the approach that a company takes in branding the set of products that they have or plan to develop. There are different brand architecture models a company can use (e.g., Ghodeswar, 2008; Junior, 2015; Keller, 2015; Strebinger, 2014). The options for such an architecture range from a branded house to a house of brands; companies can adopt a branded house strategy, a house of brands strategy, or a hybrid.

A branded house where the overall company name is used on all brands and the master brand's equity diffuses onto sub-brands (for example, Colgate, Apple, Samsung, and Philips) or a house of brands, where a company has different brands and the master's brand and the sub-brands' equities do not diffuse as closely (for example Amsterdam Brewery [the Canadian beer maker], Unilever, P&G, and Diageo). And then there are hybrids where the master's brand's equity rests on one supporting brand and diffuses onto other brands (for example, Coca-Cola, Kellogg's, Pernod Ricard, and Danone) (see Figure 8.3).

FIGURE 8.3 Different Types of Brand Architectures

These three brand architectures are expected to generate three distinct equity flow patterns (see Figure 8.4).

FIGURE 8.4 Brand Architecture

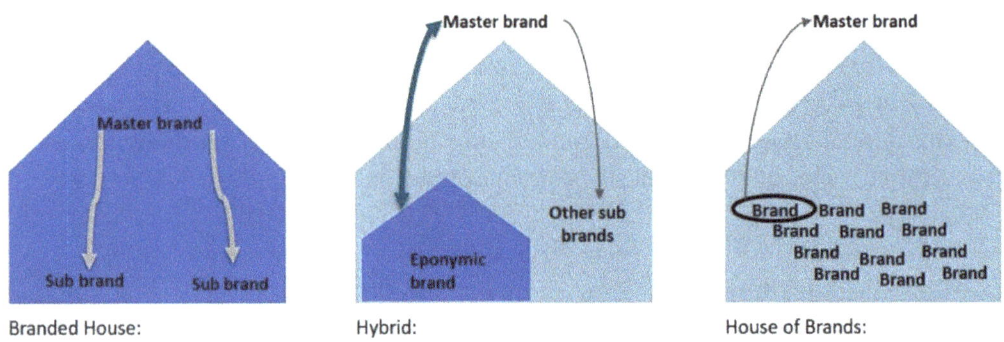

With a branded house, each of the brands needs to help strengthen the overall brand. This is the "halo" effect of sub-brands. In other words, in a strong branded house architecture where sub-brands help strengthen the master brand, there is positive equity flow between the brand and the mother brand. With house of brands architecture, there will not be much equity flow between the master brand and the different sub-brands. At most there will be a weak "echo" effect between the two. With hybrid architecture, there will be some halo effect between the master brand and the "eponymic" brand but a weak echo effect between the master brand and the other brands.

By measuring and comparing the brand equity and the brand positioning of the mother brand as well as the individual brands, the marketing research executive can see if the equity flow is working for the company. Figure 8.5 shows research that proves all three architectures have flows that go either way, with a balance between halo and echo.

FIGURE 8.5 Brand Architectures

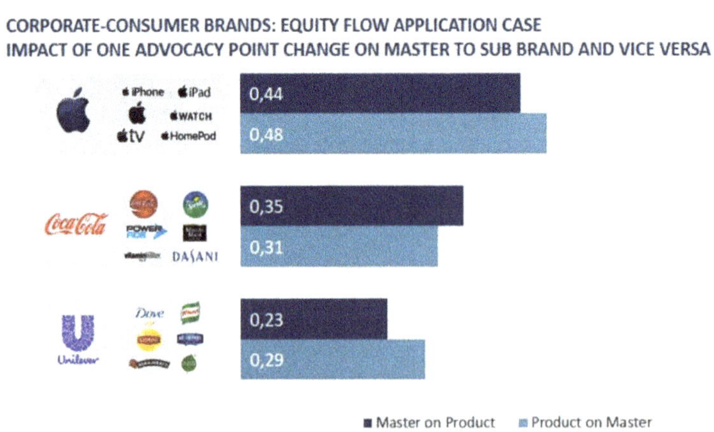

Next, we discuss various marketing research approaches used for getting insights into the brand.

8.4 INSIGHT INTO BRAND EQUITY

Brand equity research aims to answer the question "What is my brand worth?" There are two perspectives on this question: (a) a firm-level asset perspective (i.e., What is the dollar amount that should go on the financial balance sheet so that it adequately represents the brands' value?) and (b) a consumer-based perspective (i.e., How much extra would consumers be willing to pay for a product with their preferred brand?).

8.4.1 Measuring the Market-Level Brand Asset

Ailawadi et al. (2003) define brand equity as a revenue premium. For example, the equity of brand product X would be defined as the revenue premium of branded product X relative to an unbranded product Y:

> Revenue premium = {Volume of the branded product X * Price of branded product X) – {Volume of unbranded product Y * price unbranded product Y}.

Several other approaches have been proposed. It is beyond the scope of this chapter to review this topic comprehensively. One alternative is discussed by Kamakura and Russell (1993): use of scanner data to estimate a model that predicts market share based on price, promotions, advertising, and product perceptions. Brand value in their approach is the part of market share that cannot be explained by the other marketing mix variables. There are many brand-valuation approaches, each with its pros and cons. Some are published in academic journals, and some are proprietary and used by firms who sell valuation survives (for more information see Salinas & Ambler, 2009).

8.4.2 Measuring Consumer-Based Brand Equity

Consumer-based brand equity (CBBE) research can be addressed in various ways. We discuss the following approaches: (a) the attitudinal equity approach proposed by Hofmeyr et al. (2006), (b) the conjoint approach (e.g., Swait,et al., 1993; Vriens & Frazier, 2003), (c) the brand funnel, and (d) an approach based on brand associations.

The Attitudinal Equity Approach

Ipsos, a global marketing research firm, uses this approach. First, we ask in a survey what brands (in a given category) the respondents consider. For simplicity's sake, we assume we have four coffee brands and that all respondents rate/evaluate the same three brands. In many commercial studies we may have many brands. In such cases we typically ask a respondent first which brands they consider and then we ask them to evaluate only those brands. Then, for each considered brand two additional questions are asked, both a using a 10-point scale: (a) How relevant is brand [x] for you, and (b) How close are you to brand [x]? For each respondent an average is calculated for each of the brands being evaluated. In our example, we assume there are only three coffee brands and all respondents have evaluated these three brands on the attitudinal equity questions. So, for the respondent in our example we get an average for three brands. See Table 8.1.

TABLE 8.1 Attitudinal Equity of Coffee Brands (Hypothetical Example)

Brands	Green Mountain	Starbucks	Folgers	Dunkin Donuts
	Average Ratings			
How relevant is this brand for you	8.1	8.1	7.8	5.6
How close do you feel to this brand	8.3	9.5	7.4	4.5
Average attitudinal equity (average of relevance & closeness	8.2	8.8	7.6	5.1
Rank order	2	1	3	4
Zipf-distribution transformed scores into shares				

The premise of the attitudinal equity approach is that only *relative scores* matter (see also Chapter 9, as the same principle can be applied to customer satisfaction research). So, in the example in Table 8.1, Starbucks has an average (across the two attitudinal questions) of 8.8, Green Mountain, 8.2, Folgers 7.6, and Dunkin Donuts 5.1. These scores are subsequently transformed into ranks (so: Starbucks = rank 1, Green Mountain = rank 2, Folgers = rank 3, and Dunkin Donuts = rank 4). These scores can be transformed into share-of-wallet numbers using a Zipf distribution or even a simple e-base log scale ($Y=e^X$), and this can then translate into predicted market shares. Using this simple equation, the log scores for Starbucks = 6.632, Green Mountain = 3.640, Folgers = 1.998, and Dunkin Donuts = 1.64. The resulting market shares are Starbucks 53%, Green Mountain 29%, Folgers 16%, and Dunkin Donuts 2%.

The methodology has been tested on many categories and has shown that predicted market shares correlate with actual market shares very highly (0.90 or higher; Hofneyr et al., 2008).

The Conjoint-Based Approach (see Chapter 5)

Consumer Based Brand Equity (CBBE) is often used in marketing to quantify the dollar value a company can charge for a product and leads to one number that represents the dollar value of a brand vis-à-vis other brands. If two products are identical except for the brand name, say Brand A versus Brand B, the question would come down to how much more Brand A can charge for its product relative to Brand B. In this approach we can design a simple conjoint (trade-off) task where alternatives vary only by brand and price. Consider the following example. You are the brand manager for Green Mountain coffee, and you wonder what consumers are willing to pay for your brand vis-à-vis say Starbucks, Folgers, and Dunkin Donuts. We take the size of the product as a package containing 24 pods (we could vary package size too, but often we keep it simple and just select one product). Currently, the prices for a 24 pack are Green Mountain: $13.70, Starbucks: $14.40 Folgers: $14.10, and Dunkin Donuts: $13.50. For our conjoint approach we set the prices at $13.30, $13.60, $13.90, $14.20, and $14.50. Note, that we include a price level that is below the current lowest price in the market and one price level that is higher than the current highest price. We do this so that we can see the impact of moving lower or higher than the current market. It is beyond the scope of this chapter to fully discuss the conjoint approach (see Chapter 5 for an introduction). Instead, in a simple example, we will illustrate the basic components: (a) a trade-off evaluation task and (b) a calculation of utilities. Consider the following example: We have three brands: Starbucks, Green Mountain, and Seattle's Best, and we have five price levels; this means we can create 4 * 5 =2 0 price-brand combinations. See Table 8.2 for all 12 combinations.

TABLE 8.2 Brand Price Combinations of Coffee Brands

Brand-Price Combinations	Brand	Price
1	Green Mountain	$ 13.30
2	Green Mountain	$ 13.60
3	Green Mountain	$13.90
4	Green Mountain	$ 14.20
5	Green Mountain	$ 14.50
6	Starbucks	$ 13.30
7	Starbucks	$ 13.60
8	Starbucks	$13.90
9	Starbucks	$ 14.20
10	Starbucks	$ 14.50
11	Folgers	$ 13.30
12	Folgers	$ 13.60
13	Folgers	$13.90
14	Folgers	$ 14.20
15	Folgers	$ 14.50
16	Dunkin Donuts	$ 13.30
17	Dunkin Donuts	$ 13.60
18	Dunkin Donuts	$13.90
19	Dunkin Donuts	$ 14.20
20	Dunkin Donuts	$ 14.50

We could ask each respondent to tell us how likely they would be to buy a given combination, say using a 10-point rating scale, though it more common to create sets of alternatives and ask respondents what alternative in the choice set they would buy. We won't go into the details of how a conjoint study is typically set up. The data (i.e., evaluations of profiles, or stated choices) are then analyzed at the individual level or sometimes at the aggregate level, which will typically give a set of utilities for each level of both the brand and the price attribute. See Table 8.3 for hypothetical results of one hypothetical respondent.

TABLE 8.3 Utilities for Brands and Price Levels

Brands	Brand utilities	Price levels	Price level utilities
Green Mountain	0.50	$ 13.30	−0.40
Starbucks	0.60	$ 13.60	−0.20
Folgers	0.20	$ 13.90	0.00
Dunkin Donuts	−1.2	$ 14.20	0.20
		$ 14.50	0.40

As we can see from this table, Starbucks has a higher utility than Green Mountain for Respondent 1. The delta is 0.10. Recall from Chapter 5 that utilities need to interpreted relative to each other. So, how much can Green Mountain charge if it wants to be more attractive than the Starbucks alternative? Well, the difference in utility between Starbucks and Green Mountain is 0.10. A price delta of $.30 is worth $.20 utility. So, if the Starbucks product is on the shelves for, say, $14.10, then Green Mountain can make itself more attractive than Starbucks by charging $.15 less than Starbucks. Note that this calculation needs to be done for each respondent and for each brand. That's a lot of calculations and hence one typically does such calculations with the help of a simulator, as discussed in Chapter 5.

The Brand Funnel

The brand funnel can be used to get insights into brand equity. The general notion is that the more consumers know your brand, the higher the equity. Similarly, the more people consider your brand or even purchase your brand frequently, the more valuable your brand is. These metrics are often used in brand-tracking studies.

The brand funnel is based on several survey questions. First, we need to ask about awareness, and we can do this aided and unaided. Consumers won't buy a brand that they don't know. In research, one would ask an open-ended question about which brands people can think of when buying for a specific category. For example, "Thinking about coffee, what brands come to your mind?" We refer to this as unaided awareness. Any brand that the respondent lists is a brand they are aware of unaided. We can also ask a second question: "Which of the following brands have you heard of?" We would refer to this as aided awareness. The most sensitive, and most important, measure is the first brand a respondent spontaneously mentions as part of the unaided awareness question. This is the brand that is on top of the consumer's mind and the brand the respondent will be most likely to purchase.

Awareness alone is not enough. There are many brands people know that they would not consider buying. Maybe these brands do not provide the benefits people are looking for, or someone just doesn't like the brand. Therefore, brands use advertising and other marketing tools to increase the consideration rate. Marketing research often use the question, "Which of the following brands do you consider when you plan to purchase?" The total percentage of people who choose your brand from the pre-coded list shows the total consideration score. From internal research, Ipsos has seen proof that it is important to be considered, but even more important is to be considered first (Rademaker & Joosen, 2018). For example, when thinking of buying a new mobile phone, most people consider buying an iPhone or a Samsung. But when asking respondents which brand they would consider buying, more than half of the respondents would mention iPhone first spontaneously, followed by Samsung. And this "considered first" ratio matches surprisingly better with actual market shares than a "total consideration" ratio.

There may still be reasons a consumer decides not to prefer a brand over other brands. We can ask this as, "You mentioned you consider the following brands: [Insert set of considered brands]. Which of these brands do you prefer?"

The brand may not be available, it may be too expensive, or there may be another brand in the consideration set that has a better value. That's why many companies also ask people which brands they purchased. When formulating such a question, it is important to consider the exact timing. Do you ask what brands the respondent purchased in the past 2 days, the past week, the past month, or even the past year? How do you decide? In deciding what to ask, you need to consider the purchase cycle and what respondents can remember. For example, the average purchase cycle of a car is 3 years, and everyone can remember what brand of car they purchased in the past 3 years. But the purchase cycle for dishwashing liquid is roughly 2 weeks, and most people don't remember what brand they bought a month ago. Therefore, it is better to ask about the past 2 weeks for dishwashing liquid. And for beer, where the purchase cycle is roughly 2 days, and most people don't remember what beer brand they bought a week ago, it is better to ask for the past 3 days. As a marketing researcher, it is your task to decide what timeframe to use in your consideration question.

Even though the brand funnel questions are straightforward and there are no complicated calculations that need to be made, the results can be very insightful. Consider the example in Table 8.4.

TABLE 8.4 Two Brands, Two Very Different Challenges

	Brand A (number of respondents)	%	Conversion %	Brand B	%	Conversion percentages
Awareness	85	85%	85%	85	85%	85%
Consideration	76	76%	76/85=89%	44	44%	34/85=40%
Preference	24	24%	24/76=32%	24	24%	24/44=54%
Total	N=100			N=100		

As we can see from Table 8.4, both brands have the same percentage of consumers who are aware of the brand and who prefer the brand. Yet, the challenges are very different. Brand A has a high percentage of consumers who know and consider the brand. However, they struggle with closing the deal; very few consumers who consider the brand prefer it. For Brand B, there is a sharp drop-off from awareness to consideration. Once a consumer considers the brand there is a high likelihood that they will also prefer the brand. For some reason, awareness does not translate into consideration enough; maybe consumers have heard of the brand but too few know its strengths.

Brand Equity via Brand Associations

In addition to awareness, consideration, and preference, brands want to know what consumers associate their brand with. A whole variety of associations have been proposed and used. In our coffee example, we may want to know whether consumers associate our product with (a) product quality, (b) good price, (c) good taste, or (d) good variety of different flavors. These would be considered concrete product attributes. However, consumers may also have emotional reasons for liking a brand. For example, "This used to be a brand my mother used" (nostalgia). Different types of associations have been suggested (e.g., Chen, 2001). See the following examples:

- Functional versus emotional attributes
- Product versus non-product attributes
- Attributes, benefits, and values (e.g., Reynolds & Gutman, 1988)
- Brand personality (Aaker, 1997)

Examples of product attributes include color, price, quantity, packaging, and so on. Examples of functional attributes are taste, cleaning power, and affordability. Examples of what one could consider more emotional associations include "It makes me feel young," "It is a family brand," "It makes me feel excited," and "I am in control when I use this brand." Table 8.5 gives an example of functional versus emotional attributes used in a toothpaste study (from Vriens et al., 2019).

TABLE 8.5 Functional and Emotional Brand Attributes (Toothpaste)

Functional attributes	Emotional attributes
For whole family	In a good mood
Full mouth protection	Being myself among others
Trustworthy	I am a good example for others
Recommended by dentists	Secure
Preventing caries	I have total control over my oral care
Fresh breath	I made a smart choice
Whiter teeth	Seductive
Innovative	Fully stimulated

The framework that distinguishes between attributes, benefits, and values has also been successfully applied to branding. Such associations are typically first derived from qualitative laddering interviews (see Reynolds & Gutman, 1998; Vriens & ter Hofstede, 2001). The theory behind this called the means-end chain theory, and it states that consumers value attributes because they derive a benefit from them, and they value benefits because they are tied to certain values that consumers deem important. For example, a consumer may value cars with advanced safety features such as lane departure warning (a concrete attribute) because it makes them feel safer, and they value feeling safer because it makes them feel more secure and better able to care for their family (end values: security and sense of belonging). Lastly, human personality traits can also be associated with brands (Aaker, 1997). For example, Aaker (1997) defines five personality traits that apply to brands: sincerity, excitement, competence, sophistication and ruggedness. Mercedes may be associated with sophistication, Marlboro with ruggedness, and so on.

It is important to understand that, in general, it is simple for a competitor to improve their functional concrete attributes and even outperform your brand. One can build a car that is faster, accelerates better, has different colors, and so on. But it is very hard to change a brand's emotional positioning (an Android phone can be perceived as outperforming an iPhone on functionalities, but iPhone has an emotional brand equity that is very hard to match for its competitors). Therefore, it is important to add emotional attributes to any brand equity research.

In brand equity research, this process follows three steps:

1. The marketing researcher needs to determine what is relevant for consumers in the category. How do they decide what brand to choose? Through qualitative research, a list of brand attributes is generated. Attributes are short sentences that can be used to describe a brand.
2. Next, in quantitative research, the respondents are asked to score each of the brands they know from this list of attributes (e.g., "Read the next attribute and indicate how much you think this describes Brand A"). There are different approaches to rate attributes. Some prefer rating each brand on each attribute using a scale from "does not describe at all" to "completely describes." This can be an even scale (4-, 6-, 8-, 10-point scale) or an odd scale (5-, 7-, 9-point scale). Most companies prefer using an even scale so that respondents cannot use a middle point and are forced to make a choice. Another approach is to ask, for each attribute, which brand it best describes. This a much faster approach for respondents (they have only one question per attribute), but it also gives less data per brand, limiting the analytical options. There are also approaches that use a very different approach to measure attribute ratings. IRT (individual response time) is such an approach. It does ask respondents to rate each brand for each attribute, but it measures how long it takes before the respondent enters a rating. The underlying theory is that the faster a respondent answers a question, the stronger he or she feels about the relationship between the attribute and the brand. The speed of response is then used as a measure of how strongly an attribute is related to the brand.

3. Also, to measure the importance of each attribute, the respondents are asked how important each of the attributes are to them on simple numerical scale. Alternatively, the marketing researcher can use an indirect approach to determine the importance of each attribute by doing a regression analysis (see Chapter 9 on customer satisfaction where researchers also use regression to derive importance; see also Chapter 5) between the attribute scores as the dependent variables and purchase likelihood, or something similar, as de independent variable. With these brand attribute scores and attribute importance scores, a weighted average attribute score for each of the brands can be calculated. This is called a brand equity score. The higher your relative brand equity compared to your competitor, the more the consumer values your brand and the more likely the consumer is to consider your brand when it comes to making a purchase decision

8.4.3 Brand Positioning Research

So, what is a good brand positioning? A brand is considered a strong brand if it is well positioned in the mind of the consumers and has strong mental availability, so it can be easily retrieved when called on. Well-known, bigger brands tend to grow stronger than lesser-known brands. There are two, somewhat opposing, viewpoints on brand positioning. One viewpoint asserts that it only matters how many associations a brand has (e.g., Vriens et al., 2019). Another viewpoint asserts that a brand needs to decide what it "stands for" and what specific attributes it wants to be associated with stronger than the competition. However, there are several challenges with this latter view. One, the current empirical evidence does not support this viewpoint. Second, brands and products evolve. Safety for cars has evolved. Volvo certainly is not the singular safest car anymore, neither do they claim to be. For anyone doing research in branding it is useful to be aware of these two viewpoints.

Viewpoint 1

One viewpoint is that the more associations, the stronger the brand (e.g., Romaniuk, 2013; Romaniuk & Gaillard, 2007), and the more these associations are interconnected, the stronger the brand (Vriens et al., 2019). From the responses to such questions we can calculate a brand density measure, which is also a single-measure brand equity measure (see Vriens et al., 2019). However, this approach is also diagnostic as we can visualize the associations a brand has. See Figure 8.6 for an example of what we refer to as a brand association network.

We can also calculate a brand density metric and create a brand association map by using an open-ended question. For example, we may ask, "Thinking of Brand X, tell us everything that comes to your mind. This can be anything: attributes, features, usage situations, and colors." Such data need needs be text analyzed (see Vriens et al., 2019). That study also shows how such data can be used to quantify a valid brand equity number (referred to as brand density); this brand equity measure has been found to correlate highly with market shares.

FIGURE 8.6 Mental Brand Association Networks

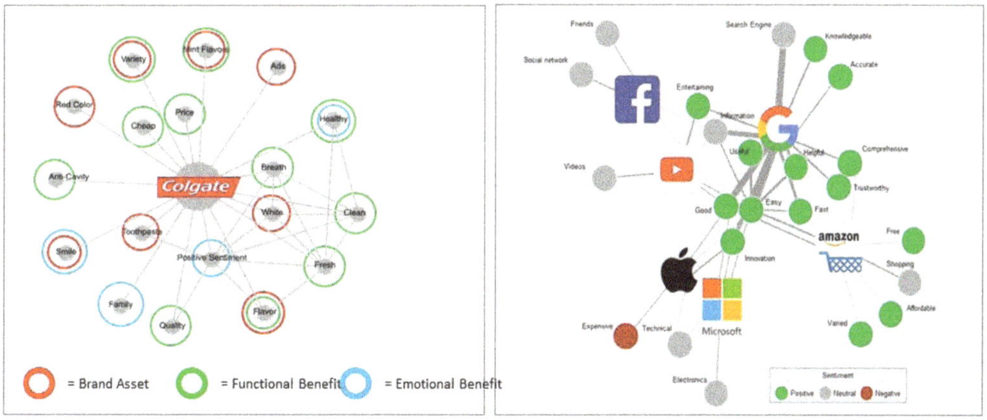

The marketing recommendations from this viewpoint are two-fold. One, increase the number of associations that evoke the brand. Two, ensure the associations themselves are as interconnected as possible.

Viewpoint 2

Another viewpoint is that a brand is stronger if it is associated with things that are relevant to consumers. Classical examples are Volvo being associated with safety, BMW associated with driving pleasure, and American Express being associated with exclusivity. For a brand to be considered at the precise moment a consumer wants to make a purchase, it needs to be relevant and positively stand out from its competitors. A consumer will not buy a brand if it is not relevant for her or him. If the brand is positioned for women and you are a man, you will probably not buy it. If the shampoo is for people with dandruff and you don't suffer from dandruff, then you won't buy it. But it also needs to be emotionally relevant. If you are a family person and the brand is positioned as an individualistic, sophisticated brand, it may not be relevant to you. And if the brand is relevant, but there are many choices equally relevant to your consumers, in other words, your brand does not stand out, then the chances are reduced that the consumer will buy your brand.

Therefore, in marketing research, the goal is to measure and track the relevance of a brand and how uniquely it is positioned on both a functional and emotional level. And with these insights, the marketing researcher can make recommendations on how to improve the brands positioning.

Brand Maps

A simple but powerful way to show a brand's positioning against its competitors is to use a multivariate map. By using brand attribute ratings ("How well does this attribute describe Brand A?"), you can create a two-dimensional map that shows how well different brands are relatively positioned against the attributes that are used in the research. If the attributes are well chosen (through qualitative research) and include both functional and emotional attributes, then these maps show how well and uniquely positioned a brand is. See the example in Figure 8.7 that shows the positioning of several chocolate bars.

FIGURE 8.7 Brand Positioning Example 1

Brand B is positioned as a bar for occasions where consumers want to indulge, Brand C is positioned as a brand used for occasions when consumers want to share, Brand F is for those moments when you want relief from hunger, and Brand H is for those moments when consumers want to stand out. Now, if the research shows that consumers eat chocolate bars to indulge or to relieve hunger, then sharing and standing out are not very relevant occasions.

If the brand you are researching is Brand A, a key insight would be that it is not strongly positioned in a relevant occasion (either indulge or hunger relief), maybe because the advertising has been focusing on breaking the bar and sharing one of the two bars with a friend. As a recommendation, a marketing researcher could propose for the Brand A brand to focus its advertising more on indulgence and move its positioning more toward Brand B. But if it would have to make sure that it still maintains its unique character (see Figure 8.8).

A key analysis in brand positioning research is to measure the size and opportunity of the different occasions or emotional positionings. How big is the indulge area for Brand A versus the hunger relief area? In other words, how many purchases are done for indulgence reasons and how many purchases are done to relieve hunger? With this information, a marketing researcher can predict how many more Brand As can be sold by repositioning the brand on a larger purchase occasion. This is a powerful analysis to predict the monetary impact of a planned repositioning strategy.

FIGURE 8.8 Brand Positioning Example 2

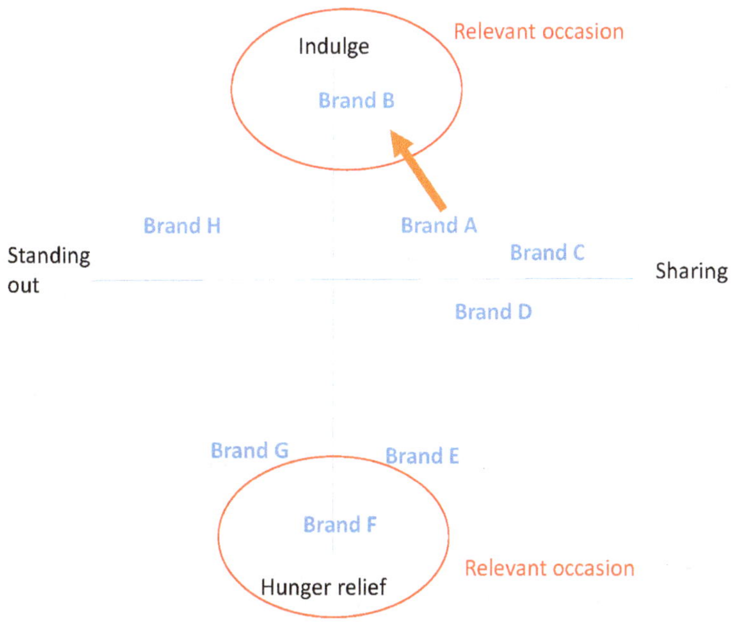

Brand managers and marketers' job is to consider the emotional positioning their brands should have in the mind of the consumers. They use marketing research to understand the emotions, feelings, needs, and attitudes of people who purchase and use their products. With this information, brands can decide on brand positioning that is relevant for these usage occasions, stand out from their competitors, and spark the right emotions.

8.4.4 Brand-Tracking Research

The primary reason why tracking research or brand tracking research is being commissioned is because the firm wants to know if its marketing is working. Maybe the marketing team has set some new awareness goals it wants to achieve for its brand; maybe the CMO has decided the brand needs to be repositioned. In such cases a budget is determined to develop an advertising and promotion campaign to achieve the set goals. How does a firm know whether these goals are accomplished? They know by executing a tracking study.

The basic concept of tracking research is to conduct the same research over and over and see how the responses to the questions change over time. The important word in this definition is *same*. In doing tracking research it is important to not change the design. If you want to compare results over time, you need to make sure the sample design, the questionnaire, and the analysis remain the same. Any small change to the questionnaire, to the sample, or to the analysis may result in a change in brand equity caused by design changes and not by real changes in consumer perception. In Table 8.6 we show a few examples of design mistakes we have seen in brand tracking research, the impact on the results, and what was done to solve the problem.

TABLE 8.6 What Happened/Impact/Resolve

What happened	What was the impact	What was done to resolve
The company accidentally interviewed slightly more males than females in one wave	Since men had a slightly more positive perception of the brand, the overall brand equity seemed to have improved	The sample was weighted to match the original sample design and the results were re-analyzed. It showed that the brand equity had not changed
Some new attributes were added to the list of brand attributes about ecommerce	The brand had a strong online presence and scored high on these new attributes resulting in a higher brand equity. The results made is seem that the brand equity improved over time	The brand equity was re-analyzed as using only the attributes from the original design. This showed that the brand actually went down over time
The company decided to move the tracking research to a competitive supplier, but leaving the design exactly the same	Since the panel used by the competitor was managed in a different way, the respondents responded slightly different to the questionnaire, The brand equity of all brands showed lower results	The company asked the original company AND the new supplier to do a parallel test. The differences were used to calibrate the results from the past and allowed comparison over time with the new supplier
The company used a new Baysian driver analysis in its brand equity analysis instead of a simple regression analysis	The new driver analysis gave different weights to the attributes resulting in a lower brand equity for the companies brand compared to its competitors	The company went back to its original driver analysis and saw no change to its brand equity over time

How do you design brand tracking research? The precise design parameters depend on the specific situation at hand. If the marketing team has decided to reposition the brand, then twice a year might work sufficiently well because brand perceptions don't change very quickly. In some cases, it can take years. In such cases, executing more than two "waves" per year will not show any significant changes to the brand equity and is basically a waste of money.

It is different, however, if you want to measure the impact of marketing campaigns (the company's own campaign or competitive campaigns). In this case, you want to do more regular waves, or even, continuous research, where you can include questions about the campaign (Have you seen the campaign? What do you think of the campaign? Does the campaign fit your ideas of the brand?, etc.). And if you want to see how the campaign influenced the brand, you want to see results before, during, and after the campaign is "on the air." In this case, the company can decide to do more frequent research, for example, monthly, weekly, or even ongoing. In the case of ongoing research, the company can choose any interval and analyze the questionnaires from that period.

The great thing about doing many waves of a tracking study is that you can analyze how perceptions change over time (longitudinal analysis). By comparing shifts in consumer perception with marketing activities or real sales data, you can predict the impact of these marketing activities on your consumer's brand perceptions. You can also analyze how shifts in brand perceptions influence sales. This kind of analysis is called marketing mix modeling. Predicting actual sales through consumer research is complicated though, as there are many more factors than consumer brand perceptions influencing sales: Are the products available in all stores? Is the price acceptable? Are there any other purchase barriers? and so on.

In most brand-tracking research studies, companies track their brand equity versus the competition, their brand positioning, and the brand funnel (awareness, consideration, and usage). For companies with many global brands, this brand-tracking research can become a costly exercise if they choose large global samples sizes, biannual waves, and long questionnaires. Often, companies spend many millions of dollars on brand-tracking research. Increasingly, companies are looking for ways to reduce the costs and are looking for more agile, social, and efficient ways to do brand-tracking research.

More agile means shorter mobile questionnaires focusing only on the key measures. Brand-tracking questionnaires, over the years, have shrunk from a half hour to less than 10 minutes. Shorter questionnaires means that these tracking studies can be done on a mobile phone, and respondents can complete them when- and wherever they are, and the result can be analyzed and reported back very quickly.

More social means that companies want to rely more on tracking what consumers say about their brands on social platforms than what people say in a questionnaire. Market research companies increasingly complement short brand-tracking questionnaires with analyzing product scores (and comments) on Amazon and Alibaba, comments people make on brands on Facebook, and what and where people post on Instagram.

Finally, companies increasingly want fully automated consumer feedback systems where consumer responses to mobile questionnaires are automatically uploaded in the cloud, analyzed, and reported on a digital dashboard where the client can (almost) real-time track consumer attitudes toward their brands.

8.5 INSURGENT BRANDS

Many companies operate in a world that is hyper-connected, always on, and changing at a lightning pace. Technology has changed every aspect of consumers' lives—how they communicate, how they travel, how they listen to music, how they shop, and so on. At the same time, definitions of gender, family, and nationality are shifting, as are political views and eco-consciousness. It is fair to say that we now live in a world that is volatile, uncertain, complex, and ambiguous. Products that are successes today can be failures tomorrow (e.g., Blackberry). Uncertainty makes it impossible to predict things; for example, vinyl records, once a dying breed, are now a sudden revival. Complexity is reflected in the fact that simple cause-and-effect chains have been replaced by complex interconnected forces (e.g., the Internet of Things). And, ambiguity is everywhere: Is chocolate good for your or bad for you? Is it worth it to own a car?

In this disruptive world, the door opened to new companies and brands who think differently than traditional companies, operate under different business models, and use technology, social media, and e-commerce to innovate faster and connect with consumers more deeply. These new brands are making an impact—stealing market share from big brands and seeing double- and even triple-digit revenue growth. They create their own rules, attacking big brands like fast and nimble military insurgents. Here are just a few examples of these new insurgent brands: Airbnb, Netflix, Monster energy drinks.

Big brands can win against these insurgents, not just by thinking and acting more like them but also by leveraging what insurgent brands don't have: strong brand mental networks, distinctive brand assets and brand equity, not to mention a wealth of data and much more capital, which enables them to invest in new technology and new distribution outlets and even acquire insurgent brands.

8.6 QUIZ AND EXERCISES

1. What is the role of a brand?
2. What is a brand key?
3. There are several options to choose for your brand architecture.
    a. Which ones?
    b. What type of brand architecture do the following brands have:
        I. Kimberly Clark
        II. Zumba
        III. Coca-Cola
        IV. Amsterdam Craft Beer Brewery (Canada)
        V. Marriott hotels
4. What is brand equity? Describe two ways in which brand equity can be approached.
5. Consider the following brand funnel (Table 8E.1). These are three brands in your portfolio, and you are responsible for their next year's growth.

TABLE 8E.1: Brand A-C

	Brand A	Brand B	Brand C
Awareness	85	85	44
Consideration	76	32	38
Preference	24	22	35
Total	N=100	N=100	N=100

a. Interpret the table. What would you conclude from this table in terms of the status and challenges of your various brands?
b. Say you have $3 million to invest. What percentage of your budget would you allocate to what brand and why (note you can use your budget to advertise and promote, or you can use it to do marketing research, or both).

6 You are asked to come up with branding research project for 23andme. This is a start-up company. How would you go about it?

7 Uber has been doing extremely well. The CEO now wants to invest in a strong brand. They have done some qualitative research and found that consumers cite mostly utilitarian reasons why they choose Uber. What would you recommend they do?

REFERENCES

Aaker, J. (1997). Dimensions of brand personality. *Journal of Marketing Research*, *34*, 347–356.

Ailawadi, K. L., Lehmann, D. R., & Neslin, S. A. (2003). Revenue premium as an outcome measure of brand equity. Journal of Marketing, *67*(4), 1–17.

Anderson, J. R. (1983). A spreading activation theory of memory. *Journal of Verbal Learning and Verbal Behavior, 22*(3), 261–295.

Attaman, B., & Ülengin, B. (2003). A note on the effect of brand image on sales. *Journal of Product and Brand Management*, *122*(4), 237–250.

Bargh, J. A. (2002). Losing consciousness: Automatic influences on consumer judgment, behavior and motivation. *Journal of Consumer Research, 29*(2), 280–285.

Brand Finance. (2019, January 22). *Brand Finance global 500 2019*. https://brandfinance.com/knowledge-centre/reports/brand-finance-global-500-2019/

Chen, A.C. (2001), "Using free associations to examine the relationship between characteristics of brand associations and brand equity", *Journal of Product and Brand Management*, Vol. 10, No. 7, pp. 449–451.

Chen, Y-P., Nelson, L. D., & Hsu, M. (2015). From "where" to "what": Distributed representations of brand associations in the brain. Journal of Marketing Research, *52*(4), 453–466.

Coates, S. L., Butler, L. T., & Berry, D. C. (2004). Implicit memory: A prime example for consideration and choice. *Applied Cognitive Psychology, 18*(9), 1195–1211.

Cobb-Walgren, C. J., Ruble, C. A., & Donthu, N. (1995). Brand equity, brand preference, and purchase intent. *Journal of Advertising*, *24*(3), 25–40.

Ehrenberg, A. S. C., Goodhardt, G. J., & Barwise, P.T. (1990). Double jeopardy revised. *Journal of Marketing, 54*(3), 82–91.

Evans, J., S., & Stanovich, K. E. (2013). Dual-processing theories of higher cognition: Advancing the debate. *Perspectives on Psychological Science, 8*(3), 223–241.

Ghodeswar, B. M. (2008). Building brand identity in competitive markets: A conceptual model. *Journal of Product and Brand Management*, *17*(1), 4–12.

Gigerenzer, G., & Gaissmaier, W. (2011). Heuristic decision making. *Annual Review of Psychology, 62,* 451–482.

Heath, R. (2009). Emotional engagement: How television brands build big brands at low attention. *Journal of Advertising Research, 49*(1), 62–73.

Heath, R., Brandt, D., & Nairn, A. (2006). Brand relationships: Strengthened by emotion, weakened by attention. *Journal of Advertising Research, 46*(4), 410–419.

Heckler, S. E., Keller, K. L., Houston, M. J., & Avery, J. (2014). Building brand knowledge structures: Elaboration and interference effects on the processing of sequentially advertised brand benefit claims. *Journal of Marketing Communications, 20*(3), 176–196.

Hofmeyr, J., Goodall, V., Bongers, M., & Holzman, P. (2007). A new measure of brand attitudinal equity based on the Zipf distribution. *International Journal of Market Research*, *50*(2), 181–202.

Hollis, N. (2013). *The meaningful brand: How strong brands make more money*. Palgrave.

Ison, M. J., Quiroga, R. Q., & Itzhak, F. (2015). Rapid encoding of new memories by individual neurons in the human brain. *Neuron, 87*(1), 220–230.

Junior, E. C. S. S. (2018). Brand portfolio strategy and brand architecture: A comparative study. *Cogent Business & Management, 5*(1), 1–10.

Kamakura, W.A., and Russell, G.J. (1993), "Measuring brand value with scanner data", *International Journal of Research in Marketing*, Vol. 10 (April), pp. 9–22.

Keller, K. L. (2015). Designing and implementing brand architecture strategies. *Journal of Brand Management, 21*(9), 702–715.

Keller, A., Marino, R., & Wallace, D. (2016). *The physics of branding*. HOW Books.

Mitzik, N., & Jacobson, R. (2008). The financial value impact of perceptual brand attributes. *Journal of Marketing Research*, *45*(1), 15–32.

Nedungadi, P. (1990). Recall and consumer consideration sets: Influencing choice without altering brand associations. *Journal of Consumer Research, 17*(3), 263–276.

Quillian, M. R. (1967). Word concepts: A theory and simulation of some basic semantic qualities. *Behavioral Science*, *12*(5), 410–430.

Rademaker, D., & Joosen, B. (2018). *Brands don't buy brands, people do*. Ipsos. https://www.ipsos.com/en/brands-dont-buy-brands-people-do

Reynolds, T. J., & Gutman, J. (1988). Laddering theory, method, analysis, and interpretation. *Journal of Advertising Research*, 28, 1, 11–31.

Romaniuk, J. (2013). Modeling mental market share. *Journal of Business Research, 66*(2), 188–195.

Romaniuk, J., & Gaillard, E. (2007). The relationship between unique brand associations, brand usage, and brand performance: An analysis across eight categories. *Journal of Marketing Management, 23*(3–4), 267–284.

Salinas, G. & Ambler, TY. (2009). A taxonomy of brand valuation practice: Methodologies and purposes. Journal of Brand Management, 17, 1, 39-61.

Schaefer, M., Knuth, M., & Rumpel, F. (2011). Striatal response to favorite brands as a function of neuroticism and extraversion. *Brain Research, 1425*, 83–89.

Schaefer, M., & Rotte, M. (2007). Favorite brands as cultural objects modulate reward circuit. *Neuroreport, 18*(2), 141–145.

Sharp, B. (2010). *How brands grow: What marketers don't know*. Oxford University Press.

Strebinger, A. (2014). Rethinking brand architecture: A study on industry-, company- and product-level drivers of branding strategy. *European Journal of Marketing*, 48(9–10), 1782–1804.

Swait, J., Erdem, T., Louviere, J., & Dubelaar, C. (1993). The equalization price: A measure of consumer-perceived brand equity. *International Journal of Research in Marketing, 10*(1), 23–45.

Thelen, E.M. and Woodside, A.G. (1997), "What evokes the brand or store? Consumer research on accessibility theory applied to modeling primary choice", International Journal of Research in Marketing, Vol. 14, pp. 125–145.

van Praet, D. (2012). *Unconscious branding: How neuroscience can empower (and inspire) marketing.* Palgrave.

Vriens, M., & ter Hofstede (2001). Linking attributes, benefits and values: A powerful approach to market segmentation, brand positioning and advertising strategy. *Marketing Research Magazine*, 3–8.

Vriens, M., & Frazier, C. (2003). The hard impact of the soft touch: How to use brand positioning attributes in conjoint analysis. *Marketing Research Magazine*, 22–27.

Vriens, M., & A. Martins Alves (2017). Modeling the implicit brand: Capturing the hidden drivers. *Journal of Product and Brand Management*, *26*(6), 600–615.

Vriens, M., Chen, S., & Schomaker, J. (2019). The evaluation of a brand density metric. *Journal of Product and Brand Management, 28*(1), 104–116.

Walvis, T. H. (2008). Three laws of branding: Neuroscientific foundations of effective brand building. *Journal of Brand Management*, *16*(3), 176–194.

Weinberg, P. & Gottwald, W. (1982). Impulsive consumer buying as a result of emotions. *Journal of Business Research*, 10, 43–57

Yoo, B., & Donthu, N. (2001). Developing and validating a multidimensional consumer-based brand equity scale. *Journal of Business Research*, *52*(1), 1–14.

Zajonc, R. B., (1968). Attitudinal effects of mere exposure. *Journal of Personality and Social Psychology Monographs, 9*(2), 1–27.

Image Credits

Fig. 8.3j: Copyright © by Diageo.
Fig. 8.5: Copyright © by Ipsos. Reprinted with permission.
Fig. 8.5a: Copyright © by Apple.
Fig. 8.5b: Copyright © by Apple.
Fig. 8.5c: Copyright © by Apple.
Fig. 8.5d: Copyright © by Apple.
Fig. 8.5e: Copyright © by Apple.
Fig. 8.5f: Copyright © by Apple.
Fig. 8.5g: Copyright © by Apple.
Fig. 8.5h: Copyright © by Coca-Cola Company.
Fig. 8.5i: Copyright © by Coca-Cola Company.
Fig. 8.5j: Copyright © by Coca-Cola Company.
Fig. 8.5k: Copyright © by Coca-Cola Company.
Fig. 8.5l: Copyright © by Coca-Cola Company.
Fig. 8.5m: Copyright © by Coca-Cola Company.
Fig. 8.5n: Copyright © by Coca-Cola Company.
Fig. 8.5o: Copyright © by Unilever.
Fig. 8.5p: Copyright © by Unilever.
Fig. 8.5q: Copyright © by Unilever.
Fig. 8.5r: Copyright © by Unilever.
Fig. 8.5s: Copyright © by Unilever.
Fig. 8.5t: Copyright © by Unilever.
Fig. 8.5u: Copyright © by Unilever.
Fig. 8.6a: Copyright © by Colgate.
Fig. 8.6b: Copyright © by Facebook.
Fig. 8.6c: Copyright © by Google.
Fig. 8.6d: Copyright © by YouTube.
Fig. 8.6e: Copyright © by Apple.
Fig. 8.6f: Copyright © by Microsoft.
Fig. 8.6g: Copyright © by Amazon.

CHAPTER 9

CUSTOMER SATISFACTION RESEARCH

9.1 WHAT AM I GOING TO LEARN?

In this chapter we outline customer satisfaction research. There is a tremendous amount of research on this topic, and we do not attempt to cover everything that has been proposed and discussed. Rather, more practically, we aim that after reading this chapter you will be prepared to (a) know why measuring and managing is a top priority in many firms; (b) understand how we define and can measure customer satisfaction; (c) understand how to design a customer satisfaction survey or program; (d) know how to analyze customer satisfaction data, including identifying and quantifying customer satisfaction drivers; and (e) know how to embed a customer satisfaction program into the fabric of business decision making. The latter includes reporting, target setting, and understanding the political sensitivities that come with it.

9.1.1 Terminology

In the customer satisfaction research literature, and in practice, a number of different terms and concepts are used:

> *Customer satisfaction*: This is measured most commonly via surveys and can be measured at the level of overall customer experience with a company's products, or it can pertain to a specific product. Customer satisfaction measures aim to capture how a customer feels about the entire experience with a firm. This may include the pre-purchase experience, the purchase experience, and the post-purchase experience (e.g., using the product, experience with how problems are handled, etc.). For example, "Thinking of your experience with the Mercedes E-Class you bought last month, how satisfied are you overall with this car, using a scale from 1 to 5, 1 meaning very dissatisfied, 2 meaning somewhat dissatisfied, 3 meaning neither satisfied nor dissatisfied, 4 meaning somewhat satisfied, and 5 meaning very satisfied?"
>
> *Likelihood to recommend.* Quite a bit is now known about the importance of positive word of mouth. Some research has suggested that every negative review or comment about a product or firm requires six positive reviews to neutralize that one negative review. To measure consumers' intent to spread positive word

of mouth, firms use a likelihood to recommend question. Typically, likelihood to recommend is asked in surveys via a standard question (e.g., "How likely are you to recommend this product [or this brand, this firm] to your friends, family, or colleagues?"). A 10-point scale is often used for this, where a 0 means not likely at all to recommend and a 10 means very likely to recommend.

Net promoter score. A very popular metric in practice is the use of what is referred to as the net promoter score, which is an aggregate measure that is calculated from responses to a likelihood to recommend question. The calculation of the net promoter score is the proportion of respondents who rated likelihood to recommend a 9 or a 10 (this group is referred to as the promoters) minus the proportion of respondents who rated the product/brand/firm anywhere between 0 and 6 (this group is referred to as the detractors). The result is a score between −100 and +100.

Key Driver Analysis

Measuring customer satisfaction is one side of the customer satisfaction research coin. The other side involves identifying and quantifying the importance of different sub-components of overall satisfaction. For example, a hotel experience, will be comprised of several components: the check-in process (Was it timely and efficient? Were the clerks friendly?), the actual room (Was it clean? Did it have the amenities you expected? Was the bed comfortable, the room quiet, etc.?). In key driver analysis (KDA) we want to quantify the relative importance of these sub-components. The goal is to prioritize what components can or should be improved.

9.2 WHY MEASURE CUSTOMER SATISFACTION?

We measure customer satisfaction because (1) it is important to consumers, and (2) it is important for businesses.

9.2.1 It is Important to Consumers

Customer experience is more important for differentiation than price and product (Walker, 2013), particularly in the business-to-business (B2B) space, and increasingly in business to consumer (B2C) as more business moves online. The underlying driver is that consumers have much more bargaining power than ever before and are at the center of a successful company's competitive strategy (Porter, 1979). The process for researching, evaluating, choosing, and purchasing a product has moved almost entirely to a digital world. It has created platforms such as Amazon, Yelp, and Google shopping, where consumers can now publicly share their opinions, rate products, and leave reviews. These opinions get significant visibility and are important in the purchase decisions of new consumers. On average, consumers evaluate at least two to three online reviews before deciding (Evans,

2017). A 2016 Nielsen Harris poll revealed that more than 80% of Americans rely on peer recommendations before making a purchase. Word of mouth remains one of the most powerful ways for a business to grow, and the internet is enabling that on a massive scale. If consumers rate products and services negatively or positively it has a dramatic impact on the company's reputation to effectively compete. Customer experiences have moved to the public domain: they can immediately share their experience via Facebook, Twitter, Instagram, Snapchat, YouTube, via special online user discussion groups, etc. This directly affects a brand's image and thereby shifting the balance of power to buyers. To stay ahead and be competitive, companies have no other choice than to listen to the voice of the consumer and act immediately if experiences are not meeting the desired expectations. It has become imperative that companies proactively invest in mechanisms to analyze and prioritize customer feedback. Many companies measure product satisfaction or some aspect of the customer experience. It's a top priority for internal market research functions to understand the health of the business.

9.2.2 It is Important to Businesses

Customer satisfaction research is strategically important for firms and quite often can be the single biggest line item in the company's marketing research budget. Just to give an example, for one Fortune 500 company, having operations in more than 35 countries, the annual budget for customer satisfaction research was over $6 million. Inside Research (2012) interviewed a small number of market research firms and estimated that customer satisfaction research in the United States exceeded $750 million (Keiningham et al., 2015). The real number is likely to be much bigger. The customer experience management (CEM) industry is worth $6 billion and is expected to grow to $17 billion by 2022, according to Customer Experience Management Market by Touch Point.

Academic research has widely shown that if your customers are more satisfied than the customers of your competitors your business will thrive. Customer satisfaction has been found to be positively related to business performance (Gupta & Zeithaml, 2007; Morgan & Rego, 2006), higher average product price, sales growth (Smith & Wright, 2004), analysts' stock recommendations (Luo et al., 2010) and firm value (Luo et al., 2010; O'Sullivan & McCallig, 2012). Bain's loyalty practice estimates that companies who systematically measure net promoter score (we will explain this metric later) and act on customer feedback have a two-times higher compound annual growth rate (CAGR) than the average growth rate of peers in the industry (see Figure 9.1). They are better able to attract new customers, retain existing ones, and improve profitability.

Superior customer satisfaction has also been shown to increase customers' inclination to recommend the company or the brand to others (Vavra, 1997).

Not surprisingly, then, for many companies the measurement and management of customer satisfaction has become a top priority.

1

FIGURE 9.1 NPS and Business Growth

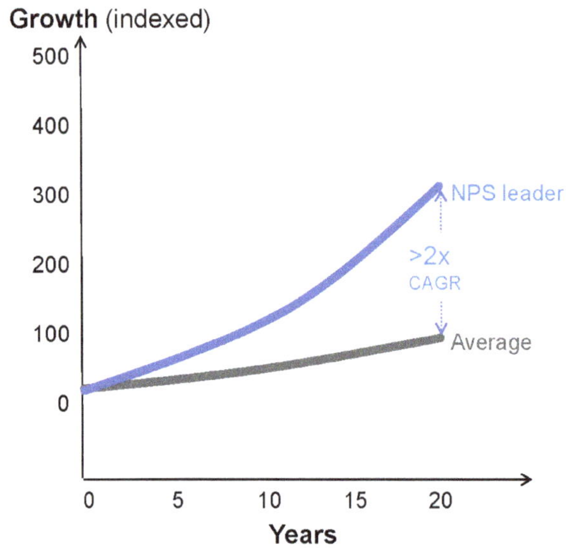

It is used to do the following:

1. Understand the health of the business (and this means it becomes part of a scorecard used in business review meetings).
2. Evaluate and reward executives if they achieve the given, set customer satisfaction goals. It has been shown that CEO compensation is a factor in explaining customer satisfaction and firm value (e.g., Luo et al., 2012; Basuroy et al., 2014).
3. Understand customers better in terms of who is likely to defect (churn) and in terms of customer prioritization (i.e., if our most valuable customers are happy with us; sometimes referred to as customer lifetime value research). Companies grow in large part through successful customer retention and the extent to which customers share positive word of mouth.

Customer satisfaction and related scores (customer loyalty and net promoter scores) are often referenced on earnings calls, along with other financial metrics to signal to investors the health of the business. For example, on Apple's Q3 2018 Earnings call, Tim Cook said that "iPhone X was the most popular iPhone in the quarter once again, with a customer satisfaction score of 98% according to 451 Research." At LinkedIn, there is a similarly strong focus on customer satisfaction, and we run large-scale market research studies to measure all aspects of the customer experience (some customer groups are referred to as members). Customer satisfaction measurement is the single biggest in spending, accounting for 40–50% of the market research budget. The executive team is focused on delivering experiences that help retain and grow the business. "Members first" is one of the cultural tenets, and business decisions are often evaluated through that lens. As such, LinkedIn regularly measures how well its products are meeting the expectations of members and customers and makes product changes based on customer feedback.

9.3 DEFINITION AND MEASUREMENT

Customer satisfaction has been defined in two ways (Yi, 1991): as a process and as an outcome. The process refers to the entire set of experiences, from obtaining a product or service to using the product or service, to post-purchase experiences, to the evaluative, perceptual, and psychological steps along the way. The customer's response refers to the evaluation of the perceived discrepancy between prior expectations and the actual performance of the product as perceived after its consumption (Tse & Wilton, 1988). The outcome refers to how the product experience makes someone feel—the emotional response and the cognitive state of being adequately or inadequately rewarded for the sacrifice (usually the price paid for a product) (Howard & Seth, 1969).

Different customer satisfaction conceptualizations have been proposed or are in use: (a) absolute measurements, (b) gap measurements, and (c) relative measurements:

1. Absolute approach. Using this approach, we ask respondents about how satisfied they are overall with your firm, product, or service. Once the firm settles on this approach you will need to decide how many categories on the rating scale you will use (e.g., a 5-point scale, a 7-point scale, a 9-point scale, or a 10-point scale). It is the responses to this overall satisfaction question that will be tracked over time and used as dependent variable in driver models.
2. Parasuraman et al. (1985) state that customer satisfaction is a function of the gap between customer expectations and customer perceptions. For example, if you go to an expensive restaurant, you expect more from your salmon order than what you get at Olive Garden. The customer gap is the difference between these two—an experience that doesn't meet an expectation leads to dissatisfaction and an experience that is perceived to meet an expectation leads to satisfaction; exceeding it will delight a customer. Parasuraman et al. (1985) proceed by saying that customer expectation is what the customer expects according to available resources and is influenced by cultural background, family lifestyle, personality, demographics, advertising, experience with similar products, and information available online. For example, research has found that higher educated people tend to be more critical and have higher expectations, making it harder to match those. At LinkedIn we have detected similar trends, where members who have fewer years of education tend to rate LinkedIn much higher yet engage us less frequently (all other factors being held constant). This is somewhat counterintuitive when you consider other cohorts that engage as frequently but have much lower satisfaction. This underlines the point that not every customer is created equal, and one needs to really consider the variations in different cohorts when measuring satisfaction for the

overall customer database to make the right recommendations for improvement. We will come back to this topic when we discuss product engagement as a factor to control in customer satisfaction research. Customer perception is completely subjective and based on the customer's interaction with the product or service. Perception is derived from the customer's satisfaction of the specific product or service and the quality of service delivery.

3 Relative measurements are typically done at the brand level. Usually, the measurement is done in two steps. First is an absolute measurement (i.e., each product or brand is evaluated in terms of overall satisfaction). The same is done for competing brands. Then the brands are evaluated relative to each other and are ranked. These rankings can be transformed to likely shares of wallet (using a Zipf distribution; see Zipf, 1935; see also Hofmeyr et al., 2008). Keiningham et al. (2015) compared absolute and relative metrics and found that relative metrics were much better able to explain share of wallet than absolute satisfaction metrics.

9.3.1 NPS Versus Customer Satisfaction Measurement

Note that NPS is being calculated, and it is an aggregate-level metric (meaning it cannot be calculated at the individual level). The survey question from which NPS is calculated is based on how likely customers and members recommend a company and its specific products and services: "How likely are you to recommend X or Y for [be specific about the product or service] to a friend or colleague?" This question is measured on an 11-point scale, with 0 being "not at all" and 10 being "extremely likely" (See Figure 9.2).

FIGURE 9.2 The Likelihood to Recommend Scale

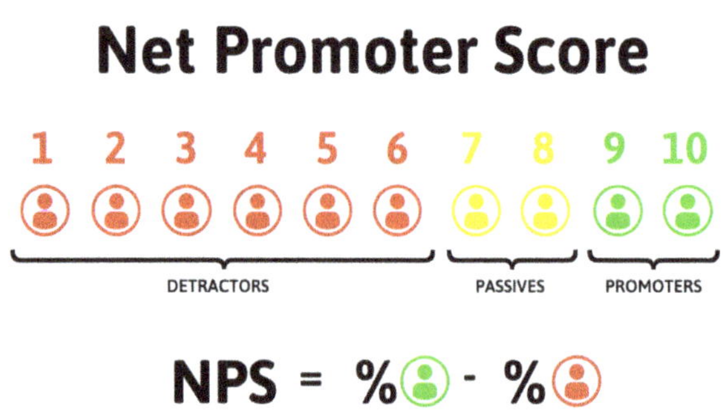

The responses are bucketed into three groups: those who rate 0–6 are called "detractors," 7–8 are "passives," and 9–10 are "promoters." You may ask, "Why 0–6 and not 0–4 or 0–5?" Research has shown that when you listen to how the 6s talk about a company they really sound different than the 7's. The 6's are more negative and may be more like a 4 or 5 than a 7. The 6s are more likely to defect or churn than the 7s. From each grouping you then calculate a net score by subtracting the proportion of promoters from the proportion of detractors; the resulting metric is called NPS and can be anywhere between -100 to +100. Scores above zero are considered good. Over the last 17 years, NPS has been popularized by Reichheld (2003) and Bain and Co., who have proven that it's a leading indicator of growth, beating traditional customer satisfaction metrics and other loyalty-oriented metrics. Later, we will return to the different ways in which NPS data can be analyzed.

The way NPS is calculated is sensitive; it is affected by the proportion of promoters and detractors, and over time small changes in either direction will have a large impact. NPS can change not only by growing or shrinking the proportion of promoters, but also by growing or shrinking detractors. For that reason, some companies have decided to only report promoters, and the metric is sometimes called a promoter metric or ambassador metric and is more stable than NPS. What you choose and how you report on it is somewhat of a subjective decision and depends on the objectives, desired simplicity, category you operate in, and type of consumption patterns—whether there is a frequent/infrequent consumption use case and whether you operate in a high/low involvement product category. We have found that what matters most is that when you decide on a metric you stick with it.

Satisfaction, on the other hand, can be asked by using a question such as "How satisfied are you with X, Y, or Z?" along with a typical Likert scale (Likert, 1932) or rating scale, say a 5-point scale with each score anchored to a satisfaction label with 5 being "very satisfied," 4 "somewhat satisfied," 3 "neutral," 2 "somewhat dissatisfied," and 1 "very dissatisfied." We have seen variations in scales. Microsoft uses a 4-point satisfaction scale, and in other cases companies use 7- or 10-point scales. It's important to be as specific as possible about what is being recommended or what aspect you ask of a satisfaction rating and whether you allow a neutral answer (odd scales) or force respondents to pick a negative or positive score (even scales). "How likely are you to recommend Company X?" is not as effective as asking "How likely are you to recommend Company X *for searching for jobs*?" The recommended question usually doesn't work well for very specific features: "How likely are you to recommend the editing feature in the LinkedIn blogging functionality?" It doesn't make much sense as people will typically think of recommending the overall experience that is tied to an overall goal; editing is one piece of the task of writing a blog (the goal). Satisfaction works better in that situation. The recommended scale is longer (11 points versus 5 points), allows for more granularity in the responses, and results in higher variance. This means that it works better when running multivariate analysis and generally produces a better-fitting model. But, a larger scale has practical implications and makes it more difficult to administer when a respondent uses a mobile device with limited screen space. Microsoft for that reason has reduced the 11-point recommend scale to a 5-point one as it found no material difference in its ability to track movements and answer what drives a propensity to recommend. Some have argued that asking a recommended question doesn't make sense when a company or product is the only option, such as a market where there is a near monopoly or where a product has virtually ubiquitous use, such as Facebook. Intel grappled with that, and to some extent at LinkedIn we debated this issue. Rather than saying, "How likely are you to recommend

X"? you may instead ask, "How likely are you to recommend using X *more?*" At LinkedIn we haven't seen it being too much of a problem, and it's more of a hypothetical question. For example, if I could, would I put my reputation on the line to vouch for this company or product? Companies such as Netflix ask more of a behavioral oriented question, "In the last month did you recommend Netflix to someone else?" followed by a binary response of yes or no. A binary (yes/no) question is very simple to administer, and it requires less thought than a hypothetical question such as "I *would* recommend a product or service" question.

Satisfaction can be measured at many different levels—for a specific product, for a specific feature, for a consumption experience, or for any transaction. Essentially any touchpoint a company has with a customer should be taken into consideration. Figure 9.3 shows the different ways in which a member touches LinkedIn when they try and accomplish different tasks. All of these touch points play an important role in the overall evaluation of LinkedIn and are measured for how well they meet expectations.

FIGURE 9.3 Different touchpoints on LinkedIn.com

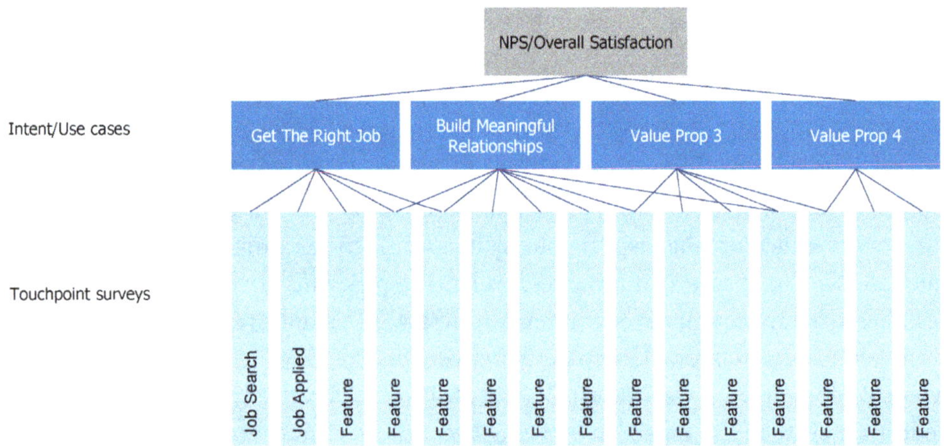

9.4 HOW TO DESIGN SUCCESSFUL CUSTOMER SATISFACTION SURVEYS

To design a successful customer satisfaction study (or net promoter study [NPS]), there are many considerations and trade-offs to be made, including (a) stakeholder alignment and presence of an executive sponsor, (b) choice of the metric and measurement approach, (c) competition, (d) drill-down questions, and (e) whether to execute the survey blindly or non-blindly. We discuss these considerations next.

9.4.1 Stakeholders and Sponsorship

Prior to embarking on scoping and designing a customer satisfaction study, it is important to bring everyone who is involved in decisions related to the customer experience along; this often cuts across all functions. In a heavily digitized world there is no distinction between back and front office, and everyone touches the customer directly in some way or shape. You also need to make sure that there is an executive sponsor, someone who is high up in the organization and can make sure it is being held accountable for the findings and recommendations. Often this is the chief marketing officer (CMO) or chief executive officer (CEO); at LinkedIn the CMO and CEO are the sponsors and the most important stakeholders. It's key that the sponsor is brought into the approach and understands how the research is being executed and what is being reported on and that they receive regular updates. Often this takes several cycles of discussions and education. Research-based findings are different from financial or behavioral metrics in that the method of data collection is based on sampling and statistical representativeness. We simply cannot get a survey response from every customer, whereas we can ascertain how much *every* customer is spending on products. Based on the responses from our sample, a subset of customers (the population), we need to make accurate assertions about the entire customer database at large, and the data is subject to non-response bias (the fact that certain groups of customers are more or less likely to respond than others) and therefore to the laws of statistics. More on this later.

When we talk about customer satisfaction it's often not one survey but a series of surveys. These can be surveys across different time periods (when looking at trends), across different audiences (e.g., end-customers and distributors), or across different parts of the business or the customer experience: satisfaction with the overall company or satisfaction for defined experiences or moments of truth—those moments that have a substantial impact on the overall perception of a company such as the onboarding, billing, or purchase process. We demonstrated the various moments of truth in Figure 9.2 for LinkedIn. This program of discrete surveys adds additional complexity in how to evaluate customer satisfaction findings, but it is necessary to understand the full end-to-end customer journey.

In the last few years a lot has been discussed about the metric and the pitfalls of net promoter score. NPS has been heavily scrutinized for its claim that it's the one metric that is a leading indicator of growth and the ultimate loyalty metric a company should focus on (Reichheld, 2003; Reichheld & Markey, 2011). Thus far, we have used the idea of customer satisfaction as a concept synonymous with the net promoter concept—a way to get an understanding of how customers feel about a product or service that they have recently consumed. A tendency to recommend follows being highly satisfied with a product. There are many other variations on this metrics such as *actual* NPS or customer advocacy which determines if someone recommended or discouraged your product to someone else rather than measuring a propensity which is what the traditional NPS is based on. The net actual NPS is the difference between the proportion who recommended minus the proportion who discouraged using the product [https://hbr.org/2019/10/where-net-promoter-score-goes-wrong]. Another metric that has been in vogue among product managers is a Product Market Fit metric that asks customers "How they would feel if they could no longer use the product?" And if more than 40% say 'very disappointed' it is being argued that you have product market fit and a product that drives satisfaction and loyalty (https://en.wikipedia.org/wiki/Product/market_fit). Often NPS is equated to Customer Value as a way of understanding what the benefits are that a customer receives from a product or service minus the costs which includes the price paid but also the time invested to make effective use of the product. These are all useful metrics to explore when someone embarks on designing a customer satisfaction survey. Before deciding on what metric to use, always make sure to correlate it to business outcomes such as revenue, profit and new customer growth (number of new customers added over a specific time period). If there is no strong correlation, it's not the right metric for your organization. For simplicity sake we will stay focused on the two that are the most common—satisfaction and recommend.

9.4.2 The Metric and Measurement

An important component of customer satisfaction research involves the "metric": How precisely do we measure customer satisfaction? Basically, we choose an absolute, a gap or relative approach (see previous section). Once a company decides it needs to stick with this metric, changing it will not be easy and is usually discouraged. This metric is used in both financial reporting, analysts' calls, and executive compensation, and hence will be heavily scrutinized.

9.4.3 Competitive Context

There has been a lot of debate around whether you ask about NPS or satisfaction in a competitive context or as an individual question for only your product or company—relative gap versus absolute measurement. In other words, based on the alternatives that someone uses, you ask how satisfied or how likely they are to recommend each one. Often a usage question precedes the NPS question: "In the last 3 months which sites did you use to search for jobs?" Note that it's important to make the question timebound and as recent as possible. We suggest not going back longer than 3 months, but that depends on the category, the intensity, or how involved customers are (i.e., how much of a sacrifice a consumer had to make to obtain and consume a product and how frequent customers typically use your products). The more recent the focus the better, as respondents will have the clearest memory of the moment they consumed your product or service and can provide the most reliable assessment. Once you know what competitive products or services have been used, you then ask how satisfied they were with each. The alternatives are typically presented in a grid format, so respondents are mentally comparing each solution. The scores you derive from it versus asking only about your company or product are often very different; this is caused by an anchoring effect (Kahneman, 2011). Depending on the competitive set, respondents will calibrate their evaluation based on a competitor who has the strongest or the weakest performing offering. The actual score is therefore subject to how people anchor on a competitor that in theory should have no impact on your company or product evaluation. But in everyday life we don't walk around actively thinking about products independent of some sort of mental yardstick. In the moment we create a frame of reference for ourselves and calibrate each competitor. This is not very different than when we buy a product in the store and compare different options.

At LinkedIn, we once ran an experiment using randomly pulled samples in which we asked half the respondents how likely they were to recommend LinkedIn when evaluating

LinkedIn by itself and the other half based on a set of competitors and peers that operate in the same space. We used the same NPS question for each group; the only thing that changed was the addition of a competitive context. The results showed that the NPS score for LinkedIn differed materially by roughly 30 NPS points. This underscores two things:

1. Competitive context matters and provides a helpful frame of reference, but relatives are therefore ultimately more important than absolutes (i.e., people don't think in absolute scores when providing an NPS score), and how that trends over time is what matters. Obviously a negative NPS is bad in either situation, competitive context or not.
2. Be thoughtful about what competitors to include as who you include impacts your score. We suggest deciding all the alternatives for accomplishing the same task that your product achieves and not to limit yourself to pure play competitors. For example, Intuit also includes paper and pencil as one of the alternatives for filing taxes and asks NPS of TurboTax in that context. Mars not only competes with Snickers and other chocolate bars but is also up against Haagen-Dazs ice cream as a snack in the snack category at large, which is how consumers make choices. And at LinkedIn we include "free LinkedIn" in the competitive set since "free" is part of the consideration set when we sell, for example, paid recruiting solutions. We are competing against ourselves. Some practitioners argue asking for each competitor separately, but that decision depends on how many competitors a respondent needs to evaluate and how well it mimics real-world decision-making situations.

9.4.4 Blind Versus Non-Blind

As a rule, it's good to ask NPS in a competitive context because it provides a mechanism to benchmark your products and company. If you also have a way and the budget of fielding a blind survey through a third-party supplier, using third-party lists, we recommend using the competitive context *only* in the blind survey and without a competitive context in any internally fielded NPS or satisfaction surveys (i.e., when surveying your own customers, you don't want to start thinking about competing alternatives). This is to avoid internal confusion with obtaining potentially two different sets of scores but also to maintain separation in the objectives of each survey. The third party can provide competitive benchmarks for customers of not only your company but also customers at companies who only use other products and not yours. As such, it provides more of a market-based and objective overview of the category at large. To this date though, it's still difficult to obtain reliable third-party lists from panels or other sources, so be careful when you engage third-party providers and make sure that you clearly understand how the panel is recruited, what the clean-out rules are, and how the provider guarantees authenticity of not only who the panelists say they are but what they do professionally in case of B2B studies. It's important to recognize that if an internal NPS survey gets sent to your customers there will be bias simply from the fact that it's obvious who it's originating from. We have found that when customers know that you are listening, the ones who are more negative are more likely to respond, and the delta can be significant. We detected a difference of 20–30 NPS points in one case. Internal customer satisfaction and NPS surveys are sometimes referred to as "complainer magnets" and used as a mechanism to identify who requires extra attention and follow-through on the issues they voice. In a blind survey, customers don't know who is sending out the survey and will provide a more objective evaluation. If you have both an internal (non-blind) and external (blind) survey in place, make sure your stakeholders are aware that although the key question is phrased the same, the scores will most likely not be the same simply because of the context, the audience selection and so you are effectively asking a different question. We have seen scenarios in which internal and external NPS move in opposite directions and often that causes confusion but its important to dissect what's driving it. External may be picking up a different composition of newer or first-time users or subscribers who tend to have lower NPS as they are still getting used to the product and many will churn whereas internal may have a more tenured set of your users who have survived for longer and have higher NPS. These compositions can change over time. Or external NPS may have been more susceptible to the actions that competitors are taking—if one made a material improvement that could have shifted of what users have come to expect of your product may result in lower or higher NPS. We will discuss how to analyze the data effectively to tease out these effects. It is important to understand these nuances and communicate these to your stakeholders. Often teams need to spend time keeping a close watch on what competitors are doing so that they can calibrate findings against competitive moves in NPS.

9.4.5 How and Who to Sample and Size

This is one of the most important decisions you must make and one where we see the greatest risk of failure. Who you select and how you sample your customers has a dramatic impact on your results, your interpretation of the data, and its implications. In the following section, we discuss several principles you should follow to minimize these risks:

1. *Define your audience*. It sounds trivial, but a lot of companies struggle with this. Should we include free trialists? Should customers be included who lapsed—they used the product once over 3 months and never used it again? Should we include dormant customers? Should we include customers who fully churned? Should we include customers who didn't use any of the premium features in their premium subscription? Should we only focus on power users? We have found that the answer should be no most of the time. Not every customer is created equal; customers have different expectations based on socioeconomic, demographic, lifestyle and education factors. It's important to understand the composition of your users and target those who have had recent enough experiences that they can recall the experience. If I can't recollect an experience very well, my answers will not be very articulate and accurate. Research shows that after 1 month our memory greatly deteriorates (see forgetting curve, e.g., Murre & Dross, 2015). Not only does it deteriorate, but our mind also plays tricks on us and we recollect an episode very differently and incorrectly as time goes by (e.g.,

see Nenycz et al., 2013; Tourangeau, 2000). But isn't it important to know why certain customers didn't come back? Yes, it is, but you are most likely not going to get great insights if you try to solve for both improving customer experiences with recent customers and lapsed ones. These are two different types of problems to solve, and they require different types of questions and hypotheses to test. In one case, low usage may simply be due to lack of awareness, but that's a different issue than someone having had a bad experience. We need to research the former differently. The customers of your product who should be included are those who have had recent and meaningful interactions. These are the most valuable customers and, using the 80/20 rule, those who contribute 80% of your revenue, usage, or engagement. In B2B you often have two types of "users": the end users of the product, the people who interact with the features and functionalities of your product, which is who we have been discussing thus far, and decision makers who may or may not be end users as well. The decision makers usually have budgetary responsibility or a significant influence on the purchase decision-making process, but they don't interact with the end product in a regular way. They interact with your account managers and billing or other administration touchpoints. Typically, we survey these groups differently because the experiences are different, and thus the way we ask the question is different. There are different factors that drive their satisfaction. Decision makers are more concerned with price/value trade-offs and may not consider individual end solutions but evaluate a company on the portfolio of products they purchase if there is more than one. In subsequent sections we will point out how to survey this group differently, but they are an important group to include and design for.

2 *Determine engagement levels.* Our economy is increasingly more intangible, driven by services that are non-physical and digital in nature; think of consumers playing video games, listening to music streaming services, buying photo prints off Etsy, using Airbnb, or other digital market places (Haskel & Westlake, 2018). The intangible economy is very different from the tangible one in the sense that the way the products are obtained and consumed are different. In fact, they are not consumed in a physical and discrete way but engaged with, subscribed to, and reused over and over. Even if products are still physical, more and more products are purchased online. So, the question of who *consumes* the product is not a simple one to answer or a binary one. Companies need to understand how *engagement* correlates with product success and at what level of engagement customers become invested and find true value in the offering. At LinkedIn, we define someone as a meaningful member if they have a quality profile and consistently engage the site at least once a month. Lots of analysis has gone into arriving at that conclusion, and it's a key determinant for the success of LinkedIn's network growth and one of the true north metrics the company pursues. From a member perspective, if someone has very little information on their profile and no or only a few connections, it's difficult to derive value from the LinkedIn platform as LinkedIn doesn't know what content to serve in the news

feed or what jobs to recommend. Someone who purchases a subscription but rarely engages with the premium features won't be able to provide meaningful clues about what to improve, so the person who purchased the subscription doesn't automatically constitute the "user." This same pattern plays out for most other companies that are currently moving all of their business online. We recommend defining your audience as anyone who has used the product within a set timeframe that is no longer than 1–3 months and to carefully identify heavy, medium, and light users so that each can be uniquely understood and acted on.

3. *Sampling*. We could dedicate an entire book to sampling. In a nutshell, there are four things to factor in. Once you have determined your population, which should be a subset of the total customer database of meaningful and recent users, do the following:
   a. We highly recommend not including anyone who has not used the product for 3 months unless forced to by the 80/20 rule and unless it was for a high-involvement purchase that is heavily infrequent or where the buying cycles are long; for example, the job-seeking process can be lengthy and span multiple months between writing the resume and applying to jobs.
   b. The sample should be large enough to derive statistically significant results and not be smaller than 30–50. At sizes of 30 to 50, a normal distribution curve typically appears, and one can calculate a t-test to understand if results are significant at a 90 to 95% confidence interval.
   c. If you use NPS, which is a more sensitive metric and has a greater margin of error around the aggregate metric, we suggest aiming for more completes. Obviously if you are capturing customer feedback in the product through a pop-up survey you may have less control over who responds, but at least they are recent users. Most sites nowadays require some sort of log-in account so that the company can identify your past usage patterns, classify you appropriately, and decide how the responses should be reported as part of the overall data set and whether free trialists should be removed.
   d. Often many other surveys are fielded to customers at the same time, and it's important to set up a system where you randomly select a group for each survey ahead of time so that there is no sample selection bias from competing surveys running at the same time.

9.4.6 What Drill-Down Questions to Ask

The value of NPS and the satisfaction survey comes from the questions asked following the main NPS or overall satisfaction question. These are the questions that explain why someone gives a high or low rating. We recommend always asking the satisfaction and recommended question at the beginning of the survey, as the very first question. Some people argue for asking it at the end after respondents have been asked about the components of the experience and are sufficiently primed to provide a more well-rounded and well-thought-out NPS or satisfaction rating for the overall product or service. It's a valid consideration, but it has the downside that not everyone makes it that far into the survey, and you end up with missing data on a key question, or, if a question changes in the survey leading up to the overall satisfaction or NPS question, it will be impossible to interpret the trend data; it breaks trends due to survey question bias, bias caused by the question being asked and the frame of mind it puts someone in.

The questions following overall satisfaction or NPS are meant to shed more light on what is driving the overall rating. In NPS, a typical follow-up question is an open-ended question such as "Why did you give that rating?" It's important that you encourage customers to elaborate as much as possible and prompt them to say more if they simply respond: "everything is good." The technology is advancing, so we can predict in real time how to probe deeper using messaging bots that predict what the right response sentence is to encourage responsiveness or to clarify a written response. For example, a respondent may type that the product was "easy to use," and based on that word combination the messaging bot may suggest, in real time, "Did you mean it was easy to navigate the site or easy to discover how to accomplish a task or easy to understand the instructions?" The respondent can simply select the appropriate follow-up response.

You can continue to probe deeper based on a machine-learned algorithm. If the sample is large, at some point text mining the results may become challenging and cannot be done manually. In that case we have to rely on semi-automatic text analytics (e.g., Chen et al., 2018). Often there are still a few closed questions to get a more structured data set. It's important that the subsequent questions are comprehensive and mutually exclusive of all the aspects that influence the overall evaluation of the product (Vavra, 1997). Often these questions are formulated as statements with performance ratings or statements that people can select from (binary): "Which of the following influenced your rating of X? *Select all that apply*."

In some cases, you may also want to ask an importance rating, but if you had to make a trade-off because of survey length, at least include performance statements. You can always derive importance later through regression analysis. Often these statements are informed by prior research, qualitative interviews, customer support feedback, discussions with frontline staff, and use language and verbiage that customers use, not marketing speak. They should cover all aspects of the experience: functional and emotional ones such as the ease of use, product quality, price, support, and value, but also how the products make customers feel—accomplished, fulfilled, productive, effective, and so on (see Forrester, 2015, for determinants). A good balance across these elements is important so that the overall rating can be accurately decomposed, and any modeling exercise produces a good-fitting model that explains the variance in ratings. The performance ratings can either be satisfaction based or performance based. It is important that the attributes are formulated as neutral statements, covering a single aspect versus many (e.g., quality and value, a double barrel) and are not leading and clearly understood (e.g., see Babin & Zikmund, 2010).

Today, it's rare to see questionnaires longer than 3–5 minutes. Attention spans and response rates have dramatically gone down. At the same time, text analytics has greatly improved, so asking the overall questions is often enough to determine what drives NPS or satisfaction and provides a robust sample size to drill deeper into different segments. For example, Uber pre-populates an algorithmically derived list of reasons people may have for their rating after every ride. We believe that this is the future with how to administer customer satisfaction research: more in-the-moment–type surveying, with probing questions that adjust to the situation and background characteristics of the user. See Figure 9.4 for an example.

FIGURE 9.4 Examples of Drill Down Questions

USAA sends a text message with simple questions that are quick to administer after an insurance claim is filed or roadside assist has been delivered. At LinkedIn we ask respondents to select a reason from a list of pre-selected items that we have found to drive NPS or satisfaction with an "other, specify" in case we missed something. Respondents can simply select what drove their satisfaction and which ones drove it most. The last aspect that typically gets asked is the intent question, the reason why someone purchased and used the product. For most products this may be very straightforward, as there is only one, but many digital products and services can be used for many different needs, and people have a variety of tasks that they need to achieve. It's important to understand goal and task motivation and how the findings differ across different motivations. For example, at LinkedIn members use the site to find and get a job, to learn, to connect with others, to grow their business, to join events and groups, and to stay informed. This is important because these different intents or uses have an impact on how someone experiences the product, even if everyone uses the same features.

9.4.7 Merging Additional Data

Most companies, especially the ones who have undergone digital transformation, have a lot of information they can append about all customer behaviors (clicks, time spent, etc.) on the site, and about past purchases, right up against when they cast the evaluation. So, in essence, a company is not only collecting overall satisfaction but has a huge dataset at their disposal that can be leveraged to understand what drives satisfaction in addition to the stated answers. Even companies that are traditional brick-and-mortar ones are trying to collect as much information about a customer through getting them to download their app and sign up. In 2018 Burger King ran a promotion for a 1-cent burger for which you needed to download the Burger King app, then drive to McDonald's (BK says getting within 600 feet of their competitor should be close enough), order your sandwich, then drive to the nearest Burger King to pick it up. And Chipotle has developed an app where you can sign in and order ahead to avoid the line. Most restaurant chains now offer an option to pay through their app rather than waiting for the waiter to show up with the bill. In all these instances, companies are expanding their data and understanding of their customer behavioral patterns. At LinkedIn we combine the data collected from the survey with site information that helps us better understand which behaviors lead to higher satisfaction when combined with open-ended responses. For example, if a member had a low rating on NPS and indicated in the open end that the rating was driven by a poor experience with the jobs that we recommended—they were too junior—we could analyze what jobs surfaced leading up to the survey, her title and current responsibilities, her years of experience, and where there has been a mismatch. For example, if it appears that the jobs that we recommended were too junior based on that specific title group, we can then make actionable recommendations to tweak the relevance algorithm and consider years of experience versus purely looking at title.

9.4.8 Frequency

Once you have a customer satisfaction survey up and running you want to collect information ideally on an ongoing basis through a drip method (e-mail-based surveys) or through impressions (in-product surveys) as frequently as possible without over-surveying your customers and causing survey fatigue. Some companies take this to great extreme and survey the same customers every week, but a lot depends on the environment, how engaged your customers are, and the usage patterns. At LinkedIn, we survey members and customers not more than once every 3 months, and we implement cool-off periods to suppress customers who have already responded to a survey. It's important that you have a clear policy in place, build the database tables to track survey touches, and track responses. This time period is somewhat arbitrary, but we track response rates, the same respondents over time, and satisfaction with the survey to better understand if we need to adjust the timing of surveys and cool-off periods. An externally fielded survey is expensive, so a competitive benchmark study happens every 3 to 6 months. The market often doesn't shift dramatically in such short time intervals, so 3 to 6 months is reasonable. The same goes for ongoing surveys that are fielded in house through the research operations team: *The product doesn't change frequently enough for customers to detect changes unless a major overhaul is happening on the site or in the packaging*. In psychology this phenomenon is called the just noticeable difference (JND), also known as the difference threshold, and is the minimum level of stimulation that a person can detect 50% of the time (Norwich & Wong, 1997). Many product improvements are so gradual that consumers don't detect them unless the changes constitute a major shift from how they have been using the product or it changes a workflow, causing initial "sticker shock." In digital interfaces, they are usually the result of changes in the user interface, causing a temporary dip in customer satisfaction until customers start getting used to the new design. At first it's hard for a product team to accept this effect, so it's important to be up front about what product changes truly make an impact; often many gradual improvements over time lift the overall experience slowly, but major shifts in the user interface can cause sudden declines that usually bounce back as time goes by. Most digital applications therefore roll out changes slowly and allow users to temporarily continue using the old version.

9.4.9 Intercept Versus E-mail

As mentioned earlier we strongly recommend surveying end users in the product at the point of interaction. In retail outlets you will often find stands where people can enter how satisfied they were, or at the bottom of receipts you will find a web link to a survey, and on websites it's common to get a pop-up survey asking about the experience. Some of these pop-ups can be triggered based on certain usage patterns. The response rate tends to be much higher (up to five times) than through e-mail-based survey invites, which is important because it allows you to better achieve a representative sample. Email-based surveys can sometimes be targeted a little more directly to certain user groups, but in general we prefer to capture responses as in the moment as possible. The only exception is if the process and outcome (Yi, 1991) we discussed earlier are separated by time, where the outcome does not coincide with the process. For example, if someone purchases a product at the store and consumes the product at a later stage, we can only get a good read on the in-store experience of purchasing the product but not capture the overall experience until after the product is consumed (the outcome). So, you need to decide what exactly you are trying to measure: the process, the outcome, or both.

Another example is at LinkedIn where we measure a lot of experiences in real time, but for some, we can only get a partial read of how well the overall experience was. When someone posts something or publishes a blog with their network, that person will not be able to fully evaluate the blogging or posting experience until after a few days have passed. The experience is dependent on whether someone is getting views, likes, and comments on their post and experiences enough engagement on their post (the outcome). No one posts for the sake of posting. Often the notion of what the experience entails is ill defined, and there are enough examples where companies interpret success or failure based on a partial view of the experience. It's important to decide if a "delayed" e-mail-based intercept is more effective, depending on the goal and type of experience. Some companies have also started to disseminate surveys through text messages. The drawback of in-product surveys is that you have limited real estate to ask deeper, probing questions to understand all the aspects of the experience, but it's worth the tradeoff. When you survey decision makers you may only be left with e-mail or traditional phone or personal depth interviews.

Lastly, once you have decided on your design, the medium for collecting the data, the scope, and the target audiences and you start fielding the surveys, it will be difficult to make changes. Any change you make after you have established a baseline, no matter how mundane, will impact your ability to trend results wave over wave. As we have demonstrated, changing to a competitive context or even changing the subject line of your e-mail survey invite will impact your results. When you do need to make changes, always experiment before implementing them so you maintain the purity of your metric and program and can adjust gradually or calibrate scores.

9.5 DATA ANALYSIS

Once you have collected your data, the first thing you must analyze is the composition of your sample. Did we get responses from a representative group of our target population?

9.5.1 Weighting

To answer the question just asked, we need to determine the composition or frequencies in demographics, firmographics, and usage patterns and determine if these deviate from the overall population. If you detect large deviations in the frequencies between sample and population, this is often a sign that there may be response bias, and you need to adjust. Specifically, when certain segments of the population are not responding to a survey for whatever reason, despite everyone having an equal opportunity to respond and their opinions are different from segments of respondents who did respond, you get non-response bias. This matters when we are doing surveys to get a representative read for a population at large *and* there is a lot of variation in the responses. Non-response bias left unaddressed is a real problem (see the polls leading up to the 2016 election) and can often lead to an inaccurate conclusion. We encounter far too often that surveys do not analyze the effect of non-response bias. It's a time-consuming exercise to determine all the different segments, or combinations on which you can dissect a population (gender, income, geography, industry, frequency of usage, education, etc.), and often the sample sizes are not large enough to properly understand the effect of non-response bias when multiple variables are involved. There are statistical packages from R, SPSS (Statistical Package for the Social Science), and others that make the process of identifying non-response bias in a large data set easier. And the good news is that across the many surveys we have conducted to date, we are starting to see a pattern on which non-response bias is likely to happen, making the process of identifying the right variables to control for easier.

The level of engagement (and strength of motivation) to use a product plays a critical role in whether someone is likely to respond to a survey, and the responses between a heavy and light user are typically different. To illustrate, here is an example with rescaled figures to preserve confidentiality. Despite the fact that we invited all users of a product to the survey, the heavy users were much more likely to respond than the light users, causing the sample to come back with a different distribution than the overall population (see Table 9.1); we ended up with three times as many heavy users than actually exist in the population at large—a result that is common in many of the surveys we do. Heavy users have a greater affinity with the company and the product and are more eager to provide feedback, an effect also found in polls where "decided" voters are more likely to respond than "undecided" or "swing" voters. NPS in Table 9.1 is the net promoter score for each segment that we captured with the likelihood to recommend question. There is quite a bit of variation in the NPS scores across the three segments. Heavy users have a much higher NPS and are more likely to recommend the product (see Table 9.1).

TABLE 9.1 NPS Across Different Types of User Intensity

Type of user	NPS	% of customers who responded to the survey (n=20000) -A-	% of all customers in the database (20mln) -B-
Heavy	30	30%	10%
Medium	10	40%	30%
Light	−20	30%	60%

If we were to calculate the NPS for the total sample, we would get = 30 * 30% + 10 * 40% + −20 * 30% = 7 (column A). However, if we adjust for non-response bias from light users and map the scores to the actual population distribution, it will make the overall NPS = 30 * 10% + 10 * 30% + −20 * 60% = −6 (column B).

These results are significantly different given the sample size and difference in NPS, and we can therefore conclude that non-response from light users is a problem and causes bias. If we didn't adjust and simply reported the overall NPS figure it would create a false sense that NPS is good and positive. Because the difference is driven by underlying segment variations, the conclusions, urgency to act, and direction the product team needs to take to improve NPS are inaccurate. For any company to grow its user base, which is the goal of the product manager, it's important to understand how to cater to both heavy and light users in a balanced and measured way that is an accurate reflection of the total user base. There are different ways to adjust for this effect, but our favored approach is to make the adjustment after the fact rather than stratify the sample and set quotas at the outset to make up for the imbalance. Because customer satisfaction measurement and NPS is big business and there is a lot at stake, applying this rigor is a must, more so than in any other type of descriptive research being conducted.

9.5.2 Common Reporting Views

Most of the time what you report has been decided well in advance as part of the sample and scope considerations and is aligned with how the company thinks about target segments.

Typically, organizations want to look at customers in different regions by different engagement levels, by different intents, and, in the case of B2B, by enterprise versus small businesses or by industry and function. In the design phase you set the sample size requirements in such a way that you can report on these views using the lowest common denominator. The findings from this type of research are split by different levels of satisfaction, or by promoters and detractors if you use NPS, so that we can quickly see how the aggregate score breaks down and where to focus the analysis.

9.5.3 Key Driver Analysis

Aside from reporting overall satisfaction and NPS, we also want to analyze what is driving satisfaction or what is driving NPS so that the organization can prioritize what to focus on. Driver analysis can be conducted in multiple ways:

1. You can simply determine what people selected as their top reasons for dissatisfaction and top reasons for satisfaction. It helps determine what we need to do for those for whom we didn't meet expectations and what we need to do to maintain high levels of satisfaction for whom we have met expectations or exceeded them.
2. We can use statistical analysis (e.g., Vriens et al., 2018), such as driver analysis, which is usually done via some variety of regression analysis (i.e., linear regression or logistic regression).

Let's look at an example: You are the CEO of Salesforce's support software portal (an online software product that can help companies with all their sales efforts. Twice a year you run a short customer satisfaction survey among active customers. The survey has one overall customer satisfaction question measured on a 10-point scale ranging from "not satisfied at all" to "very satisfied." The survey also asks customers how satisfied they are with specific components of the product and service; in this example using the same 10-point rating scale. See Table 9.2 for some hypothetical components of this product. These questions are asked for the company but also for two competing brands.

TABLE 9.2 Component of a Salesforce Software Product

Component of satisfaction of a Salesforce software portal
Ability to reach target audience
Increase awareness of the company's services
Ability to target the right content to your customers
Ability to analyze customers comments
Interface ease of use
The ability to generate leads for the business
Satisfaction with the text ads
Generate sign-ups for newsletter
Increase sales
The ease of managing content

The CEO has several questions in mind: (a) How overall satisfied are our customers and is this changing? (b) How satisfied are they with the various components of our product and service? and (c) Which of these components, if we were to improve satisfaction on them, would result in the (likely) highest increase in overall satisfaction? The average ratings of the company and its competitors on the various components can be used to identify any components on which it already scores better than the competition. That doesn't mean it can completely ignore such components, but at least these do not seem the urgent priorities. What about the components on which at least one competitor is better than the company? This question is important because the firm may not have the resources to improve all the components; but it can be (at least partially) answered with key driver analysis (KDA) using regression. When we apply linear regression, we take the overall satisfaction variable and as the dependent variable and the satisfaction ratings of the components as independent variables (see Chapter 10 for details). We run the model and find something like what is shown in Table 9.3.

TABLE 9.3 Results of Linear Regression Model (As Presented to Client)

Driver Variable	Driver Strength: (1 SD increase)
The ability to generate leads for the business	0.18
Ability to analyze customer comments	0.26
The ability to reach your target audience	0.10
Overall ease of managing content	0.03

Model Accuracy: 77% (r-squared—percentage explained variance)
Note: The average standard deviation for driver variables is 2.240t

In this table, for simplicity, we do not show the regression coefficients (for that see Chapter 10), but calculated hypothetically how much overall satisfaction would be improved if we improved each of the components by one standard deviation? Now we can see the value of this analysis. First, out of the original 10 components only 4 seem to have a statistically significant impact in terms of explained variation in overall satisfaction. So, maybe our limited budget should go to improving these components first, especially those, within the set of four, on which our company is behind the competition. Before we go further, typically create importance-performance maps are created. Then, the results show us the relative importance (i.e., if we do not have enough budget to improve all four components, we can initially just focus on the most important ones: the ability to generate leads and the ability to analyze customer data).

Often in customer satisfaction studies we go even further and compare importance with performance data (see Table 9.4 and Figure 9.5). Table 9.4 gives us some interesting insights. First, on the two most important components our competition performs better than we do. However, equally interesting, on the most important component (ability to analyze customer comments) neither our company nor the competition does particularly well. Importance

TABLE 9.4 Results of Linear Regression Model (As Presented to Client)

Driver Variable	Driver Strength: (1 SD increase)	Average Rating	
The ability to generate leads for the business	0.18	6.5	8.5
Ability to analyze customer comments	0.26	2	3
The ability to reach your target audience	0.10	5	8
Overall ease of managing content	0.03	7	5

Model Accuracy: 77% (r-squared—percentage explained variance)
Note: The average standard deviation for driver variables is 2.240t

FIGURE 9.5 The Importance Versus Importance Map

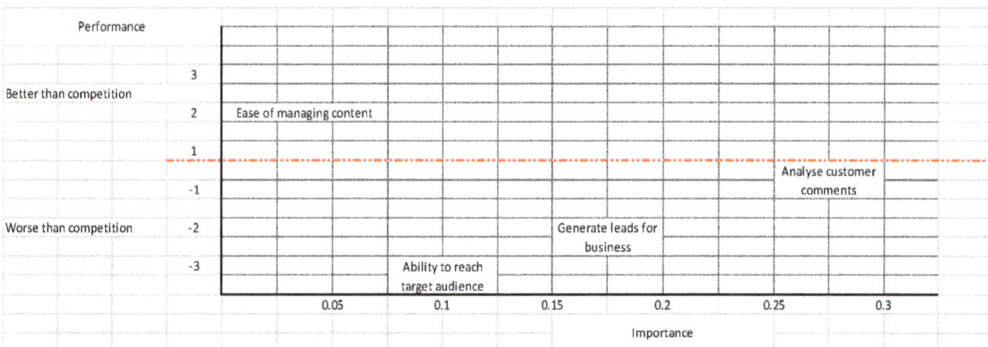

and performance are often visualized in an importance-performance map (see Figure 9.5 for an example).

When a company uses NPS as its standard metric (recall that NPS is derived from responses to a likelihood to recommend scale) the KDA is done on the underlying likelihood to recommend scale. Although we can apply linear regression to such a scale, often this scale is modeled via two logistic regression variables (see Figure 9.6). A logistic regression is a regression where the dependent variable is binary.

So, in the example in Figure 9.6, one logistic regression would aim to explain what drives the difference between detractors and passives, and a second model would aim to explain what drives the difference between passives and promoters. The output from a logistic regression analysis tells you two things: (a) what attributes of all the attributes we included in the model are significantly classifying someone as passive instead of as a detractor, or what classifies someone as promoter instead of passive; and (b) the expected relative impact of making an improvement on each driver (e.g., an increase on average by 1 point). Key driver analysis is valuable because it helps the organization stay focused on where to apply most of its energy, especially if you overlay current performance with importance (see Figures 9.6 and 9.7). Note that Figure 9.7 is not quite the same as Figure 9.6. In Figure 9.7 the performance is only shown for the LinkedIn brand. This map also contains more components.

FIGURE 9.6 Creating Binary Variables From the Likelihood to Recommend Scale

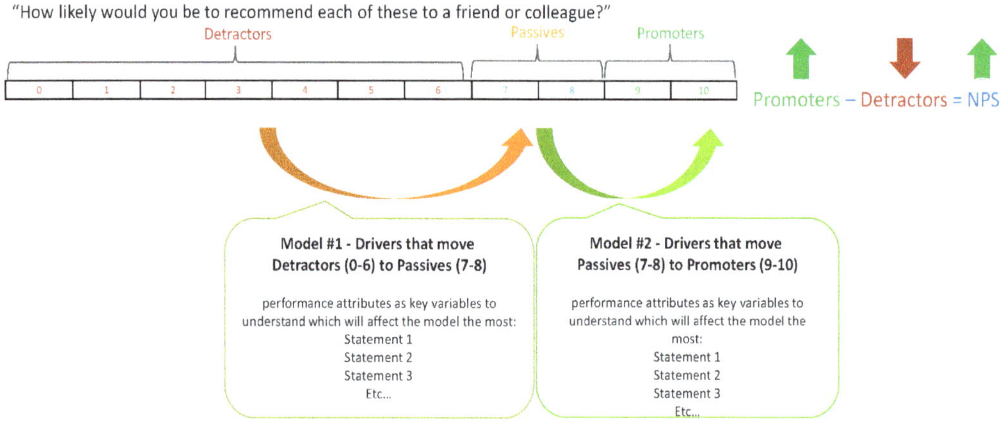

FIGURE 9.7 An Example of a Performance-Importance Map

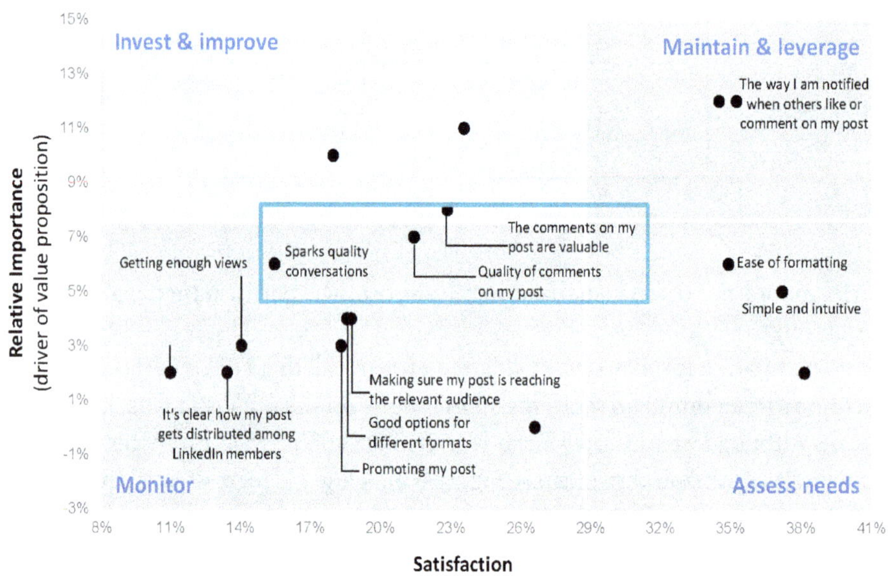

You can further overlay a third dimension of the effort it takes to address each driver to determine how to allocate the appropriate resources. Over time you can track how you are performing against these drivers.

9.5.4 Waterfall Analysis

Another common approach in business is what is referred to as a waterfall analysis (Wikipedia, 2020): analyzing shifts in what people select as their main driver for the recommend rating, tracked from one time period to another. It essentially looks at the lift or decline in NPS wave over wave and deconstructs what proportion of the change in score can be attributed to changes in the individual drivers, the reasons for the overall satisfaction or recommend score to go up or down. This is a very useful technique to explain wave-over-wave moves. Consider the hypothetical example in Table 9.5 to further explain how a waterfall analysis works.

TABLE 9.5 Example of a Waterfall Analysis

Reasons for the recommend rating	2018 Proportion	2019 Proportion	2018 NPS	2019 NPS
Experience with news Feed	80%	20%	10	0
Experience with Job Searching	20%	80%	50	45
Weighted overall NPS			18	36

Imagine a LinkedIn member can only select one or two reasons (news feed or job searching) for the stated recommend score across 2 subsequent years of surveying (2018 and 2019). The proportions in 2018 and 2019 of the selections made, and the NPS among those who either selected one or the other reason, are provided, including the overall weighted NPS.

First, the waterfall analysis looks at the NPS change caused by changes in what reasons are being selected; for example, more people may select job searching in 2018 simply because of a less favorable economy and lay-offs. In 2018, job searching has a higher likelihood of being selected regardless of whether the experience was a good or bad one. In other words, the fact that people selected it was simply based on external factors rather than a change in the experience, and we need to isolate that effect. Mathematically this would look something like the following:

1. Effect on NPS from a change in selection composition of the reasons: NPS * (2019 proportion – 2018 proportion) summed across both reasons:

   [0 * (20% – 80%)] + [45 * (80% – 20%)] = +27
   This results in a + 27 lift in NPS score.

2. We then look at the NPS change caused by what was selected as the reason for the NPS rating and the individual features or drivers of NPS by comparing the delta in NPS between 2018 and 2019:

   (2019 NPS – 2018 NPS) * 2018 proportion summed across both reasons: (0 – 10) * 80% + (45 – 50) * 20% = –9:

   - News feed contribution = (0 – 10) * 80% = –8
   - Job search contribution = (45 – 50) * 20% = –1

The change in selection composition due to the economy contributes 27 NPS points, and the changes in the product experience had a negative impact of –9 NPS with a net NPS impact of +18. Obviously, you need to ensure that the sample size is large enough to include the meaningful reasons across both waves, and it assumes that we capture all possible reasons for a change in NPS. An example of how the waterfall chart is presented is provided in Figure 9.8. This example is provided as a courtesy by Yukai Zhong (staff data scientist at LinkedIn).

FIGURE 9.8 Example of a Waterfall Analysis

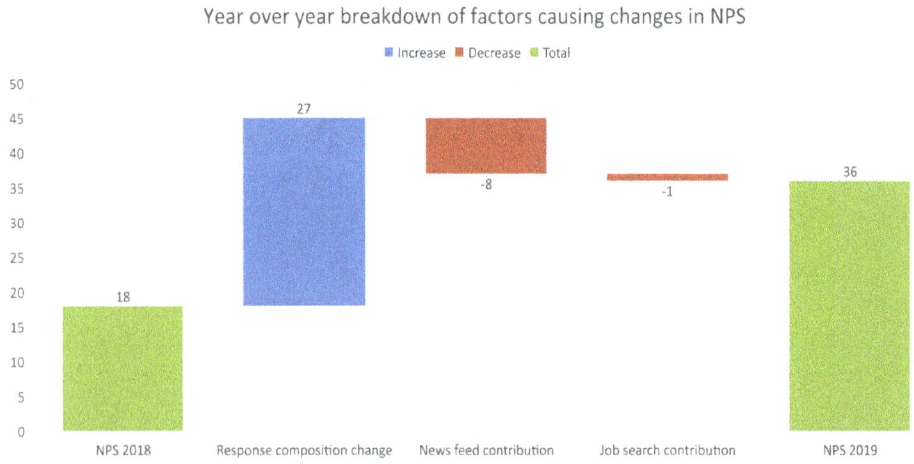

Often, we have access to a lot more information, not only from the survey but also from all the behaviors leading up to the customer taking the survey. We therefore highly recommend including everything in the model to determine what best drove a rating. Once the data set gets too large, you run into issues with overfitting, and so the number of responses is usually not large enough relative to the degrees of freedom from the attributes being included; there aren't enough respondents relative to the total number of metrics. In those instances, one may decide to use machine learning techniques, such as random forest modeling or bayes network.

9.5.5 Analyzing Open-Ended Responses

Open-ended responses are some of the most valuable pieces of information you will receive from the survey and are most helpful in providing actionable insights since they provide more color on the drivers and bring things to life. Drivers are sometimes not comprehensive enough, and there are various ways customers will interpret the same driver. For example, a stated response and rating to "quality of the product" doesn't allow the product team to focus on exactly what aspect needs to be improved, but combining this driver with the open-ended responses will shed more light on the prevalent interpretations. There are many packages out there that use NLP or k-means clustering to quickly find themes within your rich verbatim comments that teams can use to action against. You can also create word clouds as a quick way to visualize what words people use most frequently to describe dissatisfaction or satisfaction. (for more detailed information see Vriens et al., 2018, and Chen et al., 2018). Not only can you use text analytics to group verbatim comments in meaningful ways, but you can also analyze the sentiment and whether some quotes are more or less strongly worded and positive or negative.

9.5.6 Controllable and Uncontrollable Factors

When you start trending your satisfaction or NPS data from wave to wave, you will eventually find situations where the drivers don't explain why satisfaction is up or down. Your driver ratings are flat wave over wave, for example, but the NPS is down or up. If there is no sample selection bias and you have adjusted for any non-response bias or accounted for natural evolution of the business, this usually indicates there is a factor impacting the score that cannot be explained in the dataset you collected. There are several reasons why this can happen:

1. The identified drivers are not truly causally related to satisfaction. Remember, driver analysis is based on correlation, and correlation is not necessarily causation.
2. You didn't capture all the possible drivers or attribute statements that fully explain the overall experience. In other words, there are factors/variables that are causally related to satisfaction but that were simply not included in your survey. You won't know what happened with these drivers and if/how they might have affected customer satisfaction. Maybe verbatims from open-ended questions show things that respondents brought up that weren't part of the closed questions before and are new emerging trends that need to be codified in closed questions in future waves. Follow-up conversations may be necessary to get more clarity. Or, there is something happening in the macro environment or some other form of seasonality. If you included competitive benchmarking, which we recommend, and the decline is happening across the board, it's often a sign that something is happening in the macro economy or for the product category. How people feel about the macro economy and their personal finances often has an impact on how likely they are to recommend a product or service. These are factors that are entirely out of the control of the company. At LinkedIn, we track these trends carefully and include questions about people's feelings about the economy or their financial outlook. For example, when the economy is not doing well and there aren't as many jobs, we will see a decline of the job posts available on LinkedIn that is compounded by a general negative mood. As a result, people will have a poorer experience with LinkedIn, not because the product is poorer, but because there are fewer jobs to search for and a souring general mood. On the flipside, if the economy is doing well, sales professionals or outbound professionals, for example, who are compensated based on commission, are most likely to reap the benefits from a strong and growing economy. Leads are more likely to respond to outreach, and the tools sales professionals use for that are considered more effective, resulting in stronger ratings; it's not that the products are much better, but that they are simply having more success with them. LinkedIn noticed this effect in the surveys that were targeted at this segment. To properly understand these dynamics, one needs to collect enough data over at least a year to potentially correct for this and understand any other seasonality effects. But having the competitive benchmarks helps the organization to constantly recalibrate and determine if the organization is making true progress against improving satisfaction.

Competitive benchmarks are also useful to offset cultural bias when comparing different countries and to answer in which countries customers are more or less satisfied. Cultural bias stems from respondents in different regions of the world using the scale differently when responding due to cultural norms. For example, respondents in Germany and Japan tend to be more cautious and give lower ratings than respondents in Latin America. It's not that the product is much better in Latin America, but it's more of a function of how respondents use the scale differently. Knowing the gaps between you and the top competitor in each market can be used to determine relative strength and offset any cultural bias that exists in the absolute scores.

9.5.7 Social Listening and Online Reviews

Companies that operate in the B2C space and sell their products online have access to reviews and star ratings that can be used to track how well products are meeting expectations. Hotels and entertainment services can leverage sites such as Tripadvisor to mine ratings and feedback and in some cases integrate this back into their own feedback systems for ongoing improvement efforts and to close the loop with customers. Sentiment analysis can be performed to determine how strong the positive or negative reactions are. Furthermore, well-recognized brands can leverage discussions, comments, and likes that are organically happening on the internet, on social media, and in discussion forums.

9.6 HOW TO REPORT FOR IMPACT

At minimum, when you report the findings there are four overarching questions you are trying to answer: How is the company doing? What's working? What's not working? What does the company need to do to continue to make progress? The lens that organizations use can differ. At LinkedIn we look through two to four lenses along two dimensions for each product. How is the company doing in the marketplace relative to its competitors and available alternatives? How is the company doing internally when only looking at internal customers? Often, we have much more data from our internal NPS studies, and we can leverage that rich behavioral data for deeper insights and stronger product recommendations. We are also answering how we are doing with distinct groups of customers, such as end users and decision makers in the case of B2B markets. We split out the findings by end users, the users of the product, and decision makers, each with a different set of drivers. The top rows in the table in Figure 9.9 show the NPS scores for LinkedIn and competitors split by end users and decision makers. Each can come from different surveys and are conducted anonymously through a third-party panel provider to cover our own customers and customers of competitors. End users provide a view into how the product is performing from a user perspective, and the decision makers evaluate the performance of the company on things such as price, value, and account management. The bottom two quadrants represent surveys that are conducted internally among existing customers, again split by end users and decision makers. The figures are NPS ratings tracked every 6 months. The top two provide

FIGURE 9.9 End Users Decision Makers Chart

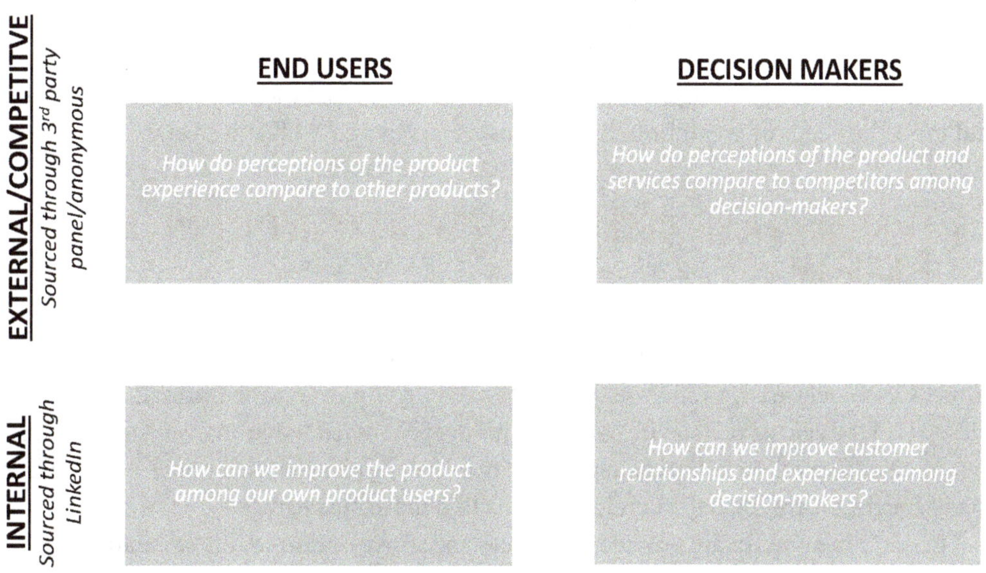

a market-based assessment and an objective read on how the products are performing vis-a-vis top competitors (i.e., how we do in the marketplace at large). The bottom two provide granular insights into what we need to do among our own customers to improve NPS. Absolutes cannot be compared across each quadrant, but over time they should move together. Reporting NPS this way can be challenging and requires a bit of education before it sticks, but if explained well it can provide valuable insights into how a company's internal actions affect its customers and standing in the marketplace.

We have found this framework to be most useful for executives to interpret and to help focus their attention. It clarifies what each survey does and doesn't answer, and while you cannot compare findings across surveys, it highlights how trends are correlated. The trend over time is looked at quarterly, monthly, and annually and changes in the trend (NPS delta) that are significant are highlighted against previous quarter and year over year. The time intervals depend on the rhythm of the business and how frequent you survey and can aggregate data points across a reliable sample. Scorecards are a useful way to describe the state of a customer's health and often we correlate these metrics with churn and revenue growth.

9.7 TARGET SETTING AND SIMULATIONS

A lot of companies set targets on NPS or satisfaction based on historical fluctuations from wave to wave and projecting what is achievable. Targets help drive accountability and provide focus and urgency. Absolute targets are tricky to determine given that there are many uncontrollable variables, but the best practice is to use the competitive benchmark of the top competitor's score. Beating that score or exceeding it by a certain amount is the goal.

The fluctuations from wave to wave justify going for a relative goal—relative to a competitor. In some cases, companies develop simulations leveraging the logistic regression models we discussed earlier to map out "what-if" scenarios: What if we pulled this driver or that driver and overlay cost/benefit analysis to determine the most optimal way to maximize satisfaction and meet the needs of greater numbers of customers in a cost-effective way?

9.8 EMBEDDING A SUCCESSFUL CUSTOMER EXPERIENCE MEASUREMENT PROGRAM

Customer satisfaction research has evolved far beyond the walls of the market research group. Customer satisfaction measurement is no longer purely done through a standalone survey for strategic or tactical insights, but it's deeply embedded in many organizations as part of customer relationship management; the survey in and of itself opens opportunities to engage the customer, have a dialogue, and close more business.

There are many software providers that offer extensive options to measure and integrate customer satisfaction measurement into Salesforce or Dynamics or create sophisticated systems to manage the customer touchpoints along a customer journey. A lot of the surveying is automated, trigger based, and always on; the responses come in on a daily basis and are triggered based on an experience—after a support call, when onboarding a new customer, and so on. Large amounts of data are collected, and in some cases the feedback is addressed in real time. Microsoft is building systems that suggest automated solutions to customer complaints from survey-based responses leveraging AI and advanced text analytics. Most companies have feedback loops where they follow up with customers and, based on the feedback, share what they have done to improve experiences as another way to engage the customer and drive upsells. Some respondents over time are being tracked to determine what interactions yield what types of outcomes and to determine more conclusively what actions have a causal effect.

Customer satisfaction has become so important that executives are being compensated and rewarded if annual satisfaction goals are met. We recommend against those practices for several reasons: (a) The NPS or satisfaction program becomes subject to auditing and monitoring rules, and most research teams are not staffed to address that; often the operations of NPS measurement move to the finance team, who is not equipped to analyze and drive effective action plans. Individual functions control aspects of the experience but not the entire experience, and often experiences are heavily integral to each other, leading teams to optimize for subsystems as opposed to the overall system. Goals need to be signed off on as a companywide objective for this to work, with executive stakeholders collectively being held accountable. NPS and satisfaction therefore needs to be considered a means to an end, and not an end in and of itself. High NPS drives revenue growth, so being customer centric is good for the customer and good for the company. There are lots of solutions from companies such as Medallia, Satmetrix, Qualtrics, and Maritz CX that provide sophisticated reporting and real-time tracking with automated alerts of drivers and issues that go to different functions to act on the insights and make ongoing improvements. The most sophisticated organizations rate green against areas highlighted in Table 9.6, and they often vary by business unit (BU) or product. These companies have embedded NPS or customer satisfaction in all their operations and apply sophisticated analyses to understand the causal relationship between their actions and the impact on the bottom line. Customer satisfaction has evolved from simply measuring things to a system of engagement to drive marketing and sales opportunities.

In conclusion, customer satisfaction is a field that is still rapidly growing, and every market researcher should be deeply aware of how to best go about measuring it and leverage it in a way that supports the company in becoming more customer centric and thus results in higher revenue. Engaging in customer satisfaction research provides the market research function with an opportunity to impact key decisions spanning product/marketing and sales. It's a jumping-off point into other interesting research and offers senior visibility and career growth opportunities.

TABLE 9.6 Best Practices

Best practices	BU1	BU2	BU3	BU4
Does our customer feedback data mirror our business/composition?	Green	Yellow	Yellow	Green
Is NPS formulated in a way that is comprehensive of overall relationship?	Green	Yellow	Green	Yellow
Cohort analysis to better understand detractors	Yellow	Yellow	Yellow	Yellow
Closing the loop w Customers through sales & marketing	Green	Orange	Yellow	Yellow
Communication strategy—results are clear and land well with sales, prod and mrkt	Green	Yellow	Yellow	Yellow
NPS integrated in rhythm of business	Green	Green	Green	Green
Mobilizing promoters for marketing purposes	Orange	Orange	Yellow	Yellow
NPS covers entire customer journey at all key interaction points across product suite	Orange	Orange	Orange	Orange
Data and results easily available, real time to the org	Orange	Orange	Orange	Orange
Business has a customer retention strategy	Yellow	Orange	Orange	Orange
Impact in taking action	Green	Orange	Yellow	Yellow
NPS linked to revenue	Green	Orange	Yellow	Orange
Longitudinal analysis (same respondent over time)	Orange	Orange	Orange	Orange

9.9 QUIZ AND EXERCISES

1. There are three measurement concepts described in the chapter. What is the most distinguishing benefit of each?
2. In the chapter we talk about the process and the outcome of customer satisfaction; how are these two terms different?
3. What is the difference between a blind and non-blind study?
4. Why do we need to weigh the data sometimes?
5. What is a key driver analysis?
6. What is an importance performance map? Can you think of two ways of creating these?
7. Look at Figure 9.6. What information is missing in this visualization? Can you think of a way to make it more insightful?
8. What is a waterfall analysis? Why and when is it useful?

REFERENCES

Babin, B., & Zikmund, W. (2010). *Exploring marketing research*. Cengage.

Basuroy, S., Gleason, K. C., & Kannan, Y. H. (2014). CEO compensation, customer satisfaction, and firm value. *Review of Accounting & Finance*, *13*(4), 326–352.

Chen, S., Vidden, C., Nelson, N., & Vriens, M. (2018). Topic modeling for open-ended survey responses. *Applied Marketing Analytics*, *4*(1), 53–62.

Evans, D. (2017). *Bottlenecks: Aligning UX design with user psychology*. Apress.

Fechner, G.T. (1966) Elements of psychophysics. Holt, Rinehart and Winston in New York.

Megan Burns with Michael E. Gazala, Carla O'Connor, Ryan Trafton, Rachel Birrell (2015). Understanding the impact of emotion on customer experience: Emotionally savvy brands combine CX discipline with empathy to make customers smile. Forrester

Gupta, S., & Zeithaml, V. (2006). Customer metrics and their impact on financial performance. *Marketing Science*, *25*(6), 718–739.

Haskel, J., & Westlake S. (2018). *Capitalism without capital*. Princeton University Press.

Hofmeyr, J., Goodall, V., Bongers, M., & Holzman, P. (2008). A new measure of brand attitudinal equity based on the Zipf distribution. *International Journal of Market Research*, 50(2), 181–202.

Howard, J. A. & Sheth, J. N. (1969). *The theory of buyer behavior*. Wiley.

Inside Research. (2012). Special report: US CSM spend back. 23, 289, 3, p. 16.

Kahneman, D. (2011). *Thinking, fast and slow*. Farrar, Straus and Giroux.

Keiningham, T. L., Cooil, B., Malthouse, E. C., Buoye, A., & Laviviere, B. (2015). Perceptions are relative: An examination of the relationship between relative satisfaction metrics and share of wallet. *Journal of Service Management*, *26*(1), 2–43.

Likert, R. (1932). A technique for the measurement of attitudes. *Archives of Psychology*, *140*, 1–55.

Luo, X., Homburg, C., & Wieseke, J. (2010). Customer satisfaction, analysts' stock recommendations, and firm value. *Journal of Marketing Research*, *47*(6), 1041–1058.

Luo, X., Homburg, C., & Wieseke, J. (2012). Incentivizing CEOs to build customer- and employee-firm relations for higher customer satisfaction and firm value. *Journal of the Academy of Marketing Science, 40*(6), 745–758.

Nenycz, M., Beal, V., Ludwichowska, G., & Romaniuk, J. (2013). Investigating the accuracy of self-reports of brand usage behavior. *Journal of Business Research, 66*(2), 224–232.

Morgan, N. A., & Rego, L. L. (2006). The value of different customer satisfaction and loyalty metrics in predicting business performance. *Marketing Science, 25*(5), 426–439.

Murre, J. M. J., & Dross, J. (2015). Replication and analysis of Ebbinghaus forgetting curve. *PLOS One, 10*(7), 1–23.

Norwich, K. H., & Wong, W. (1997). Unification of psychophysical phenomena: The complete form of Fechner's Law. *Perception & Psychophysics, 59*(6), 929–940.

O'Sullivan, D., & McCallig, J. (2012). Customer satisfaction, earnings, and firm value. *European Journal of Marketing*, 46(6), 827–843.

Parasuraman A., Zeithaml V. A., & Berry L. L. (1985). A conceptual model of service quality and its implications for future research. *Journal of Marketing, 49*(4), 41–50.

Porter, M. (1979). How competitive forces shape strategy. *Harvard Business Review, 57*(2), 137–145.

Reichheld, F. (2003). The one number that you need to grow. *Harvard Business Review, 81*(12), 46–54.

Sharp, B. (2010). *How brands grow: What marketers don't know*. Oxford University Press.

Smith, R. E., & Wright, W. F. (2004). Determinants of customer loyalty and financial performance. *Journal of Management Accounting Research, 16*(1), 183–205.

The Harris Poll. (2016). 28th annual EquiTrend Study.

Tourangeau, R. (2000). Remembering what happened: Memory errors and survey reports. In A. A. Stone, J. S. Turkkan, C. A. Bachrach, J. B. Jobe, H. S. Kurtzman, & V. S. Cain (Eds.), *The science of self-reports: Implications for research and practice* (pp. 29–47). Lawrence Erlbaum & Associates.

Tse, D. K., & Wilton, P. C. (1988). Models of consumer satisfaction formation: An extension. *Journal of Marketing Research, 25*(2), 204–212.

Vavra, T. (1997). Improving your measurement of customer satisfaction: A guide to creating, conducting, analyzing, and reporting customer satisfaction measurement programs. ASQ.

Vriens, M., Chen, S., & Vidden, C. (2018). *From data to decision: Handbook for the modern business analyst*. Cognella.

Wikipedia. (2020, January 4). Waterfall chart. https://en.wikipedia.org/wiki/Waterfall_chart

Yi, Y. (1991). A critical review of consumer satisfaction. In V. A. Zeithaml (Ed.), *Review of marketing 1990* (pp. 68–123). American Marketing Association.

Zipf, G. K. (1935). *The psycho-biology of language: An introduction to dynamic philology*. Houghton-Mifflin.

Image Credits

Fig. 9.2: Copyright © 2018 Depositphotos/goodstocker.yandex.ru.

Fig. 9.4a: Copyright © by Uber.

CHAPTER 10

NEURO MARKETING RESEARCH

10.1 WHAT AM I GOING TO LEARN?

Consumers are not always rational people who make decisions in their own best interests; they are not always able to tell us in a survey what they want or what they would like. Sometimes they may simply lie, or they may feel ashamed to reveal what they really like. An example is the Enron office chair. When it was first developed and tested, consumers apparently hated it, only to become later one of the most successful office chairs (Gladwell, 2005; 2016). This is not the only example where marketing research sometimes can fail decision-makers.

The new field of neuro marketing research offers new tools to gain insight into consumers' behavior and may let us understand deeper subconscious and sometimes (seemingly) irrational behaviors, behaviors that consumers cannot explain themselves. We may get more valid answers. Though considered an emerging field, iconic companies such as Coca-Cola, Campbell's, and Kimberly Clark have commercially adopted these once academic-only methods (e.g., Lin et al., 2018).

In this chapter, we first start with the reasons why should YOU know about this field. Second, we briefly review the following approaches:

- *Biometric methods.* This includes (a) measuring brain activity via functional magnetic resonance imaging (fMRI), (b) electroencephalogram (EEG) and magnetoencephalogram (MEG), (c) eye tracking (this involves measuring where the eyes fixate and for how long and can possibly measure pupil width (all indications of interest and preference), and (d) galvanic skin response.
- *Implicit attitudes.* These are measured via response-time solutions: neuro marketing research tools that measure the speed at which respondents answer closed survey questions. This response speed is an indication of emotional conviction to the chosen answer.
- *Facial coding.* When consumers look at something (e.g., a brand, a (new) product, an ad, a video, etc.), the facial expressions can reveal how people feel about something and can predict behavior. Initially facial coding was done manually, but developments in AI and machine learning have led to automatic ways to measure human emotions through their facial expressions.

10.2 WHY NEUROSCIENCE?

The field of neuroscience research has exploded in recent years and we are starting to understand more about how the brain operates and processes information—how neurons fire and wire together to form emotions, memories, and impressions. Consider the following examples:

The Effect of Irrelevant Cues

In a recent study (Vriens & Schomaker, 2019), respondents were shown a series of two snacks, one of the left-side of the screen, and the other on the right side of the screen. Snacks, of course, differ in appeal. Some might prefer a chocolate bar over a bag of chips or vice versa. When preference differences are large, respondents will typically choose the snack they like most. However, when presented with snacks that are somewhat equal in appeal, we found that we could get them to choose one snack over the other simply by showing an arrow pointing to that snack. The arrow had no relation to the snack and did not offer any information, yet by simply redirecting respondents' attention to one of the snacks, that snack had a higher probability of being chosen.

The Effect of Subtle Ad Differences

Ohme et al. (2009) tested two different ads for female skincare products. Both ads were very similar. There was only a slight difference: In one version the female in the ad made a small manual gesture that was barely noticeable. Both ads were shown to two groups of females. Participants in the study watched a program interrupted by ads (one of which was either version 1 or version 2 of the tested ad). The version with the subtle manual gesture scored significantly higher in terms of their knowledge of the products benefits (consumer learning) and were significantly more likely to choose the target skincare product as a complimentary gift (at the end of the experiment).

Priming

Priming refers to the phenomenon that seeing something associated with a brand, product, or consumption occasion, yet at the same time unrelated, can induce or change behavior toward that brand. Several studies have investigated this effect, sometimes from different angles. One angle comes from the spreading activation theory (Anderson, 1983; Collins & Loftus, 1975; Quillian, 1967), which states that human memory involves networks of associations. For example, I may associate toothpaste with Colgate, fresh breath, and gum health. When concerns about gum health or fresh breath come up, the brand Colgate may also pop up (e.g., Vriens et al., 2019). But, I may also associate Colgate with red; and hence seeing red prior to me walking into the toothpaste aisle may already have "primed" the brand name Colgate in my mind, and I may be more likely to buy Colgate. When NASA landed its Pathfinder on the planet Mars, Mars candy bars also noticed an increase in sales (White, 1997; see also Berger & Fitzsimons, 2008). Phenomena like this are called priming effects. Through the news on NASA the name "Mars" was primed in consumers' mind, and this was associated with candy, and resulted in higher brand sales. Berger and Fitzsimons (2008) did several interesting experiments on priming. In one experiment they used students; some of them had recently traveled to campus, and some were already there. The students were shown different slogans for a CD player, a slogan that linked CD players to traveling and a control slogan (no specific association). A week later, they were asked about their likelihood to buy and willingness to pay for CD players. Those who had been exposed to the traveling slogan were significantly more likely to buy a CD player and were significantly more willing to pay for it.

The effect of context or contrast is important in how consumers make decisions—the surroundings in which we make decisions or consume a product or see an ad has an impact on how we interpret things.

For example, which line is longer in Figure 10.1?

FIGURE 10.1 Perception Versus Reality Adapted From Müller-Lyer Illusion

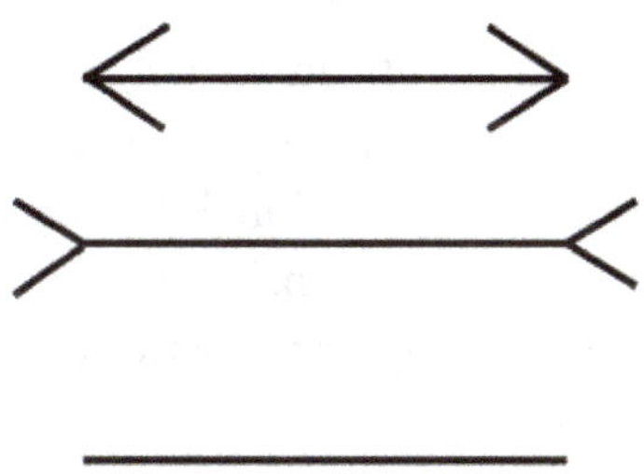

The answer is that they are all the same size. Our brains get tripped up because of the arrows, making the same line look smaller or larger depending on whether its outward or inward facing. The gray color in Figure 10.2 looks darker on the right, but it's the same color. The lighter frame around it makes it look darker; this is called a framing effect.

FIGURE 10.2 Perception Versus Reality

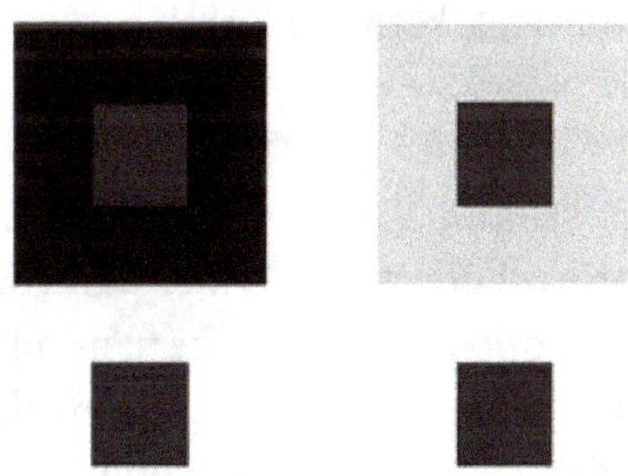

Imagine an ad being shown within a context or in a series of other ads preceding it, or the movie or TV show it is shown in—all of these surrounding events have an impact on someone's perceptions and are difficult for people to rationalize or express how these impact decisions.

Humans are notoriously bad at isolating cause and effect from individual factors. Neuroscience tools are more effective at picking up these sensitivities and how the environment interacts with the ad so that we can isolate the true effect of it from the environment. Color, sound, and anything that stimulates our senses have predisposed meanings in our brain; they are engrained to stand for something. Red stands for energy and passion, while yellow radiates warmth, and blue is often associated with depth and stability. Logos, which is a brand's most valuable cue and anchor to help consumers quickly identify and process what the commercial is for and all that a brand stands for plays a key role in advertising. Some of the world's most well-known brands don't need to spell out the name anymore because the shape of a logo is engrained in people's brains; think of the Apple symbol in the Apple logo, the red circles of Target, or the imagery of nautical character in the Starbucks logo.

If you were asked to think of the last time you purchased toothpaste in a store, can you remember all the brands you looked at? Can you remember which aisles you walked to find what you needed? If you were asked to look at a TV commercial, can you tell precisely what you looked at in the commercial? Can you indicate how your attention wavered across the screen while you were watching, or how your emotions changed during the ad? You will probably not be able to answer these questions. But these are important questions for marketers. Understanding consumer's emotions, their attention span, their behavior, and their immediate responses to marketing decisions, like commercials and packaging, will help improve the impact of commercials, will drive sales, and will improve brand positioning against competitors. Neuro marketing is designed to help explain the parts of human's actions that cannot be observed directly through a survey or an interview. Neuro marketing can help address questions around emotion, attention, and memory by measuring people's unconscious responses instead of asking respondents to translate their emotions in an answer to a closed question in a questionnaire.

Research has shown how poor we are at identifying and labeling our feelings. Feelings are simply not considered important in many cultures around the globe. "Our repertoire of words for calling people names is often larger than our vocabulary of words to clearly describe our emotional states," yet emotion plays such a key role in how we make decisions (Rosenberg, 2015, p. 37). Furthermore, Binet and Field (2017) have demonstrated that emotional ad campaigns are two times as likely to be effective in driving profit and market share as rational ones.

10.2.1 Key Applications

Getting a better understanding of emotions, memory, and attention helps marketers come up with better working marketing programs. Following are some key applications where neuro marketing research has been shown to add to our understanding.

Advertising Development and Testing

In traditional research, respondents are asked to watch a commercial reel and are asked a series of questions. Which advertisements can you recall? What do you remember from the ad? Do you remember the name of the brands? What aspects did you like or dislike? But these questions cannot measure how the commercials made them feel. Traditional research has difficulty answering respondents' more emotional state of mind. Which parts of the commercial are more engaging? At which point in the commercial do people start tuning out? Which elements of the commercial are more exciting? For advertisers, feedback to these more emotional questions can help turn a good commercial in a great commercial. In today's world, with so many options for consumers to switch away from commercials, and consumers' short attention span, it is only the great advertisements that break through the clutter and grasp people's attention. Neuro marketing can help answer these questions. For example, Figure 10.3 shows the results of a test where respondents' skin perspiration is measured while they watch a KIA commercial to track their level of arousal. It clearly shows two areas where the respondents were truly engaged and the areas where they were tuning out. This information can be used to improve the commercial's storyline and improve the overall level of arousal.

FIGURE 10.3 Enhancing Focus Groups with Galvanic Skin Response

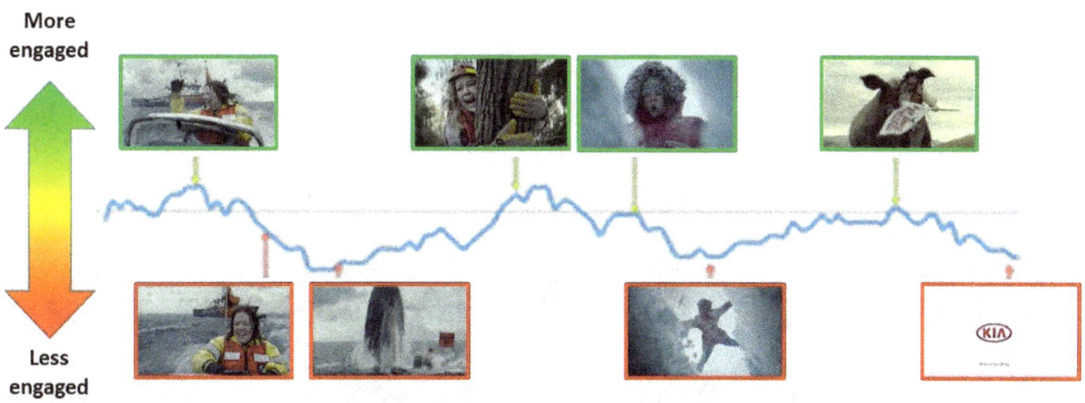

Packaging and Design

In developing new product concepts or designing new packaging in traditional research, respondents are asked what the first thing is that they looked at. But, as we said in the introduction, it is hard to control your eye movements. It is also hard to remember the first thing you looked at. Your eyes flicker very fast over a product when you pick it up, and in a fraction of a second you have decided if you like the packaging. But in that fraction of a second, what caught your eye to make such a decision? Can you tell? Try it for yourself and you will see how hard it is to put in words what your eyes did, and in which order your eyes flickered over a product. A common tool from neuro marketing is to track your eye movements through sophisticated eye-tracking glasses. With this tool, the researcher can track precisely how your eyes moved over the product or packages to see what caught your eye. In an increasingly digital world, neuro marketing research is also starting to play a key role in web usability research and in identifying what parts of a site are causing barriers for effective engagement or in understanding how emotions during the product experience affect brand perceptions.

Shopper Research

In shopper research, researchers want to understand how people shop—what routes they take through a store, what products they consider, pick up, and put in their basket. With so many choices, most of these decisions are unconscious. Shoppers love routines when they shop. People take the same route through the store, find their usual brands, and look for the shortest checkout line. For brands to break through these routines, they need to stand out on the shelf. Market researchers want to understand these subconscious shopper routines and how the shopper selects a product from the shelf. Do they scan all the products on the shelf to search for their usual brands? Do they check prices? Do they look at the packaging? Neuro marketing is a noninvasive way to track people's shopper behavior. Eye-tracking glasses show how shoppers look at shelves and at packaging in a real store. Alternatively, respondents can be asked to wear a virtual reality head set and move through a virtual store, often indistinguishable from real stores.

Political Polling and Public Opinion Research

Neuro marketing is widely used in testing and improving political speeches. Figure 10.4 shows the results of study where people's perspiration was measured while watching a political debate.

FIGURE 10.4 Using Neuromarketing in Politics

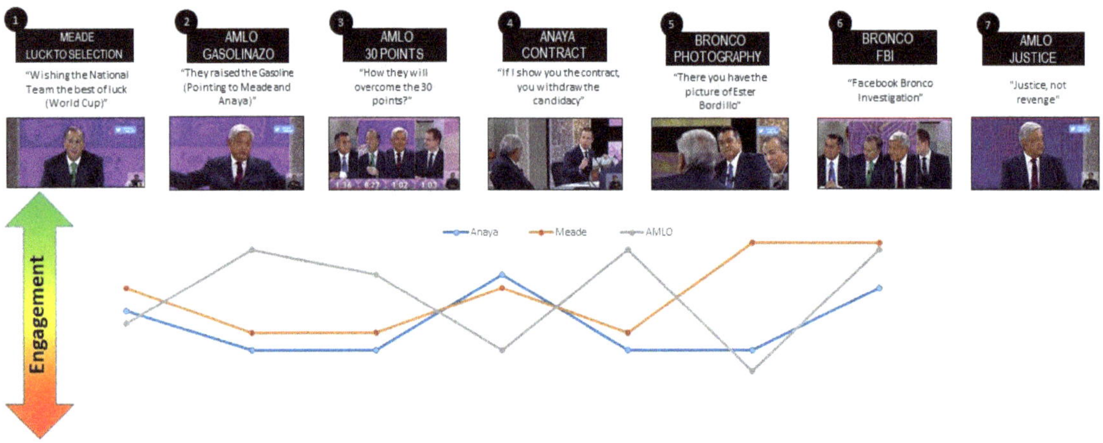

In this example the results were used to test the likeability of the different candidates and which arguments were most powerful. But they can also be used to finetune the content and the delivery of a speech to a target audience.

10.3 OVERVIEW OF KEY METHODOLOGIES

In this section we briefly review the key neuro marketing research methods (e.g., fMRI, EEG, eye tracking, implicit attitudes, and facial coding) (for more detail on some methods, see Sebastian, 2014).

10.3.1 fMRI

Functional magnetic resonance imaging is a technique (a very expensive technique) that reveals changes in blood flows in the brain. fMRI yields static images (e.g., across 10 second intervals). The benefit of fMRI is high resolution and the ability to look deep in the brain (e.g., amygdala, where emotion resides). The limitation is the time delay between images (Vecchiato et al., 2011), and currently this method is very expensive and not practical for commercial marketing research.

10.3.2 EEG

EEG is a monitoring method to record electrical activity of the brain; sometimes the electrical activity is referred to as brainwaves (e.g., Lin et al., 2018). With noninvasive monitoring devices, sensors are placed along the scalp. Figure 10.5 shows an example of a wearable EEG device used by market researchers.

FIGURE 10.5 EEG Headset

These EEG devices measure voltage fluctuations in the brain and can therefore detect brief neuronal events. Thanks to this property, it can detect and measure sudden implicit customers' reactions to various stimuli, such as an advertisement or new packaging. EEG has much shorter time intervals than fMRI (milliseconds), but the downside is that the recorded brain waves mainly stem from the cerebral cortex.

EEG is commonly used to detect (a) emotional arousal, how much consumers are aroused by an ad, a product, or an experience; (b) emotional motivation, the valence of the emotional response; and (c) cognitive load, if people are actively processing the information given or if they are experiencing information overload and stress.

Figure 10.6 shows an example of an output from study where EEG was used to evaluate three advertisement concepts.

FIGURE 10.6 Using Neuroscience in Shopping Research

EEG can help us understand cognitive and emotional brain processes better. For example, Ohme et al. (2009, 2010) used EEG to observe brain waves as respondents looked at TV commercials. In Ohme et al. (2009), a subtle difference in ads was shown to have big behavioral impact. Both EEG and galvanic skin response showed significant differences at the moment the subtle hand movement happened. Respondents were not able to verbally articulate the impact of this hand movement. In the 2010 Ohme et al. study, TV commercials that respondents remembered correlated with the degree of cortical spectral activity. According to Ohme et al. (2010), one benefit of using neuroscience methods is that it can pick up effects of advertising that consumers may not be able to verbalize yet. Some effects of learning may happen subconsciously. EEG has also been shown to be predictive. For example, Boksem and Smidts (2015) predicted box office sales and Ma et al. (2007) predicted success of brand extension.

10.3.3 Eye Tracking

The use of eye tracking has become common in marketing research. It tracks what you are looking at while you are watching an ad, walking through a store, or looking at a product. Figure 10.7 shows a real example of a respondent wearing both an EEG and an eye-tracking device while she shops for face care products.

FIGURE 10.7 Example of an Eye Tracking Heatmap

The results of an eye-tracking study are often visualized in a heatmap (see Figure 10.7).

Areas where the eyes spend more time are color-coded red, and areas where the eyes briefly pause are coded yellow or green. And, areas that are not actively noticed are not color coded. In this example, the heatmap shows that most respondents focus on the woman's face and the copy text and focus less on the brand name.

It is very hard to consciously control your eye movements; try it for yourself. Take a product in your hand and try not to look at a certain area. As you probably notice, your eyes have a will of their own.

Eye tracking is therefore a very powerful tool to figure out what respondents are really focusing on (i.e., it is a way to determine what attracts a consumer's attention and how much attention consumers are giving to various stimuli (say, potential ads, products on a shelf etc.)). It is used to understand which visuals are seen and which are missed and where visual attention is focused, for how long, and in what order.

In addition to the heatmaps, eye tracking yields several interesting and actionable measures:

- Fixation time and count. For example, if people stand in front of a supermarket shelf, how long are they looking at each product (fixation time)? How often do they switch back and forth (resulting fixation count)?
- The scan path. What items are they looking at and in which order?

It is often used for pack and communication design optimization, understanding user experience, and POS and shelf-set optimization.

FIGURE 10.8 Ipsos panel

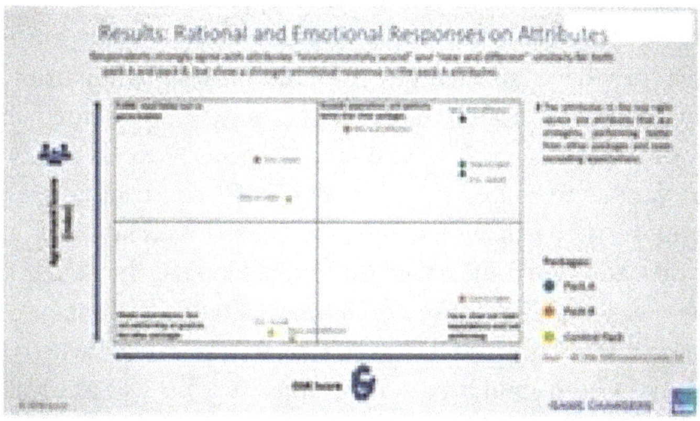

10.3.4 Galvanic Skin Response

Galvanic skin response (GSR) measures changes in galvanic skin response through small changes in skin perspiration on the fingers (see Figure 10.8).

These changes are driven by factors such as intensity of emotional response and stress. Skin response is automatic and changes without our conscious control, modulated by our autonomic nervous system. Obviously, this method cannot indicate whether this emotional response is positive or negative. It does not give us detail on the emotional response. It should therefore always be paired with a survey or other conscious research method to gain a complete understanding of the respondents' response. Figure 10.8 shows an example where people were asked to watch a few concept ads while their skin response was tracked. After this they were interviewed in one-on-one interviews to get a deeper understanding of the details behind their unconscious emotional responses.

If the researcher would have relied solely on the agreement score, she would have chosen a different winner.

In the 1940s and 1950s GSR was already being tested (Eckstrand & Gilliland, 1948; Golin & Lyerly, 1950). As mentioned (see section on EEG), Ohme et al. (2009) found that subtle differences in ads (a subtle, brief hand movement) were shown to have big behavioral impact and showed significant differences in GSR. One possible issue to be aware of is that GSR may be unable to differentiate between liking and disliking (e.g., Labarbera & Tucciarone, 1995; this paper discusses several case studies, and they conclude that GSR scores correlate with market performance, and interestingly that GSR responses are often in contradiction with self-report measures, while GSR being a better predictor of consumer behavior).

10.3.5 Response Time Solutions

A widely used neuro marketing solution is measuring not only what scores respondents give on questions in an online or mobile questionnaire but measuring how fast respondents choose an answer to a closed question. This is called implicit reaction time (IRT; e.g., Moses, 2015). The idea is that the faster a respondent responds, the more conviction they have in the answer and the more likely the response can be classified as an "implicit" response. Such responses are believed to be more automatic and originating from system 1 instead of system 2; they are hypothesized to more likely represent how someone truly feels about a brand or a product. For example, traditionally, in brand research, respondents are asked to rate a brand on various attributes on a scale of 1 to 5. These attributes can be "a brand I trust," or "a brand I choose when I am with friends." IRT then tracks how fast respondents chooses a rating after they are shown the question. Now we look at the data in two ways. One, we can ignore the speed of the response and just calculate the percentage of respondents who said they trust the brand (say 75% did), and two, we can calculate how many respondents said they trusted the brand and gave their response in a fast way (say this number was 56%). The 56% is said to be a more valid number than the 75%, as the responses came faster. It also has been shown that if respondents respond faster it is less likely for response style effects to kick in (e.g., Vriens & Martins Alves, 2017).

IRT is a tool that can be incorporated in many online or mobile questionnaires. But it requires some additional time on the questionnaire. Prior to the actual implicit response time test, the testing tool has to be calibrated to respondents personal response speeds: i.e., respondents have different normal response speeds. For example, say an older respondent who eyesight is not as good anymore as it used to be may just need a little more time to read the questions. Fast and slow responses hence need to be assessed in the context of this person's baseline response time. The tool will therefore first ask you a few questions to establish your normal response speed. It will then compare the speed of the response to other questions to the speed at which you answered these calibration questions.

In Figure 10.9 you can see the actual differences between an explicit yes (result from a survey question) and an empathetic yes (results from IRT). It shows that Apple is an innovative brand, but Citibank is not felt as a trustful brand as much as people say it is.

FIGURE 10.9 Explicit Versus Implicit Attitude Results

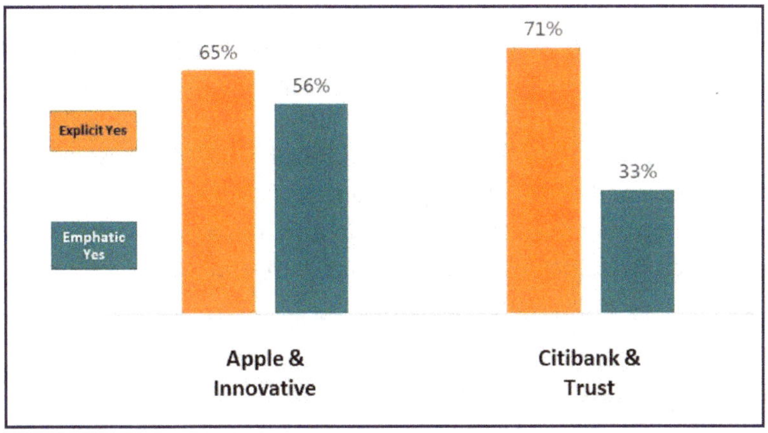

10.3.6 Facial Coding

Facial expressions are a way in which humans communicate nonverbally. We can express many emotions by simply positioning the muscles beneath the skin of our faces slightly different. There are seven basic emotions, each with their own unique and distinctive facial expressions: happiness, sadness, fear, disgust, anger, contempt, and surprise (e.g., Blaiech et al., 2013). But our faces can express various levels of these basic emotions: very happy, just happy, or even so slightly happy.

The interpretation of facial coding can be done manually or (semi) automatically. Specific coding systems have been developed for this, such as the Facial Action Coding Systems (FACS) (e.g., McDuff & el Kaliouby, 2017). This system distinguishes 28 facial actions, and trained human experts are required to apply this system (one cannot just apply this system without training). McDuff and el Kaliouby (2017) used five facial actions: (a) smiling, (b) eyebrow raise, (c) eye furrow, (d) nose wrinkle, and (e) upper lip raise or depression. They analyzed YouTube videos and showed that (within a certain category) videos that elicited higher-than-average (for the category) smiles were more successful than videos with an average number of smiles. Likewise, the other facial actions also were found to be related to video performance (albeit their effects were smaller). Teixeira, Picard, and el Kaliouby (2014) found that smiling in response to TV ads was related to purchase intent.

With the advancements of artificial intelligence algorithms, facial coding can now be done in real time and is fully automated. Webcams record the respondents' facial expressions while they are shown an ad, a product, or a brand. Computer algorithms

FIGURE 10.10 Facial Coding

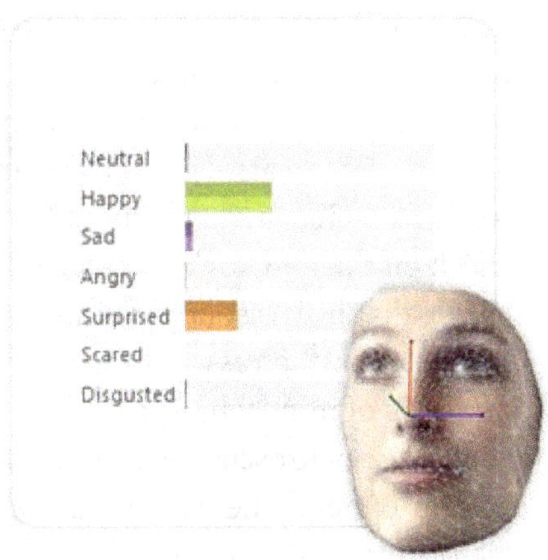

translate these facial expressions automatically in facial actions (that represent certain emotions). This facial coding is much more sophisticated than simply happy or sad. Figure 10.10 shows an example where the respondent was shown an ad while the webcam on her laptop captured her facial expressions. Her emotions were coded in real time and shared with the researcher. The computer translated her facial expressions into seven categories (neutral, happy, sad, angry, surprised, scared, and disgusted). And, in each of these categories, the bar chart showed the level of depth of this expression.

The results gave the marketer deep insights in how and where to make changes to the ad. These facial coding solutions are widely available to researchers, and they can be done online and are very easy to execute.

10.4 A PERSPECTIVE FROM LINKEDIN

At LinkedIn we leverage a combination of EEG, eye tracking, facial coding, and survey questions to determine how effective an ad (video or static) is in driving emotion, attention, relevance, and, ultimately, engagement and action intent. The goal of a campaign may be going to our website and searching for jobs, purchasing a premium subscription, humanizing the brand, or simply driving brand recognition and awareness.

EEG picks up what parts of the ad trigger heightened activities of emotion and memory before and after showing of the ad. Ads need to be emotional, to some degree, to be effective, as they are triggers for drawing someone in and getting attention. (We discussed this when we reviewed storytelling and how important it is to draw in your audience when sharing findings.) This element is no different in ad effectiveness. Emotion is a powerful way to create new neural connections and encode the brand in people's brains. We tend to remember things more easily if they are linked to a certain emotion. Memory activation, on the other hand, measures how well the ad is playing into a prior experience or something relevant to you personally, which makes retrieval of your brand more easy. Things that are personally relevant tend to draw us in, are better able to hold our attention, and have a higher likelihood of cutting through the clutter when many ads are vying for people's attention online or on TV. They capture our attention when we are busy engaging with multiple devices at once. We can link them to experiences that are familiar. For example, if we show an ad with someone drinking a cup of coffee and opening the LinkedIn app to check out the news feed, we are trying to associate a familiar morning ritual with the LinkedIn brand so that when we drink coffee in the morning "LinkedIn" is triggered and prompts consumers to use it to check on the news or accept a connection request. Of course, it will take many exposures before that link is solidified in people's mind, but the goal of ads is to develop rich neural networks through associations around a brand so that your brand and the product become more top of mind when you have a defined or undefined need.

In these neuroscience tests you typically bring in a random group of consumers, who are in your target audience, into a lab. It's important to carefully screen and determine what factors may influence the objective of your test (i.e., assess how effective the ad creative is in engaging an audience). A strong creative is an important lever for success. Usually 20–30 participants will be enough to measure whether your ad is effective, as brains work remarkably similar; the same parts of our brain get activated for emotion, memory, and attention, and the goal is to collect many observations per participant versus lots of observations from many people. The test requires these participants to be hooked up to an EEG, and sensors are directly applied to the skull. The EEG test may involve exposing your participants to a brand, its logo, competitive brands, messages you want to convey, and random words for split seconds to establish a baseline before showing the ad. The test takes place in a quiet room with no distractions. The initial read is also used to calibrate the test for everyone. The ad is then shown, and afterward we again measure reactions to the brand logos and words to determine if there was a lift in brain activity before and after exposure to the ad. Any lift can only be attributed to the campaign as everything else was held constant; therefore, a lift suggests that the ad is effective to some degree. You also want to review the results from the EEG against a normative database of other ads to see whether the lift was enough to consider it effective and creative.

The EEG output typically involves several reports: a second-by-second evaluation of how a video ad is doing on memory, attention, and emotion across the participants and an overall evaluation on how well certain key messages are coming through or how well the brand gets activated. In many categories, there are several competitors, and in highly competitive categories it's not unusual that the main competitor gets some attribution from an ad that was mostly about your brand. The reason is that many elements of the campaign activate a memory structure that is associated with elements of the category rather than the individual brand. We refer to this as co-activation. Think of Burger King ads and how they automatically make you think of McDonald's as well. Burger King features a hamburger, and the hamburger is part of the same neural network as McDonald's, so it's no surprise that unconsciously we are attributing parts of the ad to McDonald's too. It's therefore important that Burger King minimizes any co-activation by putting out a distinct ad campaign with its brand clearly visible.

Successful ads show that memory, emotion, and attention activity in the brain are moving synchronously. High attention but low memory activation suggests that an ad creative may be too complex, and people's brains must work too hard to determine what is going on, which comes with the risk of people switching off. Now imagine taking the ad outside of this lab environment where participants are focused and into their daily lives, constantly distracted when online or watching TV, it will be difficult for such an ad to do well.

For LinkedIn ads, EEG helped us realize that we needed to keep story lines very focused and simple, focusing on one key message, and that branding initially wasn't coming through as much as we wanted. These things were more difficult to pick up on when we did the focus groups. Eye tracking helps us understand what parts of the ad, static or video, people pay attention to down to specific pixels. The output is a heatmap overlay of the ad. The dark red spots highlight where people's eyes land, and it helps to understand if people are paying attention to the things we want them to pay attention to: the brand logo or a message or a product being featured. It informs the creative team on what can be done to more effectively execute the campaign and how to make changes to elements that may be too distracting.

Neuro marketing research is an exciting field, and we are seeing real advantages of this type of research when combined with more traditional survey-based research. It's important that the organization is ready for neuroscience and that people understand how to interpret the findings and limitations. And, particularly with ad creative testing, it's clear that market research is not replacing the creative process but rather strengthens it and works collaboratively with the creative studio.

10.5 QUIZ AND EXERCISES

- In what type of marketing situations would you recommend a neuromarketing research approach?
- What types of neuromarketing research did we discuss in this chapter?
- A supermarket wants to determine whether their case display for lunchmeat is optimally organized. What neuromarketing research approach could you apply best here? Explain why.
- What is a limitation of EEG methods?
- When we use eye tracking we capture the fixations of two eyes. What types of metrics do we use to capture this type of data?
- Campbell Soup developed a few new ads. They want to know how these ads are performing in terms of their ability to tell a story and creative an emotional connection with the brand. Which neuromarketing research is best and why?
- What is a distinct advantage of neuromarketing research? What is a potential downside?
- You just started working for Boeing. Given their recent issues and their struggle to deal with the recent air disasters, the marketing research team decided to commission a survey where they ask frequent travelers how much they trust Boeing and Boeing's planes. The sample size is N = 1,000. Trust was measured on a 10-point scale, ranging from 1= "I do not trust Boeing at all" to 10 = "I fully trust Boeing." The average in the sample of this question was 5.6—not super high, but overall given what happened not that bad either. However, the PR director is not convinced, and she exclaims, "People lie on surveys, or they give answers they think we want to hear." Is she right in her concerns? What would you suggest to mitigate her concerns?

REFERENCES

Anderson, J. R. (1983). A spreading activation theory of memory. *Journal of Verbal Learning and Verbal Behavior, 22*(3), 261–295.

Berger, J., & Fitzsimons (2008). Dogs on the street, Pumas on your feet: How cues in the environment influence product evaluation and choice. *Journal of Marketing Research, 45*(1), 1–14.

Binet, L. & Field, P. (2017). Media in focus: Marketing effectiveness in the digital era. Institute for Practitioners in Advertising.

Blaiech, H., Neji, M., Wali, A., & Alimi, A.M. (2013, December). Emotion recognition by analysis of EEG signals. Paper presented at the 13th International Conference on Hybrid Intelligent Systems, HAIS 2013, Tunis, Tunesia, Proceedings, pages 312-318.

Boksem, M. A. S., & Smidts, A. (2015). Brain responses to movie trailers predict individual preferences for movies and their population-wide commercial success. Journal of Marketing Research, *52*(4), 482–492.

Collins, A. M., & Loftus, E. F. (1975). A spreading activation theory of semantic processing. *Psychological Review, 82*(6), 407–428.

Eckstrand, G., & Gilliland, A. R. (1948). The psychogalvanometric method for measuring the effectiveness of advertising. *Journal of Applied Psychology, 32*(4), 415–425.

Gladwell, M. (2005). Blink: The power of thinking without thinking. Time Warner Book Group, NY, USA.

Gladwell, M. (2016). *The pitfalls of marketing research* [Video file]. https://www.youtube.com/watch?v=964va3YwPms

Golin, E., & Lyerly S. B. (1950). The galvanic skin response as a test of advertising impact. *Journal of Applied Psychology, 34*(6), 440–443.

Kandel, E. (2013). The new science of mind and the future of knowledge. *Neuron, 80*(3), 546–560.

Labarbera, P. A., & Tucciarone, J. D. (1995). GSR reconsidered: A behavior-based approach to evaluating and improving the sales potency of advertising. *Journal of Advertising Research, 35*(5), 33–53.

Lin, M-H., Cross, S. N. N., Jones, W. J., & Childers, T. L. (2018). Applying EEG in consumer neuroscience. *European Journal of Marketing, 52*(1–2), 66–91.

Ma, Q., Wang, X., Dai, S., & Liangchao, S. (2008). P300 and categorization in brand extension. *Neuroscience Letters, 431*(1), 57–67.

McDuff, D., & el Kaliouby, R. (2017). Applications of automated facial coding in media measurement. *IEEE Transactions on Effective Computing, 8*(2), 148–160.

Milosavljevic, M., & Cerf, M. (2008). First attention then intention: Insights from computational neuroscience of vision. *International Journal of Advertising, 27*(3), 381–398.

Moses, E. (2015). *Implicit reaction time (IRT) Methodology at Ipso* [White paper]. Ipso.

Ohme, R., Reykowska, D., Wiener, D., & Choromanska, A. (2009). Analysis of neurophysiological reactions to advertising stimuli by means of EEG and galvanic skin response. *Journal of Neuroscience, 2*(1), 21–31.

Ohme, R., Reykowska, D., Wiener, D., & Choromanska, A. (2010). Application of frontal EEG asymmetry to advertising research. *Journal of Economic Psychology, 31*(5), 785–793.

Quillian, M. R. (1967). Word concepts: A theory and simulation of some basic semantic qualities. *Behavioral Science, 12*(5), 410–430.

Rosenberg, M. (2015). Non-violent communication. Puddle Dancer Press.

Sebastian, V. (2014). Neuromarketing and evaluation of cognitive and emotional responses of consumers to marketing stimuli. *Procedia Social and Behavioral Sciences, 127*(2014), 753–757.

Teixeira, T., Picard, R., & el Kaliouby, R. (2014). Why, when, and how much to entertain consumers in advertisements? A web-based facial tracking field study. *Marketing Science, 33*(6), 809–827.

Vecchiato, G., Alsolfi, L., de Vico Fallani, F. Toppi, J., Aloise, F., Bez, F., Wei, D., Kong, W., Dai, J., Cincotti, F., Mattia, D., & Babiloni, F. (2011). On the use of EEG or MEG brain imaging tools in neuro-marketing research. *Computational Intelligence and Neuroscience*, https://doi.org/10.1155/2011/643489

Vriens, M., & A. Martins Alves (2017). Modeling the implicit brand: Capturing the hidden drivers. *Journal of Product and Brand Management*, *26*(6), 600–615.

Vriens, M., Chen, S., & Schomaker, J. (2019). The evaluation of a brand association density metric. *Journal of Product and Brand Management*, *28*(1), 104–116.

Vriens, M., Vidden, C. & Schomaker, J. (2020). What I see is what I want: Top down attention biasing choice behavior. Journal of Business Research, 111, 262–269.

White, M. (1997, July). Toy Rover sales soar into orbit: Mars landing puts gold shine back into space items. *Arizona Republic*, 12A.

Image Credits

Fig. 10.1: Copyright © by Fibonacci (CC BY-SA 3.0) at https://commons.wikimedia.org/wiki/File:M%C3%B-Cller-Lyer_illusion.svg.

Fig. 10.3: Copyright © by Kia Motors America.

Fig. 10.4: Adapted from Copyright © by Instituto Nacional Electoral.

Fig. 10.5: Copyright © by Chrissshe (CC BY-SA 4.0) at https://commons.wikimedia.org/wiki/File:Emotiv_EPOC%2B.png.

Fig. 10.6: Copyright © by iMotions.

Fig. 10.7: Copyright © by Bartosz Mozyrko (CC BY-SA 4.0) at https://image.slidesharecdn.com/ixda-et-110503140521-phpapp02/95/eye-tracking-ixda-2011-28-728.jpg?cb=1364913296.

Fig. 10.8: Copyright © 2018 by Ipsos. Reprinted with permission.

Fig. 10.9: Copyright © by Ipsos. Reprinted with permission.

Fig. 10.10: Copyright © by VicarVision.

CHAPTER 11

PUTTING IT ALL TOGETHER AND LOOKING FORWARD

11.1 WHAT AM I GOING TO LEARN?

Consumers have nearly infinite choices nowadays. As an example, Wikipedia shows a list of nearly 250 brands of chocolate bars. In addition to all these options, we are bombarded daily with advertising. There are estimations that the average American gets exposed to around 4,000 to 10,000 advertisements a day (Marshall, 2015).

With so many options and the massive amount of daily advertising we are exposed to, we are increasingly making choices on autopilot and using our unconscious brain to steer our choices. But then, sometimes, we break our habits and zoom in on the detailed ingredients on the back of a product and suddenly decide to buy a completely new brand of shampoo. So, how does a market researcher predict this seemingly random behavior and how can brand managers influence people's behavior? Increasingly, companies are reaching out to marketing research managers to help them understand consumers in this complicated world and develop new brand strategies.

Consumers' choices, it may seem, are increasingly difficult to predict because they have so much information at their fingertips and so many choices to choose from. Having more options for consumers does not always higher revenues or profits. On the other hand, the information that firms have access to also has exploded. In many cases, a firm will no longer rely on the results of one survey (Vriens, 2012); instead, they may have access to several survey studies, often complemented by non-survey data, to weave the customer and consumer story together. There are several reasons why organizations rely more on behavioral data than in the past.

One, advances in technology have made it easier to organize and use internally collected data.

Two, in the digital world customers leave more and more breadcrumbs that researchers can use to help understand what consumers do and why they do it. Browsing history, credit card data, tracking devices on your mobile phone, loyalty cards, in-store payments, cookies on websites, Siri listening to your conversations, in-store cameras, your connected fridge, and even your connected in-home security system knows exactly when you are home, where you are in your home, how many people live in your household, when you eat, sleep, or watch TV together, and much more. All this data can be used by market researchers, analysts, and data scientists.

Three, new methodologies have given rise to new types of data. In the previous chapter we discussed neuro marketing research, an area that has increasingly become a standard part of firm's marketing research toolbox as has the use of virtual reality, where consumers walk around in a virtual store and make virtual decisions (see Figure 11.1).

FIGURE 11.1 Virtual Reality in Shopping Research

We also have Big Data that is increasingly used (scraped consumer-generated content from the Internet). With the latter, be careful, as the output in some cases may look the same as the output from standard surveys, but that doesn't mean the output from Big Data is the same as the output from survey data. We have to be mindful that consumer-generated data from a sample of consumers, of which we know very little, may be very different from data coming from a survey where we ask questions and where we (the firm and the researchers) determine who we talk to (see, for example, Vriens et al., 2019; they studied the market structure of the skincare market and found substantial differences between the survey-based analysis and the analysis based on consumer-generated data).

With all this data available, we have high expectations of the possibilities for new insights from analytics and data science (Vriens et al., 2018). The data and analytics developments make it challenging for today's business student to really determine what they need to know and how to go about designing an appropriate marketing research project. In this book, we have tried to make sense of all these developments and have discussed topics we believe are most relevant for any marketing or business decision maker and for business students who are excited about building a foundation in marketing intelligence.

In today's business, there will be situations where expertise in a specific area is required. Though you certainly may be asked to set up a specific U&A study: i.e., you will get a specific request. There will also be situations where you will be asked to weigh in or analyze a business situation or problem (without a request as to what research to scope out; that is up to you to decide). In these cases, you may be expected to outline what type of data, analysis, and insights the firm needs to consider in their decision making. In these situations, we do not start with a specific methodology; we start with a business problem, and more than one methodology or research approach may give useful insights. There may not be a single best solution.

In the first part of this wrapping up chapter, we want to outline how to proceed in such situations. In the second part, we want to look ahead, as more major changes are coming to the intelligence discipline; we will briefly discuss some new developments in market research and some thoughts on the changing role of a marketing research manager in an organization.

11.2 HOW TO DESIGN A MARKETING RESEARCH PROJECT

In Chapter 2 we discussed the business problem and the marketing research problem. Designing marketing research projects is both an art and a science. For many business challenges and marketing research problems there is no single best approach. This can be a little un-nerving for students and professionals who have just or recently started their career in marketing or marketing research. Below are some tips and suggestions. This list is not comprehensive, but I will provide at least some handles:

Step 1: Analyze the business problem and identify the marketing research problem

First, in Chapter 2 we discussed the business problem and the marketing research problem. Our first tip is to separate these two concepts; they can be very different. For example, a business problem could be "sales are down". This can have many different causes and there can be, many, different ways to research a variety of possible solutions (see Grover & Vriens, 2006). Second, because there can be many different causes we recommend:

a. In this stage, you need to apply critical thinking: keep an open mind to all the possible ways you can answer a problem and be curious.
b. Talk to some colleagues, internal stakeholders (e.g., from sales, marketing, operations, etc.) and invite some possible hypotheses. Some good questions to ask stakeholders are "What do they think could be causing the problem (e.g., why do they think sales are down)? What is the problem that needs to be resolved? What do they think is causing the problem?"
c. Is there information available within the firm, e.g., previous research, insights from the CRM database, etc., that can shed light on the issue?
d. It may be necessary to do some qualitative, exploratory research to get sufficient insight into the nature of the causes.

This may lead to either a very specific cause or the problem may remain broad with few hypotheses.

Step 2a: A specific cause is identified, or we have a specific problem

If the cause is specific, identify possible decisions that could mitigate the problem and discuss with your internal stakeholders which decision they can make and are feasible. Then, apply the backward marketing research approach (Andreases, 1985). Here are some common scenarios of specific problems and decisions.

Scenario 1: Feature testing

Internal stakeholders think it may a feature issue (e.g., you sell the Canvas software and you get lots of complaints about the online web teaching feature (i.e., a feature similar to Webex and Zoom): it won't let you give control to students so they share their screen and make their PPT presentation). The research question becomes: If Canvas would add that feature would universities who chose an alternative to Canvas have selected Canvas instead.

From a research design perspective this could probably be tackled by interviewing university decision-makers and what platform they chose, and if they didn't choose Canvas would this feature have made difference. Simultaneously, for those who did choose Canvas, does the absence of the feature constitute a reason to be less or not satisfied with the platform. If feature testing involves an online service product (say: should Amazon include product reviews), then one can use A/B testing (e.g., Bojinov, Sait-Jacques, & Martin Tingley, 2020).

In many cases firms are looking at several, or even many, features at the same time, and they wonder how an optimal product looks like, or even how an optimal product line looks like. In such situations, we probably would recommend considering approaches such discrete choice modeling, and MaxDiff analysis. Related to this scenario is also pricing: What is the optimal or best price for my product? This too can be tackled with the Discrete Choice Modeling approach. There are other alternatives to getting pricing insights, e.g., Van Westendorp approach, Gabor-Granger method, and analysis of scanner data.

Scenario 2: Advertising copy testing

The marketing team is ready to launch some advertisement and they may some rough idea about potential T.V. commercials or print copy. This scenario is somewhat similar to the previous scenario and probably could research this via a survey maybe combined with focus groups. The focus groups are used for the "what I don't know, I don't know." In this case: does any of the advertising copy ideas induce unexpected reactions or emotions with consumers.

Scenario 3: Deciding on the optimal allocation of advertising & promotion budget

You don't know if your marketing is working or if you allocating your advertising dollars in the best possible way? Possible research design options: a tracking study or marketing mix models.

Step 2b: A specific cause cannot be identified, or we have a broad challenge

If the marketing research problem is not very specific, then we suggest to:

a. What you know and what you think you know (the difference is for the latter you do not have data to back you up), (2) What don't you know, and (3) Judge how much there could be of what you don't know you don't know. Critically challenge what you think you know and what you (actually) know.
b. Use the issue trees to break down the problem, visually share these with stakeholders for input, and formulate hypotheses of the cause the problem and what could resolve it.

c. An unstructured business problem should start with a qualitative step. This can include Focus Groups and social listening (by scraping the internet for discussion on a specific topic or audience and subsequently querying the data and text analyzing can set you on a path of greater discovery). This will help scoping the business problem: i.e., identify some possible root causes. If, on the other hand, no immediate decisions can be articulated and the nature of the business problem is somewhat broad but also (somewhat) structured, review common scenarios:

Scenario 1: Improving customer satisfaction

You are not sure how overall satisfied your customers are vis-à-vis the competition, and you worry that consumers don't talk positively about your brand or products. A possible research design option is: Scope out a customer satisfaction or NPS study combined with a statistical drivers' analysis. Possibly, preceded by some qualitative Focus Groups to determine if there are pain points or areas of dissatisfaction you are not aware of.

Scenario 2: Sales are down

Your brand's sales have stagnated or even declined. The product is solid as you have been marketing it for years. The brand is supported by a decent advertising budget. You are not sure what the reasons for lack of growth is. How can reignite the brand to grow? As possible research design options you first need to determine this is a category/market or a brand issue. If the category is down, then maybe consumer tastes are changing. In that case, consider U&A studies or market segmentation studies. Both are feasible and should possibly br preceded by a focus group. If it is a brand issue, then it may be that a competing brand has improved or a new brand has entered the market that has taken some share from your brand.

Scenario 4: Brand crisis

Your brand got caught in crisis. Think of the VW Diesel emission scandal, Wells Fargo, etc. In such situations social listening using consumer generated online data (CGD) are possibly a good option. First, with CGD we can go back in time which is useful because we can compare the sentiment about the brand before and after the crisis broke. Two, we can observe consumers' unfiltered discussions and comments unrestricted by someone asking questions (see for an example Vriens et al., 2017).

Scenario 5: Re-branding

You have more and more products under your brand, but a limited advertising budget. You want to have a more balanced and better aligned brand portfolio linked to a strong mother brand. Think of a brand positioning study to determine the emotional and functional positioning of the brands in your portfolio.

Another reason why your brand portfolio may need to be reviewed is when two firms merge. Each has its own set of brands: some have similar features and benefits. How do we re-brand the products in this new firm? In this case we need to have a good understanding of what our target market is looking for in terms of needs, aspirations, behaviors, etc., and we need to understand what consumer segments there are, and which brands would be good fits for which segments. We also need to find out the associations consumers have with the various brands. This can be done via an open-ended question. If two brands appeal to the same segment, there might be an opportunity to eliminate one of the two brands.

Scenario 6: Developing new products

Some research has suggested there are several white space opportunities in your market. The firm needs to come up with some new product ideas and decide which new products to pursue. Here we can use a variety of approaches to generate new product ideas, e.g.: Focus groups, pop-up communities, mining of social CGD, e.g., Twitter), and ethnography (see e.g., Lindstrom, ...). Once we have a set of ideas these can be narrowed down using Focus Groups and surveys.

Scenario 7: Market share and brand switching dynamics

For example, why are mothers switching from your brand of diapers to another brand of diapers? You can consider some focus groups or an online community with a group of mothers to discuss the differences between your brand and your competitors. We can also utilize quantitative brand switching models (e.g., see Vriens & Martins Alves, 2016).

Scenario 8: Understanding cultures globally to improve a global social media site

A global social media site wants to find a better way to deal with people's personal sites after they die. In order to come up with a solution, they want to understand the culture of mourning across the globe. In this case you can consider a global qualitative research with one-one-one interviews with people who have lost loved ones, with professionals in local markets, and desk research.

11.3 HOW TO HAVE IMPACT

We have discussed topics such as storytelling and business impact. Analyzing the data, finding the key insights, and defining an answer to the business question is like reaching the summit of a mountain. You have the results and are enjoying the view from the top. But now comes the hardest part: getting back to base. Reaching the top is only the halfway point of the journey. With the answers in your hand, you need to tell the story to the stakeholders and convince them to act (i.e., socialization and activation).

A story has a clear structure but not too many details. The audience should quickly understand what the key message is, what the "so what" is, and what the supporting evidence is. Insights that are not supporting the key message are nice to put in an appendix but should not be part of your overall story. Also, think about how to deliver the story. Sometimes a

PPT presentation is the right tool, but there are alternatives. You can think of a workshop, a nice-looking one-pager, a website, a movie, a flyer, posters, and so on.

Convincing your audience is the first step of having impact. The next steps are workshops with key stakeholders or ideation sessions to come up with products/concepts to bring the recommendations alive. Also, forecasting the potential financial impact of your recommendations on the company's bottom line is a very effective tool to make sure senior management acts on your recommendations.

11.4 THE FUTURE OF MARKETING RESEARCH

There are many new developments in market research. We are listing just a few new developments, but by no means do we try to be exhaustive with this list.

11.4.1 Blockchain Panel

Blockchain technology can enable panel members to own their personal data and rent it out for a certain fee. With such a technology, someone can monetize personal data by allowing companies to use certain data for a certain amount of time, after which it is automatically deleted. The distributed ledger will guarantee the privacy of the data as well as the automatic payout for use of the data. This technology is being piloted in the United States and some other markets but is not widely embraced yet, and the technology is in its infancy. We expect this to have a transformational impact on the use of respondent panels when this technology matures.

11.4.2 Big Brother

Market research will increasingly use behavioral data instead of questionnaires to understand consumer behaviors. Your connected car, fridge, toaster, toothbrush, lightbulbs, home security system, and performance wear generate terabytes of consumer usage data. The roll out of 5G networks will further increase the speed of connected products. Furthermore, apps and street cameras with face recognition add data to your offline behavior. The comments you leave on social media can be tracked and analyzed. Advanced cookies track your browsing history and determine what media you watch and what ads you were exposed to. And, unless you have actively switched this application off, your smartphone is in constant listening mode and records everything it hears. This data can and will be mined for consumer insights.

11.4.3 Consumer-Generated Online Data

Scraping data from the web, whether it's social data or data from forums, blogs, and articles, can be effective in exploring a topic an organization doesn't fully understand or to can help an organization get a sense of a particular audience they don't know much about in terms of pain points and challenges. In 2005, 5% of U.S. adults used social media, and as of 2019 it's now 72% (Perrin & Anderson, 2019); Reddit has over 330 million active monthly users conversing in over 1 million communities (Pardes, 2010). Consumers increasingly leave a digital footprint that forms a starting point for researchers to explore new topics and inform more traditional quantitative and qualitative research. Researchers have to be nimble and knowledgeable about how to mesh different data sources and solve problems holistically.

11.4.4 Neuroscience

As previously discussed, respondents are not always able to tell us what we want to know. They don't remember, they rationalize their decisions, or they simply don't know why they selected a certain product or brand. We also discussed how consumers use their unconscious brain to simplify their decision-making process in the face of so many choices. Traditional research is not always able to understand these unconscious processes. For this, we need to use techniques developed in the area of neuroscience (EEG, fMRI, galvanic skin response, eye tracking, and response time measures and implicit measures). While this is a fast-growing area in market research, it is still an area in development. The industry needs guidance to which methods are effective, which ones are not, and which ones are most appropriate for specific research questions. Also, the more we know about the working of the brain, the more tools will be developed to uncover the consumer unconscious mind.

11.4.5 Augmented Reality: Artificial Intelligence

The market researcher of the future will have to work closely with data scientists, artificial intelligence specialists, and Big Data experts to link these data streams together and distill powerful consumer insights. Questionnaires will get shorter and will only be used to understand why people use a product.

New developments in online 3D, virtual reality, and augmented reality are changing the respondent questionnaire experience. Ipsos is using digital 3D stores and virtual reality technology to have respondents walk through a digital store to see how they behave, what they purchase, which products they observe, which products they hold in their virtual hands, when they check products for details, and what put in their cart and buy.

11.5 THE FUTURE ROLE OF MARKETING RESEARCH

Advances in technology continue to have an impact on virtually every profession. Workers must continually update their skills and adapt to new realities to stay relevant according to LinkedIn's 2018 "Workforce Learning Report." Automation and AI will certainly have an impact, and we are already seeing some of that (interview bots, better text analytics with off-the-shelf tool kits, and advanced data analysis and reporting tools), but it is not so dramatic that it is displacing the role of a researcher, which at its core is part science, part creativity, and part humanity (understanding human emotions). So far, AI and automation have been in support of the market research function, and we expect further shifts in how research gets done. We also believe that market research is a critical function that any organization will continue to look for to answer important business questions that no other function, process, AI, or automation can answer. We see three major developments in the world of marketing research.

The first development is the move to cheaper, faster, more agile basic research. Research companies are coming with do-it-yourself platforms, brand trackers are getting simpler and faster if they are done at all, and many companies have significantly reduced their budget for concept testing while increasing the number of tests. Advances in technology make it so that new features and products can be released faster. The business is hungry for quick learning. It used to take weeks to complete a market research project but with today's tools and through the advent of insights communities (pre-screened panels of customers who volunteer to give feedback), easy-to-use analytical packages, structured answers from a reasonably representative and targeted samples can be obtained within hours. This requires market researchers to be nimble and design surveys that get at the main points quickly. Researchers need to rethink how to solve for problems in an agile way, leveraging hypothesis-based approaches to quickly get at the core of a problem and articulate solutions that address these problems head on, succinctly and simply. Another element of this development is the ease at which everyone can use survey tools and become a market researcher. SurveyMonkey and other survey platforms make it easy to launch a survey with little knowledge and with little effort. However, there is a real science and craft to sample selection: making sure it's representative of the target population, conducting hypothesis testing, designing questionnaires and analyzing and interpreting the findings in a meaningful way. This doesn't have to be time consuming; it takes knowledge, creativity, problem-solving, skills and experience.

The second development is the need for strategic advice in the face of category transformations. Companies are looking for support to help them make sense of today's consumers and how to reach their hearts—and wallets. There is a new role for market researchers to have more advisory capacity. Market researchers are being asked for advice on category trends and how these trends will affect brands; they are asked to give business recommendations based on consumer insights and whether a company should continue its planned product launch based on the results of a marketing research. This requires a deep business understanding, but it also requires a business attitude from the market researcher: the guts to stand up in a board room and give advice, even if it is not what the company expects or wants to hear.

The third development is the availability of consumer data and the science to make sense of all this data (Vriens et al., 2018). Data begets data. As mentioned, the digital transformation means that more and more companies are sitting on mountains of data. The tools to analyze data are getting easier to use, and with little technical expertise workers can mine knowledge faster and more efficiently with simple point-and-click or drop-and-drag solutions. Cloud-based database applications, Tableau, text analytics tool kits, and Power BI are examples of solutions that have made data analysis faster and much more accessible and reliable for a greater number of knowledge workers. More data spurs more questions. Often these questions cannot solely be answered with more behavioral data but require structured questions from survey research.

For all these reasons we believe that the market research industry will continue to grow year after year, as it has been over the past years. And with the field of data science, we expect it to grow even stronger. The Bureau of Labor Statistics (2015) predicts that market research jobs will grow by 23% until 2026, much faster than the average. Moreover, we expect that market research and data sciences will coalesce, requiring each to learn from each other.

As a market researcher, you will need to find your place in this very exciting new world of consumer insights, data science, and consumer strategy. We predict that this role will get increasingly important and might even overtake the role of today's marketing manager in the future.

We need to increase our skill sets and learn how to use analytics packages and data-querying tools that can be used to effectively analyze data and verbatims. And we need to realize that not every problem can or must be solved with a survey or behavioral data alone. In many organizations, market research is in a unique position to provide a holistic view of the consumer. Findings from market research transcend company silos and can bring disparate teams together to solve customer needs holistically. This means that market researchers need to deeply understand the customer and the problems they face, how the business makes money and the broader context it operates in, and where the centers of decision-making lie. This makes the market researcher a spider in the company web, a strategic player. And, as such, aspiring market researchers should consider rotating in other roles in the organization to become more in tune with how the product gets built and marketed. Influence and the ability to provide insights that change people's perspectives is a core competency for future market researchers.

As a final thought, the customer's or prospect's voice needs to be captured in a systematic way to understand underlying motivations, intent, and product/market fit before and after product launches. The adage of "pivot hard and fast" or "fail fast and fail often" is a risky proposition if one doesn't understand underlying consumer needs and behaviors. The graveyard of failed products is filled with examples of products that were built without prior research and fizzled, stagnated, were cancelled, or didn't generate the expected outcome.

For the market research function, it is important to educate the organization on the value of consumer insights. Market research must be built into the design process from the outset and not stop at testing a few users about a concept or prototype. It must be fully integrated throughout the product life cycle so that decisions at every turn are based on consumer insights. The role of market research is critical in navigating companies through a digital world. The future of market research is bright.

11.6 QUIZ AND EXERCISES

Note: The following exercises and quizzes are more holistic than some of the exercises in previous chapters. This means there is not necessarily a single best answer. So, in addition to identifying what you think is the best solution, also make sure you make a compelling case why it is the best solution.

1. You work for a large local hospital, and the CEO has decided they want to expand beyond the local town and maybe set up some subsidiaries in towns and areas in a 150-mile radius. She comes to you and wants you to gather information/data that can help with making these decisions.
   a. How do you go about gather this data? Is this a structured or unstructured problem?
   b. What research approach would you propose?
2. You just got hired by Fastenal. Fastenal, for years, has had a relatively small advertising budget. You believe they miss an opportunity and could leverage advertising and promotion tools much more than they have so far. (Note: If you are unfamiliar with this firm, look up information online so you know the basics of their business.)
   a. How do you go about convincing them of these strategies?
   b. What research approach do you propose and why?
3. You have been hired by Trane (a company that makes air conditioners) as a management trainee. Your manager comes to you and says they are thinking of developing an extra quiet air conditioner.
   a. How do you go about doing this?
   b. What type of research would you propose?
   c. If you propose a survey approach, what type of questions would you ask?
   d. If you propose focus groups, what topics do you cover?
   e. What other questions would you ask and to whom?
4. A company wants to launch a new advertising campaign, and they develop various creative options with the creative studio and agency. They create a digital ad along with some print options.
   a. How do you go about testing which one is most effective in driving recall and appeal?
5. A company that sells razors for shaving is struggling to find new ways to grow their business. Most markets are saturated, and a handful of competitors control the market. Growth has been slowing down to the single digits; there is little room to cut costs or raise prices, and few new customers are added every year. What are the different ways the market research department can explore different options and which ones are the most effective?

a. Formulate the problem either as a why or how problem.
b. Create an issue tree to determine the different ways the problem can be solved.
c. Determine what data is needed to test the different hypotheses.
d. Design the research.

6 A global petrol company is seeing the rise of electric cars and millennials owning less cars than ever. They want to understand the future for their brand.

a. What should they do?
b. Think about how to understand the trends in the industry.
c. How do consumers change their behavior?
d. How can you help the company come up with new solutions to stay relevant?

7 Management of an online job board wants to make a more informed decision about what website features to develop to attract more job seekers. It currently is successful attracting frontline workers but struggles attracting professional workers.

a. What type of structured research do you suggest doing?
b. How do you design the research study?

8 The CMO of VW opens his Monday newspaper and is shocked to learn to VW had been caught cheating on their Diesel emission by purposely installing software in their cars that adjust Diesel emission test results. She wants quick action and calls one of her senior marketing research managers, you. The assignment: Find out what effect this is going to have on the brand. She wants to commission a survey that asks about customers' view of the VW brand, the emission crisis, and if their views will change as a result of this crisis.

a. How do you go about doing this?
b. Would you construct a survey, do a focus group, or something else?
c. Review the different types of data you could use and identify which ones could be helpful and how.

9 You receive an e-mail from Colgate. They are facing increased competition from organic brands. They want to find out how they can successfully tackle the competition. One concept they would like to measure they refer to as teeth diligence.

a. What research approaches would you recommend and why?
b. How would you measure teeth diligence? Create several questions as to what reasons consumers might have to brush their teeth, how often, and with what type of toothpaste. The business objective is to determine if their profile can be predictive of how much they would be willing to pay for toothpaste.

10 Ipsos, a global market research firm, recently finished a U&A study for a medical devices firm. It turns out that a substantial number of consumers who completed the survey have negative attitudes toward medical devices. Other consumers in their sample like the devices of Ipsos's client. The firm doesn't fully understand if this is merely a branding issue or if there is something in the product that they don't like.

a. What is a good next step?

11 You just started working as a market research manager at a tools company in Milwaukee. The firm's products are being sold at stores such as Home Depot and Menards. One of the marketing managers comes to you and wants to know how to best develop a merchandising (marketing activities you do in store to promote the sales of the product) strategy for your firm. She is very specific: She wants you to do a U&A study.

a. What do you do?

12 You manage the global customer satisfaction study of a major Fortune 500 company. They market to business customers. The customer satisfaction study is done twice a year and you report the results and insights to the CEO and the leadership team. Every time you present a detailed action plan, you get the buy-in of the leadership team, and the action plan is always sufficiently funded. Year over year the results do not seem to change dramatically. Sometimes the numbers go up a little bit, and sometimes they go down.

a. What is (are) the most likely reason(s) this is happening? Outline how this/these reason(s) can be dealt with.

13 You started working at Target. The CEO is concerned with how much money they spend on advertising and wants to know if it is working. Are they overspending, underspending, or spending on the right categories? Your manager asks you to scope out a marketing mix model.

a. What is the first step you need to take?

14 You work for a manufacturer of washers & dryers and dishwashers. Sales over the past two quarters have been flat. You think it might be time to develop and introduce some new products. A first step in the new product development process is to generate new product or product improvement ideas (maybe some could be based on consumer "compensating" behaviors).

a. What type of research do you consider best for this purpose? Scope or describe briefly how you could go about.
b. After phase 1 you have generated roughly 100 ideas. How would you go about prioritizing these ideas, and what type of research would that be?

15 You are an entrepreneur and have noticed that many people's cars are filthy. You want to think of some solutions to this problem.

a. Could ethnographic research be of use here?
b. How could a pop-up community help with the above challenge?

REFERENCES

Andreasen, Al. (1985). 'Backward' market research. Harvard Business Review, 1–5.

Bojinov, Iavor I., Guillaume Sait-Jacques, and Martin Tingley (2020). "Avoid the Pitfalls of A/B Testing." Harvard Business Review, 98, 2, 48–53.

Lindstrom, M. (2016). Small data: the tiny clues that uncover huge trends. Picador Books, New York, USA.

Grover, R. and M. Vriens (2006). Trusted Advisor: How it helps lay the foundation for insights. In: Grover, R. and M. Vriens (eds.), Handbook of Marketing Research, 3–32, Sage Publishing, Thousand Oaks, CA.

Marshall, R. (2015, September 10). *How many ads do you see in one day?* Red Crow Marketing. https://www.redcrowmarketing.com/2015/09/10/many-ads-see-one-day/

Pardes, A. (2010). The Inside Story of Reddit's Redesign. https://www.wired.com/story/reddit-redesign/

Perrin, A., & Anderson, M. (2019, April 10). Social media usage in the U.S. in 2019. Pew Research Center. https://www.pewresearch.org/fact-tank/2019/04/10/share-of-u-s-adults-using-social-media-including-facebook-is-mostly-unchanged-since-2018/

Bureau of Labor Statistics. (2015). Occupational outlook handbook: Market research analyst. Retrieved from https://www.bls.gov/ooh/business-and-financial/market-research-analysts.htm

Vriens, M. (2012). The insights advantage: Knowing how to win. i-Universe.

Vriens, M. and A. Martins Alves (2015). Integrated competition and customer analysis: Managing market share efficiently. Applied Marketing Analytics, 1, 4, 350-362. (link: http://www.henrystewartpublications.com/ama/).

Vriens, M., Vidden, C., Chen, S., and Kaulartz, S. (2017). Assessing the impact of a brand crisis using Big Data: The case of the VW diesel emission crisis. In: DMA Annual Analytics Journal, 107-118.

Vriens, M., Chen, S., & Vidden, C. (2018). From data to decision: Handbook for the modern business analyst. Cognella.

Vriens, M. Chen, S., & Vidden, C. (2019). Mapping brand similarities: Comparing consumer online comments versus survey data. *International Journal of Market Research, 61*(2), 130–139.

Image Credits

Fig. 11.1: Copyright © by Ipsos. Reprinted with permission.

CPSIA information can be obtained
at www.ICGtesting.com
Printed in the USA
LVHW050605011222
734287LV00001B/19

9 781516 542772